2011 | THE LITTLE DATA BOOK
ON CLIMATE CHANGE

D0870152

THE WORLD BANK

ISBN: 978-0-8213-8959-1
eISBN: 978-0-8213-8964-5
DOI: 10.1596/978-0-8213-8959-1
SKU: 18959

The Little Data Book on Climate Change 2011 is a product of the
Development Data Group of the Development Economics Vice Presidency,
the Environment Department, and the Global Facility for Disaster
Reduction and Recovery Group of the World Bank.

Cover design by Peter Grundy Art & Design, London, U.K.
Design by Communications Development Incorporated, Washington, D.C.

Contents

Acknowledgments

The *Little Data Book on Climate Change 2011* is based on the *World Development Indicators* database. Defining, gathering, and disseminating international statistics is a collective effort of many people and organizations. The indicators presented in these resources are results of decades of work at many levels, from the field workers who administer censuses and household surveys to the committees and working parties of the national and international statistical agencies that develop the nomenclature, classifications, and standards fundamental to the international statistical system. Nongovernmental organizations have also made important contributions. We are indebted to many external partners as detailed in *World Development Indicators 2011* who have provided substantial help, guidance, and data.

The *Little Data Book on Climate Change 2011* is the result of close collaboration between the staff of the Development Data Group of the Development Economics Vice Presidency (DECDG), the Environment Department of the Sustainable Development Vice Presidency (ENV), and the Global Facility for Disaster Reduction and Recovery (GFDRR). Timothy Herzog coordinated the production of the book with substantial contributions from Philippe Ambrosi, Ana Bucher, and Fernanda Zermoglio from ENV, Milen Dyoulgerov and Ian Noble from GFDRR, and William Prince from DECDG. Additional support was provided by Azita Amjadi, Federico Escaler, Mahyar Eshragh-Tabary, Neil Fantom, Tariq Khokhar, Alison Kwong, and Sup Lee, from DECDG; Sameer Akbar, Jane Ebinger, Fernando Loayza, Elisabeth Mealey, Kiran Pandey, Kanta Kumari Rigaud, and Sari Soderstrom from ENV; Daniel Hoornweg and Marcus Lee from Financial Solutions Group; Roshin Joseph, and Ayaz Parvez from GFDRR; Richard Damania from the Latin America and the Caribbean Region (LAC); and Gabriela Elizondo Azuela from the Sustainable Energy Department (SEGEN). The book's design is done by Jomo Tariku and is based on an original design by Communications Development Incorporated. Staff from External Affairs consisting of Stephen McGroarty, Dina Towbin, and Nora Ridolfi oversaw publication and distribution of the book. The book was prepared under supervision of Shaida Badiee, director of the Development Data Group; Mary Barton-Dock, director of Environment; and Andrew Steer, Special Envoy for Climate Change.

Foreword

When President Robert Zoellick launched the World Bank's Open Data Initiative in April 2010, he said its purpose was to "open the treasure chest of the World Bank's data and knowledge to every village, to everyone everywhere." This small book and the much bigger open database behind it are part of this same goal.

Solving the problem of climate change requires that our behavior changes. Whether this happens depends on our understanding, which, in turn, depends upon our knowledge of facts and their implications. Access to freely available climate and climate-related data is essential to catalyze the changes in policies, investments, and technologies that will be needed if we are to move toward a climate-smart future.

The *Little Data Book on Climate Change* includes a diverse set of indicators selected from the global economic and scientific communities. These indicators recognize the intrinsic relationship between climate change and development and attempt to synthesize important aspects of current and projected climate conditions, exposure to climate impacts, resilience, greenhouse gas emissions, and the current state of efforts to take action. While these indicators are from standard sources and represent professional consensus, many are subject to considerable uncertainties, and the usual care must be taken in their interpretation.

The *Little Data Book on Climate Change* draws upon several online resources, including the Open Data website,[1] the Climate Change Knowledge Portal,[2] and the Open Data for Resilience initiative.[3] These resources from the World Bank and the Global Facility for Disaster Reduction and Recovery (GFDRR) provide free and open access to data and information relevant to climate risk, climate change, and development at the international, national and subnational levels. These resources contain many more indicators than are available in the limited space of this book and include interactive tools, visualizations on the use and interpretation of the data. In addition, there are other tools that will help users and programmers access World Bank data and develop applications.

We invite you to visit the online companions to the *Little Data Book on Climate Change*. In the coming months, we will continue to add to the datasets. We welcome suggestions on how we can improve these resources for everyone.

Shaida Badiee
Director
Development Data Group

Andrew Steer
Special Envoy for Climate Change
World Bank Group

---

[1] http://data.worldbank.org/

[2] http://climateknowledgeportal.worldbank.org/

[3] http://www.gfdrr.org/gfdrr/opendri/

User guide

The indicators in the *Little Data Book on Climate Change* are organized into the following categories, each of which relates to climate change, development, and the intrinsic relationship between the two. For additional information, refer to the definitions of each indicator in the Glossary.

Climate includes data on current and projected future average climate conditions, particularly precipitation and temperature.

Exposure to Impacts includes data that suggest the degree to which a country or region may be exposed to changes in the prevailing climate and natural environment, with potential impacts on human health, food security, water supply, and physical infrastructure.

Resilience includes data on the capacity of human systems to cope with the impacts of climate change, such as economic capacity, institutional capacity, and extent of public infrastructure.

GHG Emissions and Energy Use includes data on the emissions of greenhouse gases (GHG), energy use, including measures of energy efficiency and carbon intensity of economy.

National-Level Actions includes data that summarize actions being taken to address and respond to climate change at the national and international levels. Additional information is included in the "Summary of National Actions" tables in the appendices.

Carbon Markets includes data that summarize project activities under Joint Implementation and the Clean Development Mechanism, two of the flexibility mechanisms set forth under the Kyoto Protocol.

The data in this book are for the most recent year available. Regional aggregates include data for low- and middle-income economies only. No aggregate is calculated if missing data exceed specific thresholds by indicator. See *Statistical methods* in *World Development Indicators 2011* for more information.

Symbols used:

0 or 0.0	indicates zero or small enough that the number rounds to zero at the displayed number of decimal places.
..	indicates that data are not available.
n/a or blank	indicates not applicable, or for an aggregate, not analytically meaningful.
$	indicates current U.S. dollars.

Data are shown for economies with populations greater than 30,000 or for smaller economies if they are members of the World Bank. This publication also includes three additional economies: Cook Islands, Nauru, and Niue. The word *country* (used interchangeably with economy) does not imply political independence or official recognition by the World Bank but refers to any economy for which the authorities report separate social or economic statistics.

The cutoff date for data was October 21, 2011.

Regional tables

The country composition of regions is based on the World Bank's analytical regions and may differ from common geographic usage.

East Asia and Pacific

American Samoa, Cambodia, China, Cook Islands, Fiji, Indonesia, Kiribati, Democratic Republic of Korea, Lao People's Democratic Republic, Malaysia, Marshall Islands, Federated States of Micronesia, Mongolia, Myanmar, Nauru, Nuie, Palau, Papua New Guinea, Philippines, Samoa, Solomon Islands, Thailand, Timor-Leste, Tonga, Tuvalu, Vanuatu, Vietnam.

Europe and Central Asia

Albania, Armenia, Azerbaijan, Belarus, Bosnia and Herzegovina, Bulgaria, Georgia, Kazakhstan, Kosovo, Kyrgyz Republic, Latvia, Lithuania, Former Yugoslav Republic of Macedonia, Moldova, Montenegro, Romania, Russian Federation, Serbia, Tajikistan, Turkey, Turkmenistan, Ukraine, Uzbekistan.

Latin America and the Caribbean

Antigua and Barbuda, Argentina, Belize, Bolivia, Brazil, Chile, Colombia, Costa Rica, Cuba, Dominica, Dominican Republic, Ecuador, El Salvador, Grenada, Guatemala, Guyana, Haiti, Honduras, Jamaica, Mexico, Nicaragua, Panama, Paraguay, Peru, St. Kitts and Nevis, St. Lucia, St. Vincent and the Grenadines, Suriname, Uruguay, República Bolivariana de Venezuela.

Middle East and North Africa

Algeria, Djibouti, Arab Republic of Egypt, Islamic Republic of Iran, Iraq, Jordan, Lebanon, Libya, Morocco, Syrian Arab Republic, Tunisia, West Bank and Gaza, Republic of Yemen.

South Asia

Afghanistan, Bangladesh, Bhutan, India, Maldives, Nepal, Pakistan, Sri Lanka.

Sub-Saharan Africa

Angola, Benin, Botswana, Burkina Faso, Burundi, Cameroon, Cape Verde, Central African Republic, Chad, Comoros, Democratic Republic of Congo, Republic of Congo, Côte d'Ivoire, Eritrea, Ethiopia, Gabon, The Gambia, Ghana, Guinea, Guinea-Bissau, Kenya, Lesotho, Liberia, Madagascar, Malawi, Mali, Mauritania, Mauritius, Mayotte, Mozambique, Namibia, Niger, Nigeria, Rwanda, São Tomé and Príncipe, Senegal, Seychelles, Sierra Leone, Somalia, South Africa, Sudan, Swaziland, Tanzania, Togo, Uganda, Zambia, Zimbabwe.

World

Population (millions)	6,840.5	GDP ($ billions)	63,044.1
Pop. growth (avg. ann. %, 1990–2010)	1.3	GNI per capita (Atlas $)	9,116

Climate
Average daily min/max temperature (1961–90, Celsius)	
Projected annual temperature change (2045–65, Celsius)	
Average annual precipitation (1961–90, mm)	
Projected annual precipitation change (2045–65, mm)	
Projected change in annual hot days/warm nights	
Projected change in annual cool days/cold nights	

Exposure to Impacts
Land area below 5m (% of land area)	1.8
Population below 5m (% of total)	6.6
Population in urban agglomerations > 1 million (%)	20
Urban pop. growth (avg. annual %, 1990–2010)	2.1
Droughts, floods, extreme temps (% pop. avg., 1990–2009)	
Annual freshwater withdrawals (% of internal resources)	8.8
Agricultural land under irrigation (% of total ag. land)	..
Population living below $1.25 a day (% of total)	..
Nationally terrestrial protected areas (% of total land area)	12.5
Under-five mortality rate (per 1,000)	58
Child malnutrition, underweight (% of under age five)	21.4
Malaria incidence rate (per 100,000 people)	4,601

Resilience
Access to improved sanitation (% of total pop.)	61
Access to improved water source (% of total pop.)	87
Cereal yield (kg. per hectare)	3,566
Access to electricity (% of total population)	74.1
Paved roads (% of total roads)	49.1
Health workers (per 1,000 people)	4.4
Foreign direct investment, net inflows (% of GDP)	2.1
Invest. in infrastructure w/private participation ($ millions)	..
Disaster risk reduction progress score (1–5 scale; 5 = best)	
Ease of doing business (ranking 1–183; 1 = best)	
Public sector mgmt & institutions avg. (1–6 scale; 6 = best)	
Primary completion rate, total (% of relevant age group)	88
Ratio of girls to boys in primary & secondary school (%)	96

GHG Emissions and Energy Use
CO_2 emissions per capita (metric tons)	4.6
CO_2 emissions per units of GDP (kg/$1,000 of 2005 PPP $)	485.4
CO_2 emissions, total (MtCO_2)	30,649
GHG net emissions/removals by LUCF (MtCO_2e)	
Methane (CH_4) emissions, total (MtCO_2e)	7,136
Nitrous oxide (N_2O) emissions, total (MtCO_2e)	2,853
Other GHG emissions, total (MtCO_2e)	724
Energy use per capita (kilograms of oil equivalent)	1,803
Energy use per units of GDP (kg oil eq./$1,000 of 2005 PPP $)	182.9

National-Level Actions
Latest UNFCCC national communication	
Annex-I emissions reduction target	
NAMA submission	
NAPA submission	
Renewable energy target	

Carbon Markets
Hosted Clean Development Mechanism (CDM) projects	
Issued Certified Emission Reductions (CERs) from CDM (thousands)	
Hosted Joint Implementation (JI) projects	
Issued Emission Reduction Units (ERUs) from JI (thousands)	

East Asia & Pacific

Population (millions)	1,961.6	GDP ($ billions)	7,579.4
Pop. growth (avg. ann. %, 1990–2010)	1.0	GNI per capita (Atlas $)	3,683

Climate

Average daily min/max temperature (1961-90, Celsius)	
Projected annual temperature change (2045-65, Celsius)	
Average annual precipitation (1961-90, mm)	
Projected annual precipitation change (2045-65, mm)	
Projected change in annual hot days/warm nights	
Projected change in annual cool days/cold nights	

Exposure to Impacts

Land area below 5m (% of land area)	2.5
Population below 5m (% of total)	10.3
Population in urban agglomerations > 1 million (%)	..
Urban pop. growth (avg. annual %, 1990-2010)	3.3
Droughts, floods, extreme temps (% pop. avg., 1990-2009)	
Annual freshwater withdrawals (% of internal resources)	10.8
Agricultural land under irrigation (% of total ag. land)	..
Population living below $1.25 a day (% of total)	16.8
Nationally terrestrial protected areas (% of total land area)	14.9
Under-five mortality rate (per 1,000)	24
Child malnutrition, underweight (% of under age five)	9.0
Malaria incidence rate (per 100,000 people)	525

Resilience

Access to improved sanitation (% of total pop.)	59
Access to improved water source (% of total pop.)	88
Cereal yield (kg. per hectare)	4,860
Access to electricity (% of total population)	90.8
Paved roads (% of total roads)	15.9
Health workers (per 1,000 people)	2.8
Foreign direct investment, net inflows (% of GDP)	3.0
Invest. in infrastructure w/private participation ($ millions)	14,638
Disaster risk reduction progress score (1-5 scale; 5 = best)	
Ease of doing business (ranking 1-183; 1 = best)	
Public sector mgmt & institutions avg. (1-6 scale; 6 = best)	
Primary completion rate, total (% of relevant age group)	97
Ratio of girls to boys in primary & secondary school (%)	103

GHG Emissions and Energy Use

CO_2 emissions per capita (metric tons)	4.3
CO_2 emissions per units of GDP (kg/$1,000 of 2005 PPP $)	827.1
CO_2 emissions, total (MtCO_2)	8,259
GHG net emissions/removals by LUCF (MtCO_2e)	
Methane (CH_4) emissions, total (MtCO_2e)	1,928
Nitrous oxide (N_2O) emissions, total (MtCO_2e)	707
Other GHG emissions, total (MtCO_2e)	..
Energy use per capita (kilograms of oil equivalent)	1,436
Energy use per units of GDP (kg oil eq./$1,000 of 2005 PPP $)	259.5

National-Level Actions

Latest UNFCCC national communication
Annex-I emissions reduction target
NAMA submission
NAPA submission
Renewable energy target

Carbon Markets

Hosted Clean Development Mechanism (CDM) projects
Issued Certified Emission Reductions (CERs) from CDM (thousands)
Hosted Joint Implementation (JI) projects
Issued Emission Reduction Units (ERUs) from JI (thousands)

Europe & Central Asia

Population (millions)	405.1	GDP ($ billions)	3,055.0
Pop. growth (avg. ann. %, 1990–2010)	0.2	GNI per capita (Atlas $)	7,269

Climate
Average daily min/max temperature (1961–90, Celsius)
Projected annual temperature change (2045–65, Celsius)
Average annual precipitation (1961–90, mm)
Projected annual precipitation change (2045–65, mm)
Projected change in annual hot days/warm nights
Projected change in annual cool days/cold nights

Exposure to Impacts
Land area below 5m (% of land area)	2.5
Population below 5m (% of total)	3.0
Population in urban agglomerations > 1 million (%)	18
Urban pop. growth (avg. annual %, 1990–2010)	0.3
Droughts, floods, extreme temps (% pop. avg., 1990–2009)	
Annual freshwater withdrawals (% of internal resources)	6.5
Agricultural land under irrigation (% of total ag. land)	..
Population living below $1.25 a day (% of total)	3.7
Nationally terrestrial protected areas (% of total land area)	7.5
Under-five mortality rate (per 1,000)	23
Child malnutrition, underweight (% of under age five)	..
Malaria incidence rate (per 100,000 people)	..

Resilience
Access to improved sanitation (% of total pop.)	89
Access to improved water source (% of total pop.)	95
Cereal yield (kg. per hectare)	2,475
Access to electricity (% of total population)	
Paved roads (% of total roads)	85.8
Health workers (per 1,000 people)	9.9
Foreign direct investment, net inflows (% of GDP)	2.8
Invest. in infrastructure w/private participation ($ millions)	22,652
Disaster risk reduction progress score (1–5 scale; 5 = best)	
Ease of doing business (ranking 1–183; 1 = best)	
Public sector mgmt & institutions avg. (1–6 scale; 6 = best)	
Primary completion rate, total (% of relevant age group)	95
Ratio of girls to boys in primary & secondary school (%)	97

GHG Emissions and Energy Use
CO_2 emissions per capita (metric tons)	7.7
CO_2 emissions per units of GDP (kg/$1,000 of 2005 PPP $)	708.0
CO_2 emissions, total (MtCO$_2$)	3,110
GHG net emissions/removals by LUCF (MtCO$_2$e)	
Methane (CH_4) emissions, total (MtCO$_2$e)	937
Nitrous oxide (N_2O) emissions, total (MtCO$_2$e)	214
Other GHG emissions, total (MtCO$_2$e)	76
Energy use per capita (kilograms of oil equivalent)	2,833
Energy use per units of GDP (kg oil eq./$1,000 of 2005 PPP $)	276.8

National-Level Actions
Latest UNFCCC national communication
Annex-I emissions reduction target
NAMA submission
NAPA submission
Renewable energy target

Carbon Markets
Hosted Clean Development Mechanism (CDM) projects
Issued Certified Emission Reductions (CERs) from CDM (thousands)
Hosted Joint Implementation (JI) projects
Issued Emission Reduction Units (ERUs) from JI (thousands)

Latin America & Caribbean

Population (millions)	582.6	GDP ($ billions)	4,969.4
Pop. growth (avg. ann. %, 1990–2010)	1.4	GNI per capita (Atlas $)	7,741

Climate
Average daily min/max temperature (1961–90, Celsius)	
Projected annual temperature change (2045–65, Celsius)	
Average annual precipitation (1961–90, mm)	
Projected annual precipitation change (2045–65, mm)	
Projected change in annual hot days/warm nights	
Projected change in annual cool days/cold nights	

Exposure to Impacts
Land area below 5m (% of land area)	1.5
Population below 5m (% of total)	3.8
Population in urban agglomerations > 1 million (%)	35
Urban pop. growth (avg. annual %, 1990–2010)	2.0
Droughts, floods, extreme temps (% pop. avg., 1990–2009)	
Annual freshwater withdrawals (% of internal resources)	2.0
Agricultural land under irrigation (% of total ag. land)	..
Population living below $1.25 a day (% of total)	8.1
Nationally terrestrial protected areas (% of total land area)	20.8
Under-five mortality rate (per 1,000)	23
Child malnutrition, underweight (% of under age five)	3.8
Malaria incidence rate (per 100,000 people)	206

Resilience
Access to improved sanitation (% of total pop.)	79
Access to improved water source (% of total pop.)	93
Cereal yield (kg. per hectare)	3,337
Access to electricity (% of total population)	93.4
Paved roads (% of total roads)	28.1
Health workers (per 1,000 people)	6.9
Foreign direct investment, net inflows (% of GDP)	2.3
Invest. in infrastructure w/private participation ($ millions)	33,064
Disaster risk reduction progress score (1–5 scale; 5 = best)	
Ease of doing business (ranking 1–183; 1 = best)	
Public sector mgmt & institutions avg. (1–6 scale; 6 = best)	
Primary completion rate, total (% of relevant age group)	102
Ratio of girls to boys in primary & secondary school (%)	102

GHG Emissions and Energy Use
CO_2 emissions per capita (metric tons)	2.8
CO_2 emissions per units of GDP (kg/$1,000 of 2005 PPP $)	285.6
CO_2 emissions, total (MtCO$_2$)	1,584
GHG net emissions/removals by LUCF (MtCO$_2$e)	
Methane (CH_4) emissions, total (MtCO$_2$e)	1,009
Nitrous oxide (N_2O) emissions, total (MtCO$_2$e)	442
Other GHG emissions, total (MtCO$_2$e)	21
Energy use per capita (kilograms of oil equivalent)	1,245
Energy use per units of GDP (kg oil eq./$1,000 of 2005 PPP $)	130.6

National-Level Actions
Latest UNFCCC national communication	
Annex-I emissions reduction target	
NAMA submission	
NAPA submission	
Renewable energy target	

Carbon Markets
Hosted Clean Development Mechanism (CDM) projects	
Issued Certified Emission Reductions (CERs) from CDM (thousands)	
Hosted Joint Implementation (JI) projects	
Issued Emission Reduction Units (ERUs) from JI (thousands)	

Middle East & North Africa

Population (millions)	331.3	GDP ($ billions)	1,068.5
Pop. growth (avg. ann. %, 1990–2010)	1.9	GNI per capita (Atlas $)	3,903

Climate
Average daily min/max temperature (1961-90, Celsius)	
Projected annual temperature change (2045-65, Celsius)	
Average annual precipitation (1961-90, mm)	
Projected annual precipitation change (2045-65, mm)	
Projected change in annual hot days/warm nights	
Projected change in annual cool days/cold nights	

Exposure to Impacts
Land area below 5m (% of land area)	1.4
Population below 5m (% of total)	9.7
Population in urban agglomerations > 1 million (%)	20
Urban pop. growth (avg. annual %, 1990–2010)	2.5
Droughts, floods, extreme temps (% pop. avg., 1990–2009)	
Annual freshwater withdrawals (% of internal resources)	121.9
Agricultural land under irrigation (% of total ag. land)	..
Population living below $1.25 a day (% of total)	3.6
Nationally terrestrial protected areas (% of total land area)	4.0
Under-five mortality rate (per 1,000)	34
Child malnutrition, underweight (% of under age five)	6.8
Malaria incidence rate (per 100,000 people)	..

Resilience
Access to improved sanitation (% of total pop.)	84
Access to improved water source (% of total pop.)	87
Cereal yield (kg. per hectare)	2,512
Access to electricity (% of total population)	92.9
Paved roads (% of total roads)	74.3
Health workers (per 1,000 people)	3.6
Foreign direct investment, net inflows (% of GDP)	2.9
Invest. in infrastructure w/private participation ($ millions)	5,854
Disaster risk reduction progress score (1-5 scale; 5 = best)	
Ease of doing business (ranking 1-183; 1 = best)	
Public sector mgmt & institutions avg. (1-6 scale; 6 = best)	
Primary completion rate, total (% of relevant age group)	88
Ratio of girls to boys in primary & secondary school (%)	93

GHG Emissions and Energy Use
CO_2 emissions per capita (metric tons)	3.8
CO_2 emissions per units of GDP (kg/$1,000 of 2005 PPP $)	604.6
CO_2 emissions, total (MtCO_2)	1,230
GHG net emissions/removals by LUCF (MtCO_2e)	
Methane (CH_4) emissions, total (MtCO_2e)	287
Nitrous oxide (N_2O) emissions, total (MtCO_2e)	74
Other GHG emissions, total (MtCO_2e)	7
Energy use per capita (kilograms of oil equivalent)	1,399
Energy use per units of GDP (kg oil eq./$1,000 of 2005 PPP $)	213.9

National-Level Actions
Latest UNFCCC national communication	
Annex-I emissions reduction target	
NAMA submission	
NAPA submission	
Renewable energy target	

Carbon Markets
Hosted Clean Development Mechanism (CDM) projects	
Issued Certified Emission Reductions (CERs) from CDM (thousands)	
Hosted Joint Implementation (JI) projects	
Issued Emission Reduction Units (ERUs) from JI (thousands)	

South Asia

Population (millions)	1,579.5	GDP ($ billions)	2,088.2
Pop. growth (avg. ann. %, 1990-2010)	1.7	GNI per capita (Atlas $)	1,222

Climate

Average daily min/max temperature (1961-90, Celsius)	
Projected annual temperature change (2045-65, Celsius)	
Average annual precipitation (1961-90, mm)	
Projected annual precipitation change (2045-65, mm)	
Projected change in annual hot days/warm nights	
Projected change in annual cool days/cold nights	

Exposure to Impacts

Land area below 5m (% of land area)	1.5
Population below 5m (% of total)	4.4
Population in urban agglomerations > 1 million (%)	13
Urban pop. growth (avg. annual %, 1990-2010)	2.7
Droughts, floods, extreme temps (% pop. avg., 1990-2009)	
Annual freshwater withdrawals (% of internal resources)	50.6
Agricultural land under irrigation (% of total ag. land)	..
Population living below $1.25 a day (% of total)	40.3
Nationally terrestrial protected areas (% of total land area)	6.1
Under-five mortality rate (per 1,000)	67
Child malnutrition, underweight (% of under age five)	42.5
Malaria incidence rate (per 100,000 people)	1,127

Resilience

Access to improved sanitation (% of total pop.)	36
Access to improved water source (% of total pop.)	87
Cereal yield (kg. per hectare)	2,728
Access to electricity (% of total population)	62.1
Paved roads (% of total roads)	58.9
Health workers (per 1,000 people)	1.7
Foreign direct investment, net inflows (% of GDP)	1.3
Invest. in infrastructure w/private participation ($ millions)	73,548
Disaster risk reduction progress score (1-5 scale; 5 = best)	
Ease of doing business (ranking 1-183; 1 = best)	
Public sector mgmt & institutions avg. (1-6 scale; 6 = best)	
Primary completion rate, total (% of relevant age group)	86
Ratio of girls to boys in primary & secondary school (%)	92

GHG Emissions and Energy Use

CO_2 emissions per capita (metric tons)	1.3
CO_2 emissions per units of GDP (kg/$1,000 of 2005 PPP $)	504.6
CO_2 emissions, total (MtCO_2)	1,970
GHG net emissions/removals by LUCF (MtCO_2e)	
Methane (CH_4) emissions, total (MtCO_2e)	846
Nitrous oxide (N_2O) emissions, total (MtCO_2e)	268
Other GHG emissions, total (MtCO_2e)	9
Energy use per capita (kilograms of oil equivalent)	532
Energy use per units of GDP (kg oil eq./$1,000 of 2005 PPP $)	193.5

National-Level Actions

Latest UNFCCC national communication
Annex-I emissions reduction target
NAMA submission
NAPA submission
Renewable energy target

Carbon Markets

Hosted Clean Development Mechanism (CDM) projects
Issued Certified Emission Reductions (CERs) from CDM (thousands)
Hosted Joint Implementation (JI) projects
Issued Emission Reduction Units (ERUs) from JI (thousands)

Sub-Saharan Africa

Population (millions)	853.6	GDP ($ billions)	1,097.9
Pop. growth (avg. ann. %, 1990–2010)	2.6	GNI per capita (Atlas $)	1,176

Climate
Average daily min/max temperature (1961–90, Celsius)
Projected annual temperature change (2045–65, Celsius)
Average annual precipitation (1961–90, mm)
Projected annual precipitation change (2045–65, mm)
Projected change in annual hot days/warm nights
Projected change in annual cool days/cold nights

Exposure to Impacts

Land area below 5m (% of land area)	0.4
Population below 5m (% of total)	2.0
Population in urban agglomerations > 1 million (%)	14
Urban pop. growth (avg. annual %, 1990–2010)	4.0
Droughts, floods, extreme temps (% pop. avg., 1990–2009)	
Annual freshwater withdrawals (% of internal resources)	3.2
Agricultural land under irrigation (% of total ag. land)	..
Population living below $1.25 a day (% of total)	50.9
Nationally terrestrial protected areas (% of total land area)	11.7
Under-five mortality rate (per 1,000)	121
Child malnutrition, underweight (% of under age five)	24.6
Malaria incidence rate (per 100,000 people)	26,113

Resilience

Access to improved sanitation (% of total pop.)	31
Access to improved water source (% of total pop.)	60
Cereal yield (kg. per hectare)	1,297
Access to electricity (% of total population)	32.5
Paved roads (% of total roads)	18.3
Health workers (per 1,000 people)	1.2
Foreign direct investment, net inflows (% of GDP)	3.6
Invest. in infrastructure w/private participation ($ millions)	11,957
Disaster risk reduction progress score (1–5 scale; 5 = best)	
Ease of doing business (ranking 1–183; 1 = best)	
Public sector mgmt & institutions avg. (1–6 scale; 6 = best)	
Primary completion rate, total (% of relevant age group)	67
Ratio of girls to boys in primary & secondary school (%)	89

GHG Emissions and Energy Use

CO_2 emissions per capita (metric tons)	0.8
CO_2 emissions per units of GDP (kg/$1,000 of 2005 PPP $)	428.6
CO_2 emissions, total (MtCO_2)	685
GHG net emissions/removals by LUCF (MtCO_2e)	
Methane (CH_4) emissions, total (MtCO_2e)	590
Nitrous oxide (N_2O) emissions, total (MtCO_2e)	334
Other GHG emissions, total (MtCO_2e)	..
Energy use per capita (kilograms of oil equivalent)	689
Energy use per units of GDP (kg oil eq./$1,000 of 2005 PPP $)	308.4

National-Level Actions
Latest UNFCCC national communication
Annex-I emissions reduction target
NAMA submission
NAPA submission
Renewable energy target

Carbon Markets
Hosted Clean Development Mechanism (CDM) projects
Issued Certified Emission Reductions (CERs) from CDM (thousands)
Hosted Joint Implementation (JI) projects
Issued Emission Reduction Units (ERUs) from JI (thousands)

Income & other group tables

For operational and analytical purposes, the World Bank's main criterion for classifying economies is gross national income (GNI) per capita. Each economy in The *Little Data Book on Climate Change* is classified as low income, middle income, or high income. Low- and middle-income economies are sometimes referred to as *developing economies*. The use of the term is convenient; it is not intended to imply that all economies in the group are experiencing similar development or that other economies have reached a preferred or final stage of development. Classification by income does not necessarily reflect development status.

Note: Classifications are fixed during the World Bank's fiscal year (ending on June 30). Thus, countries remain in the categories in which they are classified irrespective of any revisions to their per capita income data.

Low-income economies are those with a 2010 GNI per capita of $1,005 or less.

Middle-income economies are those with a 2010 GNI per capita of more than $1,006 but less than $12,276. Lower-middle-income and upper-middle-income economies are separated at a 2010 GNI per capita of $3,975.

High-income economies are those with a GNI per capita of $12,276 or more.

Euro area includes the member states of the Economic and Monetary Union of the European Union that have adopted the euro as their currency: Austria, Belgium, Cyprus, Estonia, Finland, France, Germany, Greece, Ireland, Italy, Luxembourg, Malta, Netherlands, Portugal, Slovak Republic, Slovenia, and Spain.

Small island developing states included in this publication are American Samoa, Antigua and Barbuda, Aruba, The Bahamas, Barbados, Belize, Cape Verde, Comoros, Cook Islands, Cuba, Dominica, Dominican Republic, Fiji, French Polynesia, Grenada, Guam, Guinea-Bissau, Guyana, Haiti, Jamaica, Kiribati, Maldives, Marshall Islands, Mauritius, Federated States of Micronesia, Nauru, New Caledonia, Niue, Northern Mariana Islands, Palau, Papua New Guinea, Puerto Rico, Samoa, São Tomé and Príncipe, Seychelles, Singapore, Solomon Islands, St. Kitts and Nevis, St. Lucia, St. Vincent and the Grenadines, Suriname, Timor-Leste, Tonga, Trinidad and Tobago, Tuvalu, Vanuatu, and Virgin Islands (U.S.).

Low income

Population (millions)	796.3	GDP ($ billions)	413.9
Pop. growth (avg. ann. %, 1990–2010)	2.3	GNI per capita (Atlas $)	523

Climate
Average daily min/max temperature (1961–90, Celsius)	
Projected annual temperature change (2045–65, Celsius)	
Average annual precipitation (1961–90, mm)	
Projected annual precipitation change (2045–65, mm)	
Projected change in annual hot days/warm nights	
Projected change in annual cool days/cold nights	

Exposure to Impacts
Land area below 5m (% of land area)	0.7
Population below 5m (% of total)	5.1
Population in urban agglomerations > 1 million (%)	11
Urban pop. growth (avg. annual %, 1990–2010)	3.7
Droughts, floods, extreme temps (% pop. avg., 1990–2009)	
Annual freshwater withdrawals (% of internal resources)	3.7
Agricultural land under irrigation (% of total ag. land)	..
Population living below $1.25 a day (% of total)	..
Nationally terrestrial protected areas (% of total land area)	10.6
Under-five mortality rate (per 1,000)	108
Child malnutrition, underweight (% of under age five)	28.3
Malaria incidence rate (per 100,000 people)	16,659

Resilience
Access to improved sanitation (% of total pop.)	35
Access to improved water source (% of total pop.)	63
Cereal yield (kg. per hectare)	2,047
Access to electricity (% of total population)	23.0
Paved roads (% of total roads)	14.1
Health workers (per 1,000 people)	0.7
Foreign direct investment, net inflows (% of GDP)	3.2
Invest. in infrastructure w/private participation ($ millions)	4,471
Disaster risk reduction progress score (1–5 scale; 5 = best)	
Ease of doing business (ranking 1-183; 1 = best)	
Public sector mgmt & institutions avg. (1–6 scale; 6 = best)	
Primary completion rate, total (% of relevant age group)	65
Ratio of girls to boys in primary & secondary school (%)	91

GHG Emissions and Energy Use
CO_2 emissions per capita (metric tons)	0.3
CO_2 emissions per units of GDP (kg/$1,000 of 2005 PPP $)	270.2
CO_2 emissions, total (MtCO_2)	219
GHG net emissions/removals by LUCF (MtCO_2e)	
Methane (CH_4) emissions, total (MtCO_2e)	436
Nitrous oxide (N_2O) emissions, total (MtCO_2e)	209
Other GHG emissions, total (MtCO_2e)	..
Energy use per capita (kilograms of oil equivalent)	365
Energy use per units of GDP (kg oil eq./$1,000 of 2005 PPP $)	303.9

National-Level Actions
Latest UNFCCC national communication	
Annex-I emissions reduction target	
NAMA submission	
NAPA submission	
Renewable energy target	

Carbon Markets
Hosted Clean Development Mechanism (CDM) projects	
Issued Certified Emission Reductions (CERs) from CDM (thousands)	
Hosted Joint Implementation (JI) projects	
Issued Emission Reduction Units (ERUs) from JI (thousands)	

Middle income

Population (millions)	4,917.2	GDP ($ billions)	19,561.7
Pop. growth (avg. ann. %, 1990–2010)	1.3	GNI per capita (Atlas $)	3,763

Climate
Average daily min/max temperature (1961–90, Celsius)
Projected annual temperature change (2045–65, Celsius)
Average annual precipitation (1961–90, mm)
Projected annual precipitation change (2045–65, mm)
Projected change in annual hot days/warm nights
Projected change in annual cool days/cold nights

Exposure to Impacts
Land area below 5m (% of land area)	1.8
Population below 5m (% of total)	6.5
Population in urban agglomerations > 1 million (%)	18
Urban pop. growth (avg. annual %, 1990–2010)	2.5
Droughts, floods, extreme temps (% pop. avg., 1990–2009)	
Annual freshwater withdrawals (% of internal resources)	9.1
Agricultural land under irrigation (% of total ag. land)	..
Population living below $1.25 a day (% of total)	..
Nationally terrestrial protected areas (% of total land area)	12.5
Under-five mortality rate (per 1,000)	51
Child malnutrition, underweight (% of under age five)	20.9
Malaria incidence rate (per 100,000 people)	2,574

Resilience
Access to improved sanitation (% of total pop.)	56
Access to improved water source (% of total pop.)	88
Cereal yield (kg. per hectare)	3,256
Access to electricity (% of total population)	81.6
Paved roads (% of total roads)	45.0
Health workers (per 1,000 people)	3.5
Foreign direct investment, net inflows (% of GDP)	2.6
Invest. in infrastructure w/private participation ($ millions)	138,442
Disaster risk reduction progress score (1–5 scale; 5 = best)	
Ease of doing business (ranking 1–183; 1 = best)	
Public sector mgmt & institutions avg. (1–6 scale; 6 = best)	
Primary completion rate, total (% of relevant age group)	92
Ratio of girls to boys in primary & secondary school (%)	97

GHG Emissions and Energy Use
CO_2 emissions per capita (metric tons)	3.5
CO_2 emissions per units of GDP (kg/$1,000 of 2005 PPP $)	622.9
CO_2 emissions, total (MtCO$_2$)	16,604
GHG net emissions/removals by LUCF (MtCO$_2$e)	
Methane (CH$_4$) emissions, total (MtCO$_2$e)	5,160
Nitrous oxide (N$_2$O) emissions, total (MtCO$_2$e)	1,830
Other GHG emissions, total (MtCO$_2$e)	261
Energy use per capita (kilograms of oil equivalent)	1,268
Energy use per units of GDP (kg oil eq./$1,000 of 2005 PPP $)	224.6

National-Level Actions
Latest UNFCCC national communication
Annex-I emissions reduction target
NAMA submission
NAPA submission
Renewable energy target

Carbon Markets
Hosted Clean Development Mechanism (CDM) projects
Issued Certified Emission Reductions (CERs) from CDM (thousands)
Hosted Joint Implementation (JI) projects
Issued Emission Reduction Units (ERUs) from JI (thousands)

Lower middle income

Population (millions)	2,465.1	GDP ($ billions)	4,312.0
Pop. growth (avg. ann. %, 1990-2010)	1.7	GNI per capita (Atlas $)	1,660

Climate
Average daily min/max temperature (1961-90, Celsius)	
Projected annual temperature change (2045-65, Celsius)	
Average annual precipitation (1961-90, mm)	
Projected annual precipitation change (2045-65, mm)	
Projected change in annual hot days/warm nights	
Projected change in annual cool days/cold nights	

Exposure to Impacts
Land area below 5m (% of land area)	1.7
Population below 5m (% of total)	6.5
Population in urban agglomerations > 1 million (%)	14
Urban pop. growth (avg. annual %, 1990-2010)	2.8
Droughts, floods, extreme temps (% pop. avg., 1990-2009)	
Annual freshwater withdrawals (% of internal resources)	18.7
Agricultural land under irrigation (% of total ag. land)	..
Population living below $1.25 a day (% of total)	..
Nationally terrestrial protected areas (% of total land area)	9.5
Under-five mortality rate (per 1,000)	69
Child malnutrition, underweight (% of under age five)	31.7
Malaria incidence rate (per 100,000 people)	4,874

Resilience
Access to improved sanitation (% of total pop.)	45
Access to improved water source (% of total pop.)	84
Cereal yield (kg. per hectare)	2,754
Access to electricity (% of total population) .	67.3
Paved roads (% of total roads)	29.3
Health workers (per 1,000 people)	2.6
Foreign direct investment, net inflows (% of GDP)	2.4
Invest. in infrastructure w/private participation ($ millions)	81,789
Disaster risk reduction progress score (1-5 scale; 5 = best)	
Ease of doing business (ranking 1-183; 1 = best)	
Public sector mgmt & institutions avg. (1-6 scale; 6 = best)	
Primary completion rate, total (% of relevant age group)	88
Ratio of girls to boys in primary & secondary school (%)	93

GHG Emissions and Energy Use
CO_2 emissions per capita (metric tons)	1.6
CO_2 emissions per units of GDP (kg/$1,000 of 2005 PPP $)	523.9
CO_2 emissions, total (MtCO$_2$)	3,744
GHG net emissions/removals by LUCF (MtCO$_2$e)	
Methane (CH$_4$) emissions, total (MtCO$_2$e)	1,705
Nitrous oxide (N$_2$O) emissions, total (MtCO$_2$e)	687
Other GHG emissions, total (MtCO$_2$e)	17
Energy use per capita (kilograms of oil equivalent)	680
Energy use per units of GDP (kg oil eq./$1,000 of 2005 PPP $)	217.9

National-Level Actions
Latest UNFCCC national communication	
Annex-I emissions reduction target	
NAMA submission	
NAPA submission	
Renewable energy target	

Carbon Markets
Hosted Clean Development Mechanism (CDM) projects	
Issued Certified Emission Reductions (CERs) from CDM (thousands)	
Hosted Joint Implementation (JI) projects	
Issued Emission Reduction Units (ERUs) from JI (thousands)	

Upper middle income

Population (millions)	2,452.2	GDP ($ billions)	15,246.7
Pop. growth (avg. ann. %, 1990–2010)	0.9	GNI per capita (Atlas $)	5,876

Climate

Average daily min/max temperature (1961–90, Celsius)	
Projected annual temperature change (2045–65, Celsius)	
Average annual precipitation (1961–90, mm)	
Projected annual precipitation change (2045–65, mm)	
Projected change in annual hot days/warm nights	
Projected change in annual cool days/cold nights	

Exposure to Impacts

Land area below 5m (% of land area)	1.8
Population below 5m (% of total)	6.5
Population in urban agglomerations > 1 million (%)	22
Urban pop. growth (avg. annual %, 1990–2010)	2.3
Droughts, floods, extreme temps (% pop. avg., 1990–2009)	
Annual freshwater withdrawals (% of internal resources)	5.6
Agricultural land under irrigation (% of total ag. land)	..
Population living below $1.25 a day (% of total)	..
Nationally terrestrial protected areas (% of total land area)	13.6
Under-five mortality rate (per 1,000)	20
Child malnutrition, underweight (% of under age five)	4.1
Malaria incidence rate (per 100,000 people)	80

Resilience

Access to improved sanitation (% of total pop.)	68
Access to improved water source (% of total pop.)	92
Cereal yield (kg. per hectare)	3,690
Access to electricity (% of total population)	98.0
Paved roads (% of total roads)	50.5
Health workers (per 1,000 people)	4.5
Foreign direct investment, net inflows (% of GDP)	2.7
Invest. in infrastructure w/private participation ($ millions)	26,166
Disaster risk reduction progress score (1–5 scale; 5 = best)	
Ease of doing business (ranking 1–183; 1 = best)	
Public sector mgmt & institutions avg. (1–6 scale; 6 = best)	
Primary completion rate, total (% of relevant age group)	98
Ratio of girls to boys in primary & secondary school (%)	103

GHG Emissions and Energy Use

CO_2 emissions per capita (metric tons)	5.3
CO_2 emissions per units of GDP (kg/$1,000 of 2005 PPP $)	659.4
CO_2 emissions, total (MtCO_2)	12,860
GHG net emissions/removals by LUCF (MtCO_2e)	
Methane (CH_4) emissions, total (MtCO_2e)	3,455
Nitrous oxide (N_2O) emissions, total (MtCO_2e)	1,144
Other GHG emissions, total (MtCO_2e)	243
Energy use per capita (kilograms of oil equivalent)	1,848
Energy use per units of GDP (kg oil eq./$1,000 of 2005 PPP $)	227.1

National-Level Actions

Latest UNFCCC national communication
Annex-I emissions reduction target
NAMA submission
NAPA submission
Renewable energy target

Carbon Markets

Hosted Clean Development Mechanism (CDM) projects
Issued Certified Emission Reductions (CERs) from CDM (thousands)
Hosted Joint Implementation (JI) projects
Issued Emission Reduction Units (ERUs) from JI (thousands)

Low and middle income

Population (millions)	5,713.5	GDP ($ billions)	19,997.4
Pop. growth (avg. ann. %, 1990–2010)	1.4	GNI per capita (Atlas $)	3,315

Climate
Average daily min/max temperature (1961–90, Celsius)
Projected annual temperature change (2045–65, Celsius)
Average annual precipitation (1961–90, mm)
Projected annual precipitation change (2045–65, mm)
Projected change in annual hot days/warm nights
Projected change in annual cool days/cold nights

Exposure to Impacts
Land area below 5m (% of land area)	1.6
Population below 5m (% of total)	6.3
Population in urban agglomerations > 1 million (%)	17
Urban pop. growth (avg. annual %, 1990–2010)	2.6
Droughts, floods, extreme temps (% pop. avg., 1990–2009)	
Annual freshwater withdrawals (% of internal resources)	8.4
Agricultural land under irrigation (% of total ag. land)	..
Population living below $1.25 a day (% of total)	25.2
Nationally terrestrial protected areas (% of total land area)	12.2
Under-five mortality rate (per 1,000)	63
Child malnutrition, underweight (% of under age five)	22.5
Malaria incidence rate (per 100,000 people)	4,665

Resilience
Access to improved sanitation (% of total pop.)	54
Access to improved water source (% of total pop.)	84
Cereal yield (kg. per hectare)	3,065
Access to electricity (% of total population)	73.7
Paved roads (% of total roads)	29.3
Health workers (per 1,000 people)	3.1
Foreign direct investment, net inflows (% of GDP)	2.7
Invest. in infrastructure w/private participation ($ millions)	144,800
Disaster risk reduction progress score (1–5 scale; 5 = best)	
Ease of doing business (ranking 1–183; 1 = best)	
Public sector mgmt & institutions avg. (1–6 scale; 6 = best)	
Primary completion rate, total (% of relevant age group)	87
Ratio of girls to boys in primary & secondary school (%)	96

GHG Emissions and Energy Use
CO_2 emissions per capita (metric tons)	3.0
CO_2 emissions per units of GDP (kg/$1,000 of 2005 PPP $)	612.5
CO_2 emissions, total (MtCO$_2$)	16,822
GHG net emissions/removals by LUCF (MtCO$_2$e)	
Methane (CH_4) emissions, total (MtCO$_2$e)	5,597
Nitrous oxide (N_2O) emissions, total (MtCO$_2$e)	2,040
Other GHG emissions, total (MtCO$_2$e)	264
Energy use per capita (kilograms of oil equivalent)	1,173
Energy use per units of GDP (kg oil eq./$1,000 of 2005 PPP $)	226.1

National-Level Actions
Latest UNFCCC national communication
Annex-I emissions reduction target
NAMA submission
NAPA submission
Renewable energy target

Carbon Markets
Hosted Clean Development Mechanism (CDM) projects
Issued Certified Emission Reductions (CERs) from CDM (thousands)
Hosted Joint Implementation (JI) projects
Issued Emission Reduction Units (ERUs) from JI (thousands)

High income

Population (millions)	1,127.0	GDP ($ billions)	43,019.0
Pop. growth (avg. ann. %, 1990-2010)	0.7	GNI per capita (Atlas $)	38,517

Climate
Average daily min/max temperature (1961-90, Celsius)	
Projected annual temperature change (2045-65, Celsius)	
Average annual precipitation (1961-90, mm)	
Projected annual precipitation change (2045-65, mm)	
Projected change in annual hot days/warm nights	
Projected change in annual cool days/cold nights	

Exposure to Impacts
Land area below 5m (% of land area)	2.2
Population below 5m (% of total)	7.7
Population in urban agglomerations > 1 million (%)	..
Urban pop. growth (avg. annual %, 1990-2010)	1.0
Droughts, floods, extreme temps (% pop. avg., 1990-2009)	
Annual freshwater withdrawals (% of internal resources)	10.4
Agricultural land under irrigation (% of total ag. land)	..
Population living below $1.25 a day (% of total)	..
Nationally terrestrial protected areas (% of total land area)	13.4
Under-five mortality rate (per 1,000)	6
Child malnutrition, underweight (% of under age five)	..
Malaria incidence rate (per 100,000 people)	..

Resilience
Access to improved sanitation (% of total pop.)	100
Access to improved water source (% of total pop.)	100
Cereal yield (kg. per hectare)	5,445
Access to electricity (% of total population)	..
Paved roads (% of total roads)	87.3
Health workers (per 1,000 people)	10.7
Foreign direct investment, net inflows (% of GDP)	1.8
Invest. in infrastructure w/private participation ($ millions)	..
Disaster risk reduction progress score (1-5 scale; 5 = best)	
Ease of doing business (ranking 1-183; 1 = best)	
Public sector mgmt & institutions avg. (1-6 scale; 6 = best)	
Primary completion rate, total (% of relevant age group)	97
Ratio of girls to boys in primary & secondary school (%)	100

GHG Emissions and Energy Use
CO_2 emissions per capita (metric tons)	11.9
CO_2 emissions per units of GDP (kg/$1,000 of 2005 PPP $)	354.4
CO_2 emissions, total (MtCO_2)	13,285
GHG net emissions/removals by LUCF (MtCO_2e)	
Methane (CH_4) emissions, total (MtCO_2e)	1,539
Nitrous oxide (N_2O) emissions, total (MtCO_2e)	813
Other GHG emissions, total (MtCO_2e)	460
Energy use per capita (kilograms of oil equivalent)	4,944
Energy use per units of GDP (kg oil eq./$1,000 of 2005 PPP $)	147.0

National-Level Actions
Latest UNFCCC national communication	
Annex-I emissions reduction target	
NAMA submission	
NAPA submission	
Renewable energy target	

Carbon Markets
Hosted Clean Development Mechanism (CDM) projects	
Issued Certified Emission Reductions (CERs) from CDM (thousands)	
Hosted Joint Implementation (JI) projects	
Issued Emission Reduction Units (ERUs) from JI (thousands)	

Euro area

Population (millions)	331.7	GDP ($ billions)	12,174.5
Pop. growth (avg. ann. %, 1990–2010)	0.4	GNI per capita (Atlas $)	38,571

Climate
Average daily min/max temperature (1961-90, Celsius)	
Projected annual temperature change (2045-65, Celsius)	
Average annual precipitation (1961-90, mm)	
Projected annual precipitation change (2045-65, mm)	
Projected change in annual hot days/warm nights	
Projected change in annual cool days/cold nights	

Exposure to Impacts
Land area below 5m (% of land area)	3.6
Population below 5m (% of total)	8.5
Population in urban agglomerations > 1 million (%)	18
Urban pop. growth (avg. annual %, 1990–2010)	0.6
Droughts, floods, extreme temps (% pop. avg., 1990–2009)	
Annual freshwater withdrawals (% of internal resources)	21.5
Agricultural land under irrigation (% of total ag. land)	..
Population living below $1.25 a day (% of total)	..
Nationally terrestrial protected areas (% of total land area)	15.5
Under-five mortality rate (per 1,000)	4
Child malnutrition, underweight (% of under age five)	..
Malaria incidence rate (per 100,000 people)	..

Resilience
Access to improved sanitation (% of total pop.)	100
Access to improved water source (% of total pop.)	100
Cereal yield (kg. per hectare)	5,817
Access to electricity (% of total population)	..
Paved roads (% of total roads)	91.8
Health workers (per 1,000 people)	11.3
Foreign direct investment, net inflows (% of GDP)	2.7
Invest. in infrastructure w/private participation ($ millions)	..
Disaster risk reduction progress score (1–5 scale; 5 = best)	
Ease of doing business (ranking 1–183; 1 = best)	
Public sector mgmt & institutions avg. (1–6 scale; 6 = best)	
Primary completion rate, total (% of relevant age group)	101
Ratio of girls to boys in primary & secondary school (%)	99

GHG Emissions and Energy Use
CO_2 emissions per capita (metric tons)	8.0
CO_2 emissions per units of GDP (kg/$1,000 of 2005 PPP $)	260.0
CO_2 emissions, total (MtCO_2)	2,633
GHG net emissions/removals by LUCF (MtCO_2e)	
Methane (CH_4) emissions, total (MtCO_2e)	318
Nitrous oxide (N_2O) emissions, total (MtCO_2e)	219
Other GHG emissions, total (MtCO_2e)	84
Energy use per capita (kilograms of oil equivalent)	3,642
Energy use per units of GDP (kg oil eq./$1,000 of 2005 PPP $)	122.2

National-Level Actions
Latest UNFCCC national communication	
Annex-I emissions reduction target	
NAMA submission	
NAPA submission	
Renewable energy target	

Carbon Markets
Hosted Clean Development Mechanism (CDM) projects	
Issued Certified Emission Reductions (CERs) from CDM (thousands)	
Hosted Joint Implementation (JI) projects	
Issued Emission Reduction Units (ERUs) from JI (thousands)	

Small island dev. states

Population (millions)	63.2	GDP ($ billions)	575.3
Pop. growth (avg. ann. %, 1990-2010)	1.3	GNI per capita (Atlas $)	8,226

Climate
Average daily min/max temperature (1961-90, Celsius)	
Projected annual temperature change (2045-65, Celsius)	
Average annual precipitation (1961-90, mm)	
Projected annual precipitation change (2045-65, mm)	
Projected change in annual hot days/warm nights	
Projected change in annual cool days/cold nights	

Exposure to Impacts
Land area below 5m (% of land area)	5.4
Population below 5m (% of total)	9.8
Population in urban agglomerations > 1 million (%)	..
Urban pop. growth (avg. annual %, 1990-2010)	2.0
Droughts, floods, extreme temps (% pop. avg., 1990-2009)	
Annual freshwater withdrawals (% of internal resources)	1.4
Agricultural land under irrigation (% of total ag. land)	..
Population living below $1.25 a day (% of total)	..
Nationally terrestrial protected areas (% of total land area)	6.7
Under-five mortality rate (per 1,000)	69
Child malnutrition, underweight (% of under age five)	9.7
Malaria incidence rate (per 100,000 people)	..

Resilience
Access to improved sanitation (% of total pop.)	67
Access to improved water source (% of total pop.)	80
Cereal yield (kg. per hectare)	1,922
Access to electricity (% of total population)	81.4
Paved roads (% of total roads)	49.9
Health workers (per 1,000 people)	..
Foreign direct investment, net inflows (% of GDP)	12.2
Invest. in infrastructure w/private participation ($ millions)	186
Disaster risk reduction progress score (1-5 scale; 5 = best)	
Ease of doing business (ranking 1-183; 1 = best)	
Public sector mgmt & institutions avg. (1-6 scale; 6 = best)	
Primary completion rate, total (% of relevant age group)	..
Ratio of girls to boys in primary & secondary school (%)	..

GHG Emissions and Energy Use
CO_2 emissions per capita (metric tons)	3.7
CO_2 emissions per units of GDP (kg/$1,000 of 2005 PPP $)	351.5
CO_2 emissions, total (MtCO_2)	230
GHG net emissions/removals by LUCF (MtCO_2e)	
Methane (CH_4) emissions, total (MtCO_2e)	33
Nitrous oxide (N_2O) emissions, total (MtCO_2e)	12
Other GHG emissions, total (MtCO_2e)	..
Energy use per capita (kilograms of oil equivalent)	1,416
Energy use per units of GDP (kg oil eq./$1,000 of 2005 PPP $)	143.0

National-Level Actions
Latest UNFCCC national communication	
Annex-I emissions reduction target	
NAMA submission	
NAPA submission	
Renewable energy target	

Carbon Markets
Hosted Clean Development Mechanism (CDM) projects	
Issued Certified Emission Reductions (CERs) from CDM (thousands)	
Hosted Joint Implementation (JI) projects	
Issued Emission Reduction Units (ERUs) from JI (thousands)	

Country tables

China

Data for China do not include data for Hong Kong SAR, China; Macao SAR, China; or Taiwan, China.

Cyprus

GNI and GDP data and data calculated using GNI and GDP data refer to the area controlled by the government of the Republic of Cyprus.

Georgia

GNI, GDP, and population data and data calculated using GNI, GDP and population data exclude Abkhazia and South Ossetia.

Kosovo, Montenegro, and Serbia

Where available, data for each country are shown separately. However, some indicators for Serbia prior to 2006 include data for Montenegro. Moreover, data for most indicators for Serbia from 1999 onward exclude data for Kosovo, which in 1999 became a territory under international administration pursuant to UN Security Council Resolution 1244 (1999). Kosovo became a member of the World Bank on June 29, 2009.

Moldova

GNI, GDP and population data and data calculated using GNI, GDP population data exclude Transnistria.

Morocco

GNI and GDP data and data calculated using GNI and GDP data include Former Spanish Sahara.

Netherlands Antilles

Netherlands Antilles ceased to exist on October 10, 2010. Curaçao and Sint Maarten became countries within the Kingdom of the Netherlands. Bonaire, St. Eustatius, and Saba became special municipalities of the Netherlands.

Sudan and South Sudan

The Republic of South Sudan became an independent state on July 9, 2011. Data reported for Sudan include South Sudan.

Tanzania

GNI and GDP data and data calculated using GNI and GDP data refer to mainland Tanzania only.

For more information, see *World Development Indicators 2011* or http://data.worldbank.org/.

Afghanistan

Population (millions)	34.4	GDP ($ billions)	11.8
Pop. growth (avg. ann. %, 1990–2010)	3.0	GNI per capita (Atlas $)	290

Climate

Average daily min/max temperature (1961–90, Celsius)	6 / 20
Projected annual temperature change (2045–65, Celsius)	2.3 to 3.6
Average annual precipitation (1961–90, mm)	327
Projected annual precipitation change (2045–65, mm)	-58 to 13
Projected change in annual hot days/warm nights	3 / 7
Projected change in annual cool days/cold nights	-1 / -1

	Country data	South Asia	Low Income
Exposure to Impacts			
Land area below 5m (% of land area)	0.0	1.5	0.7
Population below 5m (% of total)	0.0	4.4	5.1
Population in urban agglomerations > 1 million (%)	11	13	11
Urban pop. growth (avg. annual %, 1990–2010)	4.5	2.7	3.7
Droughts, floods, extreme temps (% pop. avg., 1990–2009)	1.1		
Annual freshwater withdrawals (% of internal resources)	42.0	50.6	3.7
Agricultural land under irrigation (% of total ag. land)	4.8	..	..
Population living below $1.25 a day (% of total)	..	40.3	..
Nationally terrestrial protected areas (% of total land area)	0.4	6.1	10.6
Under-five mortality rate (per 1,000)	149	67	108
Child malnutrition, underweight (% of under age five)	32.9	42.5	28.3
Malaria incidence rate (per 100,000 people)	2,428	1,127	16,659
Resilience			
Access to improved sanitation (% of total pop.)	37	36	35
Access to improved water source (% of total pop.)	48	87	63
Cereal yield (kg. per hectare)	2,031	2,728	2,047
Access to electricity (% of total population)	15.6	62.1	23.0
Paved roads (% of total roads)	29.3	58.9	14.1
Health workers (per 1,000 people)	0.7	1.7	0.7
Foreign direct investment, net inflows (% of GDP)	2.6	1.3	3.2
Invest. in infrastructure w/private participation ($ millions)	60	73,548	4,471
Disaster risk reduction progress score (1–5 scale; 5 = best)	..		
Ease of doing business (ranking 1–183; 1 = best)	160		
Public sector mgmt & institutions avg. (1–6 scale; 6 = best)	2.4		
Primary completion rate, total (% of relevant age group)	39	86	65
Ratio of girls to boys in primary & secondary school (%)	62	92	91
GHG Emissions and Energy Use			
CO_2 emissions per capita (metric tons)	0.0	1.3	0.3
CO_2 emissions per units of GDP (kg/$1,000 of 2005 PPP $)	28.5	504.6	270.2
CO_2 emissions, total (MtCO_2)	0.8	1,970	219
GHG net emissions/removals by LUCF (MtCO_2e)	..		
Methane (CH_4) emissions, total (MtCO_2e)	..	846	436
Nitrous oxide (N_2O) emissions, total (MtCO_2e)	..	268	209
Other GHG emissions, total (MtCO_2e)	..	9	..
Energy use per capita (kilograms of oil equivalent)	..	532	365
Energy use per units of GDP (kg oil eq./$1,000 of 2005 PPP $)	..	193.5	303.9

National-Level Actions

Latest UNFCCC national communication	..
Annex-I emissions reduction target	n/a
NAMA submission	Yes
NAPA submission	Yes
Renewable energy target	..

Carbon Markets

Hosted Clean Development Mechanism (CDM) projects	..
Issued Certified Emission Reductions (CERs) from CDM (thousands)	..
Hosted Joint Implementation (JI) projects	n/a
Issued Emission Reduction Units (ERUs) from JI (thousands)	n/a

Albania

Population (millions)	3.2	GDP ($ billions)	11.8
Pop. growth (avg. ann. %, 1990–2010)	-0.1	GNI per capita (Atlas $)	3,960

Climate

Average daily min/max temperature (1961–90, Celsius)	6 / 17
Projected annual temperature change (2045–65, Celsius)	1.9 to 2.9
Average annual precipitation (1961–90, mm)	996
Projected annual precipitation change (2045–65, mm)	-147 to -44
Projected change in annual hot days/warm nights	3 / 7
Projected change in annual cool days/cold nights	-2 /-1

	Country data	Europe & Central Asia	Upper middle income
Exposure to Impacts			
Land area below 5m (% of land area)	5.0	2.5	1.8
Population below 5m (% of total)	8.2	3.0	6.5
Population in urban agglomerations > 1 million (%)	..	18	22
Urban pop. growth (avg. annual %, 1990–2010)	1.3	0.3	2.3
Droughts, floods, extreme temps (% pop. avg., 1990–2009)	5.3		
Annual freshwater withdrawals (% of internal resources)	6.8	6.5	5.6
Agricultural land under irrigation (% of total ag. land)	16.8	..	..
Population living below $1.25 a day (% of total)	<2	3.7	..
Nationally terrestrial protected areas (% of total land area)	9.8	7.5	13.6
Under-five mortality rate (per 1,000)	18	23	20
Child malnutrition, underweight (% of under age five)	6.6	..	4.1
Malaria incidence rate (per 100,000 people)	..	..	80
Resilience			
Access to improved sanitation (% of total pop.)	98	89	68
Access to improved water source (% of total pop.)	97	95	92
Cereal yield (kg. per hectare)	4,315	2,475	3,690
Access to electricity (% of total population)	..	..	98.0
Paved roads (% of total roads)	39.0	85.8	50.5
Health workers (per 1,000 people)	5.2	9.9	4.5
Foreign direct investment, net inflows (% of GDP)	9.4	2.8	2.7
Invest. in infrastructure w/private participation ($ millions)	137	22,652	26,166
Disaster risk reduction progress score (1–5 scale; 5 = best)	..		
Ease of doing business (ranking 1–183; 1 = best)	82		
Public sector mgmt & institutions avg. (1–6 scale; 6 = best)	3.3		
Primary completion rate, total (% of relevant age group)	90	95	98
Ratio of girls to boys in primary & secondary school (%)	100	97	103
GHG Emissions and Energy Use			
CO_2 emissions per capita (metric tons)	1.3	7.7	5.3
CO_2 emissions per units of GDP (kg/$1,000 of 2005 PPP $)	181.8	708.0	659.4
CO_2 emissions, total (MtCO_2)	4.2	3,110	12,860
GHG net emissions/removals by LUCF (1994, MtCO_2e)	1.5		
Methane (CH_4) emissions, total (MtCO_2e)	2.4	937	3,455
Nitrous oxide (N_2O) emissions, total (MtCO_2e)	1.0	214	1,144
Other GHG emissions, total (MtCO_2e)	0.1	76	243
Energy use per capita (kilograms of oil equivalent)	538	2,833	1,848
Energy use per units of GDP (kg oil eq./$1,000 of 2005 PPP $)	72.3	276.8	227.1

National-Level Actions

Latest UNFCCC national communication	11/23/2009 (2nd)
Annex-I emissions reduction target	n/a
NAMA submission	..
NAPA submission	n/a
Renewable energy target	Yes

Carbon Markets

Hosted Clean Development Mechanism (CDM) projects	1
Issued Certified Emission Reductions (CERs) from CDM (thousands)	0
Hosted Joint Implementation (JI) projects	n/a
Issued Emission Reduction Units (ERUs) from JI (thousands)	n/a

Algeria

Population (millions)	35.5	GDP ($ billions)	159.4
Pop. growth (avg. ann. %, 1990–2010)	1.7	GNI per capita (Atlas $)	4,450

Climate

Average daily min/max temperature (1961–90, Celsius)	15 / 30
Projected annual temperature change (2045–65, Celsius)	2.4 to 3.0
Average annual precipitation (1961–90, mm)	89
Projected annual precipitation change (2045–65, mm)	-39 to 4
Projected change in annual hot days/warm nights	4 / 8
Projected change in annual cool days/cold nights	-2 / -2

	Country data	Middle East & N. Africa	Upper middle income
Exposure to Impacts			
Land area below 5m (% of land area)	0.4	1.4	1.8
Population below 5m (% of total)	3.5	9.7	6.5
Population in urban agglomerations > 1 million (%)	8	20	22
Urban pop. growth (avg. annual %, 1990–2010)	2.9	2.5	2.3
Droughts, floods, extreme temps (% pop. avg., 1990–2009)	0.0		
Annual freshwater withdrawals (% of internal resources)	54.6	121.9	5.6
Agricultural land under irrigation (% of total ag. land)	2.1	..	..
Population living below $1.25 a day (% of total)	6.8	3.6	..
Nationally terrestrial protected areas (% of total land area)	6.3	4.0	13.6
Under-five mortality rate (per 1,000)	36	34	20
Child malnutrition, underweight (% of under age five)	3.7	6.8	4.1
Malaria incidence rate (per 100,000 people)	..	..	80
Resilience			
Access to improved sanitation (% of total pop.)	95	84	68
Access to improved water source (% of total pop.)	83	87	92
Cereal yield (kg. per hectare)	1,654	2,512	3,690
Access to electricity (% of total population)	99.3	92.9	98.0
Paved roads (% of total roads)	73.5	74.3	50.5
Health workers (per 1,000 people)	3.2	3.6	4.5
Foreign direct investment, net inflows (% of GDP)	1.4	2.9	2.7
Invest. in infrastructure w/private participation ($ millions)	237	5,854	26,166
Disaster risk reduction progress score (1–5 scale; 5 = best)	3.5		
Ease of doing business (ranking 1–183; 1 = best)	148		
Public sector mgmt & institutions avg. (1–6 scale; 6 = best)	..		
Primary completion rate, total (% of relevant age group)	91	88	98
Ratio of girls to boys in primary & secondary school (%)	98	93	103
GHG Emissions and Energy Use			
CO_2 emissions per capita (metric tons)	3.2	3.8	5.3
CO_2 emissions per units of GDP (kg/$1,000 of 2005 PPP $)	438.8	604.6	659.4
CO_2 emissions, total (MtCO_2)	111.3	1,230	12,860
GHG net emissions/removals by LUCF (2000, MtCO_2e)	-7.9		
Methane (CH_4) emissions, total (MtCO_2e)	54.2	287	3,455
Nitrous oxide (N_2O) emissions, total (MtCO_2e)	4.9	74	1,144
Other GHG emissions, total (MtCO_2e)	0.5	7	243
Energy use per capita (kilograms of oil equivalent)	1,138	1,399	1,848
Energy use per units of GDP (kg oil eq./$1,000 of 2005 PPP $)	153.5	213.9	227.1

National-Level Actions

Latest UNFCCC national communication	11/25/2010 (2nd)
Annex-I emissions reduction target	n/a
NAMA submission	Yes
NAPA submission	n/a
Renewable energy target	Yes

Carbon Markets

Hosted Clean Development Mechanism (CDM) projects	..
Issued Certified Emission Reductions (CERs) from CDM (thousands)	..
Hosted Joint Implementation (JI) projects	n/a
Issued Emission Reduction Units (ERUs) from JI (thousands)	n/a

American Samoa

Population (thousands)	68.4	GDP ($ millions)	..
Pop. growth (avg. ann. %, 1990–2010)	1.9	GNI per capita (Atlas $)	..

Climate

Average daily min/max temperature (1961–90, Celsius)	..
Projected annual temperature change (2045–65, Celsius)	1.3 to 1.6
Average annual precipitation (1961–90, mm)	..
Projected annual precipitation change (2045–65, mm)	–40 to 237
Projected change in annual hot days/warm nights	16 / 25
Projected change in annual cool days/cold nights	–3 / –3

	Country data	East Asia & Pacific	Upper middle income
Exposure to Impacts			
Land area below 5m (% of land area)	17.9	2.5	1.8
Population below 5m (% of total)	9.9	10.3	6.5
Population in urban agglomerations > 1 million (%)	..	..	22
Urban pop. growth (avg. annual %, 1990–2010)	2.6	3.3	2.3
Droughts, floods, extreme temps (% pop. avg., 1990–2009)	0.0		
Annual freshwater withdrawals (% of internal resources)	..	10.8	5.6
Agricultural land under irrigation (% of total ag. land)	..	..	..
Population living below $1.25 a day (% of total)	..	16.8	..
Nationally terrestrial protected areas (% of total land area)	0.3	14.9	13.6
Under-five mortality rate (per 1,000)	..	24	20
Child malnutrition, underweight (% of under age five)	..	9.0	4.1
Malaria incidence rate (per 100,000 people)	..	525	80
Resilience			
Access to improved sanitation (% of total pop.)	..	59	68
Access to improved water source (% of total pop.)	..	88	92
Cereal yield (kg. per hectare)	..	4,860	3,690
Access to electricity (% of total population)	..	90.8	98.0
Paved roads (% of total roads)	..	15.9	50.5
Health workers (per 1,000 people)	..	2.8	4.5
Foreign direct investment, net inflows (% of GDP)	..	3.0	2.7
Invest. in infrastructure w/private participation ($ millions)	..	14,638	26,166
Disaster risk reduction progress score (1–5 scale; 5 = best)	..		
Ease of doing business (ranking 1–183; 1 = best)	..		
Public sector mgmt & institutions avg. (1–6 scale; 6 = best)	..		
Primary completion rate, total (% of relevant age group)	..	97	98
Ratio of girls to boys in primary & secondary school (%)	..	103	103
GHG Emissions and Energy Use			
CO_2 emissions per capita (metric tons)	..	4.3	5.3
CO_2 emissions per units of GDP (kg/$1,000 of 2005 PPP $)	..	827.1	659.4
CO_2 emissions, total (MtCO_2)	..	8,259	12,860
GHG net emissions/removals by LUCF (MtCO_2e)	..		
Methane (CH_4) emissions, total (MtCO_2e)	..	1,928	3,455
Nitrous oxide (N_2O) emissions, total (MtCO_2e)	..	707	1,144
Other GHG emissions, total (MtCO_2e)	..	..	243
Energy use per capita (kilograms of oil equivalent)	..	1,436	1,848
Energy use per units of GDP (kg oil eq./$1,000 of 2005 PPP $)	..	259.5	227.1

National-Level Actions

Latest UNFCCC national communication	n/a
Annex-I emissions reduction target	n/a
NAMA submission	n/a
NAPA submission	n/a
Renewable energy target	..

Carbon Markets

Hosted Clean Development Mechanism (CDM) projects	n/a
Issued Certified Emission Reductions (CERs) from CDM (thousands)	n/a
Hosted Joint Implementation (JI) projects	n/a
Issued Emission Reduction Units (ERUs) from JI (thousands)	n/a

Andorra

| Population (thousands) | 84.9 | GDP ($ billions) | 3.7 |
| Pop. growth (avg. ann. %, 1990-2010) | 2.4 | GNI per capita (Atlas $) | 41,750 |

Climate

Average daily min/max temperature (1961-90, Celsius)	3 / 12
Projected annual temperature change (2045-65, Celsius)	1.8 to 2.8
Average annual precipitation (1961-90, mm)	973
Projected annual precipitation change (2045-65, mm)	-113 to -22
Projected change in annual hot days/warm nights	4 / 7
Projected change in annual cool days/cold nights	-2 / -2

	Country data	High income
Exposure to Impacts		
Land area below 5m (% of land area)	0.0	2.2
Population below 5m (% of total)	0.0	7.7
Population in urban agglomerations > 1 million (%)	..	..
Urban pop. growth (avg. annual %, 1990-2010)	2.0	1.0
Droughts, floods, extreme temps (% pop. avg., 1990-2009)	..	
Annual freshwater withdrawals (% of internal resources)	..	10.4
Agricultural land under irrigation (% of total ag. land)	..	
Population living below $1.25 a day (% of total)	..	..
Nationally terrestrial protected areas (% of total land area)	6.0	13.4
Under-five mortality rate (per 1,000)	4	6
Child malnutrition, underweight (% of under age five)	..	..
Malaria incidence rate (per 100,000 people)	..	..
Resilience		
Access to improved sanitation (% of total pop.)	100	100
Access to improved water source (% of total pop.)	100	100
Cereal yield (kg. per hectare)	..	5,445
Access to electricity (% of total population)	..	..
Paved roads (% of total roads)	..	87.3
Health workers (per 1,000 people)	7.9	10.7
Foreign direct investment, net inflows (% of GDP)	..	1.8
Invest. in infrastructure w/private participation ($ millions)	..	..
Disaster risk reduction progress score (1-5 scale; 5 = best)	..	
Ease of doing business (ranking 1-183; 1 = best)	..	
Public sector mgmt & institutions avg. (1-6 scale; 6 = best)	..	
Primary completion rate, total (% of relevant age group)	101	97
Ratio of girls to boys in primary & secondary school (%)	104	100
GHG Emissions and Energy Use		
CO_2 emissions per capita (metric tons)	6.5	11.9
CO_2 emissions per units of GDP (kg/$1,000 of 2005 PPP $)	..	354.4
CO_2 emissions, total (MtCO$_2$)	0.5	13,285
GHG net emissions/removals by LUCF (MtCO$_2$e)	..	
Methane (CH_4) emissions, total (MtCO$_2$e)	..	1,539
Nitrous oxide (N_2O) emissions, total (MtCO$_2$e)	..	813
Other GHG emissions, total (MtCO$_2$e)	..	460
Energy use per capita (kilograms of oil equivalent)	..	4,944
Energy use per units of GDP (kg oil eq./$1,000 of 2005 PPP $)	..	147.0
National-Level Actions		
Latest UNFCCC national communication		n/a
Annex-I emissions reduction target		n/a
NAMA submission		n/a
NAPA submission		n/a
Renewable energy target		..
Carbon Markets		
Hosted Clean Development Mechanism (CDM) projects		n/a
Issued Certified Emission Reductions (CERs) from CDM (thousands)		n/a
Hosted Joint Implementation (JI) projects		n/a
Issued Emission Reduction Units (ERUs) from JI (thousands)		n/a

Angola

| Population (millions) | 19.1 | GDP ($ billions) | 84.4 |
| Pop. growth (avg. ann. %, 1990–2010) | 3.1 | GNI per capita (Atlas $) | 3,940 |

Climate

Average daily min/max temperature (1961–90, Celsius)	15 / 28
Projected annual temperature change (2045–65, Celsius)	2.1 to 2.7
Average annual precipitation (1961–90, mm)	1,010
Projected annual precipitation change (2045–65, mm)	–89 to 75
Projected change in annual hot days/warm nights	7 / 20
Projected change in annual cool days/cold nights	-2 / -3

	Country data	Sub-Saharan Africa	Lower middle Income
Exposure to Impacts			
Land area below 5m (% of land area)	0.2	0.4	1.7
Population below 5m (% of total)	2.1	2.0	6.5
Population in urban agglomerations > 1 million (%)	25	14	14
Urban pop. growth (avg. annual %, 1990–2010)	5.3	4.0	2.8
Droughts, floods, extreme temps (% pop. avg., 1990–2009)	1.0		
Annual freshwater withdrawals (% of internal resources)	0.4	3.2	18.7
Agricultural land under irrigation (% of total ag. land)	..	..	..
Population living below $1.25 a day (% of total)	54.3	50.9	..
Nationally terrestrial protected areas (% of total land area)	12.4	11.7	9.5
Under-five mortality rate (per 1,000)	161	121	69
Child malnutrition, underweight (% of under age five)	27.5	24.6	31.7
Malaria incidence rate (per 100,000 people)	21,593	26,113	4,874
Resilience			
Access to improved sanitation (% of total pop.)	57	31	45
Access to improved water source (% of total pop.)	50	60	84
Cereal yield (kg. per hectare)	588	1,297	2,754
Access to electricity (% of total population)	26.2	32.5	67.3
Paved roads (% of total roads)	10.4	18.3	29.3
Health workers (per 1,000 people)	1.4	1.2	2.6
Foreign direct investment, net inflows (% of GDP)	11.8	3.6	2.4
Invest. in infrastructure w/private participation ($ millions)	534	11,957	81,789
Disaster risk reduction progress score (1–5 scale; 5 = best)	..		
Ease of doing business (ranking 1–183; 1 = best)	172		
Public sector mgmt & institutions avg. (1–6 scale; 6 = best)	2.4		
Primary completion rate, total (% of relevant age group)	..	67	88
Ratio of girls to boys in primary & secondary school (%)	..	89	93
GHG Emissions and Energy Use			
CO_2 emissions per capita (metric tons)	1.4	0.8	1.6
CO_2 emissions per units of GDP (kg/$1,000 of 2005 PPP $)	245.3	428.6	523.9
CO_2 emissions, total (MtCO_2)	24.4	685	3,744
GHG net emissions/removals by LUCF (MtCO_2e)	..		
Methane (CH_4) emissions, total (MtCO_2e)	45.4	590	1,705
Nitrous oxide (N_2O) emissions, total (MtCO_2e)	38.9	334	687
Other GHG emissions, total (MtCO_2e)	0.0	..	17
Energy use per capita (kilograms of oil equivalent)	641	689	680
Energy use per units of GDP (kg oil eq./$1,000 of 2005 PPP $)	116.9	308.4	217.9

National-Level Actions

Latest UNFCCC national communication	..
Annex-I emissions reduction target	n/a
NAMA submission	..
NAPA submission	..
Renewable energy target	..

Carbon Markets

Hosted Clean Development Mechanism (CDM) projects	..
Issued Certified Emission Reductions (CERs) from CDM (thousands)	..
Hosted Joint Implementation (JI) projects	n/a
Issued Emission Reduction Units (ERUs) from JI (thousands)	n/a

Antigua and Barbuda

Population (thousands)	88.7	GDP ($ billions)	1.0
Pop. growth (avg. ann. %, 1990–2010)	1.8	GNI per capita (Atlas $)	10,590

Climate

Average daily min/max temperature (1961–90, Celsius)	23 / 30
Projected annual temperature change (2045–65, Celsius)	1.3 to 1.7
Average annual precipitation (1961–90, mm)	2,420
Projected annual precipitation change (2045–65, mm)	-104 to 37
Projected change in annual hot days/warm nights	13 / 23
Projected change in annual cool days/cold nights	-3 / -3

	Country data	Latin America & the Carib.	Upper middle income
Exposure to Impacts			
Land area below 5m (% of land area)	32.4	1.5	1.8
Population below 5m (% of total)	32.3	3.8	6.5
Population in urban agglomerations > 1 million (%)	..	35	22
Urban pop. growth (avg. annual %, 1990–2010)	1.0	2.0	2.3
Droughts, floods, extreme temps (% pop. avg., 1990–2009)	..		
Annual freshwater withdrawals (% of internal resources)	3.3	2.0	5.6
Agricultural land under irrigation (% of total ag. land)	..		..
Population living below $1.25 a day (% of total)	..	8.1	..
Nationally terrestrial protected areas (% of total land area)	7.0	20.8	13.6
Under-five mortality rate (per 1,000)	8	23	20
Child malnutrition, underweight (% of under age five)	..	3.8	4.1
Malaria incidence rate (per 100,000 people)	..	206	80
Resilience			
Access to improved sanitation (% of total pop.)	95	79	68
Access to improved water source (% of total pop.)	91	93	92
Cereal yield (kg. per hectare)	1,737	3,337	3,690
Access to electricity (% of total population)	..	93.4	98.0
Paved roads (% of total roads)	33.0	28.1	50.5
Health workers (per 1,000 people)	..	6.9	4.5
Foreign direct investment, net inflows (% of GDP)	5.7	2.3	2.7
Invest. in infrastructure w/private participation ($ millions)	6	33,064	26,166
Disaster risk reduction progress score (1–5 scale; 5 = best)	2.8		
Ease of doing business (ranking 1–183; 1 = best)	57		
Public sector mgmt & institutions avg. (1–6 scale; 6 = best)	..		
Primary completion rate, total (% of relevant age group)	95	102	98
Ratio of girls to boys in primary & secondary school (%)	97	102	103
GHG Emissions and Energy Use			
CO_2 emissions per capita (metric tons)	5.1	2.8	5.3
CO_2 emissions per units of GDP (kg/$1,000 of 2005 PPP $)	274.0	285.6	659.4
CO_2 emissions, total (MtCO$_2$)	0.4	1,584	12,860
GHG net emissions/removals by LUCF (1990, MtCO$_2$e)	-0.1		
Methane (CH_4) emissions, total (MtCO$_2$e)	..	1,009	3,455
Nitrous oxide (N_2O) emissions, total (MtCO$_2$e)	..	442	1,144
Other GHG emissions, total (MtCO$_2$e)	..	21	243
Energy use per capita (kilograms of oil equivalent)	1,699	1,245	1,848
Energy use per units of GDP (kg oil eq./$1,000 of 2005 PPP $)	89.6	130.6	227.1

National-Level Actions

Latest UNFCCC national communication	9/10/2001 (1st)
Annex-I emissions reduction target	n/a
NAMA submission	Yes, with Goal
NAPA submission	n/a
Renewable energy target	..

Carbon Markets

Hosted Clean Development Mechanism (CDM) projects	..
Issued Certified Emission Reductions (CERs) from CDM (thousands)	..
Hosted Joint Implementation (JI) projects	n/a
Issued Emission Reduction Units (ERUs) from JI (thousands)	n/a

Argentina

Population (millions)	40.4	GDP ($ billions)	368.7
Pop. growth (avg. ann. %, 1990–2010)	1.1	GNI per capita (Atlas $)	8,500

Climate

Average daily min/max temperature (1961–90, Celsius)	8 / 21
Projected annual temperature change (2045–65, Celsius)	1.4 to 2.1
Average annual precipitation (1961–90, mm)	591
Projected annual precipitation change (2045–65, mm)	-57 to 52
Projected change in annual hot days/warm nights	3 / 7
Projected change in annual cool days/cold nights	-1 / -1

	Country data	Latin America & the Carib.	Upper middle income
Exposure to Impacts			
Land area below 5m (% of land area)	1.2	1.5	1.8
Population below 5m (% of total)	4.5	3.8	6.5
Population in urban agglomerations > 1 million (%)	39	35	22
Urban pop. growth (avg. annual %, 1990–2010)	1.4	2.0	2.3
Droughts, floods, extreme temps (% pop. avg., 1990–2009)	0.2		
Annual freshwater withdrawals (% of internal resources)	11.8	2.0	5.6
Agricultural land under irrigation (% of total ag. land)	1.1	..	..
Population living below $1.25 a day (% of total)	<2	8.1	..
Nationally terrestrial protected areas (% of total land area)	5.4	20.8	13.6
Under-five mortality rate (per 1,000)	14	23	20
Child malnutrition, underweight (% of under age five)	2.3	3.8	4.1
Malaria incidence rate (per 100,000 people)	0	206	80
Resilience			
Access to improved sanitation (% of total pop.)	90	79	68
Access to improved water source (% of total pop.)	97	93	92
Cereal yield (kg. per hectare)	3,167	3,337	3,690
Access to electricity (% of total population)	97.2	93.4	98.0
Paved roads (% of total roads)	30.0	28.1	50.5
Health workers (per 1,000 people)	3.2	6.9	4.5
Foreign direct investment, net inflows (% of GDP)	1.7	2.3	2.7
Invest. in infrastructure w/private participation ($ millions)	1,283	33,064	26,166
Disaster risk reduction progress score (1–5 scale; 5 = best)	3.3		
Ease of doing business (ranking 1–183; 1 = best)	113		
Public sector mgmt & institutions avg. (1–6 scale; 6 = best)	..		
Primary completion rate, total (% of relevant age group)	105	102	98
Ratio of girls to boys in primary & secondary school (%)	105	102	103
GHG Emissions and Energy Use			
CO_2 emissions per capita (metric tons)	4.8	2.8	5.3
CO_2 emissions per units of GDP (kg/$1,000 of 2005 PPP $)	364.9	285.6	659.4
CO_2 emissions, total (MtCO_2)	192.4	1,584	12,860
GHG net emissions/removals by LUCF (2000, MtCO_2e)	-43.3		
Methane (CH_4) emissions, total (MtCO_2e)	101.8	1,009	3,455
Nitrous oxide (N_2O) emissions, total (MtCO_2e)	49.8	442	1,144
Other GHG emissions, total (MtCO_2e)	0.8	21	243
Energy use per capita (kilograms of oil equivalent)	1,853	1,245	1,848
Energy use per units of GDP (kg oil eq./$1,000 of 2005 PPP $)	139.6	130.6	227.1

National-Level Actions

Latest UNFCCC national communication	3/7/2008 (2nd)
Annex-I emissions reduction target	n/a
NAMA submission	Yes
NAPA submission	n/a
Renewable energy target	Yes

Carbon Markets

Hosted Clean Development Mechanism (CDM) projects	24
Issued Certified Emission Reductions (CERs) from CDM (thousands)	7,697
Hosted Joint Implementation (JI) projects	n/a
Issued Emission Reduction Units (ERUs) from JI (thousands)	n/a

Armenia

Population (millions)	3.1	GDP ($ billions)	9.3
Pop. growth (avg. ann. %, 1990-2010)	-0.7	GNI per capita (Atlas $)	3,090

Climate

Average daily min/max temperature (1961-90, Celsius)	1 / 13
Projected annual temperature change (2045-65, Celsius)	2.1 to 3.3
Average annual precipitation (1961-90, mm)	562
Projected annual precipitation change (2045-65, mm)	-75 to -7
Projected change in annual hot days/warm nights	3 / 6
Projected change in annual cool days/cold nights	-1 / -1

	Country data	Europe & Central Asia	Lower middle income
Exposure to Impacts			
Land area below 5m (% of land area)	0.0	2.5	1.7
Population below 5m (% of total)	0.0	3.0	6.5
Population in urban agglomerations > 1 million (%)	36	18	14
Urban pop. growth (avg. annual %, 1990-2010)	-1.0	0.3	2.8
Droughts, floods, extreme temps (% pop. avg., 1990-2009)	0.5		
Annual freshwater withdrawals (% of internal resources)	41.2	6.5	18.7
Agricultural land under irrigation (% of total ag. land)	8.9	..	..
Population living below $1.25 a day (% of total)	<2	3.7	..
Nationally terrestrial protected areas (% of total land area)	8.0	7.5	9.5
Under-five mortality rate (per 1,000)	20	23	69
Child malnutrition, underweight (% of under age five)	4.2	..	31.7
Malaria incidence rate (per 100,000 people)	0	..	4,874
Resilience			
Access to improved sanitation (% of total pop.)	90	89	45
Access to improved water source (% of total pop.)	96	95	84
Cereal yield (kg. per hectare)	2,230	2,475	2,754
Access to electricity (% of total population)	..	..	67.3
Paved roads (% of total roads)	90.5	85.8	29.3
Health workers (per 1,000 people)	8.6	9.9	2.6
Foreign direct investment, net inflows (% of GDP)	6.2	2.8	2.4
Invest. in infrastructure w/private participation ($ millions)	98	22,652	81,789
Disaster risk reduction progress score (1-5 scale; 5 = best)	3.0		
Ease of doing business (ranking 1-183; 1 = best)	55		
Public sector mgmt & institutions avg. (1-6 scale; 6 = best)	3.7		
Primary completion rate, total (% of relevant age group)	98	95	88
Ratio of girls to boys in primary & secondary school (%)	103	97	93
GHG Emissions and Energy Use			
CO_2 emissions per capita (metric tons)	1.8	7.7	1.6
CO_2 emissions per units of GDP (kg/$1,000 of 2005 PPP $)	320.9	708.0	523.9
CO_2 emissions, total (MtCO_2)	5.5	3,110	3,744
GHG net emissions/removals by LUCF (MtCO_2e)	..		
Methane (CH_4) emissions, total (MtCO_2e)	3.0	937	1,705
Nitrous oxide (N_2O) emissions, total (MtCO_2e)	0.6	214	687
Other GHG emissions, total (MtCO_2e)	0.3	76	17
Energy use per capita (kilograms of oil equivalent)	843	2,833	680
Energy use per units of GDP (kg oil eq./$1,000 of 2005 PPP $)	175.5	276.8	217.9

National-Level Actions

Latest UNFCCC national communication	9/7/2010 (2nd)
Annex-I emissions reduction target	n/a
NAMA submission	Yes
NAPA submission	n/a
Renewable energy target	..

Carbon Markets

Hosted Clean Development Mechanism (CDM) projects	5
Issued Certified Emission Reductions (CERs) from CDM (thousands)	12
Hosted Joint Implementation (JI) projects	n/a
Issued Emission Reduction Units (ERUs) from JI (thousands)	n/a

Aruba

Population (thousands)	107.5	GDP ($ millions)	..
Pop. growth (avg. ann. %, 1990–2010)	2.7	GNI per capita (Atlas $)	..

Climate

Average daily min/max temperature (1961–90, Celsius)	..
Projected annual temperature change (2045–65, Celsius)	1.5 to 2.1
Average annual precipitation (1961–90, mm)	..
Projected annual precipitation change (2045–65, mm)	-121 to 24
Projected change in annual hot days/warm nights	14 / 27
Projected change in annual cool days/cold nights	-3 / -3

	Country data	High Income
Exposure to Impacts		
Land area below 5m (% of land area)	29.6	2.2
Population below 5m (% of total)	29.6	7.7
Population in urban agglomerations > 1 million (%)	..	
Urban pop. growth (avg. annual %, 1990–2010)	2.4	1.0
Droughts, floods, extreme temps (% pop. avg., 1990–2009)	..	
Annual freshwater withdrawals (% of internal resources)	..	10.4
Agricultural land under irrigation (% of total ag. land)	..	..
Population living below $1.25 a day (% of total)	..	..
Nationally terrestrial protected areas (% of total land area)	0.1	13.4
Under-five mortality rate (per 1,000)	..	6
Child malnutrition, underweight (% of under age five)	..	..
Malaria incidence rate (per 100,000 people)	..	..
Resilience		
Access to improved sanitation (% of total pop.)	..	100
Access to improved water source (% of total pop.)	100	100
Cereal yield (kg. per hectare)	..	5,445
Access to electricity (% of total population)	..	..
Paved roads (% of total roads)	..	87.3
Health workers (per 1,000 people)	..	10.7
Foreign direct investment, net inflows (% of GDP)	..	1.8
Invest. in infrastructure w/private participation ($ millions)	..	..
Disaster risk reduction progress score (1–5 scale; 5 = best)	..	
Ease of doing business (ranking 1–183; 1 = best)	..	
Public sector mgmt & institutions avg. (1–6 scale; 6 = best)	..	
Primary completion rate, total (% of relevant age group)	95	97
Ratio of girls to boys in primary & secondary school (%)	99	100
GHG Emissions and Energy Use		
CO_2 emissions per capita (metric tons)	21.7	11.9
CO_2 emissions per units of GDP (kg/$1,000 of 2005 PPP $)	..	354.4
CO_2 emissions, total (MtCO_2)	2.3	13,285
GHG net emissions/removals by LUCF (MtCO_2e)	..	
Methane (CH_4) emissions, total (MtCO_2e)	..	1,539
Nitrous oxide (N_2O) emissions, total (MtCO_2e)	..	813
Other GHG emissions, total (MtCO_2e)	..	460
Energy use per capita (kilograms of oil equivalent)	..	4,944
Energy use per units of GDP (kg oil eq./$1,000 of 2005 PPP $)	..	147.0
National-Level Actions		
Latest UNFCCC national communication		n/a
Annex-I emissions reduction target		n/a
NAMA submission		n/a
NAPA submission		n/a
Renewable energy target		..
Carbon Markets		
Hosted Clean Development Mechanism (CDM) projects		n/a
Issued Certified Emission Reductions (CERs) from CDM (thousands)		n/a
Hosted Joint Implementation (JI) projects		n/a
Issued Emission Reduction Units (ERUs) from JI (thousands)		n/a

Australia

Population (millions)	22.3	GDP ($ billions)	924.8
Pop. growth (avg. ann. %, 1990-2010)	1.3	GNI per capita (Atlas $)	43,590

Climate

Average daily min/max temperature (1961-90, Celsius)	15 / 28
Projected annual temperature change (2045-65, Celsius)	1.7 to 2.4
Average annual precipitation (1961-90, mm)	535
Projected annual precipitation change (2045-65, mm)	-67 to 54
Projected change in annual hot days/warm nights	4 / 9
Projected change in annual cool days/cold nights	-2 / -2

	Country data	High income
Exposure to Impacts		
Land area below 5m (% of land area)	1.1	2.2
Population below 5m (% of total)	7.2	7.7
Population in urban agglomerations > 1 million (%)	58	..
Urban pop. growth (avg. annual %, 1990-2010)	1.6	1.0
Droughts, floods, extreme temps (% pop. avg., 1990-2009)	3.0	
Annual freshwater withdrawals (% of internal resources)	4.9	10.4
Agricultural land under irrigation (% of total ag. land)	0.4	..
Population living below $1.25 a day (% of total)	..	..
Nationally terrestrial protected areas (% of total land area)	10.5	13.4
Under-five mortality rate (per 1,000)	5	6
Child malnutrition, underweight (% of under age five)	..	..
Malaria incidence rate (per 100,000 people)	..	..
Resilience		
Access to improved sanitation (% of total pop.)	100	100
Access to improved water source (% of total pop.)	100	100
Cereal yield (kg. per hectare)	1,764	5,445
Access to electricity (% of total population)	..	..
Paved roads (% of total roads)	..	87.3
Health workers (per 1,000 people)	12.6	10.7
Foreign direct investment, net inflows (% of GDP)	2.9	1.8
Invest. in infrastructure w/private participation ($ millions)	..	..
Disaster risk reduction progress score (1-5 scale; 5 = best)	4.0	
Ease of doing business (ranking 1-183; 1 = best)	15	
Public sector mgmt & institutions avg. (1-6 scale; 6 = best)	..	
Primary completion rate, total (% of relevant age group)	..	97
Ratio of girls to boys in primary & secondary school (%)	98	100
GHG Emissions and Energy Use		
CO_2 emissions per capita (metric tons)	18.6	11.9
CO_2 emissions per units of GDP (kg/$1,000 of 2005 PPP $)	539.6	354.4
CO_2 emissions, total (MtCO_2)	399.2	13,285
GHG net emissions/removals by LUCF (2009, MtCO_2e)	54.0	
Methane (CH_4) emissions, total (MtCO_2e)	126.5	1,539
Nitrous oxide (N_2O) emissions, total (MtCO_2e)	63.0	813
Other GHG emissions, total (MtCO_2e)	6.5	460
Energy use per capita (kilograms of oil equivalent)	5,636	4,944
Energy use per units of GDP (kg oil eq./$1,000 of 2005 PPP $)	174.9	147.0

National-Level Actions

Latest UNFCCC national communication	2/12/2010 (5th)
Annex-I emissions reduction target (base year: 2000)	5% / 25%
NAMA submission	n/a
NAPA submission	n/a
Renewable energy target	Yes

Carbon Markets

Hosted Clean Development Mechanism (CDM) projects	n/a
Issued Certified Emission Reductions (CERs) from CDM (thousands)	n/a
Hosted Joint Implementation (JI) projects	..
Issued Emission Reduction Units (ERUs) from JI (thousands)	..

Austria

Population (millions)	8.4	GDP ($ billions)	376.2
Pop. growth (avg. ann. %, 1990–2010)	0.4	GNI per capita (Atlas $)	46,690

Climate

Average daily min/max temperature (1961–90, Celsius)	2 / 10
Projected annual temperature change (2045–65, Celsius)	1.9 to 2.9
Average annual precipitation (1961–90, mm)	1,110
Projected annual precipitation change (2045–65, mm)	–70 to 27
Projected change in annual hot days/warm nights	3 / 5
Projected change in annual cool days/cold nights	–1 / –2

	Country data	High income
Exposure to Impacts		
Land area below 5m (% of land area)	0.0	2.2
Population below 5m (% of total)	0.0	7.7
Population in urban agglomerations > 1 million (%)	20	
Urban pop. growth (avg. annual %, 1990–2010)	0.6	1.0
Droughts, floods, extreme temps (% pop. avg., 1990–2009)	0.0	
Annual freshwater withdrawals (% of internal resources)	6.5	10.4
Agricultural land under irrigation (% of total ag. land)	1.4	..
Population living below $1.25 a day (% of total)	..	..
Nationally terrestrial protected areas (% of total land area)	22.9	13.4
Under-five mortality rate (per 1,000)	4	6
Child malnutrition, underweight (% of under age five)	..	..
Malaria incidence rate (per 100,000 people)	..	..
Resilience		
Access to improved sanitation (% of total pop.)	100	100
Access to improved water source (% of total pop.)	100	100
Cereal yield (kg. per hectare)	6,133	5,445
Access to electricity (% of total population)	..	
Paved roads (% of total roads)	100.0	87.3
Health workers (per 1,000 people)	4.7	10.7
Foreign direct investment, net inflows (% of GDP)	–7.1	1.8
Invest. in infrastructure w/private participation ($ millions)	..	..
Disaster risk reduction progress score (1–5 scale; 5 = best)	..	
Ease of doing business (ranking 1–183; 1 = best)	32	
Public sector mgmt & institutions avg. (1–6 scale; 6 = best)	..	
Primary completion rate, total (% of relevant age group)	97	97
Ratio of girls to boys in primary & secondary school (%)	97	100
GHG Emissions and Energy Use		
CO_2 emissions per capita (metric tons)	8.1	11.9
CO_2 emissions per units of GDP (kg/$1,000 of 2005 PPP $)	224.4	354.4
CO_2 emissions, total (MtCO_2)	67.7	13,285
GHG net emissions/removals by LUCF (2009, MtCO_2e)	–17.5	
Methane (CH_4) emissions, total (MtCO_2e)	8.5	1,539
Nitrous oxide (N_2O) emissions, total (MtCO_2e)	4.4	813
Other GHG emissions, total (MtCO_2e)	2.3	460
Energy use per capita (kilograms of oil equivalent)	3,944	4,944
Energy use per units of GDP (kg oil eq./$1,000 of 2005 PPP $)	111.8	147.0

National-Level Actions

Latest UNFCCC national communication	2/16/2010 (5th)
Annex-I emissions reduction target (base year: 1990)	20% / 30% (EU)
NAMA submission	n/a
NAPA submission	n/a
Renewable energy target	Yes

Carbon Markets

Hosted Clean Development Mechanism (CDM) projects	n/a
Issued Certified Emission Reductions (CERs) from CDM (thousands)	n/a
Hosted Joint Implementation (JI) projects	..
Issued Emission Reduction Units (ERUs) from JI (thousands)	..

Azerbaijan

Population (millions)	9.0	GDP ($ billions)	51.1
Pop. growth (avg. ann. %, 1990-2010)	1.2	GNI per capita (Atlas $)	5,080

Climate

Average daily min/max temperature (1961-90, Celsius)	7 / 17
Projected annual temperature change (2045-65, Celsius)	1.9 to 3.1
Average annual precipitation (1961-90, mm)	447
Projected annual precipitation change (2045-65, mm)	-58 to 3
Projected change in annual hot days/warm nights	3 / 6
Projected change in annual cool days/cold nights	-1 / -1

	Country data	Europe & Central Asia	Upper middle income
Exposure to Impacts			
Land area below 5m (% of land area)	20.0	2.5	1.8
Population below 5m (% of total)	29.8	3.0	6.5
Population in urban agglomerations > 1 million (%)	22	18	22
Urban pop. growth (avg. annual %, 1990-2010)	1.0	0.3	2.3
Droughts, floods, extreme temps (% pop. avg., 1990-2009)	1.1		
Annual freshwater withdrawals (% of internal resources)	150.5	6.5	5.6
Agricultural land under irrigation (% of total ag. land)	29.5	..	
Population living below $1.25 a day (% of total)	<2	3.7	..
Nationally terrestrial protected areas (% of total land area)	7.1	7.5	13.6
Under-five mortality rate (per 1,000)	46	23	20
Child malnutrition, underweight (% of under age five)	8.4	..	4.1
Malaria incidence rate (per 100,000 people)	1	..	80
Resilience			
Access to improved sanitation (% of total pop.)	45	89	68
Access to improved water source (% of total pop.)	80	95	92
Cereal yield (kg. per hectare)	2,607	2,475	3,690
Access to electricity (% of total population)	..	..	98.0
Paved roads (% of total roads)	50.6	85.8	50.5
Health workers (per 1,000 people)	12.2	9.9	4.5
Foreign direct investment, net inflows (% of GDP)	1.1	2.8	2.7
Invest. in infrastructure w/private participation ($ millions)	124	22,652	26,166
Disaster risk reduction progress score (1-5 scale; 5 = best)	..		
Ease of doing business (ranking 1-183; 1 = best)	66		
Public sector mgmt & institutions avg. (1-6 scale; 6 = best)	3.1		
Primary completion rate, total (% of relevant age group)	92	95	98
Ratio of girls to boys in primary & secondary school (%)	102	97	103
GHG Emissions and Energy Use			
CO_2 emissions per capita (metric tons)	5.4	7.7	5.3
CO_2 emissions per units of GDP (kg/$1,000 of 2005 PPP $)	670.4	708.0	659.4
CO_2 emissions, total (MtCO_2)	47.1	3,110	12,860
GHG net emissions/removals by LUCF (1994, MtCO_2e)	-1.1		
Methane (CH_4) emissions, total (MtCO_2e)	36.6	937	3,455
Nitrous oxide (N_2O) emissions, total (MtCO_2e)	2.6	214	1,144
Other GHG emissions, total (MtCO_2e)	0.1	76	243
Energy use per capita (kilograms of oil equivalent)	1,338	2,833	1,848
Energy use per units of GDP (kg oil eq./$1,000 of 2005 PPP $)	155.7	276.8	227.1

National-Level Actions

Latest UNFCCC national communication	6/7/2011 (2nd)
Annex-I emissions reduction target	n/a
NAMA submission	..
NAPA submission	n/a
Renewable energy target	..

Carbon Markets

Hosted Clean Development Mechanism (CDM) projects	1
Issued Certified Emission Reductions (CERs) from CDM (thousands)	0
Hosted Joint Implementation (JI) projects	n/a
Issued Emission Reduction Units (ERUs) from JI (thousands)	n/a

Bahamas, The

| Population (thousands) | 342.9 | GDP ($ billions) | 7.5 |
| Pop. growth (avg. ann. %, 1990–2010) | 1.5 | GNI per capita (Atlas $) | 20,610 |

Climate
Average daily min/max temperature (1961–90, Celsius)	20 / 30
Projected annual temperature change (2045–65, Celsius)	1.4 to 1.7
Average annual precipitation (1961–90, mm)	1,292
Projected annual precipitation change (2045–65, mm)	-96 to 74
Projected change in annual hot days/warm nights	10 / 16
Projected change in annual cool days/cold nights	-2 / -2

	Country data	High income
Exposure to Impacts		
Land area below 5m (% of land area)	72.0	2.2
Population below 5m (% of total)	46.5	7.7
Population in urban agglomerations > 1 million (%)	..	
Urban pop. growth (avg. annual %, 1990–2010)	1.7	1.0
Droughts, floods, extreme temps (% pop. avg., 1990–2009)	..	
Annual freshwater withdrawals (% of internal resources)	..	10.4
Agricultural land under irrigation (% of total ag. land)	..	..
Population living below $1.25 a day (% of total)	..	..
Nationally terrestrial protected areas (% of total land area)	13.7	13.4
Under-five mortality rate (per 1,000)	16	6
Child malnutrition, underweight (% of under age five)	..	..
Malaria incidence rate (per 100,000 people)	..	..
Resilience		
Access to improved sanitation (% of total pop.)	100	100
Access to improved water source (% of total pop.)	97	100
Cereal yield (kg. per hectare)	2,196	5,445
Access to electricity (% of total population)	..	
Paved roads (% of total roads)	57.4	87.3
Health workers (per 1,000 people)	..	10.7
Foreign direct investment, net inflows (% of GDP)	11.4	1.8
Invest. in infrastructure w/private participation ($ millions)	..	..
Disaster risk reduction progress score (1–5 scale; 5 = best)	..	
Ease of doing business (ranking 1–183; 1 = best)	85	
Public sector mgmt & institutions avg. (1–6 scale; 6 = best)	..	
Primary completion rate, total (% of relevant age group)	95	97
Ratio of girls to boys in primary & secondary school (%)	101	100
GHG Emissions and Energy Use		
CO_2 emissions per capita (metric tons)	6.5	11.9
CO_2 emissions per units of GDP (kg/$1,000 of 2005 PPP $)	263.6	354.4
CO_2 emissions, total (MtCO$_2$)	2.2	13,285
GHG net emissions/removals by LUCF (MtCO$_2$e)	..	
Methane (CH_4) emissions, total (MtCO$_2$e)	..	1,539
Nitrous oxide (N_2O) emissions, total (MtCO$_2$e)	..	813
Other GHG emissions, total (MtCO$_2$e)	..	460
Energy use per capita (kilograms of oil equivalent)	2,156	4,944
Energy use per units of GDP (kg oil eq./$1,000 of 2005 PPP $)	85.6	147.0
National-Level Actions		
Latest UNFCCC national communication		11/5/2001 (1st)
Annex-I emissions reduction target		n/a
NAMA submission		..
NAPA submission		n/a
Renewable energy target		..
Carbon Markets		
Hosted Clean Development Mechanism (CDM) projects		0
Issued Certified Emission Reductions (CERs) from CDM (thousands)		0
Hosted Joint Implementation (JI) projects		n/a
Issued Emission Reduction Units (ERUs) from JI (thousands)		n/a

Bahrain

Population (millions)	1.3	GDP ($ billions)	20.6
Pop. growth (avg. ann. %, 1990-2010)	4.7	GNI per capita (Atlas $)	18,730

Climate

Average daily min/max temperature (1961-90, Celsius)	21 / 34
Projected annual temperature change (2045-65, Celsius)	2.1 to 3.0
Average annual precipitation (1961-90, mm)	83
Projected annual precipitation change (2045-65, mm)	-19 to 4
Projected change in annual hot days/warm nights	5 / 9
Projected change in annual cool days/cold nights	-2 / -2

	Country data	High income
Exposure to Impacts		
Land area below 5m (% of land area)	39.0	2.2
Population below 5m (% of total)	66.6	7.7
Population in urban agglomerations > 1 million (%)	..	..
Urban pop. growth (avg. annual %, 1990-2010)	4.7	1.0
Droughts, floods, extreme temps (% pop. avg., 1990-2009)	..	
Annual freshwater withdrawals (% of internal resources)	6,375.0	10.4
Agricultural land under irrigation (% of total ag. land)	..	
Population living below $1.25 a day (% of total)	..	..
Nationally terrestrial protected areas (% of total land area)	1.3	13.4
Under-five mortality rate (per 1,000)	10	6
Child malnutrition, underweight (% of under age five)	..	..
Malaria incidence rate (per 100,000 people)	..	..
Resilience		
Access to improved sanitation (% of total pop.)	..	100
Access to improved water source (% of total pop.)	..	100
Cereal yield (kg. per hectare)	..	5,445
Access to electricity (% of total population)	99.4	..
Paved roads (% of total roads)	81.5	87.3
Health workers (per 1,000 people)	5.2	10.7
Foreign direct investment, net inflows (% of GDP)	1.2	1.8
Invest. in infrastructure w/private participation ($ millions)	..	..
Disaster risk reduction progress score (1-5 scale; 5 = best)	..	
Ease of doing business (ranking 1-183; 1 = best)	38	
Public sector mgmt & institutions avg. (1-6 scale; 6 = best)	..	
Primary completion rate, total (% of relevant age group)	101	97
Ratio of girls to boys in primary & secondary school (%)	101	100
GHG Emissions and Energy Use		
CO_2 emissions per capita (metric tons)	21.4	11.9
CO_2 emissions per units of GDP (kg/$1,000 of 2005 PPP $)	899.2	354.4
CO_2 emissions, total (MtCO$_2$)	22.5	13,285
GHG net emissions/removals by LUCF (MtCO$_2$e)	..	
Methane (CH_4) emissions, total (MtCO$_2$e)	2.8	1,539
Nitrous oxide (N_2O) emissions, total (MtCO$_2$e)	0.1	813
Other GHG emissions, total (MtCO$_2$e)	0.3	460
Energy use per capita (kilograms of oil equivalent)	8,096	4,944
Energy use per units of GDP (kg oil eq./$1,000 of 2005 PPP $)	369.8	147.0

National-Level Actions

Latest UNFCCC national communication	4/20/2005 (1st)
Annex-I emissions reduction target	n/a
NAMA submission	..
NAPA submission	n/a
Renewable energy target	..

Carbon Markets

Hosted Clean Development Mechanism (CDM) projects	..
Issued Certified Emission Reductions (CERs) from CDM (thousands)	..
Hosted Joint Implementation (JI) projects	n/a
Issued Emission Reduction Units (ERUs) from JI (thousands)	n/a

Bangladesh

Population (millions)	148.7	GDP ($ billions)	100.1
Pop. growth (avg. ann. %, 1990–2010)	1.7	GNI per capita (Atlas $)	700

Climate

Average daily min/max temperature (1961–90, Celsius)	20 / 30
Projected annual temperature change (2045–65, Celsius)	1.7 to 2.4
Average annual precipitation (1961–90, mm)	2,665
Projected annual precipitation change (2045–65, mm)	-126 to 120
Projected change in annual hot days/warm nights	3 / 12
Projected change in annual cool days/cold nights	-2 / -2

	Country data	South Asia	Low Income
Exposure to Impacts			
Land area below 5m (% of land area)	14.1	1.5	0.7
Population below 5m (% of total)	14.0	4.4	5.1
Population in urban agglomerations > 1 million (%)	14	13	11
Urban pop. growth (avg. annual %, 1990-2010)	3.5	2.7	3.7
Droughts, floods, extreme temps (% pop. avg., 1990-2009)	4.6		
Annual freshwater withdrawals (% of internal resources)	..	50.6	3.7
Agricultural land under irrigation (% of total ag. land)	52.6	..	..
Population living below $1.25 a day (% of total)	49.6	40.3	..
Nationally terrestrial protected areas (% of total land area)	1.6	6.1	10.6
Under-five mortality rate (per 1,000)	48	67	108
Child malnutrition, underweight (% of under age five)	41.3	42.5	28.3
Malaria incidence rate (per 100,000 people)	1,510	1,127	16,659
Resilience			
Access to improved sanitation (% of total pop.)	53	36	35
Access to improved water source (% of total pop.)	80	87	63
Cereal yield (kg. per hectare)	4,140	2,728	2,047
Access to electricity (% of total population)	41.0	62.1	23.0
Paved roads (% of total roads)	9.5	58.9	14.1
Health workers (per 1,000 people)	0.6	1.7	0.7
Foreign direct investment, net inflows (% of GDP)	1.0	1.3	3.2
Invest. in infrastructure w/private participation ($ millions)	617	73,548	4,471
Disaster risk reduction progress score (1-5 scale; 5 = best)	4.0		
Ease of doing business (ranking 1-183; 1 = best)	122		
Public sector mgmt & institutions avg. (1-6 scale; 6 = best)	3.0		
Primary completion rate, total (% of relevant age group)	61	86	65
Ratio of girls to boys in primary & secondary school (%)	108	92	91
GHG Emissions and Energy Use			
CO_2 emissions per capita (metric tons)	0.3	1.3	0.3
CO_2 emissions per units of GDP (kg/$1,000 of 2005 PPP $)	235.8	504.6	270.2
CO_2 emissions, total (MtCO$_2$)	46.5	1,970	219
GHG net emissions/removals by LUCF (1994, MtCO$_2$e)	7.8		
Methane (CH$_4$) emissions, total (MtCO$_2$e)	92.4	846	436
Nitrous oxide (N$_2$O) emissions, total (MtCO$_2$e)	21.4	268	209
Other GHG emissions, total (MtCO$_2$e)	0.0	9	..
Energy use per capita (kilograms of oil equivalent)	201	532	365
Energy use per units of GDP (kg oil eq./$1,000 of 2005 PPP $)	141.9	193.5	303.9

National-Level Actions

Latest UNFCCC national communication	11/12/2002 (1st)
Annex-I emissions reduction target	n/a
NAMA submission	..
NAPA submission	Yes
Renewable energy target	Yes

Carbon Markets

Hosted Clean Development Mechanism (CDM) projects	2
Issued Certified Emission Reductions (CERs) from CDM (thousands)	0
Hosted Joint Implementation (JI) projects	n/a
Issued Emission Reduction Units (ERUs) from JI (thousands)	n/a

Barbados

Population (thousands)	273.3	GDP ($ billions)	3.2
Pop. growth (avg. ann. %, 1990–2010)	0.3	GNI per capita (Atlas $)	12,660

Climate

Average daily min/max temperature (1961–90, Celsius)	22 / 30
Projected annual temperature change (2045–65, Celsius)	1.4 to 1.7
Average annual precipitation (1961–90, mm)	2,066
Projected annual precipitation change (2045–65, mm)	-154 to 14
Projected change in annual hot days/warm nights	14 / 24
Projected change in annual cool days/cold nights	-3 / -3

	Country data	High Income
Exposure to Impacts		
Land area below 5m (% of land area)	15.7	2.2
Population below 5m (% of total)	15.7	7.7
Population in urban agglomerations > 1 million (%)	..	
Urban pop. growth (avg. annual %, 1990–2010)	1.4	1.0
Droughts, floods, extreme temps (% pop. avg., 1990–2009)	..	
Annual freshwater withdrawals (% of internal resources)	76.1	10.4
Agricultural land under irrigation (% of total ag. land)	..	
Population living below $1.25 a day (% of total)	..	..
Nationally terrestrial protected areas (% of total land area)	0.1	13.4
Under-five mortality rate (per 1,000)	20	6
Child malnutrition, underweight (% of under age five)	..	
Malaria incidence rate (per 100,000 people)	..	..
Resilience		
Access to improved sanitation (% of total pop.)	100	100
Access to improved water source (% of total pop.)	100	100
Cereal yield (kg. per hectare)	2,640	5,445
Access to electricity (% of total population)	..	
Paved roads (% of total roads)	100.0	87.3
Health workers (per 1,000 people)	6.7	10.7
Foreign direct investment, net inflows (% of GDP)	2.5	1.8
Invest. in infrastructure w/private participation ($ millions)	..	
Disaster risk reduction progress score (1–5 scale; 5 = best)	4.0	
Ease of doing business (ranking 1–183; 1 = best)	..	
Public sector mgmt & institutions avg. (1–6 scale; 6 = best)	..	
Primary completion rate, total (% of relevant age group)	..	97
Ratio of girls to boys in primary & secondary school (%)	..	100
GHG Emissions and Energy Use		
CO$_2$ emissions per capita (metric tons)	5.0	11.9
CO$_2$ emissions per units of GDP (kg/$1,000 of 2005 PPP $)	267.5	354.4
CO$_2$ emissions, total (MtCO$_2$)	1.4	13,285
GHG net emissions/removals by LUCF (1997, MtCO$_2$e)	0.0	
Methane (CH$_4$) emissions, total (MtCO$_2$e)	..	1,539
Nitrous oxide (N$_2$O) emissions, total (MtCO$_2$e)	..	813
Other GHG emissions, total (MtCO$_2$e)	..	460
Energy use per capita (kilograms of oil equivalent)	1,476	4,944
Energy use per units of GDP (kg oil eq./$1,000 of 2005 PPP $)	79.4	147.0

National-Level Actions

Latest UNFCCC national communication	10/30/2001 (1st)
Annex-I emissions reduction target	n/a
NAMA submission	..
NAPA submission	n/a
Renewable energy target	..

Carbon Markets

Hosted Clean Development Mechanism (CDM) projects	..
Issued Certified Emission Reductions (CERs) from CDM (thousands)	..
Hosted Joint Implementation (JI) projects	n/a
Issued Emission Reduction Units (ERUs) from JI (thousands)	n/a

Belarus

Population (millions)	9.5	GDP ($ billions)	54.7
Pop. growth (avg. ann. %, 1990–2010)	-0.4	GNI per capita (Atlas $)	6,130

Climate

Average daily min/max temperature (1961–90, Celsius)	2 / 10
Projected annual temperature change (2045–65, Celsius)	2.2 to 3.1
Average annual precipitation (1961–90, mm)	618
Projected annual precipitation change (2045–65, mm)	8 to 70
Projected change in annual hot days/warm nights	2 / 5
Projected change in annual cool days/cold nights	-2 / -2

	Country data	Europe & Central Asia	Upper middle income
Exposure to Impacts			
Land area below 5m (% of land area)	0.0	2.5	1.8
Population below 5m (% of total)	0.0	3.0	6.5
Population in urban agglomerations > 1 million (%)	20	18	22
Urban pop. growth (avg. annual %, 1990–2010)	0.2	0.3	2.3
Droughts, floods, extreme temps (% pop. avg., 1990–2009)	0.0		
Annual freshwater withdrawals (% of internal resources)	11.7	6.5	5.6
Agricultural land under irrigation (% of total ag. land)	0.5	..	..
Population living below $1.25 a day (% of total)	<2	3.7	..
Nationally terrestrial protected areas (% of total land area)	7.3	7.5	13.6
Under-five mortality rate (per 1,000)	6	23	20
Child malnutrition, underweight (% of under age five)	1.3	..	4.1
Malaria incidence rate (per 100,000 people)	..	..	80
Resilience			
Access to improved sanitation (% of total pop.)	93	89	68
Access to improved water source (% of total pop.)	100	95	92
Cereal yield (kg. per hectare)	3,374	2,475	3,690
Access to electricity (% of total population)	..		98.0
Paved roads (% of total roads)	88.6	85.8	50.5
Health workers (per 1,000 people)	5.1	9.9	4.5
Foreign direct investment, net inflows (% of GDP)	2.6	2.8	2.7
Invest. in infrastructure w/private participation ($ millions)	1,045	22,652	26,166
Disaster risk reduction progress score (1–5 scale; 5 = best)	..		
Ease of doing business (ranking 1–183; 1 = best)	69		
Public sector mgmt & institutions avg. (1–6 scale; 6 = best)	..		
Primary completion rate, total (% of relevant age group)	96	95	98
Ratio of girls to boys in primary & secondary school (%)	102	97	103
GHG Emissions and Energy Use			
CO_2 emissions per capita (metric tons)	6.5	7.7	5.3
CO_2 emissions per units of GDP (kg/$1,000 of 2005 PPP $)	556.9	708.0	659.4
CO_2 emissions, total (MtCO_2)	62.8	3,110	12,860
GHG net emissions/removals by LUCF (2009, MtCO_2e)	-30.0		
Methane (CH_4) emissions, total (MtCO_2e)	11.5	937	3,455
Nitrous oxide (N_2O) emissions, total (MtCO_2e)	11.7	214	1,144
Other GHG emissions, total (MtCO_2e)	0.5	76	243
Energy use per capita (kilograms of oil equivalent)	2,815	2,833	1,848
Energy use per units of GDP (kg oil eq./$1,000 of 2005 PPP $)	236.8	276.8	227.1

National-Level Actions

Latest UNFCCC national communication	5/3/2010 (5th)
Annex-I emissions reduction target (base year: 1990)	5% to 10%
NAMA submission	n/a
NAPA submission	n/a
Renewable energy target	..

Carbon Markets

Hosted Clean Development Mechanism (CDM) projects	n/a
Issued Certified Emission Reductions (CERs) from CDM (thousands)	n/a
Hosted Joint Implementation (JI) projects	..
Issued Emission Reduction Units (ERUs) from JI (thousands)	..

Belgium

Population (millions)	10.9	GDP ($ billions)	467.5
Pop. growth (avg. ann. %, 1990–2010)	0.4	GNI per capita (Atlas $)	45,360

Climate

Average daily min/max temperature (1961–90, Celsius)	6 / 14
Projected annual temperature change (2045–65, Celsius)	1.4 to 2.4
Average annual precipitation (1961-90, mm)	847
Projected annual precipitation change (2045–65, mm)	-64 to 29
Projected change in annual hot days/warm nights	3 / 5
Projected change in annual cool days/cold nights	-1 / -2

	Country data	High income
Exposure to Impacts		
Land area below 5m (% of land area)	9.2	2.2
Population below 5m (% of total)	14.3	7.7
Population in urban agglomerations > 1 million (%)	18	..
Urban pop. growth (avg. annual %, 1990–2010)	0.5	1.0
Droughts, floods, extreme temps (% pop. avg., 1990–2009)	0.0	
Annual freshwater withdrawals (% of internal resources)	..	10.4
Agricultural land under irrigation (% of total ag. land)	0.4	..
Population living below $1.25 a day (% of total)	..	..
Nationally terrestrial protected areas (% of total land area)	0.9	13.4
Under-five mortality rate (per 1,000)	4	6
Child malnutrition, underweight (% of under age five)	..	..
Malaria incidence rate (per 100,000 people)	..	..
Resilience		
Access to improved sanitation (% of total pop.)	100	100
Access to improved water source (% of total pop.)	100	100
Cereal yield (kg. per hectare)	9,711	5,445
Access to electricity (% of total population)	..	
Paved roads (% of total roads)	78.2	87.3
Health workers (per 1,000 people)	3.3	10.7
Foreign direct investment, net inflows (% of GDP)	13.4	1.8
Invest. in infrastructure w/private participation ($ millions)	..	..
Disaster risk reduction progress score (1-5 scale; 5 = best)	..	
Ease of doing business (ranking 1-183; 1 = best)	28	
Public sector mgmt & institutions avg. (1-6 scale; 6 = best)	..	
Primary completion rate, total (% of relevant age group)	87	97
Ratio of girls to boys in primary & secondary school (%)	98	100
GHG Emissions and Energy Use		
CO_2 emissions per capita (metric tons)	9.8	11.9
CO_2 emissions per units of GDP (kg/$1,000 of 2005 PPP $)	291.8	354.4
CO_2 emissions, total (MtCO_2)	104.9	13,285
GHG net emissions/removals by LUCF (2009, MtCO_2e)	-1.6	
Methane (CH_4) emissions, total (MtCO_2e)	10.1	1,539
Nitrous oxide (N_2O) emissions, total (MtCO_2e)	6.6	813
Other GHG emissions, total (MtCO_2e)	2.1	460
Energy use per capita (kilograms of oil equivalent)	5,221	4,944
Energy use per units of GDP (kg oil eq./$1,000 of 2005 PPP $)	159.1	147.0

National-Level Actions

Latest UNFCCC national communication	3/10/2010 (5th)
Annex-I emissions reduction target (base year: 1990)	20% / 30% (EU)
NAMA submission	n/a
NAPA submission	n/a
Renewable energy target	Yes

Carbon Markets

Hosted Clean Development Mechanism (CDM) projects	n/a
Issued Certified Emission Reductions (CERs) from CDM (thousands)	n/a
Hosted Joint Implementation (JI) projects	..
Issued Emission Reduction Units (ERUs) from JI (thousands)	..

Belize

Population (thousands)	344.7	GDP ($ billions)	1.4
Pop. growth (avg. ann. %, 1990–2010)	3.0	GNI per capita (Atlas $)	3,740

Climate

Average daily min/max temperature (1961–90, Celsius)	21 / 30
Projected annual temperature change (2045–65, Celsius)	1.7 to 2.6
Average annual precipitation (1961–90, mm)	2,191
Projected annual precipitation change (2045–65, mm)	-189 to 16
Projected change in annual hot days/warm nights	8 / 21
Projected change in annual cool days/cold nights	-1 / -2

	Country data	Latin America & the Carib.	Lower middle income
Exposure to Impacts			
Land area below 5m (% of land area)	9.5	1.5	1.7
Population below 5m (% of total)	15.8	3.8	6.5
Population in urban agglomerations > 1 million (%)	..	35	14
Urban pop. growth (avg. annual %, 1990–2010)	3.5	2.0	2.8
Droughts, floods, extreme temps (% pop. avg., 1990–2009)	0.8		
Annual freshwater withdrawals (% of internal resources)	0.9	2.0	18.7
Agricultural land under irrigation (% of total ag. land)	..	..	
Population living below $1.25 a day (% of total)	12.4	8.1	..
Nationally terrestrial protected areas (% of total land area)	27.9	20.8	9.5
Under-five mortality rate (per 1,000)	17	23	69
Child malnutrition, underweight (% of under age five)	4.9	3.8	31.7
Malaria incidence rate (per 100,000 people)	210	206	4,874

	Country data	Latin America & the Carib.	Lower middle income
Resilience			
Access to improved sanitation (% of total pop.)	90	79	45
Access to improved water source (% of total pop.)	99	93	84
Cereal yield (kg. per hectare)	2,972	3,337	2,754
Access to electricity (% of total population)	..	93.4	67.3
Paved roads (% of total roads)	17.0	28.1	29.3
Health workers (per 1,000 people)	2.8	6.9	2.6
Foreign direct investment, net inflows (% of GDP)	6.7	2.3	2.4
Invest. in infrastructure w/private participation ($ millions)	22	33,064	81,789
Disaster risk reduction progress score (1–5 scale; 5 = best)	..		
Ease of doing business (ranking 1–183; 1 = best)	93		
Public sector mgmt & institutions avg. (1–6 scale; 6 = best)	..		
Primary completion rate, total (% of relevant age group)	106	102	88
Ratio of girls to boys in primary & secondary school (%)	101	102	93

	Country data	Latin America & the Carib.	Lower middle income
GHG Emissions and Energy Use			
CO_2 emissions per capita (metric tons)	1.3	2.8	1.6
CO_2 emissions per units of GDP (kg/$1,000 of 2005 PPP $)	212.0	285.6	523.9
CO_2 emissions, total (MtCO2)	0.4	1,584	3,744
GHG net emissions/removals by LUCF (1994, MtCO2e)	-4.0		
Methane (CH_4) emissions, total (MtCO2e)	..	1,009	1,705
Nitrous oxide (N_2O) emissions, total (MtCO2e)	..	442	687
Other GHG emissions, total (MtCO2e)	..	21	17
Energy use per capita (kilograms of oil equivalent)	571	1,245	680
Energy use per units of GDP (kg oil eq./$1,000 of 2005 PPP $)	92.1	130.6	217.9

National-Level Actions

Latest UNFCCC national communication	9/16/2002 (1st)
Annex-I emissions reduction target	n/a
NAMA submission	..
NAPA submission	n/a
Renewable energy target	..

Carbon Markets

Hosted Clean Development Mechanism (CDM) projects	..
Issued Certified Emission Reductions (CERs) from CDM (thousands)	..
Hosted Joint Implementation (JI) projects	n/a
Issued Emission Reduction Units (ERUs) from JI (thousands)	n/a

Benin

Population (millions)	8.8	GDP ($ billions)	6.6
Pop. growth (avg. ann. %, 1990–2010)	3.1	GNI per capita (Atlas $)	780

Climate

Average daily min/max temperature (1961–90, Celsius)	22 / 33
Projected annual temperature change (2045–65, Celsius)	2.0 to 2.5
Average annual precipitation (1961–90, mm)	1,039
Projected annual precipitation change (2045–65, mm)	-207 to 97
Projected change in annual hot days/warm nights	5 / 19
Projected change in annual cool days/cold nights	-2 / -3

	Country data	Sub-Saharan Africa	Low income
Exposure to Impacts			
Land area below 5m (% of land area)	1.2	0.4	0.7
Population below 5m (% of total)	14.1	2.0	5.1
Population in urban agglomerations > 1 million (%)	..	14	11
Urban pop. growth (avg. annual %, 1990–2010)	4.1	4.0	3.7
Droughts, floods, extreme temps (% pop. avg., 1990–2009)	0.9		
Annual freshwater withdrawals (% of internal resources)	1.3	3.2	3.7
Agricultural land under irrigation (% of total ag. land)	..	..	..
Population living below $1.25 a day (% of total)	47.3	50.9	..
Nationally terrestrial protected areas (% of total land area)	23.8	11.7	10.6
Under-five mortality rate (per 1,000)	115	121	108
Child malnutrition, underweight (% of under age five)	20.2	24.6	28.3
Malaria incidence rate (per 100,000 people)	35,555	26,113	16,659
Resilience			
Access to improved sanitation (% of total pop.)	12	31	35
Access to improved water source (% of total pop.)	75	60	63
Cereal yield (kg. per hectare)	1,424	1,297	2,047
Access to electricity (% of total population)	24.8	32.5	23.0
Paved roads (% of total roads)	9.5	18.3	14.1
Health workers (per 1,000 people)	0.8	1.2	0.7
Foreign direct investment, net inflows (% of GDP)	1.7	3.6	3.2
Invest. in infrastructure w/private participation ($ millions)	394	11,957	4,471
Disaster risk reduction progress score (1–5 scale; 5 = best)	..		
Ease of doing business (ranking 1–183; 1 = best)	175		
Public sector mgmt & institutions avg. (1–6 scale; 6 = best)	3.3		
Primary completion rate, total (% of relevant age group)	62	67	65
Ratio of girls to boys in primary & secondary school (%)	73	89	91
GHG Emissions and Energy Use			
CO$_2$ emissions per capita (metric tons)	0.5	0.8	0.3
CO$_2$ emissions per units of GDP (kg/$1,000 of 2005 PPP $)	345.0	428.6	270.2
CO$_2$ emissions, total (MtCO$_2$)	4.1	685	219
GHG net emissions/removals by LUCF (1995, MtCO$_2$e)	-47.5		
Methane (CH$_4$) emissions, total (MtCO$_2$e)	4.1	590	436
Nitrous oxide (N$_2$O) emissions, total (MtCO$_2$e)	2.9	334	209
Other GHG emissions, total (MtCO$_2$e)	0.0	..	..
Energy use per capita (kilograms of oil equivalent)	404	689	365
Energy use per units of GDP (kg oil eq./$1,000 of 2005 PPP $)	284.0	308.4	303.9

National-Level Actions

Latest UNFCCC national communication	10/21/2002 (1st)
Annex-I emissions reduction target	n/a
NAMA submission	Yes
NAPA submission	Yes
Renewable energy target	..

Carbon Markets

Hosted Clean Development Mechanism (CDM) projects	..
Issued Certified Emission Reductions (CERs) from CDM (thousands)	..
Hosted Joint Implementation (JI) projects	n/a
Issued Emission Reduction Units (ERUs) from JI (thousands)	n/a

Bermuda

Population (thousands)	64.6	GDP ($ billions)	5.7
Pop. growth (avg. ann. %, 1990–2010)	0.3	GNI per capita (Atlas $)	..

Climate

Average daily min/max temperature (1961–90, Celsius)	17 / 26
Projected annual temperature change (2045–65, Celsius)	1.3 to 1.7
Average annual precipitation (1961–90, mm)	1,506
Projected annual precipitation change (2045–65, mm)	-97 to 60
Projected change in annual hot days/warm nights	6 / 9
Projected change in annual cool days/cold nights	-2 / -2

	Country data	High Income
Exposure to Impacts		
Land area below 5m (% of land area)	82.3	2.2
Population below 5m (% of total)	82.3	7.7
Population in urban agglomerations > 1 million (%)	..	..
Urban pop. growth (avg. annual %, 1990–2010)	0.3	1.0
Droughts, floods, extreme temps (% pop. avg., 1990–2009)	..	
Annual freshwater withdrawals (% of internal resources)	..	10.4
Agricultural land under irrigation (% of total ag. land)	..	
Population living below $1.25 a day (% of total)	..	..
Nationally terrestrial protected areas (% of total land area)	5.6	13.4
Under-five mortality rate (per 1,000)	..	6
Child malnutrition, underweight (% of under age five)	..	..
Malaria incidence rate (per 100,000 people)	..	..
Resilience		
Access to improved sanitation (% of total pop.)	..	100
Access to improved water source (% of total pop.)	..	100
Cereal yield (kg. per hectare)	..	5,445
Access to electricity (% of total population)	..	..
Paved roads (% of total roads)	..	87.3
Health workers (per 1,000 people)	..	10.7
Foreign direct investment, net inflows (% of GDP)	0.6	1.8
Invest. in infrastructure w/private participation ($ millions)	..	..
Disaster risk reduction progress score (1–5 scale; 5 = best)	..	
Ease of doing business (ranking 1–183; 1 = best)	..	
Public sector mgmt & institutions avg. (1–6 scale; 6 = best)	..	
Primary completion rate, total (% of relevant age group)	93	97
Ratio of girls to boys in primary & secondary school (%)	109	100
GHG Emissions and Energy Use		
CO_2 emissions per capita (metric tons)	6.1	11.9
CO_2 emissions per units of GDP (kg/$1,000 of 2005 PPP $)	..	354.4
CO_2 emissions, total (MtCO$_2$)	0.4	13,285
GHG net emissions/removals by LUCF (MtCO$_2$e)	..	
Methane (CH$_4$) emissions, total (MtCO$_2$e)	..	1,539
Nitrous oxide (N$_2$O) emissions, total (MtCO$_2$e)	..	813
Other GHG emissions, total (MtCO$_2$e)	..	460
Energy use per capita (kilograms of oil equivalent)	..	4,944
Energy use per units of GDP (kg oil eq./$1,000 of 2005 PPP $)	..	147.0

National-Level Actions	
Latest UNFCCC national communication	n/a
Annex-I emissions reduction target	n/a
NAMA submission	n/a
NAPA submission	n/a
Renewable energy target	..
Carbon Markets	
Hosted Clean Development Mechanism (CDM) projects	n/a
Issued Certified Emission Reductions (CERs) from CDM (thousands)	n/a
Hosted Joint Implementation (JI) projects	n/a
Issued Emission Reduction Units (ERUs) from JI (thousands)	n/a

Bhutan

Population (thousands)	725.9	GDP ($ billions)	1.5
Pop. growth (avg. ann. %, 1990–2010)	1.3	GNI per capita (Atlas $)	1,880

Climate

Average daily min/max temperature (1961–90, Celsius)	1 / 14
Projected annual temperature change (2045–65, Celsius)	1.9 to 3.0
Average annual precipitation (1961–90, mm)	1,667
Projected annual precipitation change (2045–65, mm)	-112 to 298
Projected change in annual hot days/warm nights	3 / 9
Projected change in annual cool days/cold nights	-2 /-2

	Country data	South Asia	Lower middle income
Exposure to Impacts			
Land area below 5m (% of land area)	0.0	1.5	1.7
Population below 5m (% of total)	0.0	4.4	6.5
Population in urban agglomerations > 1 million (%)	..	13	14
Urban pop. growth (avg. annual %, 1990–2010)	5.4	2.7	2.8
Droughts, floods, extreme temps (% pop. avg., 1990–2009)	0.0		
Annual freshwater withdrawals (% of internal resources)	..	50.6	18.7
Agricultural land under irrigation (% of total ag. land)	6.8	..	..
Population living below $1.25 a day (% of total)	26.2	40.3	..
Nationally terrestrial protected areas (% of total land area)	28.3	6.1	9.5
Under-five mortality rate (per 1,000)	56	67	69
Child malnutrition, underweight (% of under age five)	12.0	42.5	31.7
Malaria incidence rate (per 100,000 people)	100	1,127	4,874
Resilience			
Access to improved sanitation (% of total pop.)	65	36	45
Access to improved water source (% of total pop.)	92	87	84
Cereal yield (kg. per hectare)	2,159	2,728	2,754
Access to electricity (% of total population)	..	62.1	67.3
Paved roads (% of total roads)	62.0	58.9	29.3
Health workers (per 1,000 people)	0.3	1.7	2.6
Foreign direct investment, net inflows (% of GDP)	0.8	1.3	2.4
Invest. in infrastructure w/private participation ($ millions)	201	73,548	81,789
Disaster risk reduction progress score (1–5 scale; 5 = best)	..		
Ease of doing business (ranking 1–183; 1 = best)	142		
Public sector mgmt & institutions avg. (1–6 scale; 6 = best)	3.9		
Primary completion rate, total (% of relevant age group)	88	86	88
Ratio of girls to boys in primary & secondary school (%)	100	92	93
GHG Emissions and Energy Use			
CO_2 emissions per capita (metric tons)	1.0	1.3	1.6
CO_2 emissions per units of GDP (kg/$1,000 of 2005 PPP $)	242.4	504.6	523.9
CO_2 emissions, total (MtCO_2)	0.7	1,970	3,744
GHG net emissions/removals by LUCF (1994, MtCO_2e)	-3.5		
Methane (CH_4) emissions, total (MtCO_2e)	..	846	1,705
Nitrous oxide (N_2O) emissions, total (MtCO_2e)	..	268	687
Other GHG emissions, total (MtCO_2e)	..	9	17
Energy use per capita (kilograms of oil equivalent)	354	532	680
Energy use per units of GDP (kg oil eq./$1,000 of 2005 PPP $)	84.4	193.5	217.9

National-Level Actions

Latest UNFCCC national communication	11/13/2000 (1st)
Annex-I emissions reduction target	n/a
NAMA submission	Yes, with Goal
NAPA submission	Yes
Renewable energy target	..

Carbon Markets

Hosted Clean Development Mechanism (CDM) projects	2
Issued Certified Emission Reductions (CERs) from CDM (thousands)	0
Hosted Joint Implementation (JI) projects	n/a
Issued Emission Reduction Units (ERUs) from JI (thousands)	n/a

Bolivia

Population (millions)	9.9	GDP ($ billions)	19.8
Pop. growth (avg. ann. %, 1990–2010)	2.0	GNI per capita (Atlas $)	1,810

Climate

Average daily min/max temperature (1961–90, Celsius)	15 / 28
Projected annual temperature change (2045–65, Celsius)	2.1 to 3.0
Average annual precipitation (1961–90, mm)	1,146
Projected annual precipitation change (2045–65, mm)	-91 to 137
Projected change in annual hot days/warm nights	5 / 17
Projected change in annual cool days/cold nights	-2 / -2

	Country data	Latin America & the Carib.	Lower middle income
Exposure to Impacts			
Land area below 5m (% of land area)	0.0	1.5	1.7
Population below 5m (% of total)	0.0	3.8	6.5
Population in urban agglomerations > 1 million (%)	33	35	14
Urban pop. growth (avg. annual %, 1990–2010)	2.9	2.0	2.8
Droughts, floods, extreme temps (% pop. avg., 1990–2009)	1.3		
Annual freshwater withdrawals (% of internal resources)	0.7	2.0	18.7
Agricultural land under irrigation (% of total ag. land)	..	..	..
Population living below $1.25 a day (% of total)	13.6	8.1	..
Nationally terrestrial protected areas (% of total land area)	18.2	20.8	9.5
Under-five mortality rate (per 1,000)	54	23	69
Child malnutrition, underweight (% of under age five)	4.5	3.8	31.7
Malaria incidence rate (per 100,000 people)	365	206	4,874
Resilience			
Access to improved sanitation (% of total pop.)	25	79	45
Access to improved water source (% of total pop.)	86	93	84
Cereal yield (kg. per hectare)	2,089	3,337	2,754
Access to electricity (% of total population)	77.5	93.4	67.3
Paved roads (% of total roads)	7.0	28.1	29.3
Health workers (per 1,000 people)	3.4	6.9	2.6
Foreign direct investment, net inflows (% of GDP)	3.1	2.3	2.4
Invest. in infrastructure w/private participation ($ millions)	37	33,064	81,789
Disaster risk reduction progress score (1–5 scale; 5 = best)	2.3		
Ease of doing business (ranking 1–183; 1 = best)	153		
Public sector mgmt & institutions avg. (1–6 scale; 6 = best)	3.3		
Primary completion rate, total (% of relevant age group)	99	102	88
Ratio of girls to boys in primary & secondary school (%)	99	102	93
GHG Emissions and Energy Use			
CO_2 emissions per capita (metric tons)	1.3	2.8	1.6
CO_2 emissions per units of GDP (kg/$1,000 of 2005 PPP $)	319.8	285.6	523.9
CO_2 emissions, total (MtCO_2)	12.8	1,584	3,744
GHG net emissions/removals by LUCF (2004, MtCO_2e)	48.0		
Methane (CH_4) emissions, total (MtCO_2e)	30.3	1,009	1,705
Nitrous oxide (N_2O) emissions, total (MtCO_2e)	15.1	442	687
Other GHG emissions, total (MtCO_2e)	0.0	21	17
Energy use per capita (kilograms of oil equivalent)	638	1,245	680
Energy use per units of GDP (kg oil eq./$1,000 of 2005 PPP $)	150.2	130.6	217.9

National-Level Actions

Latest UNFCCC national communication	12/2/2009 (2nd)
Annex-I emissions reduction target	n/a
NAMA submission	..
NAPA submission	n/a
Renewable energy target	..

Carbon Markets

Hosted Clean Development Mechanism (CDM) projects	4
Issued Certified Emission Reductions (CERs) from CDM (thousands)	1,118
Hosted Joint Implementation (JI) projects	n/a
Issued Emission Reduction Units (ERUs) from JI (thousands)	n/a

Bosnia and Herzegovina

Population (millions)	3.8	GDP ($ billions)	16.9
Pop. growth (avg. ann. %, 1990–2010)	-0.7	GNI per capita (Atlas $)	4,790

Climate

Average daily min/max temperature (1961–90, Celsius)	5 / 15
Projected annual temperature change (2045–65, Celsius)	1.9 to 3.0
Average annual precipitation (1961–90, mm)	1,028
Projected annual precipitation change (2045–65, mm)	-116 to -7
Projected change in annual hot days/warm nights	3 / 6
Projected change in annual cool days/cold nights	-2 / -2

	Country data	Europe & Central Asia	Upper middle income
Exposure to Impacts			
Land area below 5m (% of land area)	0.1	2.5	1.8
Population below 5m (% of total)	0.1	3.0	6.5
Population in urban agglomerations > 1 million (%)	..	18	22
Urban pop. growth (avg. annual %, 1990–2010)	0.4	0.3	2.3
Droughts, floods, extreme temps (% pop. avg., 1990–2009)	0.5		
Annual freshwater withdrawals (% of internal resources)	..	6.5	5.6
Agricultural land under irrigation (% of total ag. land)	..	..	..
Population living below $1.25 a day (% of total)	<2	3.7	..
Nationally terrestrial protected areas (% of total land area)	0.6	7.5	13.6
Under-five mortality rate (per 1,000)	8	23	20
Child malnutrition, underweight (% of under age five)	1.6	..	4.1
Malaria incidence rate (per 100,000 people)	..	..	80
Resilience			
Access to improved sanitation (% of total pop.)	95	89	68
Access to improved water source (% of total pop.)	99	95	92
Cereal yield (kg. per hectare)	4,539	2,475	3,690
Access to electricity (% of total population)	..	..	98.0
Paved roads (% of total roads)	52.3	85.8	50.5
Health workers (per 1,000 people)	6.1	9.9	4.5
Foreign direct investment, net inflows (% of GDP)	1.4	2.8	2.7
Invest. in infrastructure w/private participation ($ millions)	125	22,652	26,166
Disaster risk reduction progress score (1-5 scale; 5 = best)	..		
Ease of doing business (ranking 1-183; 1 = best)	125		
Public sector mgmt & institutions avg. (1-6 scale; 6 = best)	3.3		
Primary completion rate, total (% of relevant age group)	..	95	98
Ratio of girls to boys in primary & secondary school (%)	102	97	103
GHG Emissions and Energy Use			
CO_2 emissions per capita (metric tons)	8.3	7.7	5.3
CO_2 emissions per units of GDP (kg/$1,000 of 2005 PPP $)	1,108.3	708.0	659.4
CO_2 emissions, total (MtCO_2)	31.3	3,110	12,860
GHG net emissions/removals by LUCF (1990, MtCO_2e)	-7.4		
Methane (CH_4) emissions, total (MtCO_2e)	2.7	937	3,455
Nitrous oxide (N_2O) emissions, total (MtCO_2e)	1.2	214	1,144
Other GHG emissions, total (MtCO_2e)	0.6	76	243
Energy use per capita (kilograms of oil equivalent)	1,580	2,833	1,848
Energy use per units of GDP (kg oil eq./$1,000 of 2005 PPP $)	217.7	276.8	227.1

National-Level Actions

Latest UNFCCC national communication	5/26/2010 (1st)
Annex-I emissions reduction target	n/a
NAMA submission	..
NAPA submission	n/a
Renewable energy target	..

Carbon Markets

Hosted Clean Development Mechanism (CDM) projects	..
Issued Certified Emission Reductions (CERs) from CDM (thousands)	..
Hosted Joint Implementation (JI) projects	n/a
Issued Emission Reduction Units (ERUs) from JI (thousands)	n/a

Botswana

Population (millions)	2.0	GDP ($ billions)	14.9
Pop. growth (avg. ann. %, 1990–2010)	1.9	GNI per capita (Atlas $)	6,790

Climate

Average daily min/max temperature (1961–90, Celsius)	14 / 29
Projected annual temperature change (2045–65, Celsius)	2.5 to 3.3
Average annual precipitation (1961–90, mm)	416
Projected annual precipitation change (2045–65, mm)	-106 to 24
Projected change in annual hot days/warm nights	5 / 13
Projected change in annual cool days/cold nights	-2 / -2

	Country data	Sub-Saharan Africa	Upper middle income
Exposure to Impacts			
Land area below 5m (% of land area)	0.0	0.4	1.8
Population below 5m (% of total)	0.0	2.0	6.5
Population in urban agglomerations > 1 million (%)	..	14	22
Urban pop. growth (avg. annual %, 1990–2010)	3.8	4.0	2.3
Droughts, floods, extreme temps (% pop. avg., 1990–2009)	0.7		
Annual freshwater withdrawals (% of internal resources)	8.1	3.2	5.6
Agricultural land under irrigation (% of total ag. land)	0.0	..	..
Population living below $1.25 a day (% of total)	31.2	50.9	..
Nationally terrestrial protected areas (% of total land area)	30.9	11.7	13.6
Under-five mortality rate (per 1,000)	48	121	20
Child malnutrition, underweight (% of under age five)	10.7	24.6	4.1
Malaria incidence rate (per 100,000 people)	587	26,113	80
Resilience			
Access to improved sanitation (% of total pop.)	60	31	68
Access to improved water source (% of total pop.)	95	60	92
Cereal yield (kg. per hectare)	569	1,297	3,690
Access to electricity (% of total population)	45.4	32.5	98.0
Paved roads (% of total roads)	32.6	18.3	50.5
Health workers (per 1,000 people)	3.2	1.2	4.5
Foreign direct investment, net inflows (% of GDP)	3.6	3.6	2.7
Invest. in infrastructure w/private participation ($ millions)	59	11,957	26,166
Disaster risk reduction progress score (1-5 scale; 5 = best)	3.0		
Ease of doing business (ranking 1-183; 1 = best)	54		
Public sector mgmt & institutions avg. (1-6 scale; 6 = best)	..		
Primary completion rate, total (% of relevant age group)	95	67	98
Ratio of girls to boys in primary & secondary school (%)	100	89	103
GHG Emissions and Energy Use			
CO_2 emissions per capita (metric tons)	2.5	0.8	5.3
CO_2 emissions per units of GDP (kg/$1,000 of 2005 PPP $)	197.3	428.6	659.4
CO_2 emissions, total (MtCO$_2$)	4.8	685	12,860
GHG net emissions/removals by LUCF (1994, MtCO$_2$e)	-38.7		
Methane (CH_4) emissions, total (MtCO$_2$e)	4.5	590	3,455
Nitrous oxide (N_2O) emissions, total (MtCO$_2$e)	3.1	334	1,144
Other GHG emissions, total (MtCO$_2$e)	0.0	..	243
Energy use per capita (kilograms of oil equivalent)	1,034	689	1,848
Energy use per units of GDP (kg oil eq./$1,000 of 2005 PPP $)	87.8	308.4	227.1

National-Level Actions

Latest UNFCCC national communication	10/22/2001 (1st)
Annex-I emissions reduction target	n/a
NAMA submission	Yes
NAPA submission	n/a
Renewable energy target	Yes

Carbon Markets

Hosted Clean Development Mechanism (CDM) projects	..
Issued Certified Emission Reductions (CERs) from CDM (thousands)	..
Hosted Joint Implementation (JI) projects	n/a
Issued Emission Reduction Units (ERUs) from JI (thousands)	n/a

Brazil

Population (millions)	194.9	GDP ($ billions)	2,087.9
Pop. growth (avg. ann. %, 1990–2010)	1.3	GNI per capita (Atlas $)	9,390

Climate

Average daily min/max temperature (1961-90, Celsius)	20 / 30
Projected annual temperature change (2045-65, Celsius)	1.9 to 2.6
Average annual precipitation (1961-90, mm)	1,782
Projected annual precipitation change (2045-65, mm)	-95 to 136
Projected change in annual hot days/warm nights	6 / 20
Projected change in annual cool days/cold nights	-2 / -2

	Country data	Latin America & the Carib.	Upper middle income
Exposure to Impacts			
Land area below 5m (% of land area)	1.2	1.5	1.8
Population below 5m (% of total)	4.9	3.8	6.5
Population in urban agglomerations > 1 million (%)	41	35	22
Urban pop. growth (avg. annual %, 1990-2010)	2.0	2.0	2.3
Droughts, floods, extreme temps (% pop. avg., 1990-2009)	0.5		
Annual freshwater withdrawals (% of internal resources)	1.1	2.0	5.6
Agricultural land under irrigation (% of total ag. land)	..	..	..
Population living below $1.25 a day (% of total)	3.8	8.1	..
Nationally terrestrial protected areas (% of total land area)	28.0	20.8	13.6
Under-five mortality rate (per 1,000)	19	23	20
Child malnutrition, underweight (% of under age five)	2.2	3.8	4.1
Malaria incidence rate (per 100,000 people)	210	206	80
Resilience			
Access to improved sanitation (% of total pop.)	80	79	68
Access to improved water source (% of total pop.)	97	93	92
Cereal yield (kg. per hectare)	3,533	3,337	3,690
Access to electricity (% of total population)	98.3	93.4	98.0
Paved roads (% of total roads)	5.5	28.1	50.5
Health workers (per 1,000 people)	8.2	6.9	4.5
Foreign direct investment, net inflows (% of GDP)	2.3	2.3	2.7
Invest. in infrastructure w/private participation ($ millions)	16,733	33,064	26,166
Disaster risk reduction progress score (1-5 scale; 5 = best)	4.5		
Ease of doing business (ranking 1-183; 1 = best)	126		
Public sector mgmt & institutions avg. (1-6 scale; 6 = best)	..		
Primary completion rate, total (% of relevant age group)	106	102	98
Ratio of girls to boys in primary & secondary school (%)	103	102	103
GHG Emissions and Energy Use			
CO_2 emissions per capita (metric tons)	2.1	2.8	5.3
CO_2 emissions per units of GDP (kg/$1,000 of 2005 PPP $)	214.2	285.6	659.4
CO_2 emissions, total (MtCO$_2$)	393.2	1,584	12,860
GHG net emissions/removals by LUCF (2005, MtCO$_2$e)	1,329.1		
Methane (CH$_4$) emissions, total (MtCO$_2$e)	492.2	1,009	3,455
Nitrous oxide (N$_2$O) emissions, total (MtCO$_2$e)	236.0	442	1,144
Other GHG emissions, total (MtCO$_2$e)	11.8	21	243
Energy use per capita (kilograms of oil equivalent)	1,243	1,245	1,848
Energy use per units of GDP (kg oil eq./$1,000 of 2005 PPP $)	131.7	130.6	227.1

National-Level Actions

Latest UNFCCC national communication	11/30/2010 (2nd)
Annex-I emissions reduction target	n/a
NAMA submission	Yes, with Goal
NAPA submission	n/a
Renewable energy target	Yes

Carbon Markets

Hosted Clean Development Mechanism (CDM) projects	196
Issued Certified Emission Reductions (CERs) from CDM (thousands)	57,990
Hosted Joint Implementation (JI) projects	n/a
Issued Emission Reduction Units (ERUs) from JI (thousands)	n/a

Brunei Darussalam

Population (thousands)	398.9	GDP ($ billions)	10.7
Pop. growth (avg. ann. %, 1990–2010)	2.3	GNI per capita (Atlas $)	31,800

Climate
Average daily min/max temperature (1961–90, Celsius)	23 / 31
Projected annual temperature change (2045–65, Celsius)	1.5 to 1.9
Average annual precipitation (1961–90, mm)	2,722
Projected annual precipitation change (2045–65, mm)	-185 to 111
Projected change in annual hot days/warm nights	15 / 27
Projected change in annual cool days/cold nights	-2 / -3

	Country data	High income
Exposure to Impacts		
Land area below 5m (% of land area)	3.3	2.2
Population below 5m (% of total)	9.2	7.7
Population in urban agglomerations > 1 million (%)	..	
Urban pop. growth (avg. annual %, 1990–2010)	3.0	1.0
Droughts, floods, extreme temps (% pop. avg., 1990–2009)	..	
Annual freshwater withdrawals (% of internal resources)	1.1	10.4
Agricultural land under irrigation (% of total ag. land)	0.0	
Population living below $1.25 a day (% of total)	..	..
Nationally terrestrial protected areas (% of total land area)	42.9	13.4
Under-five mortality rate (per 1,000)	7	6
Child malnutrition, underweight (% of under age five)	..	
Malaria incidence rate (per 100,000 people)	..	..
Resilience		
Access to improved sanitation (% of total pop.)	..	100
Access to improved water source (% of total pop.)	99	100
Cereal yield (kg. per hectare)	1,291	5,445
Access to electricity (% of total population)	99.7	
Paved roads (% of total roads)	77.2	87.3
Health workers (per 1,000 people)	6.3	10.7
Foreign direct investment, net inflows (% of GDP)	3.0	1.8
Invest. in infrastructure w/private participation ($ millions)	..	..
Disaster risk reduction progress score (1–5 scale; 5 = best)	2.8	
Ease of doing business (ranking 1–183; 1 = best)	83	
Public sector mgmt & institutions avg. (1–6 scale; 6 = best)	..	
Primary completion rate, total (% of relevant age group)	104	97
Ratio of girls to boys in primary & secondary school (%)	101	100
GHG Emissions and Energy Use		
CO_2 emissions per capita (metric tons)	27.5	11.9
CO_2 emissions per units of GDP (kg/$1,000 of 2005 PPP $)	588.2	354.4
CO_2 emissions, total (MtCO_2)	10.6	13,285
GHG net emissions/removals by LUCF (MtCO_2e)	..	
Methane (CH_4) emissions, total (MtCO_2e)	5.8	1,539
Nitrous oxide (N_2O) emissions, total (MtCO_2e)	0.6	813
Other GHG emissions, total (MtCO_2e)	0.3	460
Energy use per capita (kilograms of oil equivalent)	7,971	4,944
Energy use per units of GDP (kg oil eq./$1,000 of 2005 PPP $)	176.5	147.0

National-Level Actions
Latest UNFCCC national communication	..
Annex-I emissions reduction target	n/a
NAMA submission	..
NAPA submission	n/a
Renewable energy target	..

Carbon Markets
Hosted Clean Development Mechanism (CDM) projects	..
Issued Certified Emission Reductions (CERs) from CDM (thousands)	..
Hosted Joint Implementation (JI) projects	n/a
Issued Emission Reduction Units (ERUs) from JI (thousands)	n/a

Bulgaria

Population (millions)	7.5	GDP ($ billions)	47.7
Pop. growth (avg. ann. %, 1990–2010)	-0.7	GNI per capita (Atlas $)	6,250

Climate

Average daily min/max temperature (1961–90, Celsius)	6 / 16
Projected annual temperature change (2045–65, Celsius)	1.9 to 3.1
Average annual precipitation (1961–90, mm)	608
Projected annual precipitation change (2045–65, mm)	-127 to -21
Projected change in annual hot days/warm nights	3 / 6
Projected change in annual cool days/cold nights	-1 / -1

	Country data	Europe & Central Asia	Upper middle income
Exposure to Impacts			
Land area below 5m (% of land area)	0.4	2.5	1.8
Population below 5m (% of total)	1.5	3.0	6.5
Population in urban agglomerations > 1 million (%)	16	18	22
Urban pop. growth (avg. annual %, 1990–2010)	-0.3	0.3	2.3
Droughts, floods, extreme temps (% pop. avg., 1990–2009)	0.0		
Annual freshwater withdrawals (% of internal resources)	24.2	6.5	5.6
Agricultural land under irrigation (% of total ag. land)	1.4	..	..
Population living below $1.25 a day (% of total)	<2	3.7	..
Nationally terrestrial protected areas (% of total land area)	9.1	7.5	13.6
Under-five mortality rate (per 1,000)	13	23	20
Child malnutrition, underweight (% of under age five)	1.6	..	4.1
Malaria incidence rate (per 100,000 people)	..	..	80
Resilience			
Access to improved sanitation (% of total pop.)	100	89	68
Access to improved water source (% of total pop.)	100	95	92
Cereal yield (kg. per hectare)	3,413	2,475	3,690
Access to electricity (% of total population)	..	..	98.0
Paved roads (% of total roads)	98.4	85.8	50.5
Health workers (per 1,000 people)	8.4	9.9	4.5
Foreign direct investment, net inflows (% of GDP)	4.5	2.8	2.7
Invest. in infrastructure w/private participation ($ millions)	488	22,652	26,166
Disaster risk reduction progress score (1–5 scale; 5 = best)	3.5		
Ease of doing business (ranking 1–183; 1 = best)	59		
Public sector mgmt & institutions avg. (1–6 scale; 6 = best)	..		
Primary completion rate, total (% of relevant age group)	94	95	98
Ratio of girls to boys in primary & secondary school (%)	97	97	103
GHG Emissions and Energy Use			
CO_2 emissions per capita (metric tons)	6.6	7.7	5.3
CO_2 emissions per units of GDP (kg/$1,000 of 2005 PPP $)	552.2	708.0	659.4
CO_2 emissions, total (MtCO$_2$)	50.5	3,110	12,860
GHG net emissions/removals by LUCF (2009, MtCO$_2$e)	-11.8		
Methane (CH$_4$) emissions, total (MtCO$_2$e)	10.9	937	3,455
Nitrous oxide (N$_2$O) emissions, total (MtCO$_2$e)	4.2	214	1,144
Other GHG emissions, total (MtCO$_2$e)	0.4	76	243
Energy use per capita (kilograms of oil equivalent)	2,305	2,833	1,848
Energy use per units of GDP (kg oil eq./$1,000 of 2005 PPP $)	202.1	276.8	227.1

National-Level Actions

Latest UNFCCC national communication	2/12/2010 (5th)
Annex-I emissions reduction target (base year: 1990)	20% / 30% (EU)
NAMA submission	n/a
NAPA submission	n/a
Renewable energy target	Yes

Carbon Markets

Hosted Clean Development Mechanism (CDM) projects	n/a
Issued Certified Emission Reductions (CERs) from CDM (thousands)	n/a
Hosted Joint Implementation (JI) projects	28
Issued Emission Reduction Units (ERUs) from JI (thousands)	2,556

Burkina Faso

Population (millions)	16.5	GDP ($ billions)	8.8
Pop. growth (avg. ann. %, 1990–2010)	2.8	GNI per capita (Atlas $)	550

Climate

Average daily min/max temperature (1961–90, Celsius)	22 / 35
Projected annual temperature change (2045–65, Celsius)	2.2 to 2.8
Average annual precipitation (1961–90, mm)	748
Projected annual precipitation change (2045–65, mm)	-229 to 88
Projected change in annual hot days/warm nights	5 / 17
Projected change in annual cool days/cold nights	-2 / -3

	Country data	Sub-Saharan Africa	Low income
Exposure to Impacts			
Land area below 5m (% of land area)	0.0	0.4	0.7
Population below 5m (% of total)	0.0	2.0	5.1
Population in urban agglomerations > 1 million (%)	12	14	11
Urban pop. growth (avg. annual %, 1990–2010)	4.8	4.0	3.7
Droughts, floods, extreme temps (% pop. avg., 1990–2009)	1.3		
Annual freshwater withdrawals (% of internal resources)	7.9	3.2	3.7
Agricultural land under irrigation (% of total ag. land)	..		
Population living below $1.25 a day (% of total)	56.5	50.9	..
Nationally terrestrial protected areas (% of total land area)	13.9	11.7	10.6
Under-five mortality rate (per 1,000)	176	121	108
Child malnutrition, underweight (% of under age five)	26.0	24.6	28.3
Malaria incidence rate (per 100,000 people)	45,322	26,113	16,659
Resilience			
Access to improved sanitation (% of total pop.)	11	31	35
Access to improved water source (% of total pop.)	76	60	63
Cereal yield (kg. per hectare)	1,002	1,297	2,047
Access to electricity (% of total population)	14.6	32.5	23.0
Paved roads (% of total roads)	4.2	18.3	14.1
Health workers (per 1,000 people)	0.8	1.2	0.7
Foreign direct investment, net inflows (% of GDP)	0.4	3.6	3.2
Invest. in infrastructure w/private participation ($ millions)	299	11,957	4,471
Disaster risk reduction progress score (1–5 scale; 5 = best)	..		
Ease of doing business (ranking 1–183; 1 = best)	150		
Public sector mgmt & institutions avg. (1–6 scale; 6 = best)	3.7		
Primary completion rate, total (% of relevant age group)	47	67	65
Ratio of girls to boys in primary & secondary school (%)	88	89	91
GHG Emissions and Energy Use			
CO$_2$ emissions per capita (metric tons)	0.1	0.8	0.3
CO$_2$ emissions per units of GDP (kg/$1,000 of 2005 PPP $)	113.1	428.6	270.2
CO$_2$ emissions, total (MtCO$_2$)	1.9	685	219
GHG net emissions/removals by LUCF (1994, MtCO$_2$e)	-1.4		
Methane (CH$_4$) emissions, total (MtCO$_2$e)	..	590	436
Nitrous oxide (N$_2$O) emissions, total (MtCO$_2$e)	..	334	209
Other GHG emissions, total (MtCO$_2$e)	..	..	..
Energy use per capita (kilograms of oil equivalent)	..	689	365
Energy use per units of GDP (kg oil eq./$1,000 of 2005 PPP $)	..	308.4	303.9

National-Level Actions

Latest UNFCCC national communication	5/16/2002 (1st)
Annex-I emissions reduction target	n/a
NAMA submission	..
NAPA submission	Yes
Renewable energy target	..

Carbon Markets

Hosted Clean Development Mechanism (CDM) projects	..
Issued Certified Emission Reductions (CERs) from CDM (thousands)	..
Hosted Joint Implementation (JI) projects	n/a
Issued Emission Reduction Units (ERUs) from JI (thousands)	n/a

Burundi

Population (millions)	8.4	GDP ($ billions)	1.6
Pop. growth (avg. ann. %, 1990–2010)	2.0	GNI per capita (Atlas $)	170

Climate

Average daily min/max temperature (1961–90, Celsius)	14 / 26
Projected annual temperature change (2045–65, Celsius)	2.1 to 2.4
Average annual precipitation (1961–90, mm)	1,218
Projected annual precipitation change (2045–65, mm)	-21 to 206
Projected change in annual hot days/warm nights	8 / 26
Projected change in annual cool days/cold nights	-2 / -3

	Country data	Sub-Saharan Africa	Low income
Exposure to Impacts			
Land area below 5m (% of land area)	0.0	0.4	0.7
Population below 5m (% of total)	0.0	2.0	5.1
Population in urban agglomerations > 1 million (%)	..	14	11
Urban pop. growth (avg. annual %, 1990–2010)	4.8	4.0	3.7
Droughts, floods, extreme temps (% pop. avg., 1990–2009)	2.4		
Annual freshwater withdrawals (% of internal resources)	2.9	3.2	3.7
Agricultural land under irrigation (% of total ag. land)	..	..	..
Population living below $1.25 a day (% of total)	81.3	50.9	..
Nationally terrestrial protected areas (% of total land area)	4.8	11.7	10.6
Under-five mortality rate (per 1,000)	142	121	108
Child malnutrition, underweight (% of under age five)	38.9	24.6	28.3
Malaria incidence rate (per 100,000 people)	48,475	26,113	16,659
Resilience			
Access to improved sanitation (% of total pop.)	46	31	35
Access to improved water source (% of total pop.)	72	60	63
Cereal yield (kg. per hectare)	1,319	1,297	2,047
Access to electricity (% of total population)	..	32.5	23.0
Paved roads (% of total roads)	10.4	18.3	14.1
Health workers (per 1,000 people)	0.2	1.2	0.7
Foreign direct investment, net inflows (% of GDP)	0.9	3.6	3.2
Invest. in infrastructure w/private participation ($ millions)	6	11,957	4,471
Disaster risk reduction progress score (1–5 scale; 5 = best)	3.3		
Ease of doing business (ranking 1–183; 1 = best)	169		
Public sector mgmt & institutions avg. (1–6 scale; 6 = best)	2.6		
Primary completion rate, total (% of relevant age group)	52	67	65
Ratio of girls to boys in primary & secondary school (%)	93	89	91
GHG Emissions and Energy Use			
CO_2 emissions per capita (metric tons)	0.0	0.8	0.3
CO_2 emissions per units of GDP (kg/$1,000 of 2005 PPP $)	62.9	428.6	270.2
CO_2 emissions, total (MtCO_2)	0.2	685	219
GHG net emissions/removals by LUCF (2005, MtCO_2e)	-15.3		
Methane (CH_4) emissions, total (MtCO_2e)	..	590	436
Nitrous oxide (N_2O) emissions, total (MtCO_2e)	..	334	209
Other GHG emissions, total (MtCO_2e)	..	..	..
Energy use per capita (kilograms of oil equivalent)	..	689	365
Energy use per units of GDP (kg oil eq./$1,000 of 2005 PPP $)	..	308.4	303.9

National-Level Actions

Latest UNFCCC national communication	6/28/2010 (2nd)
Annex-I emissions reduction target	n/a
NAMA submission	..
NAPA submission	Yes
Renewable energy target	Yes

Carbon Markets

Hosted Clean Development Mechanism (CDM) projects	..
Issued Certified Emission Reductions (CERs) from CDM (thousands)	..
Hosted Joint Implementation (JI) projects	n/a
Issued Emission Reduction Units (ERUs) from JI (thousands)	n/a

Cambodia

Population (millions)	14.1	GDP ($ billions)	11.3
Pop. growth (avg. ann. %, 1990-2010)	2.0	GNI per capita (Atlas $)	760

Climate

Average daily min/max temperature (1961-90, Celsius)	22 / 31
Projected annual temperature change (2045-65, Celsius)	1.6 to 2.0
Average annual precipitation (1961-90, mm)	1,903
Projected annual precipitation change (2045-65, mm)	-109 to 95
Projected change in annual hot days/warm nights	4 / 18
Projected change in annual cool days/cold nights	-2 / -2

	Country data	East Asia & Pacific	Low Income
Exposure to Impacts			
Land area below 5m (% of land area)	3.8	2.5	0.7
Population below 5m (% of total)	10.6	10.3	5.1
Population in urban agglomerations > 1 million (%)	11	..	11
Urban pop. growth (avg. annual %, 1990-2010)	4.9	3.3	3.7
Droughts, floods, extreme temps (% pop. avg., 1990-2009)	6.6		
Annual freshwater withdrawals (% of internal resources)	1.8	10.8	3.7
Agricultural land under irrigation (% of total ag. land)	..	..	..
Population living below $1.25 a day (% of total)	28.3	16.8	..
Nationally terrestrial protected areas (% of total land area)	24.0	14.9	10.6
Under-five mortality rate (per 1,000)	51	24	108
Child malnutrition, underweight (% of under age five)	28.8	9.0	28.3
Malaria incidence rate (per 100,000 people)	1,798	525	16,659
Resilience			
Access to improved sanitation (% of total pop.)	29	59	35
Access to improved water source (% of total pop.)	61	88	63
Cereal yield (kg. per hectare)	2,947	4,860	2,047
Access to electricity (% of total population)	24.0	90.8	23.0
Paved roads (% of total roads)	6.3	15.9	14.1
Health workers (per 1,000 people)	1.0	2.8	0.7
Foreign direct investment, net inflows (% of GDP)	6.9	3.0	3.2
Invest. in infrastructure w/private participation ($ millions)	1,775	14,638	4,471
Disaster risk reduction progress score (1-5 scale; 5 = best)	..		
Ease of doing business (ranking 1-183; 1 = best)	138		
Public sector mgmt & institutions avg. (1-6 scale; 6 = best)	2.7		
Primary completion rate, total (% of relevant age group)	79	97	65
Ratio of girls to boys in primary & secondary school (%)	90	103	91
GHG Emissions and Energy Use			
CO_2 emissions per capita (metric tons)	0.3	4.3	0.3
CO_2 emissions per units of GDP (kg/$1,000 of 2005 PPP $)	175.4	827.1	270.2
CO_2 emissions, total (MtCO$_2$)	4.6	8,259	219
GHG net emissions/removals by LUCF (1994, MtCO$_2$e)	-17.9		
Methane (CH_4) emissions, total (MtCO$_2$e)	20.2	1,928	436
Nitrous oxide (N_2O) emissions, total (MtCO$_2$e)	5.8	707	209
Other GHG emissions, total (MtCO$_2$e)	0.0	..	..
Energy use per capita (kilograms of oil equivalent)	371	1,436	365
Energy use per units of GDP (kg oil eq./$1,000 of 2005 PPP $)	201.3	259.5	303.9

National-Level Actions

Latest UNFCCC national communication	10/8/2002 (1st)
Annex-I emissions reduction target	n/a
NAMA submission	Yes
NAPA submission	Yes
Renewable energy target	..

Carbon Markets

Hosted Clean Development Mechanism (CDM) projects	5
Issued Certified Emission Reductions (CERs) from CDM (thousands)	11
Hosted Joint Implementation (JI) projects	n/a
Issued Emission Reduction Units (ERUs) from JI (thousands)	n/a

Cameroon

Population (millions)	19.6	GDP ($ billions) 22.4
Pop. growth (avg. ann. %, 1990–2010)	2.4	GNI per capita (Atlas $) 1,180

Climate

Average daily min/max temperature (1961-90, Celsius)	19 / 30
Projected annual temperature change (2045-65, Celsius)	2.1 to 2.4
Average annual precipitation (1961-90, mm)	1,604
Projected annual precipitation change (2045-65, mm)	-71 to 115
Projected change in annual hot days/warm nights	6 / 22
Projected change in annual cool days/cold nights	-2 / -2

	Country data	Sub-Saharan Africa	Lower middle income
Exposure to Impacts			
Land area below 5m (% of land area)	0.1	0.4	1.7
Population below 5m (% of total)	0.3	2.0	6.5
Population in urban agglomerations > 1 million (%)	20	14	14
Urban pop. growth (avg. annual %, 1990-2010)	4.2	4.0	2.8
Droughts, floods, extreme temps (% pop. avg., 1990-2009)	0.1		
Annual freshwater withdrawals (% of internal resources)	0.4	3.2	18.7
Agricultural land under irrigation (% of total ag. land)	..	..	..
Population living below $1.25 a day (% of total)	9.6	50.9	..
Nationally terrestrial protected areas (% of total land area)	9.2	11.7	9.5
Under-five mortality rate (per 1,000)	136	121	69
Child malnutrition, underweight (% of under age five)	16.6	24.6	31.7
Malaria incidence rate (per 100,000 people)	27,818	26,113	4,874
Resilience			
Access to improved sanitation (% of total pop.)	47	31	45
Access to improved water source (% of total pop.)	74	60	84
Cereal yield (kg. per hectare)	1,524	1,297	2,754
Access to electricity (% of total population)	48.7	32.5	67.3
Paved roads (% of total roads)	8.4	18.3	29.3
Health workers (per 1,000 people)	1.8	1.2	2.6
Foreign direct investment, net inflows (% of GDP)	-0.0	3.6	2.4
Invest. in infrastructure w/private participation ($ millions)	575	11,957	81,789
Disaster risk reduction progress score (1-5 scale; 5 = best)	..		
Ease of doing business (ranking 1-183; 1 = best)	161		
Public sector mgmt & institutions avg. (1-6 scale; 6 = best)	2.9		
Primary completion rate, total (% of relevant age group)	73	67	88
Ratio of girls to boys in primary & secondary school (%)	86	89	93
GHG Emissions and Energy Use			
CO_2 emissions per capita (metric tons)	0.3	0.8	1.6
CO_2 emissions per units of GDP (kg/$1,000 of 2005 PPP $)	138.4	428.6	523.9
CO_2 emissions, total (MtCO_2)	5.3	685	3,744
GHG net emissions/removals by LUCF (1994, MtCO_2e)	22.2		
Methane (CH_4) emissions, total (MtCO_2e)	18.5	590	1,705
Nitrous oxide (N_2O) emissions, total (MtCO_2e)	9.1	334	687
Other GHG emissions, total (MtCO_2e)	0.4	..	17
Energy use per capita (kilograms of oil equivalent)	361	689	680
Energy use per units of GDP (kg oil eq./$1,000 of 2005 PPP $)	177.0	308.4	217.9

National-Level Actions

Latest UNFCCC national communication	1/31/2005 (1st)
Annex-I emissions reduction target	n/a
NAMA submission	Yes
NAPA submission	n/a
Renewable energy target	..

Carbon Markets

Hosted Clean Development Mechanism (CDM) projects	2
Issued Certified Emission Reductions (CERs) from CDM (thousands)	0
Hosted Joint Implementation (JI) projects	n/a
Issued Emission Reduction Units (ERUs) from JI (thousands)	n/a

Canada

Population (millions)	34.1	GDP ($ billions)	1,574.1
Pop. growth (avg. ann. %, 1990–2010)	1.0	GNI per capita (Atlas $)	41,950

Climate

Average daily min/max temperature (1961–90, Celsius)	-10 / -1
Projected annual temperature change (2045–65, Celsius)	2.6 to 3.5
Average annual precipitation (1961–90, mm)	537
Projected annual precipitation change (2045–65, mm)	17 to 88
Projected change in annual hot days/warm nights	2 / 4
Projected change in annual cool days/cold nights	-2 / -2

	Country data	High income
Exposure to Impacts		
Land area below 5m (% of land area)	2.4	2.2
Population below 5m (% of total)	4.0	7.7
Population in urban agglomerations > 1 million (%)	44	..
Urban pop. growth (avg. annual %, 1990–2010)	1.3	1.0
Droughts, floods, extreme temps (% pop. avg., 1990–2009)	0.0	
Annual freshwater withdrawals (% of internal resources)	1.6	10.4
Agricultural land under irrigation (% of total ag. land)	..	..
Population living below $1.25 a day (% of total)	..	..
Nationally terrestrial protected areas (% of total land area)	8.0	13.4
Under-five mortality rate (per 1,000)	6	6
Child malnutrition, underweight (% of under age five)	..	..
Malaria incidence rate (per 100,000 people)	..	..
Resilience		
Access to improved sanitation (% of total pop.)	100	100
Access to improved water source (% of total pop.)	100	100
Cereal yield (kg. per hectare)	3,301	5,445
Access to electricity (% of total population)	..	..
Paved roads (% of total roads)	39.9	87.3
Health workers (per 1,000 people)	12.0	10.7
Foreign direct investment, net inflows (% of GDP)	1.5	1.8
Invest. in infrastructure w/private participation ($ millions)	..	..
Disaster risk reduction progress score (1–5 scale; 5 = best)	4.3	
Ease of doing business (ranking 1–183; 1 = best)	13	
Public sector mgmt & institutions avg. (1–6 scale; 6 = best)	..	
Primary completion rate, total (% of relevant age group)	96	97
Ratio of girls to boys in primary & secondary school (%)	99	100
GHG Emissions and Energy Use		
CO_2 emissions per capita (metric tons)	16.3	11.9
CO_2 emissions per units of GDP (kg/$1,000 of 2005 PPP $)	455.0	354.4
CO_2 emissions, total (MtCO_2)	544.1	13,285
GHG net emissions/removals by LUCF (2009, MtCO_2e)	-12.1	
Methane (CH_4) emissions, total (MtCO_2e)	89.3	1,539
Nitrous oxide (N_2O) emissions, total (MtCO_2e)	40.2	813
Other GHG emissions, total (MtCO_2e)	21.9	460
Energy use per capita (kilograms of oil equivalent)	7,486	4,944
Energy use per units of GDP (kg oil eq./$1,000 of 2005 PPP $)	212.4	147.0

National-Level Actions

Latest UNFCCC national communication	3/3/2010 (5th)
Annex-I emissions reduction target (base year: 2005)	17%
NAMA submission	n/a
NAPA submission	n/a
Renewable energy target	..

Carbon Markets

Hosted Clean Development Mechanism (CDM) projects	n/a
Issued Certified Emission Reductions (CERs) from CDM (thousands)	n/a
Hosted Joint Implementation (JI) projects	..
Issued Emission Reduction Units (ERUs) from JI (thousands)	..

Cape Verde

Population (thousands)	496.0	GDP ($ billions)	1.6
Pop. growth (avg. ann. %, 1990–2010)	1.8	GNI per capita (Atlas $)	3,270

Climate

Average daily min/max temperature (1961–90, Celsius)	20 / 27
Projected annual temperature change (2045–65, Celsius)	1.4 to 1.8
Average annual precipitation (1961–90, mm)	424
Projected annual precipitation change (2045–65, mm)	-32 to 12
Projected change in annual hot days/warm nights	8 / 15
Projected change in annual cool days/cold nights	-3 / -3

	Country data	Sub-Saharan Africa	Lower middle income
Exposure to Impacts			
Land area below 5m (% of land area)	14.5	0.4	1.7
Population below 5m (% of total)	13.8	2.0	6.5
Population in urban agglomerations > 1 million (%)	..	14	14
Urban pop. growth (avg. annual %, 1990–2010)	3.4	4.0	2.8
Droughts, floods, extreme temps (% pop. avg., 1990–2009)	0.0		
Annual freshwater withdrawals (% of internal resources)	6.8	3.2	18.7
Agricultural land under irrigation (% of total ag. land)	..	..	..
Population living below $1.25 a day (% of total)	21.0	50.9	..
Nationally terrestrial protected areas (% of total land area)	2.5	11.7	9.5
Under-five mortality rate (per 1,000)	36	121	69
Child malnutrition, underweight (% of under age five)	..	24.6	31.7
Malaria incidence rate (per 100,000 people)	23	26,113	4,874
Resilience			
Access to improved sanitation (% of total pop.)	54	31	45
Access to improved water source (% of total pop.)	84	60	84
Cereal yield (kg. per hectare)	224	1,297	2,754
Access to electricity (% of total population)	..	32.5	67.3
Paved roads (% of total roads)	69.0	18.3	29.3
Health workers (per 1,000 people)	1.9	1.2	2.6
Foreign direct investment, net inflows (% of GDP)	6.8	3.6	2.4
Invest. in infrastructure w/private participation ($ millions)	16	11,957	81,789
Disaster risk reduction progress score (1–5 scale; 5 = best)	3.5		
Ease of doing business (ranking 1–183; 1 = best)	119		
Public sector mgmt & institutions avg. (1–6 scale; 6 = best)	4.0		
Primary completion rate, total (% of relevant age group)	87	67	88
Ratio of girls to boys in primary & secondary school (%)	103	89	93
GHG Emissions and Energy Use			
CO_2 emissions per capita (metric tons)	0.6	0.8	1.6
CO_2 emissions per units of GDP (kg/$1,000 of 2005 PPP $)	189.7	428.6	523.9
CO_2 emissions, total (MtCO$_2$)	0.3	685	3,744
GHG net emissions/removals by LUCF (1995, MtCO$_2$e)	-0.1		
Methane (CH_4) emissions, total (MtCO$_2$e)	..	590	1,705
Nitrous oxide (N_2O) emissions, total (MtCO$_2$e)	..	334	687
Other GHG emissions, total (MtCO$_2$e)	..	..	17
Energy use per capita (kilograms of oil equivalent)	213	689	680
Energy use per units of GDP (kg oil eq./$1,000 of 2005 PPP $)	67.4	308.4	217.9

National-Level Actions

Latest UNFCCC national communication	11/13/2000 (1st)
Annex-I emissions reduction target	n/a
NAMA submission	..
NAPA submission	Yes
Renewable energy target	Yes

Carbon Markets

Hosted Clean Development Mechanism (CDM) projects	0
Issued Certified Emission Reductions (CERs) from CDM (thousands)	0
Hosted Joint Implementation (JI) projects	n/a
Issued Emission Reduction Units (ERUs) from JI (thousands)	n/a

Cayman Islands

Population (thousands)	56.2	GDP ($ millions)	..
Pop. growth (avg. ann. %, 1990–2010)	3.8	GNI per capita (Atlas $)	..

Climate

Average daily min/max temperature (1961–90, Celsius)	..
Projected annual temperature change (2045–65, Celsius)	1.4 to 1.8
Average annual precipitation (1961–90, mm)	..
Projected annual precipitation change (2045–65, mm)	-122 to 39
Projected change in annual hot days/warm nights	11 / 18
Projected change in annual cool days/cold nights	-2 / -2

	Country data	High Income
Exposure to Impacts		
Land area below 5m (% of land area)	60.3	2.2
Population below 5m (% of total)	59.6	7.7
Population in urban agglomerations > 1 million (%)	..	
Urban pop. growth (avg. annual %, 1990–2010)	3.8	1.0
Droughts, floods, extreme temps (% pop. avg., 1990–2009)	..	
Annual freshwater withdrawals (% of internal resources)	..	10.4
Agricultural land under irrigation (% of total ag. land)	..	
Population living below $1.25 a day (% of total)	..	..
Nationally terrestrial protected areas (% of total land area)	8.7	13.4
Under-five mortality rate (per 1,000)	..	6
Child malnutrition, underweight (% of under age five)	..	
Malaria incidence rate (per 100,000 people)	..	
Resilience		
Access to improved sanitation (% of total pop.)	96	100
Access to improved water source (% of total pop.)	95	100
Cereal yield (kg. per hectare)	..	5,445
Access to electricity (% of total population)	..	..
Paved roads (% of total roads)	..	87.3
Health workers (per 1,000 people)	..	10.7
Foreign direct investment, net inflows (% of GDP)	..	1.8
Invest. in infrastructure w/private participation ($ millions)	..	..
Disaster risk reduction progress score (1–5 scale; 5 = best)	3.0	
Ease of doing business (ranking 1–183; 1 = best)	..	
Public sector mgmt & institutions avg. (1–6 scale; 6 = best)	..	
Primary completion rate, total (% of relevant age group)	84	97
Ratio of girls to boys in primary & secondary school (%)	101	100
GHG Emissions and Energy Use		
CO_2 emissions per capita (metric tons)	10.1	11.9
CO_2 emissions per units of GDP (kg/$1,000 of 2005 PPP $)	..	354.4
CO_2 emissions, total (MtCO$_2$)	0.6	13,285
GHG net emissions/removals by LUCF (MtCO$_2$e)	..	
Methane (CH$_4$) emissions, total (MtCO$_2$e)	..	1,539
Nitrous oxide (N$_2$O) emissions, total (MtCO$_2$e)	..	813
Other GHG emissions, total (MtCO$_2$e)	..	460
Energy use per capita (kilograms of oil equivalent)	..	4,944
Energy use per units of GDP (kg oil eq./$1,000 of 2005 PPP $)	..	147.0
National-Level Actions		
Latest UNFCCC national communication		n/a
Annex-I emissions reduction target		n/a
NAMA submission		n/a
NAPA submission		n/a
Renewable energy target		..
Carbon Markets		
Hosted Clean Development Mechanism (CDM) projects		n/a
Issued Certified Emission Reductions (CERs) from CDM (thousands)		n/a
Hosted Joint Implementation (JI) projects		n/a
Issued Emission Reduction Units (ERUs) from JI (thousands)		n/a

Central African Republic

Population (millions)	4.4	GDP ($ billions)	2.0
Pop. growth (avg. ann. %, 1990–2010)	2.0	GNI per capita (Atlas $)	470

Climate

Average daily min/max temperature (1961–90, Celsius)	18 / 32
Projected annual temperature change (2045–65, Celsius)	2.1 to 2.4
Average annual precipitation (1961–90, mm)	1,343
Projected annual precipitation change (2045–65, mm)	-73 to 100
Projected change in annual hot days/warm nights	5 / 23
Projected change in annual cool days/cold nights	-2 / -2

	Country data	Sub-Saharan Africa	Low Income
Exposure to Impacts			
Land area below 5m (% of land area)	0.0	0.4	0.7
Population below 5m (% of total)	0.0	2.0	5.1
Population in urban agglomerations > 1 million (%)	..	14	11
Urban pop. growth (avg. annual %, 1990–2010)	2.3	4.0	3.7
Droughts, floods, extreme temps (% pop. avg., 1990–2009)	0.2		
Annual freshwater withdrawals (% of internal resources)	0.0	3.2	3.7
Agricultural land under irrigation (% of total ag. land)	..	..	..
Population living below $1.25 a day (% of total)	62.8	50.9	..
Nationally terrestrial protected areas (% of total land area)	14.7	11.7	10.6
Under-five mortality rate (per 1,000)	159	121	108
Child malnutrition, underweight (% of under age five)	21.8	24.6	28.3
Malaria incidence rate (per 100,000 people)	35,786	26,113	16,659
Resilience			
Access to improved sanitation (% of total pop.)	34	31	35
Access to improved water source (% of total pop.)	67	60	63
Cereal yield (kg. per hectare)	948	1,297	2,047
Access to electricity (% of total population)	..	32.5	23.0
Paved roads (% of total roads)	..	18.3	14.1
Health workers (per 1,000 people)	0.5	1.2	0.7
Foreign direct investment, net inflows (% of GDP)	3.6	3.6	3.2
Invest. in infrastructure w/private participation ($ millions)	10	11,957	4,471
Disaster risk reduction progress score (1–5 scale; 5 = best)	..		
Ease of doing business (ranking 1–183; 1 = best)	182		
Public sector mgmt & institutions avg. (1–6 scale; 6 = best)	2.5		
Primary completion rate, total (% of relevant age group)	40	67	65
Ratio of girls to boys in primary & secondary school (%)	69	89	91
GHG Emissions and Energy Use			
CO_2 emissions per capita (metric tons)	0.1	0.8	0.3
CO_2 emissions per units of GDP (kg/$1,000 of 2005 PPP $)	87.8	428.6	270.2
CO_2 emissions, total (MtCO_2)	0.3	685	219
GHG net emissions/removals by LUCF (1994, MtCO_2e)	-139.3		
Methane (CH_4) emissions, total (MtCO_2e)	..	590	436
Nitrous oxide (N_2O) emissions, total (MtCO_2e)	..	334	209
Other GHG emissions, total (MtCO_2e)	..	..	..
Energy use per capita (kilograms of oil equivalent)	..	689	365
Energy use per units of GDP (kg oil eq./$1,000 of 2005 PPP $)	..	308.4	303.9

National-Level Actions

Latest UNFCCC national communication	6/10/2003 (1st)
Annex-I emissions reduction target	n/a
NAMA submission	Yes
NAPA submission	Yes
Renewable energy target	..

Carbon Markets

Hosted Clean Development Mechanism (CDM) projects	..
Issued Certified Emission Reductions (CERs) from CDM (thousands)	..
Hosted Joint Implementation (JI) projects	n/a
Issued Emission Reduction Units (ERUs) from JI (thousands)	n/a

Chad

| Population (millions) | 11.2 | GDP ($ billions) | 7.6 |
| Pop. growth (avg. ann. %, 1990-2010) | 3.1 | GNI per capita (Atlas $) | 620 |

Climate

Average daily min/max temperature (1961-90, Celsius)	19 / 35
Projected annual temperature change (2045-65, Celsius)	2.3 to 2.6
Average annual precipitation (1961-90, mm)	322
Projected annual precipitation change (2045-65, mm)	-79 to 41
Projected change in annual hot days/warm nights	5 / 14
Projected change in annual cool days/cold nights	-2 / -2

	Country data	Sub-Saharan Africa	Low income
Exposure to Impacts			
Land area below 5m (% of land area)	0.0	0.4	0.7
Population below 5m (% of total)	0.0	2.0	5.1
Population in urban agglomerations > 1 million (%)	..	14	11
Urban pop. growth (avg. annual %, 1990-2010)	4.5	4.0	3.7
Droughts, floods, extreme temps (% pop. avg., 1990-2009)	2.7		
Annual freshwater withdrawals (% of internal resources)	2.4	3.2	3.7
Agricultural land under irrigation (% of total ag. land)	..	..	..
Population living below $1.25 a day (% of total)	61.9	50.9	..
Nationally terrestrial protected areas (% of total land area)	9.4	11.7	10.6
Under-five mortality rate (per 1,000)	173	121	108
Child malnutrition, underweight (% of under age five)	33.9	24.6	28.3
Malaria incidence rate (per 100,000 people)	39,508	26,113	16,659
Resilience			
Access to improved sanitation (% of total pop.)	9	31	35
Access to improved water source (% of total pop.)	50	60	63
Cereal yield (kg. per hectare)	880	1,297	2,047
Access to electricity (% of total population)	..	32.5	23.0
Paved roads (% of total roads)	0.8	18.3	14.1
Health workers (per 1,000 people)	0.3	1.2	0.7
Foreign direct investment, net inflows (% of GDP)	10.3	3.6	3.2
Invest. in infrastructure w/private participation ($ millions)	345	11,957	4,471
Disaster risk reduction progress score (1-5 scale; 5 = best)	..		
Ease of doing business (ranking 1-183; 1 = best)	183		
Public sector mgmt & institutions avg. (1-6 scale; 6 = best)	2.2		
Primary completion rate, total (% of relevant age group)	33	67	65
Ratio of girls to boys in primary & secondary school (%)	64	89	91
GHG Emissions and Energy Use			
CO_2 emissions per capita (metric tons)	0.0	0.8	0.3
CO_2 emissions per units of GDP (kg/$1,000 of 2005 PPP $)	36.8	428.6	270.2
CO_2 emissions, total (MtCO_2)	0.5	685	219
GHG net emissions/removals by LUCF (1993, MtCO_2e)	-46.2		
Methane (CH_4) emissions, total (MtCO_2e)	..	590	436
Nitrous oxide (N_2O) emissions, total (MtCO_2e)	..	334	209
Other GHG emissions, total (MtCO_2e)	..	..	..
Energy use per capita (kilograms of oil equivalent)	..	689	365
Energy use per units of GDP (kg oil eq./$1,000 of 2005 PPP $)	..	308.4	303.9

National-Level Actions

Latest UNFCCC national communication	10/29/2001 (1st)
Annex-I emissions reduction target	n/a
NAMA submission	Yes
NAPA submission	Yes
Renewable energy target	..

Carbon Markets

Hosted Clean Development Mechanism (CDM) projects	..
Issued Certified Emission Reductions (CERs) from CDM (thousands)	..
Hosted Joint Implementation (JI) projects	n/a
Issued Emission Reduction Units (ERUs) from JI (thousands)	n/a

Channel Islands

Population (thousands)	153.4	GDP ($ billions)	11.5
Pop. growth (avg. ann. %, 1990–2010)	0.5	GNI per capita (Atlas $)	67,960

Climate

Average daily min/max temperature (1961–90, Celsius)	..
Projected annual temperature change (2045–65, Celsius)	..
Average annual precipitation (1961–90, mm)	..
Projected annual precipitation change (2045–65, mm)	..
Projected change in annual hot days/warm nights	..
Projected change in annual cool days/cold nights	..

	Country data	High income
Exposure to Impacts		
Land area below 5m (% of land area)	..	2.2
Population below 5m (% of total)	..	7.7
Population in urban agglomerations > 1 million (%)	..	..
Urban pop. growth (avg. annual %, 1990–2010)	0.5	1.0
Droughts, floods, extreme temps (% pop. avg., 1990–2009)	..	
Annual freshwater withdrawals (% of internal resources)	..	10.4
Agricultural land under irrigation (% of total ag. land)	0.0	..
Population living below $1.25 a day (% of total)	..	..
Nationally terrestrial protected areas (% of total land area)	..	13.4
Under-five mortality rate (per 1,000)	..	6
Child malnutrition, underweight (% of under age five)	..	..
Malaria incidence rate (per 100,000 people)	..	..
Resilience		
Access to improved sanitation (% of total pop.)	..	100
Access to improved water source (% of total pop.)	..	100
Cereal yield (kg. per hectare)	..	5,445
Access to electricity (% of total population)	..	..
Paved roads (% of total roads)	..	87.3
Health workers (per 1,000 people)	..	10.7
Foreign direct investment, net inflows (% of GDP)	..	1.8
Invest. in infrastructure w/private participation ($ millions)	..	..
Disaster risk reduction progress score (1–5 scale; 5 = best)	..	
Ease of doing business (ranking 1–183; 1 = best)	..	
Public sector mgmt & institutions avg. (1–6 scale; 6 = best)	..	
Primary completion rate, total (% of relevant age group)	..	97
Ratio of girls to boys in primary & secondary school (%)	..	100
GHG Emissions and Energy Use		
CO_2 emissions per capita (metric tons)	..	11.9
CO_2 emissions per units of GDP (kg/$1,000 of 2005 PPP $)	..	354.4
CO_2 emissions, total (MtCO_2)	..	13,285
GHG net emissions/removals by LUCF (MtCO_2e)	..	
Methane (CH_4) emissions, total (MtCO_2e)	..	1,539
Nitrous oxide (N_2O) emissions, total (MtCO_2e)	..	813
Other GHG emissions, total (MtCO_2e)	..	460
Energy use per capita (kilograms of oil equivalent)	..	4,944
Energy use per units of GDP (kg oil eq./$1,000 of 2005 PPP $)	..	147.0
National-Level Actions		
Latest UNFCCC national communication		n/a
Annex-I emissions reduction target		n/a
NAMA submission		n/a
NAPA submission		n/a
Renewable energy target		..
Carbon Markets		
Hosted Clean Development Mechanism (CDM) projects		n/a
Issued Certified Emission Reductions (CERs) from CDM (thousands)		n/a
Hosted Joint Implementation (JI) projects		n/a
Issued Emission Reduction Units (ERUs) from JI (thousands)		n/a

Chile

| Population (millions) | 17.1 | GDP ($ billions) | 203.4 |
| Pop. growth (avg. ann. %, 1990–2010) | 1.3 | GNI per capita (Atlas $) | 9,950 |

Climate

Average daily min/max temperature (1961–90, Celsius)	4 / 13
Projected annual temperature change (2045–65, Celsius)	1.2 to 1.9
Average annual precipitation (1961–90, mm)	716
Projected annual precipitation change (2045–65, mm)	-118 to 24
Projected change in annual hot days/warm nights	4 / 7
Projected change in annual cool days/cold nights	-2 / -2

	Country data	Latin America & the Carib.	Upper middle income
Exposure to Impacts			
Land area below 5m (% of land area)	3.1	1.5	1.8
Population below 5m (% of total)	1.6	3.8	6.5
Population in urban agglomerations > 1 million (%)	35	35	22
Urban pop. growth (avg. annual %, 1990–2010)	1.6	2.0	2.3
Droughts, floods, extreme temps (% pop. avg., 1990–2009)	0.3		
Annual freshwater withdrawals (% of internal resources)	1.3	2.0	5.6
Agricultural land under irrigation (% of total ag. land)	5.6	..	
Population living below $1.25 a day (% of total)	<2	8.1	..
Nationally terrestrial protected areas (% of total land area)	16.5	20.8	13.6
Under-five mortality rate (per 1,000)	9	23	20
Child malnutrition, underweight (% of under age five)	0.5	3.8	4.1
Malaria incidence rate (per 100,000 people)	..	206	80
Resilience			
Access to improved sanitation (% of total pop.)	96	79	68
Access to improved water source (% of total pop.)	96	93	92
Cereal yield (kg. per hectare)	5,472	3,337	3,690
Access to electricity (% of total population)	98.5	93.4	98.0
Paved roads (% of total roads)	20.2	28.1	50.5
Health workers (per 1,000 people)	1.3	6.9	4.5
Foreign direct investment, net inflows (% of GDP)	7.4	2.3	2.7
Invest. in infrastructure w/private participation ($ millions)	1,266	33,064	26,166
Disaster risk reduction progress score (1–5 scale; 5 = best)	2.8		
Ease of doing business (ranking 1–183; 1 = best)	39		
Public sector mgmt & institutions avg. (1–6 scale; 6 = best)	..		
Primary completion rate, total (% of relevant age group)	95	102	98
Ratio of girls to boys in primary & secondary school (%)	99	102	103
GHG Emissions and Energy Use			
CO_2 emissions per capita (metric tons)	4.4	2.8	5.3
CO_2 emissions per units of GDP (kg/$1,000 of 2005 PPP $)	325.0	285.6	659.4
CO_2 emissions, total (MtCO_2)	73.1	1,584	12,860
GHG net emissions/removals by LUCF (1994, MtCO_2e)	-9.2		
Methane (CH_4) emissions, total (MtCO_2e)	18.1	1,009	3,455
Nitrous oxide (N_2O) emissions, total (MtCO_2e)	8.1	442	1,144
Other GHG emissions, total (MtCO_2e)	0.0	21	243
Energy use per capita (kilograms of oil equivalent)	1,826	1,245	1,848
Energy use per units of GDP (kg oil eq./$1,000 of 2005 PPP $)	134.3	130.6	227.1

National-Level Actions

Latest UNFCCC national communication	2/8/2000 (1st)
Annex-I emissions reduction target	n/a
NAMA submission	Yes, with Goal
NAPA submission	n/a
Renewable energy target	Yes

Carbon Markets

Hosted Clean Development Mechanism (CDM) projects	51
Issued Certified Emission Reductions (CERs) from CDM (thousands)	7,307
Hosted Joint Implementation (JI) projects	n/a
Issued Emission Reduction Units (ERUs) from JI (thousands)	n/a

China

Population (millions)	1,338.3	GDP ($ billions)	5,878.6
Pop. growth (avg. ann. %, 1990-2010)	0.8	GNI per capita (Atlas $)	4,260

Climate

Average daily min/max temperature (1961-90, Celsius)	1 / 13
Projected annual temperature change (2045-65, Celsius)	2.1 to 3.0
Average annual precipitation (1961-90, mm)	627
Projected annual precipitation change (2045-65, mm)	-37 to 86
Projected change in annual hot days/warm nights	3 / 6
Projected change in annual cool days/cold nights	-1 / -2

	Country data	East Asia & Pacific	Upper middle income
Exposure to Impacts			
Land area below 5m (% of land area)	1.4	2.5	1.8
Population below 5m (% of total)	8.1	10.3	6.5
Population in urban agglomerations > 1 million (%)	18	..	22
Urban pop. growth (avg. annual %, 1990-2010)	3.3	3.3	2.3
Droughts, floods, extreme temps (% pop. avg., 1990-2009)	8.0		
Annual freshwater withdrawals (% of internal resources)	19.7	10.8	5.6
Agricultural land under irrigation (% of total ag. land)	10.2	..	..
Population living below $1.25 a day (% of total)	15.9	16.8	..
Nationally terrestrial protected areas (% of total land area)	16.6	14.9	13.6
Under-five mortality rate (per 1,000)	18	24	20
Child malnutrition, underweight (% of under age five)	4.5	9.0	4.1
Malaria incidence rate (per 100,000 people)	3	525	80
Resilience			
Access to improved sanitation (% of total pop.)	55	59	68
Access to improved water source (% of total pop.)	89	88	92
Cereal yield (kg. per hectare)	5,450	4,860	3,690
Access to electricity (% of total population)	99.4	90.8	98.0
Paved roads (% of total roads)	53.5	15.9	50.5
Health workers (per 1,000 people)	2.8	2.8	4.5
Foreign direct investment, net inflows (% of GDP)	3.1	3.0	2.7
Invest. in infrastructure w/private participation ($ millions)	942	14,638	26,166
Disaster risk reduction progress score (1-5 scale; 5 = best)	..		
Ease of doing business (ranking 1-183; 1 = best)	91		
Public sector mgmt & institutions avg. (1-6 scale; 6 = best)	..		
Primary completion rate, total (% of relevant age group)	..	97	98
Ratio of girls to boys in primary & secondary school (%)	105	103	103
GHG Emissions and Energy Use			
CO_2 emissions per capita (metric tons)	5.3	4.3	5.3
CO_2 emissions per units of GDP (kg/$1,000 of 2005 PPP $)	929.3	827.1	659.4
CO_2 emissions, total (MtCO_2)	7,031.9	8,259	12,860
GHG net emissions/removals by LUCF (1994, MtCO_2e)	-407.5		
Methane (CH_4) emissions, total (MtCO_2e)	1,333.1	1,928	3,455
Nitrous oxide (N_2O) emissions, total (MtCO_2e)	467.2	707	1,144
Other GHG emissions, total (MtCO_2e)	141.4	..	243
Energy use per capita (kilograms of oil equivalent)	1,695	1,436	1,848
Energy use per units of GDP (kg oil eq./$1,000 of 2005 PPP $)	273.2	259.5	227.1

National-Level Actions

Latest UNFCCC national communication	12/10/2004 (1st)
Annex-I emissions reduction target	n/a
NAMA submission	Yes, with Goal
NAPA submission	n/a
Renewable energy target	Yes

Carbon Markets

Hosted Clean Development Mechanism (CDM) projects	1,604
Issued Certified Emission Reductions (CERs) from CDM (thousands)	430,696
Hosted Joint Implementation (JI) projects	n/a
Issued Emission Reduction Units (ERUs) from JI (thousands)	n/a

Colombia

Population (millions)	46.3	GDP ($ billions)	288.2
Pop. growth (avg. ann. %, 1990–2010)	1.7	GNI per capita (Atlas $)	5,510

Climate
Average daily min/max temperature (1961–90, Celsius)	20 / 29
Projected annual temperature change (2045–65, Celsius)	1.8 to 2.5
Average annual precipitation (1961–90, mm)	2,612
Projected annual precipitation change (2045–65, mm)	-80 to 199
Projected change in annual hot days/warm nights	8 / 27
Projected change in annual cool days/cold nights	-2 / -3

	Country data	Latin America & the Carib.	Upper middle income
Exposure to Impacts			
Land area below 5m (% of land area)	0.9	1.5	1.8
Population below 5m (% of total)	2.0	3.8	6.5
Population in urban agglomerations > 1 million (%)	38	35	22
Urban pop. growth (avg. annual %, 1990–2010)	2.1	2.0	2.3
Droughts, floods, extreme temps (% pop. avg., 1990–2009)	0.7		
Annual freshwater withdrawals (% of internal resources)	0.6	2.0	5.6
Agricultural land under irrigation (% of total ag. land)	..	..	..
Population living below $1.25 a day (% of total)	16.0	8.1	..
Nationally terrestrial protected areas (% of total land area)	20.4	20.8	13.6
Under-five mortality rate (per 1,000)	19	23	20
Child malnutrition, underweight (% of under age five)	5.1	3.8	4.1
Malaria incidence rate (per 100,000 people)	394	206	80
Resilience			
Access to improved sanitation (% of total pop.)	74	79	68
Access to improved water source (% of total pop.)	92	93	92
Cereal yield (kg. per hectare)	4,017	3,337	3,690
Access to electricity (% of total population)	93.6	93.4	98.0
Paved roads (% of total roads)	..	28.1	50.5
Health workers (per 1,000 people)	1.4	6.9	4.5
Foreign direct investment, net inflows (% of GDP)	2.3	2.3	2.7
Invest. in infrastructure w/private participation ($ millions)	3,549	33,064	26,166
Disaster risk reduction progress score (1–5 scale; 5 = best)	3.8		
Ease of doing business (ranking 1–183; 1 = best)	42		
Public sector mgmt & institutions avg. (1–6 scale; 6 = best)	..		
Primary completion rate, total (% of relevant age group)	115	102	98
Ratio of girls to boys in primary & secondary school (%)	105	102	103
GHG Emissions and Energy Use			
CO_2 emissions per capita (metric tons)	1.5	2.8	5.3
CO_2 emissions per units of GDP (kg/$1,000 of 2005 PPP $)	182.3	285.6	659.4
CO_2 emissions, total (MtCO$_2$)	67.7	1,584	12,860
GHG net emissions/removals by LUCF (2004, MtCO$_2$e)	26.0		
Methane (CH$_4$) emissions, total (MtCO$_2$e)	58.1	1,009	3,455
Nitrous oxide (N$_2$O) emissions, total (MtCO$_2$e)	21.3	442	1,144
Other GHG emissions, total (MtCO$_2$e)	0.1	21	243
Energy use per capita (kilograms of oil equivalent)	697	1,245	1,848
Energy use per units of GDP (kg oil eq./$1,000 of 2005 PPP $)	84.5	130.6	227.1

National-Level Actions
Latest UNFCCC national communication	12/7/2010 (2nd)
Annex-I emissions reduction target	n/a
NAMA submission	Yes, with Goal
NAPA submission	n/a
Renewable energy target	..

Carbon Markets
Hosted Clean Development Mechanism (CDM) projects	34
Issued Certified Emission Reductions (CERs) from CDM (thousands)	1,094
Hosted Joint Implementation (JI) projects	n/a
Issued Emission Reduction Units (ERUs) from JI (thousands)	n/a

Comoros

Population (thousands)	734.8	GDP ($ millions)	541.1
Pop. growth (avg. ann. %, 1990-2010)	2.6	GNI per capita (Atlas $)	750

Climate

Average daily min/max temperature (1961-90, Celsius)	22 / 30
Projected annual temperature change (2045-65, Celsius)	1.5 to 1.8
Average annual precipitation (1961-90, mm)	1,754
Projected annual precipitation change (2045-65, mm)	-9 to 140
Projected change in annual hot days/warm nights	12 / 19
Projected change in annual cool days/cold nights	-3 / -3

	Country data	Sub-Saharan Africa	Low income
Exposure to Impacts			
Land area below 5m (% of land area)	13.5	0.4	0.7
Population below 5m (% of total)	14.0	2.0	5.1
Population in urban agglomerations > 1 million (%)	..	14	11
Urban pop. growth (avg. annual %, 1990-2010)	2.6	4.0	3.7
Droughts, floods, extreme temps (% pop. avg., 1990-2009)	0.0		
Annual freshwater withdrawals (% of internal resources)	0.8	3.2	3.7
Agricultural land under irrigation (% of total ag. land)	..	..	..
Population living below $1.25 a day (% of total)	46.1	50.9	..
Nationally terrestrial protected areas (% of total land area)	0.0	11.7	10.6
Under-five mortality rate (per 1,000)	86	121	108
Child malnutrition, underweight (% of under age five)	25.0	24.6	28.3
Malaria incidence rate (per 100,000 people)	24,619	26,113	16,659
Resilience			
Access to improved sanitation (% of total pop.)	36	31	35
Access to improved water source (% of total pop.)	95	60	63
Cereal yield (kg. per hectare)	1,064	1,297	2,047
Access to electricity (% of total population)	..	32.5	23.0
Paved roads (% of total roads)	76.5	18.3	14.1
Health workers (per 1,000 people)	0.9	1.2	0.7
Foreign direct investment, net inflows (% of GDP)	1.7	3.6	3.2
Invest. in infrastructure w/private participation ($ millions)	1	11,957	4,471
Disaster risk reduction progress score (1-5 scale; 5 = best)	1.8		
Ease of doing business (ranking 1-183; 1 = best)	157		
Public sector mgmt & institutions avg. (1-6 scale; 6 = best)	2.4		
Primary completion rate, total (% of relevant age group)	81	67	65
Ratio of girls to boys in primary & secondary school (%)	84	89	91
GHG Emissions and Energy Use			
CO_2 emissions per capita (metric tons)	0.2	0.8	0.3
CO_2 emissions per units of GDP (kg/$1,000 of 2005 PPP $)	179.3	428.6	270.2
CO_2 emissions, total (MtCO$_2$)	0.1	685	219
GHG net emissions/removals by LUCF (1994, MtCO$_2$e)	-0.9		
Methane (CH$_4$) emissions, total (MtCO$_2$e)	..	590	436
Nitrous oxide (N$_2$O) emissions, total (MtCO$_2$e)	..	334	209
Other GHG emissions, total (MtCO$_2$e)	..	..	..
Energy use per capita (kilograms of oil equivalent)	60	689	365
Energy use per units of GDP (kg oil eq./$1,000 of 2005 PPP $)	59.5	308.4	303.9

National-Level Actions

Latest UNFCCC national communication	4/5/2003 (1st)
Annex-I emissions reduction target	n/a
NAMA submission	..
NAPA submission	Yes
Renewable energy target	..

Carbon Markets

Hosted Clean Development Mechanism (CDM) projects	..
Issued Certified Emission Reductions (CERs) from CDM (thousands)	..
Hosted Joint Implementation (JI) projects	n/a
Issued Emission Reduction Units (ERUs) from JI (thousands)	n/a

Congo, Dem. Rep.

Population (millions)	66.0	GDP ($ billions)	13.1
Pop. growth (avg. ann. %, 1990-2010)	3.0	GNI per capita (Atlas $)	180

Climate

Average daily min/max temperature (1961-90, Celsius)	18 / 30
Projected annual temperature change (2045-65, Celsius)	2.1 to 2.4
Average annual precipitation (1961-90, mm)	1,543
Projected annual precipitation change (2045-65, mm)	-48 to 128
Projected change in annual hot days/warm nights	6 / 25
Projected change in annual cool days/cold nights	-2 / -3

	Country data	Sub-Saharan Africa	Low income
Exposure to Impacts			
Land area below 5m (% of land area)	0.0	0.4	0.7
Population below 5m (% of total)	0.0	2.0	5.1
Population in urban agglomerations > 1 million (%)	18	14	11
Urban pop. growth (avg. annual %, 1990-2010)	4.2	4.0	3.7
Droughts, floods, extreme temps (% pop. avg., 1990-2009)	0.0		
Annual freshwater withdrawals (% of internal resources)	0.1	3.2	3.7
Agricultural land under irrigation (% of total ag. land)	..	..	..
Population living below $1.25 a day (% of total)	59.2	50.9	..
Nationally terrestrial protected areas (% of total land area)	10.0	11.7	10.6
Under-five mortality rate (per 1,000)	170	121	108
Child malnutrition, underweight (% of under age five)	28.2	24.6	28.3
Malaria incidence rate (per 100,000 people)	37,400	26,113	16,659
Resilience			
Access to improved sanitation (% of total pop.)	23	31	35
Access to improved water source (% of total pop.)	46	60	63
Cereal yield (kg. per hectare)	789	1,297	2,047
Access to electricity (% of total population)	11.1	32.5	23.0
Paved roads (% of total roads)	1.8	18.3	14.1
Health workers (per 1,000 people)	0.6	1.2	0.7
Foreign direct investment, net inflows (% of GDP)	22.4	3.6	3.2
Invest. in infrastructure w/private participation ($ millions)	174	11,957	4,471
Disaster risk reduction progress score (1-5 scale; 5 = best)	..		
Ease of doing business (ranking 1-183; 1 = best)	178		
Public sector mgmt & institutions avg. (1-6 scale; 6 = best)	2.2		
Primary completion rate, total (% of relevant age group)	56	67	65
Ratio of girls to boys in primary & secondary school (%)	77	89	91
GHG Emissions and Energy Use			
CO_2 emissions per capita (metric tons)	0.0	0.8	0.3
CO_2 emissions per units of GDP (kg/$1,000 of 2005 PPP $)	151.2	428.6	270.2
CO_2 emissions, total (MtCO_2)	2.8	685	219
GHG net emissions/removals by LUCF (2003, MtCO_2e)	-178.8		
Methane (CH_4) emissions, total (MtCO_2e)	56.4	590	436
Nitrous oxide (N_2O) emissions, total (MtCO_2e)	54.6	334	209
Other GHG emissions, total (MtCO_2e)	0.0	..	..
Energy use per capita (kilograms of oil equivalent)	357	689	365
Energy use per units of GDP (kg oil eq./$1,000 of 2005 PPP $)	1,196.4	308.4	303.9

National-Level Actions

Latest UNFCCC national communication	11/28/2009 (2nd)
Annex-I emissions reduction target	n/a
NAMA submission	..
NAPA submission	Yes
Renewable energy target	..

Carbon Markets

Hosted Clean Development Mechanism (CDM) projects	2
Issued Certified Emission Reductions (CERs) from CDM (thousands)	0
Hosted Joint Implementation (JI) projects	n/a
Issued Emission Reduction Units (ERUs) from JI (thousands)	n/a

Congo, Rep.

Population (millions)	4.0	GDP ($ billions)	11.9
Pop. growth (avg. ann. %, 1990-2010)	2.6	GNI per capita (Atlas $)	2,150

Climate

Average daily min/max temperature (1961-90, Celsius)	20 / 29
Projected annual temperature change (2045-65, Celsius)	2.0 to 2.3
Average annual precipitation (1961-90, mm)	1,646
Projected annual precipitation change (2045-65, mm)	-40 to 134
Projected change in annual hot days/warm nights	9 / 26
Projected change in annual cool days/cold nights	-2 / -3

	Country data	Sub-Saharan Africa	Lower middle income
Exposure to Impacts			
Land area below 5m (% of land area)	0.1	0.4	1.7
Population below 5m (% of total)	1.0	2.0	6.5
Population in urban agglomerations > 1 million (%)	33	14	14
Urban pop. growth (avg. annual %, 1990-2010)	3.3	4.0	2.8
Droughts, floods, extreme temps (% pop. avg., 1990-2009)	0.3		
Annual freshwater withdrawals (% of internal resources)	0.0	3.2	18.7
Agricultural land under irrigation (% of total ag. land)	..	..	..
Population living below $1.25 a day (% of total)	54.1	50.9	..
Nationally terrestrial protected areas (% of total land area)	9.4	11.7	9.5
Under-five mortality rate (per 1,000)	93	121	69
Child malnutrition, underweight (% of under age five)	11.8	24.6	31.7
Malaria incidence rate (per 100,000 people)	34,298	26,113	4,874
Resilience			
Access to improved sanitation (% of total pop.)	30	31	45
Access to improved water source (% of total pop.)	71	60	84
Cereal yield (kg. per hectare)	862	1,297	2,754
Access to electricity (% of total population)	37.1	32.5	67.3
Paved roads (% of total roads)	7.1	18.3	29.3
Health workers (per 1,000 people)	0.9	1.2	2.6
Foreign direct investment, net inflows (% of GDP)	23.7	3.6	2.4
Invest. in infrastructure w/private participation ($ millions)	77	11,957	81,789
Disaster risk reduction progress score (1-5 scale; 5 = best)	..		
Ease of doing business (ranking 1-183; 1 = best)	181		
Public sector mgmt & institutions avg. (1-6 scale; 6 = best)	2.6		
Primary completion rate, total (% of relevant age group)	74	67	88
Ratio of girls to boys in primary & secondary school (%)	92	89	93
GHG Emissions and Energy Use			
CO_2 emissions per capita (metric tons)	0.5	0.8	1.6
CO_2 emissions per units of GDP (kg/$1,000 of 2005 PPP $)	147.0	428.6	523.9
CO_2 emissions, total (MtCO_2)	1.9	685	3,744
GHG net emissions/removals by LUCF (2000, MtCO_2e)	-82.1		
Methane (CH_4) emissions, total (MtCO_2e)	5.6	590	1,705
Nitrous oxide (N_2O) emissions, total (MtCO_2e)	3.6	334	687
Other GHG emissions, total (MtCO_2e)	0.0	..	17
Energy use per capita (kilograms of oil equivalent)	356	689	680
Energy use per units of GDP (kg oil eq./$1,000 of 2005 PPP $)	99.1	308.4	217.9

National-Level Actions

Latest UNFCCC national communication	11/27/2009 (2nd)
Annex-I emissions reduction target	n/a
NAMA submission	Yes
NAPA submission	n/a
Renewable energy target	..

Carbon Markets

Hosted Clean Development Mechanism (CDM) projects	..
Issued Certified Emission Reductions (CERs) from CDM (thousands)	..
Hosted Joint Implementation (JI) projects	n/a
Issued Emission Reduction Units (ERUs) from JI (thousands)	n/a

Cook Islands

Population (thousands)	20.3	GDP ($ millions)	..
Pop. growth (avg. ann. %, 1990–2010)	0.7	GNI per capita (Atlas $)	..

Climate

Average daily min/max temperature (1961–90, Celsius)	22 / 28
Projected annual temperature change (2045–65, Celsius)	1.3 to 1.7
Average annual precipitation (1961–90, mm)	1,925
Projected annual precipitation change (2045–65, mm)	-57 to 174
Projected change in annual hot days/warm nights	11 / 16
Projected change in annual cool days/cold nights	-3 / -3

	Country data	East Asia & Pacific	Upper middle income
Exposure to Impacts			
Land area below 5m (% of land area)	87.9	2.5	1.8
Population below 5m (% of total)	62.0	10.3	6.5
Population in urban agglomerations > 1 million (%)	..	..	22
Urban pop. growth (avg. annual %, 1990–2010)	..	3.3	2.3
Droughts, floods, extreme temps (% pop. avg., 1990–2009)	..		
Annual freshwater withdrawals (% of internal resources)	..	10.8	5.6
Agricultural land under irrigation (% of total ag. land)	..	..	..
Population living below $1.25 a day (% of total)	..	16.8	..
Nationally terrestrial protected areas (% of total land area)	0.8	14.9	13.6
Under-five mortality rate (per 1,000)	9	24	20
Child malnutrition, underweight (% of under age five)	..	9.0	4.1
Malaria incidence rate (per 100,000 people)	..	525	80
Resilience			
Access to improved sanitation (% of total pop.)	100	59	68
Access to improved water source (% of total pop.)	94	88	92
Cereal yield (kg. per hectare)	..	4,860	3,690
Access to electricity (% of total population)	..	90.8	98.0
Paved roads (% of total roads)	..	15.9	50.5
Health workers (per 1,000 people)	5.9	2.8	4.5
Foreign direct investment, net inflows (% of GDP)	..	3.0	2.7
Invest. in infrastructure w/private participation ($ millions)	..	14,638	26,166
Disaster risk reduction progress score (1–5 scale; 5 = best)	3.5		
Ease of doing business (ranking 1–183; 1 = best)	..		
Public sector mgmt & institutions avg. (1–6 scale; 6 = best)	..		
Primary completion rate, total (% of relevant age group)	102	97	98
Ratio of girls to boys in primary & secondary school (%)	106	103	103
GHG Emissions and Energy Use			
CO_2 emissions per capita (metric tons)	3.4	4.3	5.3
CO_2 emissions per units of GDP (kg/$1,000 of 2005 PPP $)	..	827.1	659.4
CO_2 emissions, total (MtCO_2)	0.1	8,259	12,860
GHG net emissions/removals by LUCF (1994, MtCO_2e)	-0.2		
Methane (CH_4) emissions, total (MtCO_2e)	..	1,928	3,455
Nitrous oxide (N_2O) emissions, total (MtCO_2e)	..	707	1,144
Other GHG emissions, total (MtCO_2e)	..	..	243
Energy use per capita (kilograms of oil equivalent)	..	1,436	1,848
Energy use per units of GDP (kg oil eq./$1,000 of 2005 PPP $)	..	259.5	227.1

National-Level Actions

Latest UNFCCC national communication	10/30/1999 (1st)
Annex-I emissions reduction target	n/a
NAMA submission	..
NAPA submission	n/a
Renewable energy target	..

Carbon Markets

Hosted Clean Development Mechanism (CDM) projects	..
Issued Certified Emission Reductions (CERs) from CDM (thousands)	..
Hosted Joint Implementation (JI) projects	n/a
Issued Emission Reduction Units (ERUs) from JI (thousands)	n/a

Costa Rica

Population (millions)	4.7	GDP ($ billions)	34.6
Pop. growth (avg. ann. %, 1990-2010)	2.1	GNI per capita (Atlas $)	6,550

Climate

Average daily min/max temperature (1961-90, Celsius)	20 / 30
Projected annual temperature change (2045-65, Celsius)	1.6 to 2.3
Average annual precipitation (1961-90, mm)	2,926
Projected annual precipitation change (2045-65, mm)	-239 to 60
Projected change in annual hot days/warm nights	12 / 27
Projected change in annual cool days/cold nights	-3 / -3

	Country data	Latin America & the Carib.	Upper middle income
Exposure to Impacts			
Land area below 5m (% of land area)	2.1	1.5	1.8
Population below 5m (% of total)	0.8	3.8	6.5
Population in urban agglomerations > 1 million (%)	31	35	22
Urban pop. growth (avg. annual %, 1990-2010)	3.3	2.0	2.3
Droughts, floods, extreme temps (% pop. avg., 1990-2009)	0.7		
Annual freshwater withdrawals (% of internal resources)	2.4	2.0	5.6
Agricultural land under irrigation (% of total ag. land)	1.5	..	..
Population living below $1.25 a day (% of total)	<2	8.1	..
Nationally terrestrial protected areas (% of total land area)	20.9	20.8	13.6
Under-five mortality rate (per 1,000)	10	23	20
Child malnutrition, underweight (% of under age five)	..	3.8	4.1
Malaria incidence rate (per 100,000 people)	51	206	80
Resilience			
Access to improved sanitation (% of total pop.)	95	79	68
Access to improved water source (% of total pop.)	97	93	92
Cereal yield (kg. per hectare)	3,770	3,337	3,690
Access to electricity (% of total population)	99.3	93.4	98.0
Paved roads (% of total roads)	25.3	28.1	50.5
Health workers (per 1,000 people)	2.3	6.9	4.5
Foreign direct investment, net inflows (% of GDP)	4.1	2.3	2.7
Invest. in infrastructure w/private participation ($ millions)	144	33,064	26,166
Disaster risk reduction progress score (1-5 scale; 5 = best)	4.5		
Ease of doing business (ranking 1-183; 1 = best)	121		
Public sector mgmt & institutions avg. (1-6 scale; 6 = best)	..		
Primary completion rate, total (% of relevant age group)	96	102	98
Ratio of girls to boys in primary & secondary school (%)	102	102	103
GHG Emissions and Energy Use			
CO_2 emissions per capita (metric tons)	1.8	2.8	5.3
CO_2 emissions per units of GDP (kg/$1,000 of 2005 PPP $)	171.0	285.6	659.4
CO_2 emissions, total (MtCO_2)	8.0	1,584	12,860
GHG net emissions/removals by LUCF (2005, MtCO_2e)	-3.5		
Methane (CH_4) emissions, total (MtCO_2e)	2.6	1,009	3,455
Nitrous oxide (N_2O) emissions, total (MtCO_2e)	1.3	442	1,144
Other GHG emissions, total (MtCO_2e)	0.1	21	243
Energy use per capita (kilograms of oil equivalent)	1,067	1,245	1,848
Energy use per units of GDP (kg oil eq./$1,000 of 2005 PPP $)	106.1	130.6	227.1

National-Level Actions

Latest UNFCCC national communication	10/7/2009 (2nd)
Annex-I emissions reduction target	n/a
NAMA submission	Yes, with Goal
NAPA submission	n/a
Renewable energy target	..

Carbon Markets

Hosted Clean Development Mechanism (CDM) projects	8
Issued Certified Emission Reductions (CERs) from CDM (thousands)	320
Hosted Joint Implementation (JI) projects	n/a
Issued Emission Reduction Units (ERUs) from JI (thousands)	n/a

Côte d'Ivoire

Population (millions)	19.7	GDP ($ billions)	22.8
Pop. growth (avg. ann. %, 1990–2010)	2.3	GNI per capita (Atlas $)	1,160

Climate
Average daily min/max temperature (1961–90, Celsius)	21 / 32
Projected annual temperature change (2045–65, Celsius)	1.8 to 2.4
Average annual precipitation (1961–90, mm)	1,348
Projected annual precipitation change (2045–65, mm)	-125 to 73
Projected change in annual hot days/warm nights	7 / 23
Projected change in annual cool days/cold nights	-2 / -2

	Country data	Sub-Saharan Africa	Lower middle income
Exposure to Impacts			
Land area below 5m (% of land area)	0.2	0.4	1.7
Population below 5m (% of total)	3.2	2.0	6.5
Population in urban agglomerations > 1 million (%)	21	14	14
Urban pop. growth (avg. annual %, 1990–2010)	3.4	4.0	2.8
Droughts, floods, extreme temps (% pop. avg., 1990–2009)	0.0		
Annual freshwater withdrawals (% of internal resources)	1.8	3.2	18.7
Agricultural land under irrigation (% of total ag. land)	..	..	..
Population living below $1.25 a day (% of total)	23.8	50.9	..
Nationally terrestrial protected areas (% of total land area)	22.6	11.7	9.5
Under-five mortality rate (per 1,000)	123	121	69
Child malnutrition, underweight (% of under age five)	16.7	24.6	31.7
Malaria incidence rate (per 100,000 people)	36,482	26,113	4,874
Resilience			
Access to improved sanitation (% of total pop.)	23	31	45
Access to improved water source (% of total pop.)	80	60	84
Cereal yield (kg. per hectare)	1,900	1,297	2,754
Access to electricity (% of total population)	47.3	32.5	67.3
Paved roads (% of total roads)	7.9	18.3	29.3
Health workers (per 1,000 people)	0.6	1.2	2.6
Foreign direct investment, net inflows (% of GDP)	1.8	3.6	2.4
Invest. in infrastructure w/private participation ($ millions)	319	11,957	81,789
Disaster risk reduction progress score (1–5 scale; 5 = best)	2.5		
Ease of doing business (ranking 1–183; 1 = best)	167		
Public sector mgmt & institutions avg. (1–6 scale; 6 = best)	2.4		
Primary completion rate, total (% of relevant age group)	46	67	88
Ratio of girls to boys in primary & secondary school (%)	69	89	93
GHG Emissions and Energy Use			
CO_2 emissions per capita (metric tons)	0.4	0.8	1.6
CO_2 emissions per units of GDP (kg/$1,000 of 2005 PPP $)	223.0	428.6	523.9
CO_2 emissions, total (MtCO$_2$)	7.0	685	3,744
GHG net emissions/removals by LUCF (2000, MtCO$_2$e)	-18.4		
Methane (CH$_4$) emissions, total (MtCO$_2$e)	11.0	590	1,705
Nitrous oxide (N$_2$O) emissions, total (MtCO$_2$e)	7.4	334	687
Other GHG emissions, total (MtCO$_2$e)	0.0	..	17
Energy use per capita (kilograms of oil equivalent)	535	689	680
Energy use per units of GDP (kg oil eq./$1,000 of 2005 PPP $)	317.2	308.4	217.9

National-Level Actions
Latest UNFCCC national communication	4/26/2010 (2nd)
Annex-I emissions reduction target	n/a
NAMA submission	Yes
NAPA submission	n/a
Renewable energy target	..

Carbon Markets
Hosted Clean Development Mechanism (CDM) projects	3
Issued Certified Emission Reductions (CERs) from CDM (thousands)	0
Hosted Joint Implementation (JI) projects	n/a
Issued Emission Reduction Units (ERUs) from JI (thousands)	n/a

Croatia

Population (millions)	4.4	GDP ($ billions)	60.9
Pop. growth (avg. ann. %, 1990-2010)	-0.4	GNI per capita (Atlas $)	13,780

Climate

Average daily min/max temperature (1961-90, Celsius)	6 / 16
Projected annual temperature change (2045-65, Celsius)	1.9 to 2.9
Average annual precipitation (1961-90, mm)	1,113
Projected annual precipitation change (2045-65, mm)	-112 to -2
Projected change in annual hot days/warm nights	3 / 6
Projected change in annual cool days/cold nights	-2 / -2

	Country data	High income
Exposure to Impacts		
Land area below 5m (% of land area)	3.0	2.2
Population below 5m (% of total)	3.4	7.7
Population in urban agglomerations > 1 million (%)	..	..
Urban pop. growth (avg. annual %, 1990-2010)	0.0	1.0
Droughts, floods, extreme temps (% pop. avg., 1990-2009)	0.0	
Annual freshwater withdrawals (% of internal resources)	..	10.4
Agricultural land under irrigation (% of total ag. land)	0.4	..
Population living below $1.25 a day (% of total)	<2	..
Nationally terrestrial protected areas (% of total land area)	7.3	13.4
Under-five mortality rate (per 1,000)	6	6
Child malnutrition, underweight (% of under age five)	1.0	..
Malaria incidence rate (per 100,000 people)	..	..
Resilience		
Access to improved sanitation (% of total pop.)	99	100
Access to improved water source (% of total pop.)	99	100
Cereal yield (kg. per hectare)	6,117	5,445
Access to electricity (% of total population)	..	..
Paved roads (% of total roads)	86.9	87.3
Health workers (per 1,000 people)	2.7	10.7
Foreign direct investment, net inflows (% of GDP)	0.5	1.8
Invest. in infrastructure w/private participation ($ millions)	719	..
Disaster risk reduction progress score (1-5 scale; 5 = best)	..	
Ease of doing business (ranking 1-183; 1 = best)	80	
Public sector mgmt & institutions avg. (1-6 scale; 6 = best)	..	
Primary completion rate, total (% of relevant age group)	97	97
Ratio of girls to boys in primary & secondary school (%)	102	100
GHG Emissions and Energy Use		
CO_2 emissions per capita (metric tons)	5.3	11.9
CO_2 emissions per units of GDP (kg/$1,000 of 2005 PPP $)	303.5	354.4
CO_2 emissions, total (MtCO$_2$)	23.3	13,285
GHG net emissions/removals by LUCF (2009, MtCO$_2$e)	-8.7	
Methane (CH$_4$) emissions, total (MtCO$_2$e)	3.9	1,539
Nitrous oxide (N$_2$O) emissions, total (MtCO$_2$e)	2.9	813
Other GHG emissions, total (MtCO$_2$e)	0.1	460
Energy use per capita (kilograms of oil equivalent)	1,965	4,944
Energy use per units of GDP (kg oil eq./$1,000 of 2005 PPP $)	120.6	147.0
National-Level Actions		
Latest UNFCCC national communication		..
Annex-I emissions reduction target (base year: 1990)		5%
NAMA submission		n/a
NAPA submission		n/a
Renewable energy target		..
Carbon Markets		
Hosted Clean Development Mechanism (CDM) projects		n/a
Issued Certified Emission Reductions (CERs) from CDM (thousands)		n/a
Hosted Joint Implementation (JI) projects		..
Issued Emission Reduction Units (ERUs) from JI (thousands)		..

Cuba

Population (millions)	11.3	GDP ($ billions)	62.7
Pop. growth (avg. ann. %, 1990–2010)	0.3	GNI per capita (Atlas $)	5,520

Climate

Average daily min/max temperature (1961–90, Celsius)	20 / 30
Projected annual temperature change (2045–65, Celsius)	1.4 to 1.8
Average annual precipitation (1961–90, mm)	1,335
Projected annual precipitation change (2045–65, mm)	-108 to 39
Projected change in annual hot days/warm nights	11 / 18
Projected change in annual cool days/cold nights	-2 / -2

	Country data	Latin America & the Carib.	Upper middle income
Exposure to Impacts			
Land area below 5m (% of land area)	12.7	1.5	1.8
Population below 5m (% of total)	10.0	3.8	6.5
Population in urban agglomerations > 1 million (%)	19	35	22
Urban pop. growth (avg. annual %, 1990–2010)	0.5	2.0	2.3
Droughts, floods, extreme temps (% pop. avg., 1990–2009)	0.7		
Annual freshwater withdrawals (% of internal resources)	19.8	2.0	5.6
Agricultural land under irrigation (% of total ag. land)	..	..	..
Population living below $1.25 a day (% of total)	..	8.1	..
Nationally terrestrial protected areas (% of total land area)	6.2	20.8	13.6
Under-five mortality rate (per 1,000)	6	23	20
Child malnutrition, underweight (% of under age five)	3.4	3.8	4.1
Malaria incidence rate (per 100,000 people)	..	206	80
Resilience			
Access to improved sanitation (% of total pop.)	91	79	68
Access to improved water source (% of total pop.)	94	93	92
Cereal yield (kg. per hectare)	2,069	3,337	3,690
Access to electricity (% of total population)	97.0	93.4	98.0
Paved roads (% of total roads)	49.0	28.1	50.5
Health workers (per 1,000 people)	15.0	6.9	4.5
Foreign direct investment, net inflows (% of GDP)	0.0	2.3	2.7
Invest. in infrastructure w/private participation ($ millions)	60	33,064	26,166
Disaster risk reduction progress score (1–5 scale; 5 = best)	4.5		
Ease of doing business (ranking 1–183; 1 = best)	..		
Public sector mgmt & institutions avg. (1–6 scale; 6 = best)	..		
Primary completion rate, total (% of relevant age group)	98	102	98
Ratio of girls to boys in primary & secondary school (%)	99	102	103
GHG Emissions and Energy Use			
CO_2 emissions per capita (metric tons)	2.8	2.8	5.3
CO_2 emissions per units of GDP (kg/$1,000 of 2005 PPP $)	..	285.6	659.4
CO_2 emissions, total (MtCO_2)	31.4	1,584	12,860
GHG net emissions/removals by LUCF (1996, MtCO_2e)	-21.7		
Methane (CH_4) emissions, total (MtCO_2e)	9.5	1,009	3,455
Nitrous oxide (N_2O) emissions, total (MtCO_2e)	6.4	442	1,144
Other GHG emissions, total (MtCO_2e)	0.1	21	243
Energy use per capita (kilograms of oil equivalent)	1,022	1,245	1,848
Energy use per units of GDP (kg oil eq./$1,000 of 2005 PPP $)	..	130.6	227.1

National-Level Actions

Latest UNFCCC national communication	9/28/2001 (1st)
Annex-I emissions reduction target	n/a
NAMA submission	..
NAPA submission	n/a
Renewable energy target	..

Carbon Markets

Hosted Clean Development Mechanism (CDM) projects	2
Issued Certified Emission Reductions (CERs) from CDM (thousands)	171
Hosted Joint Implementation (JI) projects	n/a
Issued Emission Reduction Units (ERUs) from JI (thousands)	n/a

Curaçao

Population (thousands)	142.7	GDP ($ millions)	..
Pop. growth (avg. ann. %, 1990-2010)	-0.1	GNI per capita (Atlas $)	..

Climate

Average daily min/max temperature (1961-90, Celsius)	..
Projected annual temperature change (2045-65, Celsius)	..
Average annual precipitation (1961-90, mm)	..
Projected annual precipitation change (2045-65, mm)	..
Projected change in annual hot days/warm nights	..
Projected change in annual cool days/cold nights	..

	Country data	High income
Exposure to Impacts		
Land area below 5m (% of land area)	..	2.2
Population below 5m (% of total)	..	7.7
Population in urban agglomerations > 1 million (%)	..	..
Urban pop. growth (avg. annual %, 1990-2010)	..	1.0
Droughts, floods, extreme temps (% pop. avg., 1990-2009)	..	
Annual freshwater withdrawals (% of internal resources)	..	10.4
Agricultural land under irrigation (% of total ag. land)	..	
Population living below $1.25 a day (% of total)	..	..
Nationally terrestrial protected areas (% of total land area)	..	13.4
Under-five mortality rate (per 1,000)	..	6
Child malnutrition, underweight (% of under age five)	..	..
Malaria incidence rate (per 100,000 people)	..	..
Resilience		
Access to improved sanitation (% of total pop.)	..	100
Access to improved water source (% of total pop.)	..	100
Cereal yield (kg. per hectare)	..	5,445
Access to electricity (% of total population)	..	
Paved roads (% of total roads)	..	87.3
Health workers (per 1,000 people)	..	10.7
Foreign direct investment, net inflows (% of GDP)	..	1.8
Invest. in infrastructure w/private participation ($ millions)	..	..
Disaster risk reduction progress score (1-5 scale; 5 = best)	..	
Ease of doing business (ranking 1-183; 1 = best)	..	
Public sector mgmt & institutions avg. (1-6 scale; 6 = best)	..	
Primary completion rate, total (% of relevant age group)	..	97
Ratio of girls to boys in primary & secondary school (%)	..	100
GHG Emissions and Energy Use		
CO_2 emissions per capita (metric tons)	..	11.9
CO_2 emissions per units of GDP (kg/$1,000 of 2005 PPP $)	..	354.4
CO_2 emissions, total (MtCO_2)	..	13,285
GHG net emissions/removals by LUCF (MtCO_2e)	..	
Methane (CH_4) emissions, total (MtCO_2e)	..	1,539
Nitrous oxide (N_2O) emissions, total (MtCO_2e)	..	813
Other GHG emissions, total (MtCO_2e)	..	460
Energy use per capita (kilograms of oil equivalent)	..	4,944
Energy use per units of GDP (kg oil eq./$1,000 of 2005 PPP $)	..	147.0
National-Level Actions		
Latest UNFCCC national communication		n/a
Annex-I emissions reduction target		n/a
NAMA submission		n/a
NAPA submission		n/a
Renewable energy target		..
Carbon Markets		
Hosted Clean Development Mechanism (CDM) projects		n/a
Issued Certified Emission Reductions (CERs) from CDM (thousands)		n/a
Hosted Joint Implementation (JI) projects		n/a
Issued Emission Reduction Units (ERUs) from JI (thousands)		n/a

Cyprus

Population (millions)	1.1	GDP ($ billions)	25.0
Pop. growth (avg. ann. %, 1990–2010)	1.8	GNI per capita (Atlas $)	30,480

Climate
Average daily min/max temperature (1961–90, Celsius)	13 / 24
Projected annual temperature change (2045–65, Celsius)	1.7 to 2.3
Average annual precipitation (1961–90, mm)	498
Projected annual precipitation change (2045–65, mm)	-98 to -44
Projected change in annual hot days/warm nights	4 / 7
Projected change in annual cool days/cold nights	-2 / -2

	Country data	High income
Exposure to Impacts		
Land area below 5m (% of land area)	6.4	2.2
Population below 5m (% of total)	9.7	7.7
Population in urban agglomerations > 1 million (%)	..	..
Urban pop. growth (avg. annual %, 1990–2010)	2.1	1.0
Droughts, floods, extreme temps (% pop. avg., 1990–2009)	0.0	
Annual freshwater withdrawals (% of internal resources)	24.5	10.4
Agricultural land under irrigation (% of total ag. land)	20.8	..
Population living below $1.25 a day (% of total)	..	..
Nationally terrestrial protected areas (% of total land area)	11.0	13.4
Under-five mortality rate (per 1,000)	4	6
Child malnutrition, underweight (% of under age five)	..	..
Malaria incidence rate (per 100,000 people)	..	..
Resilience		
Access to improved sanitation (% of total pop.)	100	100
Access to improved water source (% of total pop.)	100	100
Cereal yield (kg. per hectare)	900	5,445
Access to electricity (% of total population)	..	
Paved roads (% of total roads)	64.6	87.3
Health workers (per 1,000 people)	6.3	10.7
Foreign direct investment, net inflows (% of GDP)	23.4	1.8
Invest. in infrastructure w/private participation ($ millions)	..	..
Disaster risk reduction progress score (1–5 scale; 5 = best)	..	
Ease of doing business (ranking 1–183; 1 = best)	40	
Public sector mgmt & institutions avg. (1–6 scale; 6 = best)	..	
Primary completion rate, total (% of relevant age group)	103	97
Ratio of girls to boys in primary & secondary school (%)	100	100
GHG Emissions and Energy Use		
CO_2 emissions per capita (metric tons)	7.9	11.9
CO_2 emissions per units of GDP (kg/$1,000 of 2005 PPP $)	410.2	354.4
CO_2 emissions, total (MtCO$_2$)	8.6	13,285
GHG net emissions/removals by LUCF (MtCO$_2$e)	..	
Methane (CH$_4$) emissions, total (MtCO$_2$e)	0.6	1,539
Nitrous oxide (N$_2$O) emissions, total (MtCO$_2$e)	0.3	813
Other GHG emissions, total (MtCO$_2$e)	0.2	460
Energy use per capita (kilograms of oil equivalent)	2,298	4,944
Energy use per units of GDP (kg oil eq./$1,000 of 2005 PPP $)	121.4	147.0

National-Level Actions
Latest UNFCCC national communication	..
Annex-I emissions reduction target (base year: 1990)	20% / 30%
NAMA submission	..
NAPA submission	n/a
Renewable energy target	Yes

Carbon Markets
Hosted Clean Development Mechanism (CDM) projects	8
Issued Certified Emission Reductions (CERs) from CDM (thousands)	0
Hosted Joint Implementation (JI) projects	n/a
Issued Emission Reduction Units (ERUs) from JI (thousands)	n/a

Czech Republic

Population (millions)	10.5	GDP ($ billions)	192.2
Pop. growth (avg. ann. %, 1990–2010)	0.1	GNI per capita (Atlas $)	17,890

Climate

Average daily min/max temperature (1961–90, Celsius)	3 / 12
Projected annual temperature change (2045–65, Celsius)	1.9 to 2.8
Average annual precipitation (1961-90, mm)	677
Projected annual precipitation change (2045–65, mm)	-43 to 55
Projected change in annual hot days/warm nights	3 / 5
Projected change in annual cool days/cold nights	-1 / -2

	Country data	High income
Exposure to Impacts		
Land area below 5m (% of land area)	0.0	2.2
Population below 5m (% of total)	0.0	7.7
Population in urban agglomerations > 1 million (%)	11	..
Urban pop. growth (avg. annual %, 1990–2010)	0.0	1.0
Droughts, floods, extreme temps (% pop. avg., 1990–2009)	0.2	
Annual freshwater withdrawals (% of internal resources)	13.6	10.4
Agricultural land under irrigation (% of total ag. land)	0.3	..
Population living below $1.25 a day (% of total)	<2	..
Nationally terrestrial protected areas (% of total land area)	15.1	13.4
Under-five mortality rate (per 1,000)	4	6
Child malnutrition, underweight (% of under age five)	2.1	..
Malaria incidence rate (per 100,000 people)	..	..
Resilience		
Access to improved sanitation (% of total pop.)	98	100
Access to improved water source (% of total pop.)	100	100
Cereal yield (kg. per hectare)	5,074	5,445
Access to electricity (% of total population)	..	..
Paved roads (% of total roads)	100.0	87.3
Health workers (per 1,000 people)	12.2	10.7
Foreign direct investment, net inflows (% of GDP)	3.5	1.8
Invest. in infrastructure w/private participation ($ millions)	..	..
Disaster risk reduction progress score (1–5 scale; 5 = best)	2.8	
Ease of doing business (ranking 1–183; 1 = best)	64	
Public sector mgmt & institutions avg. (1–6 scale; 6 = best)	..	
Primary completion rate, total (% of relevant age group)	99	97
Ratio of girls to boys in primary & secondary school (%)	101	100
GHG Emissions and Energy Use		
CO_2 emissions per capita (metric tons)	11.2	11.9
CO_2 emissions per units of GDP (kg/$1,000 of 2005 PPP $)	483.3	354.4
CO_2 emissions, total (MtCO$_2$)	117.0	13,285
GHG net emissions/removals by LUCF (2009, MtCO$_2$e)	-6.9	
Methane (CH$_4$) emissions, total (MtCO$_2$e)	11.5	1,539
Nitrous oxide (N$_2$O) emissions, total (MtCO$_2$e)	8.9	813
Other GHG emissions, total (MtCO$_2$e)	1.1	460
Energy use per capita (kilograms of oil equivalent)	4,022	4,944
Energy use per units of GDP (kg oil eq./$1,000 of 2005 PPP $)	178.3	147.0

National-Level Actions

Latest UNFCCC national communication	11/30/2009 (5th)
Annex-I emissions reduction target (base year: 1990)	20% / 30% (EU)
NAMA submission	n/a
NAPA submission	n/a
Renewable energy target	Yes

Carbon Markets

Hosted Clean Development Mechanism (CDM) projects	n/a
Issued Certified Emission Reductions (CERs) from CDM (thousands)	n/a
Hosted Joint Implementation (JI) projects	58
Issued Emission Reduction Units (ERUs) from JI (thousands)	607

Denmark

Population (millions)	5.5	GDP ($ billions)	310.4
Pop. growth (avg. ann. %, 1990–2010)	0.4	GNI per capita (Atlas $)	59,210

Climate

Average daily min/max temperature (1961–90, Celsius)	4 / 11
Projected annual temperature change (2045–65, Celsius)	1.6 to 2.5
Average annual precipitation (1961–90, mm)	703
Projected annual precipitation change (2045–65, mm)	21 to 87
Projected change in annual hot days/warm nights	3 / 5
Projected change in annual cool days/cold nights	-2 / -2

	Country data	High Income
Exposure to Impacts		
Land area below 5m (% of land area)	17.7	2.2
Population below 5m (% of total)	18.5	7.7
Population in urban agglomerations > 1 million (%)	21	..
Urban pop. growth (avg. annual %, 1990–2010)	0.5	1.0
Droughts, floods, extreme temps (% pop. avg., 1990–2009)	0.0	
Annual freshwater withdrawals (% of internal resources)	17.4	10.4
Agricultural land under irrigation (% of total ag. land)	9.6	..
Population living below $1.25 a day (% of total)	..	..
Nationally terrestrial protected areas (% of total land area)	5.0	13.4
Under-five mortality rate (per 1,000)	4	6
Child malnutrition, underweight (% of under age five)	..	..
Malaria incidence rate (per 100,000 people)	..	..
Resilience		
Access to improved sanitation (% of total pop.)	100	100
Access to improved water source (% of total pop.)	100	100
Cereal yield (kg. per hectare)	6,776	5,445
Access to electricity (% of total population)	..	
Paved roads (% of total roads)	100.0	87.3
Health workers (per 1,000 people)	18.0	10.7
Foreign direct investment, net inflows (% of GDP)	-0.2	1.8
Invest. in infrastructure w/private participation ($ millions)	..	..
Disaster risk reduction progress score (1–5 scale; 5 = best)	..	
Ease of doing business (ranking 1–183; 1 = best)	5	
Public sector mgmt & institutions avg. (1–6 scale; 6 = best)	..	
Primary completion rate, total (% of relevant age group)	97	97
Ratio of girls to boys in primary & secondary school (%)	102	100
GHG Emissions and Energy Use		
CO_2 emissions per capita (metric tons)	8.4	11.9
CO_2 emissions per units of GDP (kg/$1,000 of 2005 PPP $)	246.4	354.4
CO_2 emissions, total (MtCO_2)	46.0	13,285
GHG net emissions/removals by LUCF (2009, MtCO_2e)	-1.1	
Methane (CH_4) emissions, total (MtCO_2e)	7.9	1,539
Nitrous oxide (N_2O) emissions, total (MtCO_2e)	6.3	813
Other GHG emissions, total (MtCO_2e)	1.4	460
Energy use per capita (kilograms of oil equivalent)	3,550	4,944
Energy use per units of GDP (kg oil eq./$1,000 of 2005 PPP $)	108.9	147.0

National-Level Actions

Latest UNFCCC national communication	1/11/2010 (5th)
Annex-I emissions reduction target (base year: 1990)	20% / 30% (EU)
NAMA submission	n/a
NAPA submission	n/a
Renewable energy target	Yes

Carbon Markets

Hosted Clean Development Mechanism (CDM) projects	n/a
Issued Certified Emission Reductions (CERs) from CDM (thousands)	n/a
Hosted Joint Implementation (JI) projects	..
Issued Emission Reduction Units (ERUs) from JI (thousands)	..

Djibouti

Population (thousands)	888.7	GDP ($ billions)	1.0
Pop. growth (avg. ann. %, 1990-2010)	2.3	GNI per capita (Atlas $)	1,270

Climate

Average daily min/max temperature (1961-90, Celsius)	23 / 33
Projected annual temperature change (2045-65, Celsius)	2.0 to 2.7
Average annual precipitation (1961-90, mm)	220
Projected annual precipitation change (2045-65, mm)	-29 to 57
Projected change in annual hot days/warm nights	7 / 16
Projected change in annual cool days/cold nights	-2 / -3

	Country data	Middle East & N. Africa	Lower middle income
Exposure to Impacts			
Land area below 5m (% of land area)	2.6	1.4	1.7
Population below 5m (% of total)	7.6	9.7	6.5
Population in urban agglomerations > 1 million (%)	..	20	14
Urban pop. growth (avg. annual %, 1990-2010)	3.0	2.5	2.8
Droughts, floods, extreme temps (% pop. avg., 1990-2009)	6.8		
Annual freshwater withdrawals (% of internal resources)	6.3	121.9	18.7
Agricultural land under irrigation (% of total ag. land)	..		..
Population living below $1.25 a day (% of total)	18.8	3.6	..
Nationally terrestrial protected areas (% of total land area)	0.0	4.0	9.5
Under-five mortality rate (per 1,000)	91	34	69
Child malnutrition, underweight (% of under age five)	29.6	6.8	31.7
Malaria incidence rate (per 100,000 people)	467	..	4,874
Resilience			
Access to improved sanitation (% of total pop.)	56	84	45
Access to improved water source (% of total pop.)	92	87	84
Cereal yield (kg. per hectare)	1,111	2,512	2,754
Access to electricity (% of total population)	..	92.9	67.3
Paved roads (% of total roads)	45.0	74.3	29.3
Health workers (per 1,000 people)	0.8	3.6	2.6
Foreign direct investment, net inflows (% of GDP)	9.2	2.9	2.4
Invest. in infrastructure w/private participation ($ millions)	396	5,854	81,789
Disaster risk reduction progress score (1-5 scale; 5 = best)	..		
Ease of doing business (ranking 1-183; 1 = best)	170		
Public sector mgmt & institutions avg. (1-6 scale; 6 = best)	2.8		
Primary completion rate, total (% of relevant age group)	35	88	88
Ratio of girls to boys in primary & secondary school (%)	82	93	93
GHG Emissions and Energy Use			
CO_2 emissions per capita (metric tons)	0.6	3.8	1.6
CO_2 emissions per units of GDP (kg/$1,000 of 2005 PPP $)	302.5	604.6	523.9
CO_2 emissions, total (MtCO_2)	0.5	1,230	3,744
GHG net emissions/removals by LUCF (1994, MtCO_2e)	-0.6		
Methane (CH_4) emissions, total (MtCO_2e)	..	287	1,705
Nitrous oxide (N_2O) emissions, total (MtCO_2e)	..	74	687
Other GHG emissions, total (MtCO_2e)	..	7	17
Energy use per capita (kilograms of oil equivalent)	170	1,399	680
Energy use per units of GDP (kg oil eq./$1,000 of 2005 PPP $)	87.3	213.9	217.9

National-Level Actions

Latest UNFCCC national communication	6/2/2002 (1st)
Annex-I emissions reduction target	n/a
NAMA submission	..
NAPA submission	Yes
Renewable energy target	..

Carbon Markets

Hosted Clean Development Mechanism (CDM) projects	..
Issued Certified Emission Reductions (CERs) from CDM (thousands)	..
Hosted Joint Implementation (JI) projects	n/a
Issued Emission Reduction Units (ERUs) from JI (thousands)	n/a

Dominica

Population (thousands)	67.8	GDP ($ millions)	382.8
Pop. growth (avg. ann. %, 1990–2010)	-0.2	GNI per capita (Atlas $)	5,410

Climate

Average daily min/max temperature (1961–90, Celsius)	19 / 26
Projected annual temperature change (2045–65, Celsius)	1.3 to 1.7
Average annual precipitation (1961–90, mm)	3,436
Projected annual precipitation change (2045–65, mm)	-106 to 42
Projected change in annual hot days/warm nights	13 / 24
Projected change in annual cool days/cold nights	-3 / -3

	Country data	Latin America & the Carib.	Upper middle income
Exposure to Impacts			
Land area below 5m (% of land area)	9.4	1.5	1.8
Population below 5m (% of total)	10.4	3.8	6.5
Population in urban agglomerations > 1 million (%)	..	35	22
Urban pop. growth (avg. annual %, 1990–2010)	0.3	2.0	2.3
Droughts, floods, extreme temps (% pop. avg., 1990–2009)	..		
Annual freshwater withdrawals (% of internal resources)	..	2.0	5.6
Agricultural land under irrigation (% of total ag. land)	..	..	..
Population living below $1.25 a day (% of total)	..	8.1	..
Nationally terrestrial protected areas (% of total land area)	21.7	20.8	13.6
Under-five mortality rate (per 1,000)	12	23	20
Child malnutrition, underweight (% of under age five)	..	3.8	4.1
Malaria incidence rate (per 100,000 people)	..	206	80
Resilience			
Access to improved sanitation (% of total pop.)	81	79	68
Access to improved water source (% of total pop.)	95	93	92
Cereal yield (kg. per hectare)	1,437	3,337	3,690
Access to electricity (% of total population)	..	93.4	98.0
Paved roads (% of total roads)	50.4	28.1	50.5
Health workers (per 1,000 people)	..	6.9	4.5
Foreign direct investment, net inflows (% of GDP)	8.1	2.3	2.7
Invest. in infrastructure w/private participation ($ millions)	5	33,064	26,166
Disaster risk reduction progress score (1–5 scale; 5 = best)	..		
Ease of doing business (ranking 1–183; 1 = best)	65		
Public sector mgmt & institutions avg. (1–6 scale; 6 = best)	3.9		
Primary completion rate, total (% of relevant age group)	89	102	98
Ratio of girls to boys in primary & secondary school (%)	102	102	103
GHG Emissions and Energy Use			
CO_2 emissions per capita (metric tons)	1.9	2.8	5.3
CO_2 emissions per units of GDP (kg/$1,000 of 2005 PPP $)	214.5	285.6	659.4
CO_2 emissions, total (MtCO_2)	0.1	1,584	12,860
GHG net emissions/removals by LUCF (1994, MtCO_2e)	-0.4		
Methane (CH_4) emissions, total (MtCO_2e)	..	1,009	3,455
Nitrous oxide (N_2O) emissions, total (MtCO_2e)	..	442	1,144
Other GHG emissions, total (MtCO_2e)	..	21	243
Energy use per capita (kilograms of oil equivalent)	628	1,245	1,848
Energy use per units of GDP (kg oil eq./$1,000 of 2005 PPP $)	74.4	130.6	227.1

National-Level Actions

Latest UNFCCC national communication	12/4/2001 (1st)
Annex-I emissions reduction target	n/a
NAMA submission	..
NAPA submission	n/a
Renewable energy target	..

Carbon Markets

Hosted Clean Development Mechanism (CDM) projects	..
Issued Certified Emission Reductions (CERs) from CDM (thousands)	..
Hosted Joint Implementation (JI) projects	n/a
Issued Emission Reduction Units (ERUs) from JI (thousands)	n/a

Dominican Republic

Population (millions)	9.9	GDP ($ billions)	51.6
Pop. growth (avg. ann. %, 1990-2010)	1.6	GNI per capita (Atlas $)	5,000

Climate

Average daily min/max temperature (1961-90, Celsius)	20 / 29
Projected annual temperature change (2045-65, Celsius)	1.5 to 1.8
Average annual precipitation (1961-90, mm)	1,410
Projected annual precipitation change (2045-65, mm)	-128 to 30
Projected change in annual hot days/warm nights	12 / 24
Projected change in annual cool days/cold nights	-3 / -3

	Country data	Latin America & the Carib.	Upper middle income
Exposure to Impacts			
Land area below 5m (% of land area)	4.1	1.5	1.8
Population below 5m (% of total)	3.0	3.8	6.5
Population in urban agglomerations > 1 million (%)	22	35	22
Urban pop. growth (avg. annual %, 1990-2010)	2.8	2.0	2.3
Droughts, floods, extreme temps (% pop. avg., 1990-2009)	0.1		
Annual freshwater withdrawals (% of internal resources)	16.6	2.0	5.6
Agricultural land under irrigation (% of total ag. land)	9.0	..	..
Population living below $1.25 a day (% of total)	4.3	8.1	..
Nationally terrestrial protected areas (% of total land area)	22.1	20.8	13.6
Under-five mortality rate (per 1,000)	27	23	20
Child malnutrition, underweight (% of under age five)	3.4	3.8	4.1
Malaria incidence rate (per 100,000 people)	46	206	80
Resilience			
Access to improved sanitation (% of total pop.)	83	79	68
Access to improved water source (% of total pop.)	86	93	92
Cereal yield (kg. per hectare)	2,846	3,337	3,690
Access to electricity (% of total population)	95.9	93.4	98.0
Paved roads (% of total roads)	49.4	28.1	50.5
Health workers (per 1,000 people)	3.7	6.9	4.5
Foreign direct investment, net inflows (% of GDP)	3.2	2.3	2.7
Invest. in infrastructure w/private participation ($ millions)	69	33,064	26,166
Disaster risk reduction progress score (1-5 scale; 5 = best)	3.0		
Ease of doing business (ranking 1-183; 1 = best)	108		
Public sector mgmt & institutions avg. (1-6 scale; 6 = best)	..		
Primary completion rate, total (% of relevant age group)	90	102	98
Ratio of girls to boys in primary & secondary school (%)	97	102	103
GHG Emissions and Energy Use			
CO_2 emissions per capita (metric tons)	2.2	2.8	5.3
CO_2 emissions per units of GDP (kg/$1,000 of 2005 PPP $)	289.4	285.6	659.4
CO_2 emissions, total (MtCO_2)	21.6	1,584	12,860
GHG net emissions/removals by LUCF (2000, MtCO_2e)	-18.8		
Methane (CH_4) emissions, total (MtCO_2e)	6.1	1,009	3,455
Nitrous oxide (N_2O) emissions, total (MtCO_2e)	2.3	442	1,144
Other GHG emissions, total (MtCO_2e)	0.0	21	243
Energy use per capita (kilograms of oil equivalent)	826	1,245	1,848
Energy use per units of GDP (kg oil eq./$1,000 of 2005 PPP $)	104.7	130.6	227.1

National-Level Actions

Latest UNFCCC national communication	11/17/2009 (2nd)
Annex-I emissions reduction target	n/a
NAMA submission	..
NAPA submission	n/a
Renewable energy target	Yes

Carbon Markets

Hosted Clean Development Mechanism (CDM) projects	2
Issued Certified Emission Reductions (CERs) from CDM (thousands)	12
Hosted Joint Implementation (JI) projects	n/a
Issued Emission Reduction Units (ERUs) from JI (thousands)	n/a

Ecuador

Population (millions)	14.5	GDP ($ billions)	58.9
Pop. growth (avg. ann. %, 1990–2010)	1.7	GNI per capita (Atlas $)	4,290

Climate

Average daily min/max temperature (1961–90, Celsius)	16 / 28
Projected annual temperature change (2045–65, Celsius)	1.8 to 2.3
Average annual precipitation (1961–90, mm)	2,087
Projected annual precipitation change (2045–65, mm)	22 to 273
Projected change in annual hot days/warm nights	10 / 24
Projected change in annual cool days/cold nights	-3 / -3

	Country data	Latin America & the Carib.	Upper middle income
Exposure to Impacts			
Land area below 5m (% of land area)	2.0	1.5	1.8
Population below 5m (% of total)	7.3	3.8	6.5
Population in urban agglomerations > 1 million (%)	31	35	22
Urban pop. growth (avg. annual %, 1990–2010)	2.7	2.0	2.3
Droughts, floods, extreme temps (% pop. avg., 1990–2009)	0.3		
Annual freshwater withdrawals (% of internal resources)	3.5	2.0	5.6
Agricultural land under irrigation (% of total ag. land)	12.6	..	..
Population living below $1.25 a day (% of total)	4.4	8.1	..
Nationally terrestrial protected areas (% of total land area)	25.1	20.8	13.6
Under-five mortality rate (per 1,000)	20	23	20
Child malnutrition, underweight (% of under age five)	6.2	3.8	4.1
Malaria incidence rate (per 100,000 people)	63	206	80
Resilience			
Access to improved sanitation (% of total pop.)	92	79	68
Access to improved water source (% of total pop.)	94	93	92
Cereal yield (kg. per hectare)	2,974	3,337	3,690
Access to electricity (% of total population)	92.2	93.4	98.0
Paved roads (% of total roads)	14.8	28.1	50.5
Health workers (per 1,000 people)	3.1	6.9	4.5
Foreign direct investment, net inflows (% of GDP)	0.3	2.3	2.7
Invest. in infrastructure w/private participation ($ millions)	239	33,064	26,166
Disaster risk reduction progress score (1–5 scale; 5 = best)	4.8		
Ease of doing business (ranking 1–183; 1 = best)	130		
Public sector mgmt & institutions avg. (1–6 scale; 6 = best)	..		
Primary completion rate, total (% of relevant age group)	106	102	98
Ratio of girls to boys in primary & secondary school (%)	102	102	103
GHG Emissions and Energy Use			
CO_2 emissions per capita (metric tons)	1.9	2.8	5.3
CO_2 emissions per units of GDP (kg/$1,000 of 2005 PPP $)	263.2	285.6	659.4
CO_2 emissions, total (MtCO_2)	26.8	1,584	12,860
GHG net emissions/removals by LUCF (1990, MtCO_2e)	46.9		
Methane (CH_4) emissions, total (MtCO_2e)	17.1	1,009	3,455
Nitrous oxide (N_2O) emissions, total (MtCO_2e)	4.6	442	1,144
Other GHG emissions, total (MtCO_2e)	0.1	21	243
Energy use per capita (kilograms of oil equivalent)	796	1,245	1,848
Energy use per units of GDP (kg oil eq./$1,000 of 2005 PPP $)	111.0	130.6	227.1

National-Level Actions

Latest UNFCCC national communication	11/15/2000 (1st)
Annex-I emissions reduction target	n/a
NAMA submission	..
NAPA submission	n/a
Renewable energy target	..

Carbon Markets

Hosted Clean Development Mechanism (CDM) projects	17
Issued Certified Emission Reductions (CERs) from CDM (thousands)	1,184
Hosted Joint Implementation (JI) projects	n/a
Issued Emission Reduction Units (ERUs) from JI (thousands)	n/a

Egypt, Arab Rep.

Population (millions)	81.1	GDP ($ billions)	218.9
Pop. growth (avg. ann. %, 1990-2010)	1.8	GNI per capita (Atlas $)	2,440

Climate

Average daily min/max temperature (1961-90, Celsius)	15 / 29
Projected annual temperature change (2045-65, Celsius)	1.9 to 2.4
Average annual precipitation (1961-90, mm)	51
Projected annual precipitation change (2045-65, mm)	-20 to 1
Projected change in annual hot days/warm nights	4 / 8
Projected change in annual cool days/cold nights	-2 / -2

	Country data	Middle East & N. Africa	Lower middle income
Exposure to Impacts			
Land area below 5m (% of land area)	4.0	1.4	1.7
Population below 5m (% of total)	25.6	9.7	6.5
Population in urban agglomerations > 1 million (%)	19	20	14
Urban pop. growth (avg. annual %, 1990-2010)	1.7	2.5	2.8
Droughts, floods, extreme temps (% pop. avg., 1990-2009)	0.0		
Annual freshwater withdrawals (% of internal resources)	3,788.9	121.9	18.7
Agricultural land under irrigation (% of total ag. land)	..	..	..
Population living below $1.25 a day (% of total)	<2	3.6	..
Nationally terrestrial protected areas (% of total land area)	5.9	4.0	9.5
Under-five mortality rate (per 1,000)	22	34	69
Child malnutrition, underweight (% of under age five)	6.8	6.8	31.7
Malaria incidence rate (per 100,000 people)	0	..	4,874
Resilience			
Access to improved sanitation (% of total pop.)	94	84	45
Access to improved water source (% of total pop.)	99	87	84
Cereal yield (kg. per hectare)	7,571	2,512	2,754
Access to electricity (% of total population)	99.6	92.9	67.3
Paved roads (% of total roads)	86.9	74.3	29.3
Health workers (per 1,000 people)	6.4	3.6	2.6
Foreign direct investment, net inflows (% of GDP)	2.9	2.9	2.4
Invest. in infrastructure w/private participation ($ millions)	2,588	5,854	81,789
Disaster risk reduction progress score (1-5 scale; 5 = best)	..		
Ease of doing business (ranking 1-183; 1 = best)	110		
Public sector mgmt & institutions avg. (1-6 scale; 6 = best)	..		
Primary completion rate, total (% of relevant age group)	96	88	88
Ratio of girls to boys in primary & secondary school (%)	96	93	93
GHG Emissions and Energy Use			
CO_2 emissions per capita (metric tons)	2.7	3.8	1.6
CO_2 emissions per units of GDP (kg/$1,000 of 2005 PPP $)	514.8	604.6	523.9
CO_2 emissions, total (MtCO_2)	210.3	1,230	3,744
GHG net emissions/removals by LUCF (1990, MtCO_2e)	-9.9		
Methane (CH_4) emissions, total (MtCO_2e)	47.0	287	1,705
Nitrous oxide (N_2O) emissions, total (MtCO_2e)	19.0	74	687
Other GHG emissions, total (MtCO_2e)	3.2	7	17
Energy use per capita (kilograms of oil equivalent)	903	1,399	680
Energy use per units of GDP (kg oil eq./$1,000 of 2005 PPP $)	164.5	213.9	217.9

National-Level Actions

Latest UNFCCC national communication	6/7/2010 (2nd)
Annex-I emissions reduction target	n/a
NAMA submission	..
NAPA submission	n/a
Renewable energy target	Yes

Carbon Markets

Hosted Clean Development Mechanism (CDM) projects	9
Issued Certified Emission Reductions (CERs) from CDM (thousands)	7,012
Hosted Joint Implementation (JI) projects	n/a
Issued Emission Reduction Units (ERUs) from JI (thousands)	n/a

El Salvador

Population (millions)	6.2	GDP ($ billions)	21.8
Pop. growth (avg. ann. %, 1990–2010)	0.7	GNI per capita (Atlas $)	3,360

Climate

Average daily min/max temperature (1961-90, Celsius)	18 / 31
Projected annual temperature change (2045-65, Celsius)	1.7 to 2.9
Average annual precipitation (1961-90, mm)	1,724
Projected annual precipitation change (2045-65, mm)	-205 to 14
Projected change in annual hot days/warm nights	9 / 25
Projected change in annual cool days/cold nights	-2 / -2

	Country data	Latin America & the Carib.	Lower middle income
Exposure to Impacts			
Land area below 5m (% of land area)	2.5	1.5	1.7
Population below 5m (% of total)	1.7	3.8	6.5
Population in urban agglomerations > 1 million (%)	25	35	14
Urban pop. growth (avg. annual %, 1990-2010)	1.8	2.0	2.8
Droughts, floods, extreme temps (% pop. avg., 1990-2009)	0.4		
Annual freshwater withdrawals (% of internal resources)	7.8	2.0	18.7
Agricultural land under irrigation (% of total ag. land)	2.1	..	..
Population living below $1.25 a day (% of total)	5.1	8.1	..
Nationally terrestrial protected areas (% of total land area)	0.8	20.8	9.5
Under-five mortality rate (per 1,000)	16	23	69
Child malnutrition, underweight (% of under age five)	6.1	3.8	31.7
Malaria incidence rate (per 100,000 people)	1	206	4,874
Resilience			
Access to improved sanitation (% of total pop.)	87	79	45
Access to improved water source (% of total pop.)	87	93	84
Cereal yield (kg. per hectare)	2,727	3,337	2,754
Access to electricity (% of total population)	86.4	93.4	67.3
Paved roads (% of total roads)	19.8	28.1	29.3
Health workers (per 1,000 people)	2.0	6.9	2.6
Foreign direct investment, net inflows (% of GDP)	0.0	2.3	2.4
Invest. in infrastructure w/private participation ($ millions)	152	33,064	81,789
Disaster risk reduction progress score (1-5 scale; 5 = best)	3.3		
Ease of doing business (ranking 1-183; 1 = best)	112		
Public sector mgmt & institutions avg. (1-6 scale; 6 = best)	..		
Primary completion rate, total (% of relevant age group)	89	102	88
Ratio of girls to boys in primary & secondary school (%)	98	102	93
GHG Emissions and Energy Use			
CO_2 emissions per capita (metric tons)	1.0	2.8	1.6
CO_2 emissions per units of GDP (kg/$1,000 of 2005 PPP $)	158.9	285.6	523.9
CO_2 emissions, total (MtCO_2)	6.1	1,584	3,744
GHG net emissions/removals by LUCF (1994, MtCO_2e)	3.9		
Methane (CH_4) emissions, total (MtCO_2e)	3.1	1,009	1,705
Nitrous oxide (N_2O) emissions, total (MtCO_2e)	1.4	442	687
Other GHG emissions, total (MtCO_2e)	0.1	21	17
Energy use per capita (kilograms of oil equivalent)	828	1,245	680
Energy use per units of GDP (kg oil eq./$1,000 of 2005 PPP $)	137.5	130.6	217.9

National-Level Actions

Latest UNFCCC national communication	4/10/2000 (1st)
Annex-I emissions reduction target	n/a
NAMA submission	..
NAPA submission	n/a
Renewable energy target	..

Carbon Markets

Hosted Clean Development Mechanism (CDM) projects	6
Issued Certified Emission Reductions (CERs) from CDM (thousands)	790
Hosted Joint Implementation (JI) projects	n/a
Issued Emission Reduction Units (ERUs) from JI (thousands)	n/a

Equatorial Guinea

Population (thousands)	700.4	GDP ($ billions)	14.0
Pop. growth (avg. ann. %, 1990-2010)	3.1	GNI per capita (Atlas $)	14,540

Climate

Average daily min/max temperature (1961-90, Celsius)	21 / 29
Projected annual temperature change (2045-65, Celsius)	1.8 to 2.1
Average annual precipitation (1961-90, mm)	2,156
Projected annual precipitation change (2045-65, mm)	-16 to 129
Projected change in annual hot days/warm nights	13 / 27
Projected change in annual cool days/cold nights	-3 / -3

	Country data	High income
Exposure to Impacts		
Land area below 5m (% of land area)	0.9	2.2
Population below 5m (% of total)	2.6	7.7
Population in urban agglomerations > 1 million (%)	..	..
Urban pop. growth (avg. annual %, 1990-2010)	3.8	1.0
Droughts, floods, extreme temps (% pop. avg., 1990-2009)	..	
Annual freshwater withdrawals (% of internal resources)	0.1	10.4
Agricultural land under irrigation (% of total ag. land)	..	..
Population living below $1.25 a day (% of total)	..	..
Nationally terrestrial protected areas (% of total land area)	19.2	13.4
Under-five mortality rate (per 1,000)	121	6
Child malnutrition, underweight (% of under age five)	10.6	..
Malaria incidence rate (per 100,000 people)	27,726	..
Resilience		
Access to improved sanitation (% of total pop.)	51	100
Access to improved water source (% of total pop.)	43	100
Cereal yield (kg. per hectare)	..	5,445
Access to electricity (% of total population)	..	
Paved roads (% of total roads)	..	87.3
Health workers (per 1,000 people)	0.8	10.7
Foreign direct investment, net inflows (% of GDP)	5.0	1.8
Invest. in infrastructure w/private participation ($ millions)	..	..
Disaster risk reduction progress score (1-5 scale; 5 = best)	..	
Ease of doing business (ranking 1-183; 1 = best)	155	
Public sector mgmt & institutions avg. (1-6 scale; 6 = best)	..	
Primary completion rate, total (% of relevant age group)	50	97
Ratio of girls to boys in primary & secondary school (%)	83	100
GHG Emissions and Energy Use		
CO_2 emissions per capita (metric tons)	7.3	11.9
CO_2 emissions per units of GDP (kg/$1,000 of 2005 PPP $)	234.6	354.4
CO_2 emissions, total (MtCO_2)	4.8	13,285
GHG net emissions/removals by LUCF (MtCO_2e)	..	
Methane (CH_4) emissions, total (MtCO_2e)	..	1,539
Nitrous oxide (N_2O) emissions, total (MtCO_2e)	..	813
Other GHG emissions, total (MtCO_2e)	..	460
Energy use per capita (kilograms of oil equivalent)	2,732	4,944
Energy use per units of GDP (kg oil eq./$1,000 of 2005 PPP $)	94.9	147.0
National-Level Actions		
Latest UNFCCC national communication		..
Annex-I emissions reduction target		n/a
NAMA submission		..
NAPA submission		..
Renewable energy target		..
Carbon Markets		
Hosted Clean Development Mechanism (CDM) projects		0
Issued Certified Emission Reductions (CERs) from CDM (thousands)		0
Hosted Joint Implementation (JI) projects		n/a
Issued Emission Reduction Units (ERUs) from JI (thousands)		n/a

Eritrea

Population (millions)	5.3	GDP ($ billions)	2.1
Pop. growth (avg. ann. %, 1990–2010)	2.5	GNI per capita (Atlas $)	340

Climate

Average daily min/max temperature (1961–90, Celsius)	19 / 32
Projected annual temperature change (2045–65, Celsius)	2.1 to 2.7
Average annual precipitation (1961–90, mm)	384
Projected annual precipitation change (2045–65, mm)	-55 to 26
Projected change in annual hot days/warm nights	7 / 14
Projected change in annual cool days/cold nights	-2 / -2

	Country data	Sub-Saharan Africa	Low income
Exposure to Impacts			
Land area below 5m (% of land area)	3.1	0.4	0.7
Population below 5m (% of total)	1.2	2.0	5.1
Population in urban agglomerations > 1 million (%)	..	14	11
Urban pop. growth (avg. annual %, 1990–2010)	4.1	4.0	3.7
Droughts, floods, extreme temps (% pop. avg., 1990–2009)	7.3		
Annual freshwater withdrawals (% of internal resources)	20.8	3.2	3.7
Agricultural land under irrigation (% of total ag. land)	..		
Population living below $1.25 a day (% of total)	..	50.9	..
Nationally terrestrial protected areas (% of total land area)	5.0	11.7	10.6
Under-five mortality rate (per 1,000)	61	121	108
Child malnutrition, underweight (% of under age five)	34.5	24.6	28.3
Malaria incidence rate (per 100,000 people)	762	26,113	16,659
Resilience			
Access to improved sanitation (% of total pop.)	14	31	35
Access to improved water source (% of total pop.)	61	60	63
Cereal yield (kg. per hectare)	500	1,297	2,047
Access to electricity (% of total population)	32.0	32.5	23.0
Paved roads (% of total roads)	21.8	18.3	14.1
Health workers (per 1,000 people)	0.6	1.2	0.7
Foreign direct investment, net inflows (% of GDP)	2.6	3.6	3.2
Invest. in infrastructure w/private participation ($ millions)	40	11,957	4,471
Disaster risk reduction progress score (1–5 scale; 5 = best)	..		
Ease of doing business (ranking 1–183; 1 = best)	180		
Public sector mgmt & institutions avg. (1–6 scale; 6 = best)	2.7		
Primary completion rate, total (% of relevant age group)	48	67	65
Ratio of girls to boys in primary & secondary school (%)	77	89	91
GHG Emissions and Energy Use			
CO_2 emissions per capita (metric tons)	0.1	0.8	0.3
CO_2 emissions per units of GDP (kg/$1,000 of 2005 PPP $)	171.0	428.6	270.2
CO_2 emissions, total (MtCO$_2$)	0.4	685	219
GHG net emissions/removals by LUCF (1994, MtCO$_2$e)	1.7		
Methane (CH_4) emissions, total (MtCO$_2$e)	2.5	590	436
Nitrous oxide (N_2O) emissions, total (MtCO$_2$e)	1.2	334	209
Other GHG emissions, total (MtCO$_2$e)	0.0	..	..
Energy use per capita (kilograms of oil equivalent)	142	689	365
Energy use per units of GDP (kg oil eq./$1,000 of 2005 PPP $)	288.2	308.4	303.9

National-Level Actions

Latest UNFCCC national communication	9/16/2002 (1st)
Annex-I emissions reduction target	n/a
NAMA submission	Yes
NAPA submission	Yes
Renewable energy target	..

Carbon Markets

Hosted Clean Development Mechanism (CDM) projects	..
Issued Certified Emission Reductions (CERs) from CDM (thousands)	..
Hosted Joint Implementation (JI) projects	n/a
Issued Emission Reduction Units (ERUs) from JI (thousands)	n/a

Estonia

Population (millions)	1.3	GDP ($ billions)	18.7
Pop. growth (avg. ann. %, 1990-2010)	-0.8	GNI per capita (Atlas $)	14,370

Climate

Average daily min/max temperature (1961-90, Celsius)	2 / 9
Projected annual temperature change (2045-65, Celsius)	2.2 to 3.2
Average annual precipitation (1961-90, mm)	626
Projected annual precipitation change (2045-65, mm)	33 to 93
Projected change in annual hot days/warm nights	2 / 5
Projected change in annual cool days/cold nights	-2 / -2

	Country data	High income
Exposure to Impacts		
Land area below 5m (% of land area)	3.4	2.2
Population below 5m (% of total)	7.2	7.7
Population in urban agglomerations > 1 million (%)	..	..
Urban pop. growth (avg. annual %, 1990-2010)	-0.9	1.0
Droughts, floods, extreme temps (% pop. avg., 1990-2009)	0.0	
Annual freshwater withdrawals (% of internal resources)	1.2	10.4
Agricultural land under irrigation (% of total ag. land)	..	..
Population living below $1.25 a day (% of total)	<2	..
Nationally terrestrial protected areas (% of total land area)	20.0	13.4
Under-five mortality rate (per 1,000)	5	6
Child malnutrition, underweight (% of under age five)	..	..
Malaria incidence rate (per 100,000 people)	..	..
Resilience		
Access to improved sanitation (% of total pop.)	95	100
Access to improved water source (% of total pop.)	98	100
Cereal yield (kg. per hectare)	2,761	5,445
Access to electricity (% of total population)	..	
Paved roads (% of total roads)	28.8	87.3
Health workers (per 1,000 people)	10.2	10.7
Foreign direct investment, net inflows (% of GDP)	8.2	1.8
Invest. in infrastructure w/private participation ($ millions)	..	..
Disaster risk reduction progress score (1-5 scale; 5 = best)	..	
Ease of doing business (ranking 1-183; 1 = best)	24	
Public sector mgmt & institutions avg. (1-6 scale; 6 = best)	..	
Primary completion rate, total (% of relevant age group)	100	97
Ratio of girls to boys in primary & secondary school (%)	101	100
GHG Emissions and Energy Use		
CO_2 emissions per capita (metric tons)	13.6	11.9
CO_2 emissions per units of GDP (kg/$1,000 of 2005 PPP $)	731.7	354.4
CO_2 emissions, total (MtCO$_2$)	18.3	13,285
GHG net emissions/removals by LUCF (2009, MtCO$_2$e)	-7.0	
Methane (CH_4) emissions, total (MtCO$_2$e)	2.1	1,539
Nitrous oxide (N_2O) emissions, total (MtCO$_2$e)	0.9	813
Other GHG emissions, total (MtCO$_2$e)	0.0	460
Energy use per capita (kilograms of oil equivalent)	4,085	4,944
Energy use per units of GDP (kg oil eq./$1,000 of 2005 PPP $)	249.8	147.0

National-Level Actions

Latest UNFCCC national communication	2/12/2010 (5th)
Annex-I emissions reduction target (base year: 1990)	20% / 30% (EU)
NAMA submission	n/a
NAPA submission	n/a
Renewable energy target	Yes

Carbon Markets

Hosted Clean Development Mechanism (CDM) projects	n/a
Issued Certified Emission Reductions (CERs) from CDM (thousands)	n/a
Hosted Joint Implementation (JI) projects	12
Issued Emission Reduction Units (ERUs) from JI (thousands)	0

Ethiopia

Population (millions)	82.9	GDP ($ billions)	29.7
Pop. growth (avg. ann. %, 1990–2010)	2.7	GNI per capita (Atlas $)	390

Climate

Average daily min/max temperature (1961-90, Celsius)	16 / 29
Projected annual temperature change (2045-65, Celsius)	2.1 to 2.5
Average annual precipitation (1961-90, mm)	848
Projected annual precipitation change (2045-65, mm)	-42 to 79
Projected change in annual hot days/warm nights	7 / 21
Projected change in annual cool days/cold nights	-2 / -3

	Country data	Sub-Saharan Africa	Low income
Exposure to Impacts			
Land area below 5m (% of land area)	0.7	0.4	0.7
Population below 5m (% of total)	0.4	2.0	5.1
Population in urban agglomerations > 1 million (%)	4	14	11
Urban pop. growth (avg. annual %, 1990-2010)	4.4	4.0	3.7
Droughts, floods, extreme temps (% pop. avg., 1990-2009)	3.3		
Annual freshwater withdrawals (% of internal resources)	4.6	3.2	3.7
Agricultural land under irrigation (% of total ag. land)	0.5	..	..
Population living below $1.25 a day (% of total)	39.0	50.9	..
Nationally terrestrial protected areas (% of total land area)	18.4	11.7	10.6
Under-five mortality rate (per 1,000)	106	121	108
Child malnutrition, underweight (% of under age five)	34.6	24.6	28.3
Malaria incidence rate (per 100,000 people)	11,509	26,113	16,659
Resilience			
Access to improved sanitation (% of total pop.)	12	31	35
Access to improved water source (% of total pop.)	38	60	63
Cereal yield (kg. per hectare)	1,677	1,297	2,047
Access to electricity (% of total population)	17.0	32.5	23.0
Paved roads (% of total roads)	13.7	18.3	14.1
Health workers (per 1,000 people)	0.3	1.2	0.7
Foreign direct investment, net inflows (% of GDP)	0.6	3.6	3.2
Invest. in infrastructure w/private participation ($ millions)	4	11,957	4,471
Disaster risk reduction progress score (1-5 scale; 5 = best)	..		
Ease of doing business (ranking 1-183; 1 = best)	111		
Public sector mgmt & institutions avg. (1-6 scale; 6 = best)	3.2		
Primary completion rate, total (% of relevant age group)	55	67	65
Ratio of girls to boys in primary & secondary school (%)	88	89	91
GHG Emissions and Energy Use			
CO_2 emissions per capita (metric tons)	0.1	0.8	0.3
CO_2 emissions per units of GDP (kg/$1,000 of 2005 PPP $)	109.9	428.6	270.2
CO_2 emissions, total (MtCO$_2$)	7.1	685	219
GHG net emissions/removals by LUCF (1995, MtCO$_2$e)	-9.9		
Methane (CH$_4$) emissions, total (MtCO$_2$e)	52.2	590	436
Nitrous oxide (N$_2$O) emissions, total (MtCO$_2$e)	30.5	334	209
Other GHG emissions, total (MtCO$_2$e)	0.0	..	..
Energy use per capita (kilograms of oil equivalent)	402	689	365
Energy use per units of GDP (kg oil eq./$1,000 of 2005 PPP $)	464.6	308.4	303.9

National-Level Actions

Latest UNFCCC national communication	10/16/2001 (1st)
Annex-I emissions reduction target	n/a
NAMA submission	Yes
NAPA submission	Yes
Renewable energy target	..

Carbon Markets

Hosted Clean Development Mechanism (CDM) projects	1
Issued Certified Emission Reductions (CERs) from CDM (thousands)	0
Hosted Joint Implementation (JI) projects	n/a
Issued Emission Reduction Units (ERUs) from JI (thousands)	n/a

Faeroe Islands

Population (thousands)	48.7	GDP ($ billions)	2.2
Pop. growth (avg. ann. %, 1990-2010)	0.1	GNI per capita (Atlas $)	..

Climate

Average daily min/max temperature (1961-90, Celsius)	4 / 8
Projected annual temperature change (2045-65, Celsius)	0.6 to 1.6
Average annual precipitation (1961-90, mm)	1,578
Projected annual precipitation change (2045-65, mm)	16 to 95
Projected change in annual hot days/warm nights	4 / 5
Projected change in annual cool days/cold nights	-1 / -1

	Country data	High Income
Exposure to Impacts		
Land area below 5m (% of land area)	14.5	2.2
Population below 5m (% of total)	11.0	7.7
Population in urban agglomerations > 1 million (%)	..	..
Urban pop. growth (avg. annual %, 1990-2010)	1.8	1.0
Droughts, floods, extreme temps (% pop. avg., 1990-2009)	..	
Annual freshwater withdrawals (% of internal resources)	..	10.4
Agricultural land under irrigation (% of total ag. land)	..	..
Population living below $1.25 a day (% of total)	..	..
Nationally terrestrial protected areas (% of total land area)	..	13.4
Under-five mortality rate (per 1,000)	..	6
Child malnutrition, underweight (% of under age five)	..	..
Malaria incidence rate (per 100,000 people)	..	..
Resilience		
Access to improved sanitation (% of total pop.)	..	100
Access to improved water source (% of total pop.)	..	100
Cereal yield (kg. per hectare)	..	5,445
Access to electricity (% of total population)	..	..
Paved roads (% of total roads)	..	87.3
Health workers (per 1,000 people)	..	10.7
Foreign direct investment, net inflows (% of GDP)	..	1.8
Invest. in infrastructure w/private participation ($ millions)	..	..
Disaster risk reduction progress score (1-5 scale; 5 = best)	..	
Ease of doing business (ranking 1-183; 1 = best)	..	
Public sector mgmt & institutions avg. (1-6 scale; 6 = best)	..	
Primary completion rate, total (% of relevant age group)	..	97
Ratio of girls to boys in primary & secondary school (%)	..	100
GHG Emissions and Energy Use		
CO_2 emissions per capita (metric tons)	14.6	11.9
CO_2 emissions per units of GDP (kg/$1,000 of 2005 PPP $)	..	354.4
CO_2 emissions, total (MtCO$_2$)	0.7	13,285
GHG net emissions/removals by LUCF (MtCO$_2$e)	..	
Methane (CH_4) emissions, total (MtCO$_2$e)	..	1,539
Nitrous oxide (N_2O) emissions, total (MtCO$_2$e)	..	813
Other GHG emissions, total (MtCO$_2$e)	..	460
Energy use per capita (kilograms of oil equivalent)	..	4,944
Energy use per units of GDP (kg oil eq./$1,000 of 2005 PPP $)	..	147.0
National-Level Actions		
Latest UNFCCC national communication		n/a
Annex-I emissions reduction target		n/a
NAMA submission		n/a
NAPA submission		n/a
Renewable energy target		..
Carbon Markets		
Hosted Clean Development Mechanism (CDM) projects		n/a
Issued Certified Emission Reductions (CERs) from CDM (thousands)		n/a
Hosted Joint Implementation (JI) projects		n/a
Issued Emission Reduction Units (ERUs) from JI (thousands)		n/a

Fiji

Population (thousands)	860.6	GDP ($ billions)	3.0
Pop. growth (avg. ann. %, 1990–2010)	0.8	GNI per capita (Atlas $)	3,580

Climate

Average daily min/max temperature (1961–90, Celsius)	21 / 28
Projected annual temperature change (2045–65, Celsius)	1.3 to 1.7
Average annual precipitation (1961–90, mm)	2,593
Projected annual precipitation change (2045–65, mm)	-93 to 271
Projected change in annual hot days/warm nights	10 / 18
Projected change in annual cool days/cold nights	-3 / -3

	Country data	East Asia & Pacific	Lower middle income
Exposure to Impacts			
Land area below 5m (% of land area)	11.4	2.5	1.7
Population below 5m (% of total)	11.0	10.3	6.5
Population in urban agglomerations > 1 million (%)	..	..	14
Urban pop. growth (avg. annual %, 1990–2010)	2.1	3.3	2.8
Droughts, floods, extreme temps (% pop. avg., 1990–2009)	1.7		
Annual freshwater withdrawals (% of internal resources)	0.3	10.8	18.7
Agricultural land under irrigation (% of total ag. land)	..	..	..
Population living below $1.25 a day (% of total)	..	16.8	..
Nationally terrestrial protected areas (% of total land area)	1.3	14.9	9.5
Under-five mortality rate (per 1,000)	17	24	69
Child malnutrition, underweight (% of under age five)	..	9.0	31.7
Malaria incidence rate (per 100,000 people)	..	525	4,874
Resilience			
Access to improved sanitation (% of total pop.)	..	59	45
Access to improved water source (% of total pop.)	..	88	84
Cereal yield (kg. per hectare)	2,458	4,860	2,754
Access to electricity (% of total population)	..	90.8	67.3
Paved roads (% of total roads)	49.2	15.9	29.3
Health workers (per 1,000 people)	2.4	2.8	2.6
Foreign direct investment, net inflows (% of GDP)	4.3	3.0	2.4
Invest. in infrastructure w/private participation ($ millions)	90	14,638	81,789
Disaster risk reduction progress score (1–5 scale; 5 = best)	2.8		
Ease of doing business (ranking 1–183; 1 = best)	77		
Public sector mgmt & institutions avg. (1–6 scale; 6 = best)	..		
Primary completion rate, total (% of relevant age group)	92	97	88
Ratio of girls to boys in primary & secondary school (%)	103	103	93
GHG Emissions and Energy Use			
CO_2 emissions per capita (metric tons)	1.5	4.3	1.6
CO_2 emissions per units of GDP (kg/$1,000 of 2005 PPP $)	348.5	827.1	523.9
CO_2 emissions, total (MtCO$_2$)	1.3	8,259	3,744
GHG net emissions/removals by LUCF (1994, MtCO$_2$e)	-7.7		
Methane (CH_4) emissions, total (MtCO$_2$e)	..	1,928	1,705
Nitrous oxide (N_2O) emissions, total (MtCO$_2$e)	..	707	687
Other GHG emissions, total (MtCO$_2$e)	..	..	17
Energy use per capita (kilograms of oil equivalent)	627	1,436	680
Energy use per units of GDP (kg oil eq./$1,000 of 2005 PPP $)	145.9	259.5	217.9

National-Level Actions

Latest UNFCCC national communication	5/18/2006 (1st)
Annex-I emissions reduction target	n/a
NAMA submission	..
NAPA submission	n/a
Renewable energy target	Yes

Carbon Markets

Hosted Clean Development Mechanism (CDM) projects	2
Issued Certified Emission Reductions (CERs) from CDM (thousands)	36
Hosted Joint Implementation (JI) projects	n/a
Issued Emission Reduction Units (ERUs) from JI (thousands)	n/a

Finland

| Population (millions) | 5.4 | GDP ($ billions) | 238.8 |
| Pop. growth (avg. ann. %, 1990–2010) | 0.4 | GNI per capita (Atlas $) | 47,160 |

Climate

Average daily min/max temperature (1961–90, Celsius)	-2 / 6
Projected annual temperature change (2045–65, Celsius)	2.4 to 3.7
Average annual precipitation (1961–90, mm)	536
Projected annual precipitation change (2045–65, mm)	37 to 103
Projected change in annual hot days/warm nights	2 / 4
Projected change in annual cool days/cold nights	-2 / -2

	Country data	High income
Exposure to Impacts		
Land area below 5m (% of land area)	1.1	2.2
Population below 5m (% of total)	4.4	7.7
Population in urban agglomerations > 1 million (%)	21	..
Urban pop. growth (avg. annual %, 1990–2010)	0.6	1.0
Droughts, floods, extreme temps (% pop. avg., 1990–2009)	0.0	
Annual freshwater withdrawals (% of internal resources)	2.1	10.4
Agricultural land under irrigation (% of total ag. land)	2.8	
Population living below $1.25 a day (% of total)	..	..
Nationally terrestrial protected areas (% of total land area)	9.1	13.4
Under-five mortality rate (per 1,000)	3	6
Child malnutrition, underweight (% of under age five)	..	
Malaria incidence rate (per 100,000 people)	..	..
Resilience		
Access to improved sanitation (% of total pop.)	100	100
Access to improved water source (% of total pop.)	100	100
Cereal yield (kg. per hectare)	3,760	5,445
Access to electricity (% of total population)		
Paved roads (% of total roads)	65.5	87.3
Health workers (per 1,000 people)	2.7	10.7
Foreign direct investment, net inflows (% of GDP)	1.8	1.8
Invest. in infrastructure w/private participation ($ millions)	..	..
Disaster risk reduction progress score (1–5 scale; 5 = best)	3.5	
Ease of doing business (ranking 1–183; 1 = best)	11	
Public sector mgmt & institutions avg. (1–6 scale; 6 = best)	..	
Primary completion rate, total (% of relevant age group)	97	97
Ratio of girls to boys in primary & secondary school (%)	102	100
GHG Emissions and Energy Use		
CO_2 emissions per capita (metric tons)	10.6	11.9
CO_2 emissions per units of GDP (kg/$1,000 of 2005 PPP $)	316.3	354.4
CO_2 emissions, total (MtCO_2)	56.5	13,285
GHG net emissions/removals by LUCF (2009, MtCO_2e)	-40.6	
Methane (CH_4) emissions, total (MtCO_2e)	9.7	1,539
Nitrous oxide (N_2O) emissions, total (MtCO_2e)	7.1	813
Other GHG emissions, total (MtCO_2e)	0.8	460
Energy use per capita (kilograms of oil equivalent)	6,639	4,944
Energy use per units of GDP (kg oil eq./$1,000 of 2005 PPP $)	210.6	147.0

National-Level Actions

Latest UNFCCC national communication	12/23/2009 (5th)
Annex-I emissions reduction target (base year: 1990)	20% / 30% (EU)
NAMA submission	n/a
NAPA submission	n/a
Renewable energy target	Yes

Carbon Markets

Hosted Clean Development Mechanism (CDM) projects	n/a
Issued Certified Emission Reductions (CERs) from CDM (thousands)	n/a
Hosted Joint Implementation (JI) projects	3
Issued Emission Reduction Units (ERUs) from JI (thousands)	245

France

Population (millions)	64.9	GDP ($ billions)	2,560.0
Pop. growth (avg. ann. %, 1990–2010)	0.5	GNI per capita (Atlas $)	42,390

Climate

Average daily min/max temperature (1961–90, Celsius)	7 / 15
Projected annual temperature change (2045–65, Celsius)	1.6 to 2.6
Average annual precipitation (1961–90, mm)	867
Projected annual precipitation change (2045–65, mm)	–112 to 2
Projected change in annual hot days/warm nights	4 / 6
Projected change in annual cool days/cold nights	–1 / –1

	Country data	High Income
Exposure to Impacts		
Land area below 5m (% of land area)	2.1	2.2
Population below 5m (% of total)	4.0	7.7
Population in urban agglomerations > 1 million (%)	22	..
Urban pop. growth (avg. annual %, 1990–2010)	0.8	1.0
Droughts, floods, extreme temps (% pop. avg., 1990–2009)	0.0	
Annual freshwater withdrawals (% of internal resources)	15.9	10.4
Agricultural land under irrigation (% of total ag. land)	5.1	..
Population living below $1.25 a day (% of total)	..	..
Nationally terrestrial protected areas (% of total land area)	15.1	13.4
Under-five mortality rate (per 1,000)	4	6
Child malnutrition, underweight (% of under age five)	..	..
Malaria incidence rate (per 100,000 people)	..	..
Resilience		
Access to improved sanitation (% of total pop.)	100	100
Access to improved water source (% of total pop.)	100	100
Cereal yield (kg. per hectare)	7,456	5,445
Access to electricity (% of total population)	..	
Paved roads (% of total roads)	100.0	87.3
Health workers (per 1,000 people)	8.9	10.7
Foreign direct investment, net inflows (% of GDP)	1.3	1.8
Invest. in infrastructure w/private participation ($ millions)	..	..
Disaster risk reduction progress score (1–5 scale; 5 = best)	..	
Ease of doing business (ranking 1–183; 1 = best)	29	
Public sector mgmt & institutions avg. (1–6 scale; 6 = best)	..	
Primary completion rate, total (% of relevant age group)	98	97
Ratio of girls to boys in primary & secondary school (%)	100	100
GHG Emissions and Energy Use		
CO_2 emissions per capita (metric tons)	5.9	11.9
CO_2 emissions per units of GDP (kg/$1,000 of 2005 PPP $)	193.5	354.4
CO_2 emissions, total (MtCO$_2$)	377.0	13,285
GHG net emissions/removals by LUCF (2009, MtCO$_2$e)	–63.9	
Methane (CH$_4$) emissions, total (MtCO$_2$e)	77.3	1,539
Nitrous oxide (N$_2$O) emissions, total (MtCO$_2$e)	49.1	813
Other GHG emissions, total (MtCO$_2$e)	15.5	460
Energy use per capita (kilograms of oil equivalent)	4,073	4,944
Energy use per units of GDP (kg oil eq./$1,000 of 2005 PPP $)	137.4	147.0

National-Level Actions

Latest UNFCCC national communication	2/8/2010 (5th)
Annex-I emissions reduction target (base year: 1990)	20% / 30% (EU)
NAMA submission	n/a
NAPA submission	n/a
Renewable energy target	Yes

Carbon Markets

Hosted Clean Development Mechanism (CDM) projects	n/a
Issued Certified Emission Reductions (CERs) from CDM (thousands)	n/a
Hosted Joint Implementation (JI) projects	17
Issued Emission Reduction Units (ERUs) from JI (thousands)	3,535

French Polynesia

Population (thousands)	270.8	GDP ($ millions)	..
Pop. growth (avg. ann. %, 1990-2010)	1.6	GNI per capita (Atlas $)	..

Climate

Average daily min/max temperature (1961-90, Celsius)	..
Projected annual temperature change (2045-65, Celsius)	1.3 to 1.7
Average annual precipitation (1961-90, mm)	..
Projected annual precipitation change (2045-65, mm)	-79 to 283
Projected change in annual hot days/warm nights	16 / 25
Projected change in annual cool days/cold nights	-3 / -3

	Country data	High income
Exposure to Impacts		
Land area below 5m (% of land area)	37.6	2.2
Population below 5m (% of total)	19.8	7.7
Population in urban agglomerations > 1 million (%)	..	..
Urban pop. growth (avg. annual %, 1990-2010)	1.2	1.0
Droughts, floods, extreme temps (% pop. avg., 1990-2009)	..	
Annual freshwater withdrawals (% of internal resources)	..	10.4
Agricultural land under irrigation (% of total ag. land)	..	..
Population living below $1.25 a day (% of total)	..	..
Nationally terrestrial protected areas (% of total land area)	0.4	13.4
Under-five mortality rate (per 1,000)	..	6
Child malnutrition, underweight (% of under age five)	..	..
Malaria incidence rate (per 100,000 people)	..	..
Resilience		
Access to improved sanitation (% of total pop.)	98	100
Access to improved water source (% of total pop.)	100	100
Cereal yield (kg. per hectare)	..	5,445
Access to electricity (% of total population)	..	..
Paved roads (% of total roads)	..	87.3
Health workers (per 1,000 people)	1.7	10.7
Foreign direct investment, net inflows (% of GDP)	..	1.8
Invest. in infrastructure w/private participation ($ millions)	..	..
Disaster risk reduction progress score (1-5 scale; 5 = best)	..	
Ease of doing business (ranking 1-183; 1 = best)	..	
Public sector mgmt & institutions avg. (1-6 scale; 6 = best)	..	
Primary completion rate, total (% of relevant age group)	..	97
Ratio of girls to boys in primary & secondary school (%)	..	100
GHG Emissions and Energy Use		
CO$_2$ emissions per capita (metric tons)	3.4	11.9
CO$_2$ emissions per units of GDP (kg/$1,000 of 2005 PPP $)	..	354.4
CO$_2$ emissions, total (MtCO$_2$)	0.9	13,285
GHG net emissions/removals by LUCF (MtCO$_2$e)	..	
Methane (CH$_4$) emissions, total (MtCO$_2$e)	..	1,539
Nitrous oxide (N$_2$O) emissions, total (MtCO$_2$e)	..	813
Other GHG emissions, total (MtCO$_2$e)	..	460
Energy use per capita (kilograms of oil equivalent)	..	4,944
Energy use per units of GDP (kg oil eq./$1,000 of 2005 PPP $)	..	147.0

National-Level Actions

Latest UNFCCC national communication	n/a
Annex-I emissions reduction target	n/a
NAMA submission	n/a
NAPA submission	n/a
Renewable energy target	..

Carbon Markets

Hosted Clean Development Mechanism (CDM) projects	n/a
Issued Certified Emission Reductions (CERs) from CDM (thousands)	n/a
Hosted Joint Implementation (JI) projects	n/a
Issued Emission Reduction Units (ERUs) from JI (thousands)	n/a

Gabon

Population (millions)	1.5	GDP ($ billions)	13.0
Pop. growth (avg. ann. %, 1990–2010)	2.4	GNI per capita (Atlas $)	7,740

Climate

Average daily min/max temperature (1961–90, Celsius)	21 / 29
Projected annual temperature change (2045–65, Celsius)	1.8 to 2.2
Average annual precipitation (1961–90, mm)	1,831
Projected annual precipitation change (2045–65, mm)	-51 to 148
Projected change in annual hot days/warm nights	14 / 27
Projected change in annual cool days/cold nights	-3 / -3

	Country data	Sub-Saharan Africa	Upper middle income
Exposure to Impacts			
Land area below 5m (% of land area)	0.5	0.4	1.8
Population below 5m (% of total)	5.9	2.0	6.5
Population in urban agglomerations > 1 million (%)	..	14	22
Urban pop. growth (avg. annual %, 1990–2010)	3.5	4.0	2.3
Droughts, floods, extreme temps (% pop. avg., 1990–2009)	..		
Annual freshwater withdrawals (% of internal resources)	0.1	3.2	5.6
Agricultural land under irrigation (% of total ag. land)	..	..	..
Population living below $1.25 a day (% of total)	4.8	50.9	..
Nationally terrestrial protected areas (% of total land area)	14.9	11.7	13.6
Under-five mortality rate (per 1,000)	74	121	20
Child malnutrition, underweight (% of under age five)	8.8	24.6	4.1
Malaria incidence rate (per 100,000 people)	29,451	26,113	80
Resilience			
Access to improved sanitation (% of total pop.)	33	31	68
Access to improved water source (% of total pop.)	87	60	92
Cereal yield (kg. per hectare)	2,389	1,297	3,690
Access to electricity (% of total population)	36.7	32.5	98.0
Paved roads (% of total roads)	10.2	18.3	50.5
Health workers (per 1,000 people)	5.3	1.2	4.5
Foreign direct investment, net inflows (% of GDP)	1.3	3.6	2.7
Invest. in infrastructure w/private participation ($ millions)	125	11,957	26,166
Disaster risk reduction progress score (1–5 scale; 5 = best)	..		
Ease of doing business (ranking 1–183; 1 = best)	156		
Public sector mgmt & institutions avg. (1–6 scale; 6 = best)	..		
Primary completion rate, total (% of relevant age group)	70	67	98
Ratio of girls to boys in primary & secondary school (%)	96	89	103
GHG Emissions and Energy Use			
CO_2 emissions per capita (metric tons)	1.7	0.8	5.3
CO_2 emissions per units of GDP (kg/$1,000 of 2005 PPP $)	126.8	428.6	659.4
CO_2 emissions, total (MtCO_2)	2.5	685	12,860
GHG net emissions/removals by LUCF (1994, MtCO_2e)	-500.9		
Methane (CH_4) emissions, total (MtCO_2e)	8.2	590	3,455
Nitrous oxide (N_2O) emissions, total (MtCO_2e)	0.5	334	1,144
Other GHG emissions, total (MtCO_2e)	0.0	..	243
Energy use per capita (kilograms of oil equivalent)	1,214	689	1,848
Energy use per units of GDP (kg oil eq./$1,000 of 2005 PPP $)	93.3	308.4	227.1

National-Level Actions

Latest UNFCCC national communication	12/22/2004 (1st)
Annex-I emissions reduction target	n/a
NAMA submission	Yes
NAPA submission	n/a
Renewable energy target	Yes

Carbon Markets

Hosted Clean Development Mechanism (CDM) projects	..
Issued Certified Emission Reductions (CERs) from CDM (thousands)	..
Hosted Joint Implementation (JI) projects	n/a
Issued Emission Reduction Units (ERUs) from JI (thousands)	n/a

Gambia, The

Population (millions)	1.7	
Pop. growth (avg. ann. %, 1990-2010)	2.9	
GDP ($ millions)		806.5
GNI per capita (Atlas $)		450

Climate

Average daily min/max temperature (1961-90, Celsius)	20 / 35
Projected annual temperature change (2045-65, Celsius)	2.1 to 2.7
Average annual precipitation (1961-90, mm)	837
Projected annual precipitation change (2045-65, mm)	-87 to 26
Projected change in annual hot days/warm nights	7 / 17
Projected change in annual cool days/cold nights	-2 / -3

	Country data	Sub-Saharan Africa	Low income
Exposure to Impacts			
Land area below 5m (% of land area)	16.6	0.4	0.7
Population below 5m (% of total)	33.4	2.0	5.1
Population in urban agglomerations > 1 million (%)	..	14	11
Urban pop. growth (avg. annual %, 1990-2010)	5.0	4.0	3.7
Droughts, floods, extreme temps (% pop. avg., 1990-2009)	0.2		
Annual freshwater withdrawals (% of internal resources)	2.4	3.2	3.7
Agricultural land under irrigation (% of total ag. land)	..	..	..
Population living below $1.25 a day (% of total)	34.3	50.9	..
Nationally terrestrial protected areas (% of total land area)	1.5	11.7	10.6
Under-five mortality rate (per 1,000)	98	121	108
Child malnutrition, underweight (% of under age five)	15.8	24.6	28.3
Malaria incidence rate (per 100,000 people)	31,925	26,113	16,659
Resilience			
Access to improved sanitation (% of total pop.)	67	31	35
Access to improved water source (% of total pop.)	92	60	63
Cereal yield (kg. per hectare)	1,049	1,297	2,047
Access to electricity (% of total population)	..	32.5	23.0
Paved roads (% of total roads)	19.3	18.3	14.1
Health workers (per 1,000 people)	0.6	1.2	0.7
Foreign direct investment, net inflows (% of GDP)	4.6	3.6	3.2
Invest. in infrastructure w/private participation ($ millions)	35	11,957	4,471
Disaster risk reduction progress score (1-5 scale; 5 = best)	..		
Ease of doing business (ranking 1-183; 1 = best)	149		
Public sector mgmt & institutions avg. (1-6 scale; 6 = best)	3.0		
Primary completion rate, total (% of relevant age group)	72	67	65
Ratio of girls to boys in primary & secondary school (%)	100	89	91
GHG Emissions and Energy Use			
CO_2 emissions per capita (metric tons)	0.3	0.8	0.3
CO_2 emissions per units of GDP (kg/$1,000 of 2005 PPP $)	209.4	428.6	270.2
CO_2 emissions, total (MtCO_2)	0.4	685	219
GHG net emissions/removals by LUCF (1993, MtCO_2e)	-50.0		
Methane (CH_4) emissions, total (MtCO_2e)	..	590	436
Nitrous oxide (N_2O) emissions, total (MtCO_2e)	..	334	209
Other GHG emissions, total (MtCO_2e)	..	..	..
Energy use per capita (kilograms of oil equivalent)	84	689	365
Energy use per units of GDP (kg oil eq./$1,000 of 2005 PPP $)	71.5	308.4	303.9

National-Level Actions

Latest UNFCCC national communication	10/6/2003 (1st)
Annex-I emissions reduction target	n/a
NAMA submission	..
NAPA submission	Yes
Renewable energy target	..

Carbon Markets

Hosted Clean Development Mechanism (CDM) projects	..
Issued Certified Emission Reductions (CERs) from CDM (thousands)	..
Hosted Joint Implementation (JI) projects	n/a
Issued Emission Reduction Units (ERUs) from JI (thousands)	n/a

Georgia

Population (millions)	4.5	GDP ($ billions)	11.7
Pop. growth (avg. ann. %, 1990–2010)	-0.4	GNI per capita (Atlas $)	2,690

Climate

Average daily min/max temperature (1961–90, Celsius)	0 / 11
Projected annual temperature change (2045–65, Celsius)	1.9 to 3.0
Average annual precipitation (1961–90, mm)	1,026
Projected annual precipitation change (2045–65, mm)	-77 to -3
Projected change in annual hot days/warm nights	3 / 6
Projected change in annual cool days/cold nights	-1 / -1

	Country data	Europe & Central Asia	Lower middle income
Exposure to Impacts			
Land area below 5m (% of land area)	1.4	2.5	1.7
Population below 5m (% of total)	3.3	3.0	6.5
Population in urban agglomerations > 1 million (%)	25	18	14
Urban pop. growth (avg. annual %, 1990–2010)	-0.6	0.3	2.8
Droughts, floods, extreme temps (% pop. avg., 1990–2009)	0.8		
Annual freshwater withdrawals (% of internal resources)	2.8	6.5	18.7
Agricultural land under irrigation (% of total ag. land)	4.0	..	..
Population living below $1.25 a day (% of total)	15.3	3.7	..
Nationally terrestrial protected areas (% of total land area)	3.7	7.5	9.5
Under-five mortality rate (per 1,000)	22	23	69
Child malnutrition, underweight (% of under age five)	2.3	..	31.7
Malaria incidence rate (per 100,000 people)	0	..	4,874
Resilience			
Access to improved sanitation (% of total pop.)	95	89	45
Access to improved water source (% of total pop.)	98	95	84
Cereal yield (kg. per hectare)	1,918	2,475	2,754
Access to electricity (% of total population)	..	..	67.3
Paved roads (% of total roads)	94.1	85.8	29.3
Health workers (per 1,000 people)	8.4	9.9	2.6
Foreign direct investment, net inflows (% of GDP)	4.7	2.8	2.4
Invest. in infrastructure w/private participation ($ millions)	61	22,652	81,789
Disaster risk reduction progress score (1–5 scale; 5 = best)	2.8		
Ease of doing business (ranking 1–183; 1 = best)	16		
Public sector mgmt & institutions avg. (1–6 scale; 6 = best)	3.9		
Primary completion rate, total (% of relevant age group)	107	95	88
Ratio of girls to boys in primary & secondary school (%)	96	97	93
GHG Emissions and Energy Use			
CO_2 emissions per capita (metric tons)	1.2	7.7	1.6
CO_2 emissions per units of GDP (kg/$1,000 of 2005 PPP $)	262.8	708.0	523.9
CO_2 emissions, total (MtCO$_2$)	5.2	3,110	3,744
GHG net emissions/removals by LUCF (1994, MtCO$_2$e)	1.0		
Methane (CH_4) emissions, total (MtCO$_2$e)	4.4	937	1,705
Nitrous oxide (N_2O) emissions, total (MtCO$_2$e)	2.0	214	687
Other GHG emissions, total (MtCO$_2$e)	0.0	76	17
Energy use per capita (kilograms of oil equivalent)	723	2,833	680
Energy use per units of GDP (kg oil eq./$1,000 of 2005 PPP $)	167.4	276.8	217.9

National-Level Actions

Latest UNFCCC national communication	10/2/2009 (2nd)
Annex-I emissions reduction target	n/a
NAMA submission	Yes
NAPA submission	n/a
Renewable energy target	..

Carbon Markets

Hosted Clean Development Mechanism (CDM) projects	2
Issued Certified Emission Reductions (CERs) from CDM (thousands)	53
Hosted Joint Implementation (JI) projects	n/a
Issued Emission Reduction Units (ERUs) from JI (thousands)	n/a

Germany

Population (millions)	81.7	GDP ($ billions)	3,309.7
Pop. growth (avg. ann. %, 1990-2010)	0.1	GNI per capita (Atlas $)	43,290

Climate

Average daily min/max temperature (1961-90, Celsius)	5 / 12
Projected annual temperature change (2045-65, Celsius)	1.7 to 2.6
Average annual precipitation (1961-90, mm)	700
Projected annual precipitation change (2045-65, mm)	-38 to 57
Projected change in annual hot days/warm nights	3 / 5
Projected change in annual cool days/cold nights	-1 / -2

	Country data	High income
Exposure to Impacts		
Land area below 5m (% of land area)	4.9	2.2
Population below 5m (% of total)	4.4	7.7
Population in urban agglomerations > 1 million (%)	8	..
Urban pop. growth (avg. annual %, 1990-2010)	0.2	1.0
Droughts, floods, extreme temps (% pop. avg., 1990-2009)	0.0	
Annual freshwater withdrawals (% of internal resources)	36.6	10.4
Agricultural land under irrigation (% of total ag. land)	..	
Population living below $1.25 a day (% of total)	..	..
Nationally terrestrial protected areas (% of total land area)	40.5	13.4
Under-five mortality rate (per 1,000)	4	6
Child malnutrition, underweight (% of under age five)	1.1	..
Malaria incidence rate (per 100,000 people)	..	..
Resilience		
Access to improved sanitation (% of total pop.)	100	100
Access to improved water source (% of total pop.)	100	100
Cereal yield (kg. per hectare)	7,201	5,445
Access to electricity (% of total population)	..	..
Paved roads (% of total roads)	100.0	87.3
Health workers (per 1,000 people)	14.4	10.7
Foreign direct investment, net inflows (% of GDP)	1.4	1.8
Invest. in infrastructure w/private participation ($ millions)	..	..
Disaster risk reduction progress score (1-5 scale; 5 = best)	4.3	
Ease of doing business (ranking 1-183; 1 = best)	19	
Public sector mgmt & institutions avg. (1-6 scale; 6 = best)	..	
Primary completion rate, total (% of relevant age group)	104	97
Ratio of girls to boys in primary & secondary school (%)	96	100
GHG Emissions and Energy Use		
CO_2 emissions per capita (metric tons)	9.6	11.9
CO_2 emissions per units of GDP (kg/$1,000 of 2005 PPP $)	283.8	354.4
CO_2 emissions, total (MtCO$_2$)	786.7	13,285
GHG net emissions/removals by LUCF (2009, MtCO$_2$e)	17.6	
Methane (CH_4) emissions, total (MtCO$_2$e)	67.6	1,539
Nitrous oxide (N_2O) emissions, total (MtCO$_2$e)	56.6	813
Other GHG emissions, total (MtCO$_2$e)	31.5	460
Energy use per capita (kilograms of oil equivalent)	4,057	4,944
Energy use per units of GDP (kg oil eq./$1,000 of 2005 PPP $)	121.1	147.0

National-Level Actions

Latest UNFCCC national communication	2/11/2010 (5th)
Annex-I emissions reduction target (base year: 1990)	20% / 30% (EU)
NAMA submission	n/a
NAPA submission	n/a
Renewable energy target	Yes

Carbon Markets

Hosted Clean Development Mechanism (CDM) projects	n/a
Issued Certified Emission Reductions (CERs) from CDM (thousands)	n/a
Hosted Joint Implementation (JI) projects	11
Issued Emission Reduction Units (ERUs) from JI (thousands)	2,087

Ghana

Population (millions)	24.4	GDP ($ billions)	31.3
Pop. growth (avg. ann. %, 1990–2010)	2.5	GNI per capita (Atlas $)	1,230

Climate

Average daily min/max temperature (1961–90, Celsius)	22 / 32
Projected annual temperature change (2045–65, Celsius)	1.8 to 2.4
Average annual precipitation (1961–90, mm)	1,187
Projected annual precipitation change (2045–65, mm)	-159 to 83
Projected change in annual hot days/warm nights	7 / 22
Projected change in annual cool days/cold nights	-2 / -2

	Country data	Sub-Saharan Africa	Lower middle income
Exposure to Impacts			
Land area below 5m (% of land area)	0.8	0.4	1.7
Population below 5m (% of total)	2.3	2.0	6.5
Population in urban agglomerations > 1 million (%)	17	14	14
Urban pop. growth (avg. annual %, 1990–2010)	4.2	4.0	2.8
Droughts, floods, extreme temps (% pop. avg., 1990–2009)	1.0		
Annual freshwater withdrawals (% of internal resources)	3.2	3.2	18.7
Agricultural land under irrigation (% of total ag. land)	..	..	..
Population living below $1.25 a day (% of total)	30.0	50.9	..
Nationally terrestrial protected areas (% of total land area)	14.0	11.7	9.5
Under-five mortality rate (per 1,000)	74	121	69
Child malnutrition, underweight (% of under age five)	14.3	24.6	31.7
Malaria incidence rate (per 100,000 people)	31,179	26,113	4,874
Resilience			
Access to improved sanitation (% of total pop.)	13	31	45
Access to improved water source (% of total pop.)	82	60	84
Cereal yield (kg. per hectare)	1,660	1,297	2,754
Access to electricity (% of total population)	60.5	32.5	67.3
Paved roads (% of total roads)	14.9	18.3	29.3
Health workers (per 1,000 people)	1.1	1.2	2.6
Foreign direct investment, net inflows (% of GDP)	8.1	3.6	2.4
Invest. in infrastructure w/private participation ($ millions)	290	11,957	81,789
Disaster risk reduction progress score (1-5 scale; 5 = best)	3.3		
Ease of doing business (ranking 1-183; 1 = best)	63		
Public sector mgmt & institutions avg. (1-6 scale; 6 = best)	3.7		
Primary completion rate, total (% of relevant age group)	83	67	88
Ratio of girls to boys in primary & secondary school (%)	95	89	93
GHG Emissions and Energy Use			
CO_2 emissions per capita (metric tons)	0.4	0.8	1.6
CO_2 emissions per units of GDP (kg/$1,000 of 2005 PPP $)	267.6	428.6	523.9
CO_2 emissions, total (MtCO$_2$)	8.6	685	3,744
GHG net emissions/removals by LUCF (1996, MtCO$_2$e)	-19.0		
Methane (CH$_4$) emissions, total (MtCO$_2$e)	9.0	590	1,705
Nitrous oxide (N$_2$O) emissions, total (MtCO$_2$e)	4.9	334	687
Other GHG emissions, total (MtCO$_2$e)	0.0	..	17
Energy use per capita (kilograms of oil equivalent)	388	689	680
Energy use per units of GDP (kg oil eq./$1,000 of 2005 PPP $)	275.0	308.4	217.9
National-Level Actions			
Latest UNFCCC national communication	5/2/2001 (1st)		
Annex-I emissions reduction target	n/a		
NAMA submission	Yes		
NAPA submission	n/a		
Renewable energy target	Yes		
Carbon Markets			
Hosted Clean Development Mechanism (CDM) projects	0		
Issued Certified Emission Reductions (CERs) from CDM (thousands)	0		
Hosted Joint Implementation (JI) projects	n/a		
Issued Emission Reduction Units (ERUs) from JI (thousands)	n/a		

Gibraltar

Population (thousands)	29.2	GDP ($ millions)	..
Pop. growth (avg. ann. %, 1990–2010)	0.4	GNI per capita (Atlas $)	..

Climate

Average daily min/max temperature (1961–90, Celsius)	13 / 22
Projected annual temperature change (2045–65, Celsius)	1.8 to 2.7
Average annual precipitation (1961–90, mm)	618
Projected annual precipitation change (2045–65, mm)	-100 to -26
Projected change in annual hot days/warm nights	3 / 8
Projected change in annual cool days/cold nights	-2 / -2

	Country data	High income
Exposure to Impacts		
Land area below 5m (% of land area)	100.0	2.2
Population below 5m (% of total)	100.0	7.7
Population in urban agglomerations > 1 million (%)	..	
Urban pop. growth (avg. annual %, 1990–2010)	..	1.0
Droughts, floods, extreme temps (% pop. avg., 1990–2009)	..	
Annual freshwater withdrawals (% of internal resources)	..	10.4
Agricultural land under irrigation (% of total ag. land)	..	
Population living below $1.25 a day (% of total)	..	..
Nationally terrestrial protected areas (% of total land area)	4.7	13.4
Under-five mortality rate (per 1,000)	..	6
Child malnutrition, underweight (% of under age five)	..	
Malaria incidence rate (per 100,000 people)	..	..
Resilience		
Access to improved sanitation (% of total pop.)	..	100
Access to improved water source (% of total pop.)	..	100
Cereal yield (kg. per hectare)	..	5,445
Access to electricity (% of total population)	..	
Paved roads (% of total roads)	..	87.3
Health workers (per 1,000 people)	..	10.7
Foreign direct investment, net inflows (% of GDP)	..	1.8
Invest. in infrastructure w/private participation ($ millions)	..	..
Disaster risk reduction progress score (1–5 scale; 5 = best)	..	
Ease of doing business (ranking 1–183; 1 = best)	..	
Public sector mgmt & institutions avg. (1–6 scale; 6 = best)	..	
Primary completion rate, total (% of relevant age group)	..	97
Ratio of girls to boys in primary & secondary school (%)	..	100
GHG Emissions and Energy Use		
CO_2 emissions per capita (metric tons)	14.4	11.9
CO_2 emissions per units of GDP (kg/$1,000 of 2005 PPP $)	..	354.4
CO_2 emissions, total (MtCO_2)	0.4	13,285
GHG net emissions/removals by LUCF (MtCO_2e)	..	
Methane (CH_4) emissions, total (MtCO_2e)	0.0	1,539
Nitrous oxide (N_2O) emissions, total (MtCO_2e)	0.0	813
Other GHG emissions, total (MtCO_2e)	0.0	460
Energy use per capita (kilograms of oil equivalent)	5,597	4,944
Energy use per units of GDP (kg oil eq./$1,000 of 2005 PPP $)	..	147.0
National-Level Actions		
Latest UNFCCC national communication		n/a
Annex-I emissions reduction target		n/a
NAMA submission		n/a
NAPA submission		n/a
Renewable energy target		..
Carbon Markets		
Hosted Clean Development Mechanism (CDM) projects		n/a
Issued Certified Emission Reductions (CERs) from CDM (thousands)		n/a
Hosted Joint Implementation (JI) projects		n/a
Issued Emission Reduction Units (ERUs) from JI (thousands)		n/a

Greece

Population (millions)	11.3	GDP ($ billions)	304.9
Pop. growth (avg. ann. %, 1990–2010)	0.5	GNI per capita (Atlas $)	27,260

Climate
Average daily min/max temperature (1961–90, Celsius)	11 / 20
Projected annual temperature change (2045–65, Celsius)	1.7 to 2.6
Average annual precipitation (1961–90, mm)	652
Projected annual precipitation change (2045–65, mm)	-110 to -40
Projected change in annual hot days/warm nights	3 / 6
Projected change in annual cool days/cold nights	-2 / -2

	Country data	High Income
Exposure to Impacts		
Land area below 5m (% of land area)	6.3	2.2
Population below 5m (% of total)	9.9	7.7
Population in urban agglomerations > 1 million (%)	29	..
Urban pop. growth (avg. annual %, 1990–2010)	0.8	1.0
Droughts, floods, extreme temps (% pop. avg., 1990–2009)	0.0	
Annual freshwater withdrawals (% of internal resources)	12.2	10.4
Agricultural land under irrigation (% of total ag. land)	16.9	..
Population living below $1.25 a day (% of total)	..	..
Nationally terrestrial protected areas (% of total land area)	13.8	13.4
Under-five mortality rate (per 1,000)	4	6
Child malnutrition, underweight (% of under age five)	..	..
Malaria incidence rate (per 100,000 people)	..	..
Resilience		
Access to improved sanitation (% of total pop.)	98	100
Access to improved water source (% of total pop.)	100	100
Cereal yield (kg. per hectare)	4,103	5,445
Access to electricity (% of total population)	..	
Paved roads (% of total roads)	91.8	87.3
Health workers (per 1,000 people)	9.7	10.7
Foreign direct investment, net inflows (% of GDP)	0.7	1.8
Invest. in infrastructure w/private participation ($ millions)	..	
Disaster risk reduction progress score (1–5 scale; 5 = best)	..	
Ease of doing business (ranking 1–183; 1 = best)	100	
Public sector mgmt & institutions avg. (1–6 scale; 6 = best)	..	
Primary completion rate, total (% of relevant age group)	101	97
Ratio of girls to boys in primary & secondary school (%)	97	100
GHG Emissions and Energy Use		
CO_2 emissions per capita (metric tons)	8.7	11.9
CO_2 emissions per units of GDP (kg/$1,000 of 2005 PPP $)	323.6	354.4
CO_2 emissions, total (MtCO$_2$)	97.8	13,285
GHG net emissions/removals by LUCF (2009, MtCO$_2$e)	-3.0	
Methane (CH_4) emissions, total (MtCO$_2$e)	7.3	1,539
Nitrous oxide (N_2O) emissions, total (MtCO$_2$e)	6.0	813
Other GHG emissions, total (MtCO$_2$e)	1.8	460
Energy use per capita (kilograms of oil equivalent)	2,387	4,944
Energy use per units of GDP (kg oil eq./$1,000 of 2005 PPP $)	95.5	147.0

National-Level Actions
Latest UNFCCC national communication	1/18/2010 (5th)
Annex-I emissions reduction target (base year: 1990)	20% / 30% (EU)
NAMA submission	n/a
NAPA submission	n/a
Renewable energy target	Yes

Carbon Markets
Hosted Clean Development Mechanism (CDM) projects	n/a
Issued Certified Emission Reductions (CERs) from CDM (thousands)	n/a
Hosted Joint Implementation (JI) projects	..
Issued Emission Reduction Units (ERUs) from JI (thousands)	..

Greenland

Population (thousands)	56.5	GDP ($ billions)	1.3
Pop. growth (avg. ann. %, 1990–2010)	0.1	GNI per capita (Atlas $)	26,020

Climate

Average daily min/max temperature (1961–90, Celsius)	-23 / -10
Projected annual temperature change (2045–65, Celsius)	1.9 to 3.0
Average annual precipitation (1961–90, mm)	585
Projected annual precipitation change (2045–65, mm)	6 to 74
Projected change in annual hot days/warm nights	2 / 5
Projected change in annual cool days/cold nights	-1 / -2

	Country data	High income
Exposure to Impacts		
Land area below 5m (% of land area)	16.3	2.2
Population below 5m (% of total)	52.2	7.7
Population in urban agglomerations > 1 million (%)	..	..
Urban pop. growth (avg. annual %, 1990–2010)	0.3	1.0
Droughts, floods, extreme temps (% pop. avg., 1990–2009)	..	
Annual freshwater withdrawals (% of internal resources)		10.4
Agricultural land under irrigation (% of total ag. land)	..	..
Population living below $1.25 a day (% of total)	..	..
Nationally terrestrial protected areas (% of total land area)	40.5	13.4
Under-five mortality rate (per 1,000)	..	6
Child malnutrition, underweight (% of under age five)	..	..
Malaria incidence rate (per 100,000 people)	..	..
Resilience		
Access to improved sanitation (% of total pop.)	..	100
Access to improved water source (% of total pop.)	..	100
Cereal yield (kg. per hectare)	..	5,445
Access to electricity (% of total population)	..	..
Paved roads (% of total roads)	..	87.3
Health workers (per 1,000 people)	..	10.7
Foreign direct investment, net inflows (% of GDP)	..	1.8
Invest. in infrastructure w/private participation ($ millions)	..	..
Disaster risk reduction progress score (1–5 scale; 5 = best)	..	
Ease of doing business (ranking 1–183; 1 = best)	..	
Public sector mgmt & institutions avg. (1–6 scale; 6 = best)	..	
Primary completion rate, total (% of relevant age group)	..	97
Ratio of girls to boys in primary & secondary school (%)	..	100
GHG Emissions and Energy Use		
CO$_2$ emissions per capita (metric tons)	10.2	11.9
CO$_2$ emissions per units of GDP (kg/$1,000 of 2005 PPP $)	..	354.4
CO$_2$ emissions, total (MtCO$_2$)	0.6	13,285
GHG net emissions/removals by LUCF (MtCO$_2$e)	..	
Methane (CH$_4$) emissions, total (MtCO$_2$e)	..	1,539
Nitrous oxide (N$_2$O) emissions, total (MtCO$_2$e)	..	813
Other GHG emissions, total (MtCO$_2$e)	..	460
Energy use per capita (kilograms of oil equivalent)	..	4,944
Energy use per units of GDP (kg oil eq./$1,000 of 2005 PPP $)	..	147.0
National-Level Actions		
Latest UNFCCC national communication		n/a
Annex-I emissions reduction target		n/a
NAMA submission		n/a
NAPA submission		n/a
Renewable energy target		..
Carbon Markets		
Hosted Clean Development Mechanism (CDM) projects		n/a
Issued Certified Emission Reductions (CERs) from CDM (thousands)		n/a
Hosted Joint Implementation (JI) projects		n/a
Issued Emission Reduction Units (ERUs) from JI (thousands)		n/a

Grenada

Population (thousands)	104.5	GDP ($ millions)	627.9
Pop. growth (avg. ann. %, 1990-2010)	0.4	GNI per capita (Atlas $)	5,550

Climate

Average daily min/max temperature (1961-90, Celsius)	23 / 31
Projected annual temperature change (2045-65, Celsius)	1.5 to 1.9
Average annual precipitation (1961-90, mm)	1,535
Projected annual precipitation change (2045-65, mm)	-245 to 7
Projected change in annual hot days/warm nights	15 / 26
Projected change in annual cool days/cold nights	-3 / -3

	Country data	Latin America & the Carib.	Upper middle income
Exposure to Impacts			
Land area below 5m (% of land area)	21.7	1.5	1.8
Population below 5m (% of total)	21.7	3.8	6.5
Population in urban agglomerations > 1 million (%)	..	35	22
Urban pop. growth (avg. annual %, 1990-2010)	0.2	2.0	2.3
Droughts, floods, extreme temps (% pop. avg., 1990-2009)	..		
Annual freshwater withdrawals (% of internal resources)	..	2.0	5.6
Agricultural land under irrigation (% of total ag. land)	0.0	..	..
Population living below $1.25 a day (% of total)	..	8.1	..
Nationally terrestrial protected areas (% of total land area)	1.7	20.8	13.6
Under-five mortality rate (per 1,000)	11	23	20
Child malnutrition, underweight (% of under age five)	..	3.8	4.1
Malaria incidence rate (per 100,000 people)	..	206	80
Resilience			
Access to improved sanitation (% of total pop.)	97	79	68
Access to improved water source (% of total pop.)	95	93	92
Cereal yield (kg. per hectare)	989	3,337	3,690
Access to electricity (% of total population)	..	93.4	98.0
Paved roads (% of total roads)	61.0	28.1	50.5
Health workers (per 1,000 people)	..	6.9	4.5
Foreign direct investment, net inflows (% of GDP)	10.1	2.3	2.7
Invest. in infrastructure w/private participation ($ millions)	14	33,064	26,166
Disaster risk reduction progress score (1-5 scale; 5 = best)	..		
Ease of doing business (ranking 1-183; 1 = best)	73		
Public sector mgmt & institutions avg. (1-6 scale; 6 = best)	3.7		
Primary completion rate, total (% of relevant age group)	126	102	98
Ratio of girls to boys in primary & secondary school (%)	97	102	103
GHG Emissions and Energy Use			
CO_2 emissions per capita (metric tons)	2.4	2.8	5.3
CO_2 emissions per units of GDP (kg/$1,000 of 2005 PPP $)	290.2	285.6	659.4
CO_2 emissions, total (MtCO_2)	0.2	1,584	12,860
GHG net emissions/removals by LUCF (1994, MtCO_2e)	-0.1		
Methane (CH_4) emissions, total (MtCO_2e)	..	1,009	3,455
Nitrous oxide (N_2O) emissions, total (MtCO_2e)	..	442	1,144
Other GHG emissions, total (MtCO_2e)	..	21	243
Energy use per capita (kilograms of oil equivalent)	784	1,245	1,848
Energy use per units of GDP (kg oil eq./$1,000 of 2005 PPP $)	96.5	130.6	227.1

National-Level Actions

Latest UNFCCC national communication	11/21/2000 (1st)
Annex-I emissions reduction target	n/a
NAMA submission	..
NAPA submission	n/a
Renewable energy target	..

Carbon Markets

Hosted Clean Development Mechanism (CDM) projects	..
Issued Certified Emission Reductions (CERs) from CDM (thousands)	..
Hosted Joint Implementation (JI) projects	n/a
Issued Emission Reduction Units (ERUs) from JI (thousands)	n/a

Population (thousands)	179.9	GDP ($ millions)	..
Pop. growth (avg. ann. %, 1990-2010)	1.5	GNI per capita (Atlas $)	..

Climate

Average daily min/max temperature (1961-90, Celsius)	..
Projected annual temperature change (2045-65, Celsius)	1.3 to 1.7
Average annual precipitation (1961-90, mm)	..
Projected annual precipitation change (2045-65, mm)	-25 to 230
Projected change in annual hot days/warm nights	19 / 27
Projected change in annual cool days/cold nights	-3 / -3

	Country data	High income
Exposure to Impacts		
Land area below 5m (% of land area)	20.4	2.2
Population below 5m (% of total)	26.6	7.7
Population in urban agglomerations > 1 million (%)	..	..
Urban pop. growth (avg. annual %, 1990-2010)	1.6	1.0
Droughts, floods, extreme temps (% pop. avg., 1990-2009)	..	
Annual freshwater withdrawals (% of internal resources)	..	10.4
Agricultural land under irrigation (% of total ag. land)	..	..
Population living below $1.25 a day (% of total)	..	..
Nationally terrestrial protected areas (% of total land area)	26.4	13.4
Under-five mortality rate (per 1,000)	..	6
Child malnutrition, underweight (% of under age five)	..	..
Malaria incidence rate (per 100,000 people)	..	..
Resilience		
Access to improved sanitation (% of total pop.)	99	100
Access to improved water source (% of total pop.)	100	100
Cereal yield (kg. per hectare)	3,333	5,445
Access to electricity (% of total population)	..	..
Paved roads (% of total roads)	..	87.3
Health workers (per 1,000 people)	..	10.7
Foreign direct investment, net inflows (% of GDP)	..	1.8
Invest. in infrastructure w/private participation ($ millions)	..	..
Disaster risk reduction progress score (1-5 scale; 5 = best)	..	
Ease of doing business (ranking 1-183; 1 = best)	..	
Public sector mgmt & institutions avg. (1-6 scale; 6 = best)	..	
Primary completion rate, total (% of relevant age group)	..	97
Ratio of girls to boys in primary & secondary school (%)	..	100
GHG Emissions and Energy Use		
CO$_2$ emissions per capita (metric tons)	..	11.9
CO$_2$ emissions per units of GDP (kg/$1,000 of 2005 PPP $)	..	354.4
CO$_2$ emissions, total (MtCO$_2$)	..	13,285
GHG net emissions/removals by LUCF (1994, MtCO$_2$e)	..	
Methane (CH$_4$) emissions, total (MtCO$_2$e)	..	1,539
Nitrous oxide (N$_2$O) emissions, total (MtCO$_2$e)	..	813
Other GHG emissions, total (MtCO$_2$e)	..	460
Energy use per capita (kilograms of oil equivalent)	..	4,944
Energy use per units of GDP (kg oil eq./$1,000 of 2005 PPP $)	..	147.0
National-Level Actions		
Latest UNFCCC national communication		n/a
Annex-I emissions reduction target		n/a
NAMA submission		n/a
NAPA submission		n/a
Renewable energy target		..
Carbon Markets		
Hosted Clean Development Mechanism (CDM) projects		n/a
Issued Certified Emission Reductions (CERs) from CDM (thousands)		n/a
Hosted Joint Implementation (JI) projects		n/a
Issued Emission Reduction Units (ERUs) from JI (thousands)		n/a

Guatemala

Population (millions)	14.4	GDP ($ billions)	41.2
Pop. growth (avg. ann. %, 1990–2010)	2.4	GNI per capita (Atlas $)	2,730

Climate

Average daily min/max temperature (1961–90, Celsius)	18 / 29
Projected annual temperature change (2045–65, Celsius)	1.7 to 2.8
Average annual precipitation (1961–90, mm)	2,712
Projected annual precipitation change (2045–65, mm)	-186 to 22
Projected change in annual hot days/warm nights	8 / 22
Projected change in annual cool days/cold nights	-2 / -2

	Country data	Latin America & the Carib.	Lower middle income
Exposure to Impacts			
Land area below 5m (% of land area)	0.6	1.5	1.7
Population below 5m (% of total)	0.3	3.8	6.5
Population in urban agglomerations > 1 million (%)	8	35	14
Urban pop. growth (avg. annual %, 1990–2010)	3.3	2.0	2.8
Droughts, floods, extreme temps (% pop. avg., 1990–2009)	1.3		
Annual freshwater withdrawals (% of internal resources)	2.7	2.0	18.7
Agricultural land under irrigation (% of total ag. land)	..	..	..
Population living below $1.25 a day (% of total)	11.7	8.1	..
Nationally terrestrial protected areas (% of total land area)	30.6	20.8	9.5
Under-five mortality rate (per 1,000)	32	23	69
Child malnutrition, underweight (% of under age five)	17.7	3.8	31.7
Malaria incidence rate (per 100,000 people)	184	206	4,874
Resilience			
Access to improved sanitation (% of total pop.)	81	79	45
Access to improved water source (% of total pop.)	94	93	84
Cereal yield (kg. per hectare)	1,966	3,337	2,754
Access to electricity (% of total population)	80.5	93.4	67.3
Paved roads (% of total roads)	34.5	28.1	29.3
Health workers (per 1,000 people)	..	6.9	2.6
Foreign direct investment, net inflows (% of GDP)	1.7	2.3	2.4
Invest. in infrastructure w/private participation ($ millions)	971	33,064	81,789
Disaster risk reduction progress score (1-5 scale; 5 = best)	3.3		
Ease of doing business (ranking 1-183; 1 = best)	97		
Public sector mgmt & institutions avg. (1-6 scale; 6 = best)	..		
Primary completion rate, total (% of relevant age group)	80	102	88
Ratio of girls to boys in primary & secondary school (%)	94	102	93
GHG Emissions and Energy Use			
CO_2 emissions per capita (metric tons)	0.9	2.8	1.6
CO_2 emissions per units of GDP (kg/$1,000 of 2005 PPP $)	199.4	285.6	523.9
CO_2 emissions, total (MtCO_2)	11.9	1,584	3,744
GHG net emissions/removals by LUCF (1990, MtCO_2e)	-39.5		
Methane (CH_4) emissions, total (MtCO_2e)	8.3	1,009	1,705
Nitrous oxide (N_2O) emissions, total (MtCO_2e)	5.4	442	687
Other GHG emissions, total (MtCO_2e)	0.5	21	17
Energy use per capita (kilograms of oil equivalent)	701	1,245	680
Energy use per units of GDP (kg oil eq./$1,000 of 2005 PPP $)	163.8	130.6	217.9

National-Level Actions

Latest UNFCCC national communication	2/1/2002 (1st)
Annex-I emissions reduction target	n/a
NAMA submission	..
NAPA submission	n/a
Renewable energy target	..

Carbon Markets

Hosted Clean Development Mechanism (CDM) projects	11
Issued Certified Emission Reductions (CERs) from CDM (thousands)	1,023
Hosted Joint Implementation (JI) projects	n/a
Issued Emission Reduction Units (ERUs) from JI (thousands)	n/a

Guinea

Population (millions)	10.0	GDP ($ billions)	4.5
Pop. growth (avg. ann. %, 1990–2010)	2.7	GNI per capita (Atlas $)	400

Climate

Average daily min/max temperature (1961-90, Celsius)	20 / 32
Projected annual temperature change (2045-65, Celsius)	2.0 to 2.6
Average annual precipitation (1961-90, mm)	1,651
Projected annual precipitation change (2045-65, mm)	-122 to 104
Projected change in annual hot days/warm nights	7 / 20
Projected change in annual cool days/cold nights	-2 / -2

	Country data	Sub-Saharan Africa	Low income
Exposure to Impacts			
Land area below 5m (% of land area)	1.1	0.4	0.7
Population below 5m (% of total)	3.6	2.0	5.1
Population in urban agglomerations > 1 million (%)	17	14	11
Urban pop. growth (avg. annual %, 1990-2010)	3.9	4.0	3.7
Droughts, floods, extreme temps (% pop. avg., 1990-2009)	0.2		
Annual freshwater withdrawals (% of internal resources)	0.7	3.2	3.7
Agricultural land under irrigation (% of total ag. land)	..	..	..
Population living below $1.25 a day (% of total)	43.3	50.9	..
Nationally terrestrial protected areas (% of total land area)	6.8	11.7	10.6
Under-five mortality rate (per 1,000)	130	121	108
Child malnutrition, underweight (% of under age five)	20.8	24.6	28.3
Malaria incidence rate (per 100,000 people)	40,585	26,113	16,659
Resilience			
Access to improved sanitation (% of total pop.)	19	31	35
Access to improved water source (% of total pop.)	71	60	63
Cereal yield (kg. per hectare)	1,339	1,297	2,047
Access to electricity (% of total population)	..	32.5	23.0
Paved roads (% of total roads)	9.8	18.3	14.1
Health workers (per 1,000 people)	0.1	1.2	0.7
Foreign direct investment, net inflows (% of GDP)	2.2	3.6	3.2
Invest. in infrastructure w/private participation ($ millions)	71	11,957	4,471
Disaster risk reduction progress score (1-5 scale; 5 = best)	..		
Ease of doing business (ranking 1-183; 1 = best)	179		
Public sector mgmt & institutions avg. (1-6 scale; 6 = best)	2.6		
Primary completion rate, total (% of relevant age group)	62	67	65
Ratio of girls to boys in primary & secondary school (%)	77	89	91
GHG Emissions and Energy Use			
CO_2 emissions per capita (metric tons)	0.1	0.8	0.3
CO_2 emissions per units of GDP (kg/$1,000 of 2005 PPP $)	145.0	428.6	270.2
CO_2 emissions, total (MtCO_2)	1.4	685	219
GHG net emissions/removals by LUCF (1994, MtCO_2e)	-17.6		
Methane (CH_4) emissions, total (MtCO_2e)	..	590	436
Nitrous oxide (N_2O) emissions, total (MtCO_2e)	..	334	209
Other GHG emissions, total (MtCO_2e)	..	..	..
Energy use per capita (kilograms of oil equivalent)	..	689	365
Energy use per units of GDP (kg oil eq./$1,000 of 2005 PPP $)	..	308.4	303.9

National-Level Actions

Latest UNFCCC national communication	10/28/2002 (1st)
Annex-I emissions reduction target	n/a
NAMA submission	..
NAPA submission	Yes
Renewable energy target	..

Carbon Markets

Hosted Clean Development Mechanism (CDM) projects	..
Issued Certified Emission Reductions (CERs) from CDM (thousands)	..
Hosted Joint Implementation (JI) projects	n/a
Issued Emission Reduction Units (ERUs) from JI (thousands)	n/a

Guinea-Bissau

Population (millions)	1.5	GDP ($ millions)	878.5
Pop. growth (avg. ann. %, 1990–2010)	2.0	GNI per capita (Atlas $)	590

Climate

Average daily min/max temperature (1961–90, Celsius)	21 / 33
Projected annual temperature change (2045–65, Celsius)	1.8 to 2.2
Average annual precipitation (1961–90, mm)	1,577
Projected annual precipitation change (2045–65, mm)	-69 to 130
Projected change in annual hot days/warm nights	10 / 22
Projected change in annual cool days/cold nights	-3 / -3

	Country data	Sub-Saharan Africa	Low income
Exposure to Impacts			
Land area below 5m (% of land area)	9.5	0.4	0.7
Population below 5m (% of total)	18.8	2.0	5.1
Population in urban agglomerations > 1 million (%)	..	14	11
Urban pop. growth (avg. annual %, 1990–2010)	2.3	4.0	3.7
Droughts, floods, extreme temps (% pop. avg., 1990–2009)	0.5		
Annual freshwater withdrawals (% of internal resources)	1.1	3.2	3.7
Agricultural land under irrigation (% of total ag. land)	..	..	..
Population living below $1.25 a day (% of total)	48.8	50.9	..
Nationally terrestrial protected areas (% of total land area)	16.1	11.7	10.6
Under-five mortality rate (per 1,000)	150	121	108
Child malnutrition, underweight (% of under age five)	17.4	24.6	28.3
Malaria incidence rate (per 100,000 people)	34,043	26,113	16,659
Resilience			
Access to improved sanitation (% of total pop.)	21	31	35
Access to improved water source (% of total pop.)	61	60	63
Cereal yield (kg. per hectare)	1,445	1,297	2,047
Access to electricity (% of total population)	..	32.5	23.0
Paved roads (% of total roads)	27.9	18.3	14.1
Health workers (per 1,000 people)	0.6	1.2	0.7
Foreign direct investment, net inflows (% of GDP)	1.0	3.6	3.2
Invest. in infrastructure w/private participation ($ millions)	19	11,957	4,471
Disaster risk reduction progress score (1–5 scale; 5 = best)	1.0		
Ease of doing business (ranking 1–183; 1 = best)	176		
Public sector mgmt & institutions avg. (1–6 scale; 6 = best)	2.6		
Primary completion rate, total (% of relevant age group)	31	67	65
Ratio of girls to boys in primary & secondary school (%)	65	89	91
GHG Emissions and Energy Use			
CO_2 emissions per capita (metric tons)	0.2	0.8	0.3
CO_2 emissions per units of GDP (kg/$1,000 of 2005 PPP $)	186.6	428.6	270.2
CO_2 emissions, total (MtCO_2)	0.3	685	219
GHG net emissions/removals by LUCF (MtCO_2e)	..		
Methane (CH_4) emissions, total (MtCO_2e)	..	590	436
Nitrous oxide (N_2O) emissions, total (MtCO_2e)	..	334	209
Other GHG emissions, total (MtCO_2e)	..	..	..
Energy use per capita (kilograms of oil equivalent)	67	689	365
Energy use per units of GDP (kg oil eq./$1,000 of 2005 PPP $)	64.8	308.4	303.9

National-Level Actions

Latest UNFCCC national communication	12/1/2005 (1st)
Annex-I emissions reduction target	n/a
NAMA submission	..
NAPA submission	Yes
Renewable energy target	..

Carbon Markets

Hosted Clean Development Mechanism (CDM) projects	..
Issued Certified Emission Reductions (CERs) from CDM (thousands)	..
Hosted Joint Implementation (JI) projects	n/a
Issued Emission Reduction Units (ERUs) from JI (thousands)	n/a

Guyana

Population (thousands)	754.5	GDP ($ billions)	2.2
Pop. growth (avg. ann. %, 1990-2010)	0.2	GNI per capita (Atlas $)	3,300

Climate

Average daily min/max temperature (1961-90, Celsius)	22 / 30
Projected annual temperature change (2045-65, Celsius)	1.9 to 3.0
Average annual precipitation (1961-90, mm)	2,387
Projected annual precipitation change (2045-65, mm)	-158 to 72
Projected change in annual hot days/warm nights	9 / 26
Projected change in annual cool days/cold nights	-3 / -3

	Country data	Latin America & the Carib.	Lower middle income
Exposure to Impacts			
Land area below 5m (% of land area)	2.7	1.5	1.7
Population below 5m (% of total)	31.3	3.8	6.5
Population in urban agglomerations > 1 million (%)	..	35	14
Urban pop. growth (avg. annual %, 1990-2010)	0.0	2.0	2.8
Droughts, floods, extreme temps (% pop. avg., 1990-2009)	7.2		
Annual freshwater withdrawals (% of internal resources)	0.7	2.0	18.7
Agricultural land under irrigation (% of total ag. land)	..	..	..
Population living below $1.25 a day (% of total)	8.7	8.1	..
Nationally terrestrial protected areas (% of total land area)	4.9	20.8	9.5
Under-five mortality rate (per 1,000)	30	23	69
Child malnutrition, underweight (% of under age five)	10.8	3.8	31.7
Malaria incidence rate (per 100,000 people)	2,194	206	4,874
Resilience			
Access to improved sanitation (% of total pop.)	81	79	45
Access to improved water source (% of total pop.)	94	93	84
Cereal yield (kg. per hectare)	2,568	3,337	2,754
Access to electricity (% of total population)	..	93.4	67.3
Paved roads (% of total roads)	7.4	28.1	29.3
Health workers (per 1,000 people)	2.8	6.9	2.6
Foreign direct investment, net inflows (% of GDP)	8.4	2.3	2.4
Invest. in infrastructure w/private participation ($ millions)	26	33,064	81,789
Disaster risk reduction progress score (1-5 scale; 5 = best)	..		
Ease of doing business (ranking 1-183; 1 = best)	114		
Public sector mgmt & institutions avg. (1-6 scale; 6 = best)	3.0		
Primary completion rate, total (% of relevant age group)	109	102	88
Ratio of girls to boys in primary & secondary school (%)	100	102	93
GHG Emissions and Energy Use			
CO$_2$ emissions per capita (metric tons)	2.0	2.8	1.6
CO$_2$ emissions per units of GDP (kg/$1,000 of 2005 PPP $)	780.2	285.6	523.9
CO$_2$ emissions, total (MtCO$_2$)	1.5	1,584	3,744
GHG net emissions/removals by LUCF (1998, MtCO$_2$e)	-30.9		
Methane (CH$_4$) emissions, total (MtCO$_2$e)	..	1,009	1,705
Nitrous oxide (N$_2$O) emissions, total (MtCO$_2$e)	..	442	687
Other GHG emissions, total (MtCO$_2$e)	..	21	17
Energy use per capita (kilograms of oil equivalent)	667	1,245	680
Energy use per units of GDP (kg oil eq./$1,000 of 2005 PPP $)	260.8	130.6	217.9

National-Level Actions

Latest UNFCCC national communication	5/16/2002 (1st)
Annex-I emissions reduction target	n/a
NAMA submission	..
NAPA submission	n/a
Renewable energy target	...

Carbon Markets

Hosted Clean Development Mechanism (CDM) projects	1
Issued Certified Emission Reductions (CERs) from CDM (thousands)	0
Hosted Joint Implementation (JI) projects	n/a
Issued Emission Reduction Units (ERUs) from JI (thousands)	n/a

Haiti

Population (millions)	10.0	GDP ($ billions)	6.7
Pop. growth (avg. ann. %, 1990–2010)	1.7	GNI per capita (Atlas $)	650

Climate

Average daily min/max temperature (1961–90, Celsius)	20 / 30
Projected annual temperature change (2045–65, Celsius)	1.5 to 1.8
Average annual precipitation (1961–90, mm)	1,440
Projected annual precipitation change (2045–65, mm)	-125 to 34
Projected change in annual hot days/warm nights	13 / 23
Projected change in annual cool days/cold nights	-3 /-3

	Country data	Latin America & the Carib.	Low Income
Exposure to Impacts			
Land area below 5m (% of land area)	3.9	1.5	0.7
Population below 5m (% of total)	5.4	3.8	5.1
Population in urban agglomerations > 1 million (%)	21	35	11
Urban pop. growth (avg. annual %, 1990–2010)	4.5	2.0	3.7
Droughts, floods, extreme temps (% pop. avg., 1990–2009)	0.8		
Annual freshwater withdrawals (% of internal resources)	9.2	2.0	3.7
Agricultural land under irrigation (% of total ag. land)	..	..	..
Population living below $1.25 a day (% of total)	54.9	8.1	..
Nationally terrestrial protected areas (% of total land area)	0.3	20.8	10.6
Under-five mortality rate (per 1,000)	165	23	108
Child malnutrition, underweight (% of under age five)	18.9	3.8	28.3
Malaria incidence rate (per 100,000 people)	1,891	206	16,659
Resilience			
Access to improved sanitation (% of total pop.)	17	79	35
Access to improved water source (% of total pop.)	63	93	63
Cereal yield (kg. per hectare)	991	3,337	2,047
Access to electricity (% of total population)	38.5	93.4	23.0
Paved roads (% of total roads)	24.3	28.1	14.1
Health workers (per 1,000 people)	..	6.9	0.7
Foreign direct investment, net inflows (% of GDP)	2.2	2.3	3.2
Invest. in infrastructure w/private participation ($ millions)	1	33,064	4,471
Disaster risk reduction progress score (1–5 scale; 5 = best)	..		
Ease of doing business (ranking 1-183; 1 = best)	174		
Public sector mgmt & institutions avg. (1–6 scale; 6 = best)	2.5		
Primary completion rate, total (% of relevant age group)	..	102	65
Ratio of girls to boys in primary & secondary school (%)	..	102	91
GHG Emissions and Energy Use			
CO_2 emissions per capita (metric tons)	0.3	2.8	0.3
CO_2 emissions per units of GDP (kg/$1,000 of 2005 PPP $)	238.9	285.6	270.2
CO_2 emissions, total (MtCO_2)	2.4	1,584	219
GHG net emissions/removals by LUCF (1994, MtCO_2e)	1.0		
Methane (CH_4) emissions, total (MtCO_2e)	4.0	1,009	436
Nitrous oxide (N_2O) emissions, total (MtCO_2e)	1.4	442	209
Other GHG emissions, total (MtCO_2e)	0.0	21	..
Energy use per capita (kilograms of oil equivalent)	263	1,245	365
Energy use per units of GDP (kg oil eq./$1,000 of 2005 PPP $)	247.5	130.6	303.9

National-Level Actions

Latest UNFCCC national communication	1/3/2002 (1st)
Annex-I emissions reduction target	n/a
NAMA submission	..
NAPA submission	Yes
Renewable energy target	..

Carbon Markets

Hosted Clean Development Mechanism (CDM) projects	..
Issued Certified Emission Reductions (CERs) from CDM (thousands)	..
Hosted Joint Implementation (JI) projects	n/a
Issued Emission Reduction Units (ERUs) from JI (thousands)	n/a

Honduras

Population (millions)	7.6	GDP ($ billions)	15.4
Pop. growth (avg. ann. %, 1990–2010)	2.2	GNI per capita (Atlas $)	1,880

Climate

Average daily min/max temperature (1961–90, Celsius)	19 / 28
Projected annual temperature change (2045–65, Celsius)	1.6 to 2.6
Average annual precipitation (1961–90, mm)	1,976
Projected annual precipitation change (2045–65, mm)	-204 to 15
Projected change in annual hot days/warm nights	10 / 25
Projected change in annual cool days/cold nights	-2 / -2

	Country data	Latin America & the Carib.	Lower middle income
Exposure to Impacts			
Land area below 5m (% of land area)	3.0	1.5	1.7
Population below 5m (% of total)	2.2	3.8	6.5
Population in urban agglomerations > 1 million (%)	14	35	14
Urban pop. growth (avg. annual %, 1990–2010)	3.2	2.0	2.8
Droughts, floods, extreme temps (% pop. avg., 1990–2009)	1.3		
Annual freshwater withdrawals (% of internal resources)	1.2	2.0	18.7
Agricultural land under irrigation (% of total ag. land)	..	..	..
Population living below $1.25 a day (% of total)	23.3	8.1	..
Nationally terrestrial protected areas (% of total land area)	18.2	20.8	9.5
Under-five mortality rate (per 1,000)	24	23	69
Child malnutrition, underweight (% of under age five)	8.6	3.8	31.7
Malaria incidence rate (per 100,000 people)	335	206	4,874
Resilience			
Access to improved sanitation (% of total pop.)	71	79	45
Access to improved water source (% of total pop.)	86	93	84
Cereal yield (kg. per hectare)	1,752	3,337	2,754
Access to electricity (% of total population)	70.3	93.4	67.3
Paved roads (% of total roads)	20.4	28.1	29.3
Health workers (per 1,000 people)	1.9	6.9	2.6
Foreign direct investment, net inflows (% of GDP)	5.2	2.3	2.4
Invest. in infrastructure w/private participation ($ millions)	321	33,064	81,789
Disaster risk reduction progress score (1–5 scale; 5 = best)	3.8		
Ease of doing business (ranking 1–183; 1 = best)	128		
Public sector mgmt & institutions avg. (1–6 scale; 6 = best)	3.3		
Primary completion rate, total (% of relevant age group)	90	102	88
Ratio of girls to boys in primary & secondary school (%)	107	102	93
GHG Emissions and Energy Use			
CO_2 emissions per capita (metric tons)	1.2	2.8	1.6
CO_2 emissions per units of GDP (kg/$1,000 of 2005 PPP $)	326.6	285.6	523.9
CO_2 emissions, total (MtCO_2)	8.7	1,584	3,744
GHG net emissions/removals by LUCF (1995, MtCO_2e)	4.6		
Methane (CH_4) emissions, total (MtCO_2e)	5.2	1,009	1,705
Nitrous oxide (N_2O) emissions, total (MtCO_2e)	2.9	442	687
Other GHG emissions, total (MtCO_2e)	0.0	21	17
Energy use per capita (kilograms of oil equivalent)	592	1,245	680
Energy use per units of GDP (kg oil eq./$1,000 of 2005 PPP $)	169.2	130.6	217.9

National-Level Actions

Latest UNFCCC national communication	11/15/2000 (1st)
Annex-I emissions reduction target	n/a
NAMA submission	..
NAPA submission	n/a
Renewable energy target	..

Carbon Markets

Hosted Clean Development Mechanism (CDM) projects	19
Issued Certified Emission Reductions (CERs) from CDM (thousands)	568
Hosted Joint Implementation (JI) projects	n/a
Issued Emission Reduction Units (ERUs) from JI (thousands)	n/a

Hong Kong SAR, China

Population (millions)	7.1	GDP ($ billions)	224.5
Pop. growth (avg. ann. %, 1990–2010)	1.1	GNI per capita (Atlas $)	32,780

Climate

Average daily min/max temperature (1961-90, Celsius)	19 / 26
Projected annual temperature change (2045-65, Celsius)	1.4 to 1.9
Average annual precipitation (1961-90, mm)	2,240
Projected annual precipitation change (2045-65, mm)	-83 to 73
Projected change in annual hot days/warm nights	7 / 10
Projected change in annual cool days/cold nights	-1 / -1

	Country data	High income
Exposure to Impacts		
Land area below 5m (% of land area)	24.6	2.2
Population below 5m (% of total)	26.2	7.7
Population in urban agglomerations > 1 million (%)	100	..
Urban pop. growth (avg. annual %, 1990-2010)	1.1	1.0
Droughts, floods, extreme temps (% pop. avg., 1990-2009)	0.0	
Annual freshwater withdrawals (% of internal resources)	..	10.4
Agricultural land under irrigation (% of total ag. land)	..	..
Population living below $1.25 a day (% of total)	..	..
Nationally terrestrial protected areas (% of total land area)	41.8	13.4
Under-five mortality rate (per 1,000)	..	6
Child malnutrition, underweight (% of under age five)	..	..
Malaria incidence rate (per 100,000 people)	..	..
Resilience		
Access to improved sanitation (% of total pop.)	..	100
Access to improved water source (% of total pop.)	..	100
Cereal yield (kg. per hectare)	..	5,445
Access to electricity (% of total population)	..	
Paved roads (% of total roads)	100.0	87.3
Health workers (per 1,000 people)	..	10.7
Foreign direct investment, net inflows (% of GDP)	30.7	1.8
Invest. in infrastructure w/private participation ($ millions)	..	..
Disaster risk reduction progress score (1-5 scale; 5 = best)	..	
Ease of doing business (ranking 1-183; 1 = best)	2	
Public sector mgmt & institutions avg. (1-6 scale; 6 = best)	..	
Primary completion rate, total (% of relevant age group)	93	97
Ratio of girls to boys in primary & secondary school (%)	102	100
GHG Emissions and Energy Use		
CO_2 emissions per capita (metric tons)	5.5	11.9
CO_2 emissions per units of GDP (kg/$1,000 of 2005 PPP $)	136.2	354.4
CO_2 emissions, total (MtCO_2)	38.6	13,285
GHG net emissions/removals by LUCF (MtCO_2e)	..	
Methane (CH_4) emissions, total (MtCO_2e)	2.8	1,539
Nitrous oxide (N_2O) emissions, total (MtCO_2e)	0.4	813
Other GHG emissions, total (MtCO_2e)	0.1	460
Energy use per capita (kilograms of oil equivalent)	2,133	4,944
Energy use per units of GDP (kg oil eq./$1,000 of 2005 PPP $)	54.2	147.0
National-Level Actions		
Latest UNFCCC national communication		n/a
Annex-I emissions reduction target		n/a
NAMA submission		n/a
NAPA submission		n/a
Renewable energy target		..
Carbon Markets		
Hosted Clean Development Mechanism (CDM) projects		n/a
Issued Certified Emission Reductions (CERs) from CDM (thousands)		n/a
Hosted Joint Implementation (JI) projects		n/a
Issued Emission Reduction Units (ERUs) from JI (thousands)		n/a

Hungary

Population (millions)	10.0	GDP ($ billions)	130.4
Pop. growth (avg. ann. %, 1990-2010)	-0.2	GNI per capita (Atlas $)	12,980

Climate

Average daily min/max temperature (1961-90, Celsius)	5 / 15
Projected annual temperature change (2045-65, Celsius)	2.0 to 3.0
Average annual precipitation (1961-90, mm)	589
Projected annual precipitation change (2045-65, mm)	-75 to 23
Projected change in annual hot days/warm nights	3 / 5
Projected change in annual cool days/cold nights	-1 / -2

	Country data	High income
Exposure to Impacts		
Land area below 5m (% of land area)	0.0	2.2
Population below 5m (% of total)	0.0	7.7
Population in urban agglomerations > 1 million (%)	17	..
Urban pop. growth (avg. annual %, 1990-2010)	0.0	1.0
Droughts, floods, extreme temps (% pop. avg., 1990-2009)	0.1	
Annual freshwater withdrawals (% of internal resources)	89.6	10.4
Agricultural land under irrigation (% of total ag. land)	1.8	..
Population living below $1.25 a day (% of total)	<2	..
Nationally terrestrial protected areas (% of total land area)	5.1	13.4
Under-five mortality rate (per 1,000)	6	6
Child malnutrition, underweight (% of under age five)	..	..
Malaria incidence rate (per 100,000 people)	..	..
Resilience		
Access to improved sanitation (% of total pop.)	100	100
Access to improved water source (% of total pop.)	100	100
Cereal yield (kg. per hectare)	4,712	5,445
Access to electricity (% of total population)	..	..
Paved roads (% of total roads)	37.7	87.3
Health workers (per 1,000 people)	9.4	10.7
Foreign direct investment, net inflows (% of GDP)	-32.2	1.8
Invest. in infrastructure w/private participation ($ millions)	2,645	..
Disaster risk reduction progress score (1-5 scale; 5 = best)	..	
Ease of doing business (ranking 1-183; 1 = best)	51	
Public sector mgmt & institutions avg. (1-6 scale; 6 = best)	..	
Primary completion rate, total (% of relevant age group)	95	97
Ratio of girls to boys in primary & secondary school (%)	99	100
GHG Emissions and Energy Use		
CO_2 emissions per capita (metric tons)	5.4	11.9
CO_2 emissions per units of GDP (kg/$1,000 of 2005 PPP $)	312.1	354.4
CO_2 emissions, total (MtCO_2)	54.6	13,285
GHG net emissions/removals by LUCF (2009, MtCO_2e)	-3.0	
Methane (CH_4) emissions, total (MtCO_2e)	7.8	1,539
Nitrous oxide (N_2O) emissions, total (MtCO_2e)	7.0	813
Other GHG emissions, total (MtCO_2e)	1.6	460
Energy use per capita (kilograms of oil equivalent)	2,542	4,944
Energy use per units of GDP (kg oil eq./$1,000 of 2005 PPP $)	153.9	147.0

National-Level Actions

Latest UNFCCC national communication	12/10/2009 (5th)
Annex-I emissions reduction target (base year: 1990)	20% / 30% (EU)
NAMA submission	n/a
NAPA submission	n/a
Renewable energy target	Yes

Carbon Markets

Hosted Clean Development Mechanism (CDM) projects	n/a
Issued Certified Emission Reductions (CERs) from CDM (thousands)	n/a
Hosted Joint Implementation (JI) projects	11
Issued Emission Reduction Units (ERUs) from JI (thousands)	1,321

Iceland

Population (thousands)	317.4	GDP ($ billions)	12.6
Pop. growth (avg. ann. %, 1990–2010)	1.1	GNI per capita (Atlas $)	33,990

Climate

Average daily min/max temperature (1961–90, Celsius)	–1 / 5
Projected annual temperature change (2045–65, Celsius)	0.9 to 2.3
Average annual precipitation (1961–90, mm)	978
Projected annual precipitation change (2045–65, mm)	–1 to 101
Projected change in annual hot days/warm nights	3 / 6
Projected change in annual cool days/cold nights	–1 / –1

	Country data	High income
Exposure to Impacts		
Land area below 5m (% of land area)	4.4	2.2
Population below 5m (% of total)	13.1	7.7
Population in urban agglomerations > 1 million (%)	..	..
Urban pop. growth (avg. annual %, 1990–2010)	1.2	1.0
Droughts, floods, extreme temps (% pop. avg., 1990–2009)	..	
Annual freshwater withdrawals (% of internal resources)	0.1	10.4
Agricultural land under irrigation (% of total ag. land)	..	..
Population living below $1.25 a day (% of total)	..	..
Nationally terrestrial protected areas (% of total land area)	9.7	13.4
Under-five mortality rate (per 1,000)	2	6
Child malnutrition, underweight (% of under age five)	..	..
Malaria incidence rate (per 100,000 people)	..	..
Resilience		
Access to improved sanitation (% of total pop.)	100	100
Access to improved water source (% of total pop.)	100	100
Cereal yield (kg. per hectare)	..	5,445
Access to electricity (% of total population)	..	..
Paved roads (% of total roads)	36.6	87.3
Health workers (per 1,000 people)	20.4	10.7
Foreign direct investment, net inflows (% of GDP)	23.4	1.8
Invest. in infrastructure w/private participation ($ millions)	..	..
Disaster risk reduction progress score (1–5 scale; 5 = best)	..	
Ease of doing business (ranking 1–183; 1 = best)	9	
Public sector mgmt & institutions avg. (1–6 scale; 6 = best)	..	
Primary completion rate, total (% of relevant age group)	98	97
Ratio of girls to boys in primary & secondary school (%)	102	100
GHG Emissions and Energy Use		
CO_2 emissions per capita (metric tons)	7.0	11.9
CO_2 emissions per units of GDP (kg/$1,000 of 2005 PPP $)	191.5	354.4
CO_2 emissions, total (MtCO_2)	2.2	13,285
GHG net emissions/removals by LUCF (2009, MtCO_2e)	0.7	
Methane (CH_4) emissions, total (MtCO_2e)	0.4	1,539
Nitrous oxide (N_2O) emissions, total (MtCO_2e)	0.4	813
Other GHG emissions, total (MtCO_2e)	0.2	460
Energy use per capita (kilograms of oil equivalent)	16,876	4,944
Energy use per units of GDP (kg oil eq./$1,000 of 2005 PPP $)	512.0	147.0

National-Level Actions

Latest UNFCCC national communication	3/12/2010 (5th)
Annex-I emissions reduction target (base year: 1990)	30%
NAMA submission	n/a
NAPA submission	n/a
Renewable energy target	..

Carbon Markets

Hosted Clean Development Mechanism (CDM) projects	n/a
Issued Certified Emission Reductions (CERs) from CDM (thousands)	n/a
Hosted Joint Implementation (JI) projects	..
Issued Emission Reduction Units (ERUs) from JI (thousands)	..

India

Population (millions)	1,170.9	GDP ($ billions)	1,729.0
Pop. growth (avg. ann. %, 1990-2010)	1.6	GNI per capita (Atlas $)	1,340

Climate

Average daily min/max temperature (1961-90, Celsius)	18 / 30
Projected annual temperature change (2045-65, Celsius)	1.9 to 2.6
Average annual precipitation (1961-90, mm)	1,083
Projected annual precipitation change (2045-65, mm)	-91 to 135
Projected change in annual hot days/warm nights	5 / 13
Projected change in annual cool days/cold nights	-2 / -2

	Country data	South Asia	Lower middle income
Exposure to Impacts			
Land area below 5m (% of land area)	1.4	1.5	1.7
Population below 5m (% of total)	3.8	4.4	6.5
Population in urban agglomerations > 1 million (%)	13	13	14
Urban pop. growth (avg. annual %, 1990-2010)	2.4	2.7	2.8
Droughts, floods, extreme temps (% pop. avg., 1990-2009)	4.4		
Annual freshwater withdrawals (% of internal resources)	47.8	50.6	18.7
Agricultural land under irrigation (% of total ag. land)	35.1	..	..
Population living below $1.25 a day (% of total)	41.6	40.3	..
Nationally terrestrial protected areas (% of total land area)	5.3	6.1	9.5
Under-five mortality rate (per 1,000)	63	67	69
Child malnutrition, underweight (% of under age five)	43.5	42.5	31.7
Malaria incidence rate (per 100,000 people)	1,124	1,127	4,874
Resilience			
Access to improved sanitation (% of total pop.)	31	36	45
Access to improved water source (% of total pop.)	88	87	84
Cereal yield (kg. per hectare)	2,572	2,728	2,754
Access to electricity (% of total population)	66.3	62.1	67.3
Paved roads (% of total roads)	49.3	58.9	29.3
Health workers (per 1,000 people)	1.9	1.7	2.6
Foreign direct investment, net inflows (% of GDP)	1.4	1.3	2.4
Invest. in infrastructure w/private participation ($ millions)	71,898	73,548	81,789
Disaster risk reduction progress score (1-5 scale; 5 = best)	3.3		
Ease of doing business (ranking 1-183; 1 = best)	132		
Public sector mgmt & institutions avg. (1-6 scale; 6 = best)	3.6		
Primary completion rate, total (% of relevant age group)	95	86	88
Ratio of girls to boys in primary & secondary school (%)	92	92	93
GHG Emissions and Energy Use			
CO_2 emissions per capita (metric tons)	1.5	1.3	1.6
CO_2 emissions per units of GDP (kg/$1,000 of 2005 PPP $)	549.8	504.6	523.9
CO_2 emissions, total (MtCO_2)	1,742.7	1,970	3,744
GHG net emissions/removals by LUCF (1994, MtCO_2e)	14.3		
Methane (CH_4) emissions, total (MtCO_2e)	584.0	846	1,705
Nitrous oxide (N_2O) emissions, total (MtCO_2e)	212.9	268	687
Other GHG emissions, total (MtCO_2e)	8.4	9	17
Energy use per capita (kilograms of oil equivalent)	585	532	680
Energy use per units of GDP (kg oil eq./$1,000 of 2005 PPP $)	195.4	193.5	217.9

National-Level Actions

Latest UNFCCC national communication	6/22/2004 (1st)
Annex-I emissions reduction target	n/a
NAMA submission	Yes, with Goal
NAPA submission	n/a
Renewable energy target	Yes

Carbon Markets

Hosted Clean Development Mechanism (CDM) projects	727
Issued Certified Emission Reductions (CERs) from CDM (thousands)	118,184
Hosted Joint Implementation (JI) projects	n/a
Issued Emission Reduction Units (ERUs) from JI (thousands)	n/a

Indonesia

Population (millions)	239.9	GDP ($ billions)	706.6
Pop. growth (avg. ann. %, 1990–2010)	1.3	GNI per capita (Atlas $)	2,500

Climate

Average daily min/max temperature (1961–90, Celsius)	21 / 31
Projected annual temperature change (2045–65, Celsius)	1.5 to 1.8
Average annual precipitation (1961–90, mm)	2,702
Projected annual precipitation change (2045–65, mm)	-160 to 234
Projected change in annual hot days/warm nights	17 / 27
Projected change in annual cool days/cold nights	-3 / -3

	Country data	East Asia & Pacific	Lower middle income
Exposure to Impacts			
Land area below 5m (% of land area)	5.5	2.5	1.7
Population below 5m (% of total)	11.2	10.3	6.5
Population in urban agglomerations > 1 million (%)	9	..	14
Urban pop. growth (avg. annual %, 1990–2010)	4.1	3.3	2.8
Droughts, floods, extreme temps (% pop. avg., 1990–2009)	0.2		
Annual freshwater withdrawals (% of internal resources)	5.6	10.8	18.7
Agricultural land under irrigation (% of total ag. land)	16.0	..	..
Population living below $1.25 a day (% of total)	18.7	16.8	..
Nationally terrestrial protected areas (% of total land area)	14.1	14.9	9.5
Under-five mortality rate (per 1,000)	35	24	69
Child malnutrition, underweight (% of under age five)	17.5	9.0	31.7
Malaria incidence rate (per 100,000 people)	1,645	525	4,874
Resilience			
Access to improved sanitation (% of total pop.)	52	59	45
Access to improved water source (% of total pop.)	80	88	84
Cereal yield (kg. per hectare)	4,813	4,860	2,754
Access to electricity (% of total population)	64.5	90.8	67.3
Paved roads (% of total roads)	59.1	15.9	29.3
Health workers (per 1,000 people)	2.3	2.8	2.6
Foreign direct investment, net inflows (% of GDP)	1.9	3.0	2.4
Invest. in infrastructure w/private participation ($ millions)	3,408	14,638	81,789
Disaster risk reduction progress score (1–5 scale; 5 = best)	3.3		
Ease of doing business (ranking 1–183; 1 = best)	129		
Public sector mgmt & institutions avg. (1–6 scale; 6 = best)	3.2		
Primary completion rate, total (% of relevant age group)	109	97	88
Ratio of girls to boys in primary & secondary school (%)	98	103	93
GHG Emissions and Energy Use			
CO_2 emissions per capita (metric tons)	1.7	4.3	1.6
CO_2 emissions per units of GDP (kg/$1,000 of 2005 PPP $)	484.1	827.1	523.9
CO_2 emissions, total (MtCO_2)	406.0	8,259	3,744
GHG net emissions/removals by LUCF (1994, MtCO_2e)	164.1		
Methane (CH_4) emissions, total (MtCO_2e)	208.9	1,928	1,705
Nitrous oxide (N_2O) emissions, total (MtCO_2e)	123.3	707	687
Other GHG emissions, total (MtCO_2e)	1.0	..	17
Energy use per capita (kilograms of oil equivalent)	851	1,436	680
Energy use per units of GDP (kg oil eq./$1,000 of 2005 PPP $)	230.3	259.5	217.9

National-Level Actions

Latest UNFCCC national communication	10/27/1999 (1st)
Annex-I emissions reduction target	n/a
NAMA submission	Yes, with Goal
NAPA submission	n/a
Renewable energy target	Yes

Carbon Markets

Hosted Clean Development Mechanism (CDM) projects	70
Issued Certified Emission Reductions (CERs) from CDM (thousands)	3,007
Hosted Joint Implementation (JI) projects	n/a
Issued Emission Reduction Units (ERUs) from JI (thousands)	n/a

Iran, Islamic Rep.

Population (millions)	74.0	GDP ($ billions)	331.0
Pop. growth (avg. ann. %, 1990–2010)	1.5	GNI per capita (Atlas $)	4,520

Climate

Average daily min/max temperature (1961-90, Celsius)	10 / 24
Projected annual temperature change (2045-65, Celsius)	2.2 to 3.3
Average annual precipitation (1961-90, mm)	228
Projected annual precipitation change (2045-65, mm)	-51 to 6
Projected change in annual hot days/warm nights	3 / 7
Projected change in annual cool days/cold nights	-1 / -1

	Country data	Middle East & N. Africa	Upper middle income
Exposure to Impacts			
Land area below 5m (% of land area)	1.6	1.4	1.8
Population below 5m (% of total)	5.0	9.7	6.5
Population in urban agglomerations > 1 million (%)	24	20	22
Urban pop. growth (avg. annual %, 1990-2010)	2.5	2.5	2.3
Droughts, floods, extreme temps (% pop. avg., 1990-2009)	3.1		
Annual freshwater withdrawals (% of internal resources)	72.5	121.9	5.6
Agricultural land under irrigation (% of total ag. land)	19.0	..	..
Population living below $1.25 a day (% of total)	<2	3.6	..
Nationally terrestrial protected areas (% of total land area)	7.1	4.0	13.6
Under-five mortality rate (per 1,000)	26	34	20
Child malnutrition, underweight (% of under age five)	..	6.8	4.1
Malaria incidence rate (per 100,000 people)	18	..	80
Resilience			
Access to improved sanitation (% of total pop.)	83	84	68
Access to improved water source (% of total pop.)	93	87	92
Cereal yield (kg. per hectare)	2,289	2,512	3,690
Access to electricity (% of total population)	98.4	92.9	98.0
Paved roads (% of total roads)	73.3	74.3	50.5
Health workers (per 1,000 people)	2.5	3.6	4.5
Foreign direct investment, net inflows (% of GDP)	0.9	2.9	2.7
Invest. in infrastructure w/private participation ($ millions)	486	5,854	26,166
Disaster risk reduction progress score (1-5 scale; 5 = best)	..		
Ease of doing business (ranking 1-183; 1 = best)	144		
Public sector mgmt & institutions avg. (1-6 scale; 6 = best)	..		
Primary completion rate, total (% of relevant age group)	101	88	98
Ratio of girls to boys in primary & secondary school (%)	97	93	103
GHG Emissions and Energy Use			
CO_2 emissions per capita (metric tons)	7.4	3.8	5.3
CO_2 emissions per units of GDP (kg/$1,000 of 2005 PPP $)	716.3	604.6	659.4
CO_2 emissions, total (MtCO$_2$)	538.4	1,230	12,860
GHG net emissions/removals by LUCF (1994, MtCO$_2$e)	31.6		
Methane (CH_4) emissions, total (MtCO$_2$e)	114.6	287	3,455
Nitrous oxide (N_2O) emissions, total (MtCO$_2$e)	26.6	74	1,144
Other GHG emissions, total (MtCO$_2$e)	2.6	7	243
Energy use per capita (kilograms of oil equivalent)	2,951	1,399	1,848
Energy use per units of GDP (kg oil eq./$1,000 of 2005 PPP $)	282.1	213.9	227.1

National-Level Actions

Latest UNFCCC national communication	3/31/2003 (1st)
Annex-I emissions reduction target	n/a
NAMA submission	..
NAPA submission	n/a
Renewable energy target	..

Carbon Markets

Hosted Clean Development Mechanism (CDM) projects	7
Issued Certified Emission Reductions (CERs) from CDM (thousands)	0
Hosted Joint Implementation (JI) projects	n/a
Issued Emission Reduction Units (ERUs) from JI (thousands)	n/a

Iraq

Population (millions)	32.0	GDP ($ billions)	82.2
Pop. growth (avg. ann. %, 1990–2010)	2.8	GNI per capita (Atlas $)	2,340

Climate

Average daily min/max temperature (1961–90, Celsius)	14 / 29
Projected annual temperature change (2045–65, Celsius)	2.3 to 3.2
Average annual precipitation (1961–90, mm)	216
Projected annual precipitation change (2045–65, mm)	-38 to -2
Projected change in annual hot days/warm nights	3 / 7
Projected change in annual cool days/cold nights	-2 / -1

	Country data	Middle East & N. Africa	Lower middle income
Exposure to Impacts			
Land area below 5m (% of land area)	4.0	1.4	1.7
Population below 5m (% of total)	6.5	9.7	6.5
Population in urban agglomerations > 1 million (%)	23	20	14
Urban pop. growth (avg. annual %, 1990–2010)	2.6	2.5	2.8
Droughts, floods, extreme temps (% pop. avg., 1990–2009)	0.0		
Annual freshwater withdrawals (% of internal resources)	187.5	121.9	18.7
Agricultural land under irrigation (% of total ag. land)	..	..	..
Population living below $1.25 a day (% of total)	4.0	3.6	..
Nationally terrestrial protected areas (% of total land area)	0.1	4.0	9.5
Under-five mortality rate (per 1,000)	39	34	69
Child malnutrition, underweight (% of under age five)	7.1	6.8	31.7
Malaria incidence rate (per 100,000 people)	0	..	4,874
Resilience			
Access to improved sanitation (% of total pop.)	73	84	45
Access to improved water source (% of total pop.)	79	87	84
Cereal yield (kg. per hectare)	1,222	2,512	2,754
Access to electricity (% of total population)	86.0	92.9	67.3
Paved roads (% of total roads)	84.3	74.3	29.3
Health workers (per 1,000 people)	2.1	3.6	2.6
Foreign direct investment, net inflows (% of GDP)	1.7	2.9	2.4
Invest. in infrastructure w/private participation ($ millions)	956	5,854	81,789
Disaster risk reduction progress score (1–5 scale; 5 = best)	..		
Ease of doing business (ranking 1–183; 1 = best)	164		
Public sector mgmt & institutions avg. (1–6 scale; 6 = best)	..		
Primary completion rate, total (% of relevant age group)	64	88	88
Ratio of girls to boys in primary & secondary school (%)	81	93	93
GHG Emissions and Energy Use			
CO_2 emissions per capita (metric tons)	3.4	3.8	1.6
CO_2 emissions per units of GDP (kg/$1,000 of 2005 PPP $)	1,057.0	604.6	523.9
CO_2 emissions, total (MtCO$_2$)	102.9	1,230	3,744
GHG net emissions/removals by LUCF (MtCO$_2$e)	..		
Methane (CH$_4$) emissions, total (MtCO$_2$e)	15.9	287	1,705
Nitrous oxide (N$_2$O) emissions, total (MtCO$_2$e)	3.4	74	687
Other GHG emissions, total (MtCO$_2$e)	0.1	7	17
Energy use per capita (kilograms of oil equivalent)	1,035	1,399	680
Energy use per units of GDP (kg oil eq./$1,000 of 2005 PPP $)	317.1	213.9	217.9

National-Level Actions

Latest UNFCCC national communication	..
Annex-I emissions reduction target	n/a
NAMA submission	..
NAPA submission	n/a
Renewable energy target	..

Carbon Markets

Hosted Clean Development Mechanism (CDM) projects	..
Issued Certified Emission Reductions (CERs) from CDM (thousands)	..
Hosted Joint Implementation (JI) projects	n/a
Issued Emission Reduction Units (ERUs) from JI (thousands)	n/a

Ireland

Population (millions)	4.5	GDP ($ billions)	203.9
Pop. growth (avg. ann. %, 1990-2010)	1.2	GNI per capita (Atlas $)	40,720

Climate

Average daily min/max temperature (1961-90, Celsius)	6 / 13
Projected annual temperature change (2045-65, Celsius)	0.9 to 1.4
Average annual precipitation (1961-90, mm)	1,118
Projected annual precipitation change (2045-65, mm)	-13 to 78
Projected change in annual hot days/warm nights	3 / 6
Projected change in annual cool days/cold nights	-1 / -1

	Country data	High income
Exposure to Impacts		
Land area below 5m (% of land area)	4.0	2.2
Population below 5m (% of total)	6.6	7.7
Population in urban agglomerations > 1 million (%)	25	..
Urban pop. growth (avg. annual %, 1990-2010)	1.6	1.0
Droughts, floods, extreme temps (% pop. avg., 1990-2009)	0.0	
Annual freshwater withdrawals (% of internal resources)	..	10.4
Agricultural land under irrigation (% of total ag. land)	..	..
Population living below $1.25 a day (% of total)	..	..
Nationally terrestrial protected areas (% of total land area)	1.0	13.4
Under-five mortality rate (per 1,000)	4	6
Child malnutrition, underweight (% of under age five)	..	..
Malaria incidence rate (per 100,000 people)	..	..
Resilience		
Access to improved sanitation (% of total pop.)	99	100
Access to improved water source (% of total pop.)	100	100
Cereal yield (kg. per hectare)	6,798	5,445
Access to electricity (% of total population)	..	
Paved roads (% of total roads)	100.0	87.3
Health workers (per 1,000 people)	15.7	10.7
Foreign direct investment, net inflows (% of GDP)	13.3	1.8
Invest. in infrastructure w/private participation ($ millions)	..	..
Disaster risk reduction progress score (1-5 scale; 5 = best)	..	
Ease of doing business (ranking 1-183; 1 = best)	10	
Public sector mgmt & institutions avg. (1-6 scale; 6 = best)	..	
Primary completion rate, total (% of relevant age group)	97	97
Ratio of girls to boys in primary & secondary school (%)	103	100
GHG Emissions and Energy Use		
CO_2 emissions per capita (metric tons)	9.9	11.9
CO_2 emissions per units of GDP (kg/$1,000 of 2005 PPP $)	252.9	354.4
CO_2 emissions, total (MtCO$_2$)	43.6	13,285
GHG net emissions/removals by LUCF (2009, MtCO$_2$e)	-2.2	
Methane (CH$_4$) emissions, total (MtCO$_2$e)	15.3	1,539
Nitrous oxide (N$_2$O) emissions, total (MtCO$_2$e)	7.5	813
Other GHG emissions, total (MtCO$_2$e)	1.2	460
Energy use per capita (kilograms of oil equivalent)	3,333	4,944
Energy use per units of GDP (kg oil eq./$1,000 of 2005 PPP $)	94.7	147.0

National-Level Actions

Latest UNFCCC national communication	3/3/2010 (5th)
Annex-I emissions reduction target (base year: 1990)	20% / 30% (EU)
NAMA submission	n/a
NAPA submission	n/a
Renewable energy target	Yes

Carbon Markets

Hosted Clean Development Mechanism (CDM) projects	n/a
Issued Certified Emission Reductions (CERs) from CDM (thousands)	n/a
Hosted Joint Implementation (JI) projects	..
Issued Emission Reduction Units (ERUs) from JI (thousands)	..

Isle of Man

Population (thousands)	82.9	GDP ($ billions)	4.1
Pop. growth (avg. ann. %, 1990–2010)	0.8	GNI per capita (Atlas $)	48,910

Climate

Average daily min/max temperature (1961–90, Celsius)	..
Projected annual temperature change (2045–65, Celsius)	1.3 to 1.8
Average annual precipitation (1961–90, mm)	..
Projected annual precipitation change (2045–65, mm)	-13 to 56
Projected change in annual hot days/warm nights	3 / 5
Projected change in annual cool days/cold nights	-1 / -1

	Country data	High income
Exposure to Impacts		
Land area below 5m (% of land area)	12.1	2.2
Population below 5m (% of total)	27.8	7.7
Population in urban agglomerations > 1 million (%)	..	..
Urban pop. growth (avg. annual %, 1990–2010)	0.7	1.0
Droughts, floods, extreme temps (% pop. avg., 1990–2009)	..	
Annual freshwater withdrawals (% of internal resources)	..	10.4
Agricultural land under irrigation (% of total ag. land)	..	..
Population living below $1.25 a day (% of total)	..	..
Nationally terrestrial protected areas (% of total land area)	..	13.4
Under-five mortality rate (per 1,000)	..	6
Child malnutrition, underweight (% of under age five)	..	
Malaria incidence rate (per 100,000 people)	..	..
Resilience		
Access to improved sanitation (% of total pop.)	..	100
Access to improved water source (% of total pop.)	..	100
Cereal yield (kg. per hectare)	..	5,445
Access to electricity (% of total population)	..	
Paved roads (% of total roads)	..	87.3
Health workers (per 1,000 people)	..	10.7
Foreign direct investment, net inflows (% of GDP)	..	1.8
Invest. in infrastructure w/private participation ($ millions)	..	..
Disaster risk reduction progress score (1–5 scale; 5 = best)	..	
Ease of doing business (ranking 1–183; 1 = best)	..	
Public sector mgmt & institutions avg. (1–6 scale; 6 = best)	..	
Primary completion rate, total (% of relevant age group)	..	97
Ratio of girls to boys in primary & secondary school (%)	..	100
GHG Emissions and Energy Use		
CO_2 emissions per capita (metric tons)	..	11.9
CO_2 emissions per units of GDP (kg/$1,000 of 2005 PPP $)	..	354.4
CO_2 emissions, total (MtCO_2)	..	13,285
GHG net emissions/removals by LUCF (MtCO_2e)	..	
Methane (CH_4) emissions, total (MtCO_2e)	..	1,539
Nitrous oxide (N_2O) emissions, total (MtCO_2e)	..	813
Other GHG emissions, total (MtCO_2e)	..	460
Energy use per capita (kilograms of oil equivalent)	..	4,944
Energy use per units of GDP (kg oil eq./$1,000 of 2005 PPP $)	..	147.0
National-Level Actions		
Latest UNFCCC national communication		n/a
Annex-I emissions reduction target		n/a
NAMA submission		n/a
NAPA submission		n/a
Renewable energy target		..
Carbon Markets		
Hosted Clean Development Mechanism (CDM) projects		n/a
Issued Certified Emission Reductions (CERs) from CDM (thousands)		n/a
Hosted Joint Implementation (JI) projects		n/a
Issued Emission Reduction Units (ERUs) from JI (thousands)		n/a

Israel

| Population (millions) | 7.6 | GDP ($ billions) | 217.3 |
| Pop. growth (avg. ann. %, 1990–2010) | 2.5 | GNI per capita (Atlas $) | 27,170 |

Climate
Average daily min/max temperature (1961–90, Celsius)	13 / 25
Projected annual temperature change (2045–65, Celsius)	1.9 to 2.7
Average annual precipitation (1961–90, mm)	435
Projected annual precipitation change (2045–65, mm)	–41 to –11
Projected change in annual hot days/warm nights	4 / 8
Projected change in annual cool days/cold nights	–2 / –2

	Country data	High income
Exposure to Impacts		
Land area below 5m (% of land area)	7.8	2.2
Population below 5m (% of total)	8.3	7.7
Population in urban agglomerations > 1 million (%)	57	..
Urban pop. growth (avg. annual %, 1990–2010)	2.5	1.0
Droughts, floods, extreme temps (% pop. avg., 1990–2009)	0.0	
Annual freshwater withdrawals (% of internal resources)	241.9	10.4
Agricultural land under irrigation (% of total ag. land)	28.4	..
Population living below $1.25 a day (% of total)	..	..
Nationally terrestrial protected areas (% of total land area)	18.7	13.4
Under-five mortality rate (per 1,000)	5	6
Child malnutrition, underweight (% of under age five)	..	
Malaria incidence rate (per 100,000 people)	..	..
Resilience		
Access to improved sanitation (% of total pop.)	100	100
Access to improved water source (% of total pop.)	100	100
Cereal yield (kg. per hectare)	3,182	5,445
Access to electricity (% of total population)	99.7	..
Paved roads (% of total roads)	100.0	87.3
Health workers (per 1,000 people)	9.8	10.7
Foreign direct investment, net inflows (% of GDP)	2.4	1.8
Invest. in infrastructure w/private participation ($ millions)	..	..
Disaster risk reduction progress score (1–5 scale; 5 = best)	..	
Ease of doing business (ranking 1–183; 1 = best)	34	
Public sector mgmt & institutions avg. (1–6 scale; 6 = best)	..	
Primary completion rate, total (% of relevant age group)	102	97
Ratio of girls to boys in primary & secondary school (%)	102	100
GHG Emissions and Energy Use		
CO_2 emissions per capita (metric tons)	5.2	11.9
CO_2 emissions per units of GDP (kg/$1,000 of 2005 PPP $)	200.2	354.4
CO_2 emissions, total (MtCO$_2$)	37.7	13,285
GHG net emissions/removals by LUCF (2007, MtCO$_2$e)	–0.4	
Methane (CH_4) emissions, total (MtCO$_2$e)	3.5	1,539
Nitrous oxide (N_2O) emissions, total (MtCO$_2$e)	1.8	813
Other GHG emissions, total (MtCO$_2$e)	2.0	460
Energy use per capita (kilograms of oil equivalent)	2,873	4,944
Energy use per units of GDP (kg oil eq./$1,000 of 2005 PPP $)	110.4	147.0

National-Level Actions
Latest UNFCCC national communication	12/7/2010 (2nd)
Annex-I emissions reduction target	n/a
NAMA submission	Yes, with Goal
NAPA submission	n/a
Renewable energy target	Yes

Carbon Markets
Hosted Clean Development Mechanism (CDM) projects	22
Issued Certified Emission Reductions (CERs) from CDM (thousands)	1,160
Hosted Joint Implementation (JI) projects	n/a
Issued Emission Reduction Units (ERUs) from JI (thousands)	n/a

Italy

Population (millions)	60.5	GDP ($ billions)	2,051.4
Pop. growth (avg. ann. %, 1990–2010)	0.3	GNI per capita (Atlas $)	35,150

Climate

Average daily min/max temperature (1961–90, Celsius)	10 / 17
Projected annual temperature change (2045–65, Celsius)	1.8 to 2.6
Average annual precipitation (1961–90, mm)	832
Projected annual precipitation change (2045–65, mm)	-108 to -11
Projected change in annual hot days/warm nights	4 / 7
Projected change in annual cool days/cold nights	-2 / -2

	Country data	High Income
Exposure to Impacts		
Land area below 5m (% of land area)	5.2	2.2
Population below 5m (% of total)	7.5	7.7
Population in urban agglomerations > 1 million (%)	17	..
Urban pop. growth (avg. annual %, 1990–2010)	0.4	1.0
Droughts, floods, extreme temps (% pop. avg., 1990–2009)	0.0	
Annual freshwater withdrawals (% of internal resources)	24.8	10.4
Agricultural land under irrigation (% of total ag. land)	18.8	..
Population living below $1.25 a day (% of total)	..	..
Nationally terrestrial protected areas (% of total land area)	9.9	13.4
Under-five mortality rate (per 1,000)	4	6
Child malnutrition, underweight (% of under age five)	..	..
Malaria incidence rate (per 100,000 people)	..	..
Resilience		
Access to improved sanitation (% of total pop.)	..	100
Access to improved water source (% of total pop.)	100	100
Cereal yield (kg. per hectare)	5,035	5,445
Access to electricity (% of total population)		
Paved roads (% of total roads)	100.0	87.3
Health workers (per 1,000 people)	6.5	10.7
Foreign direct investment, net inflows (% of GDP)	0.5	1.8
Invest. in infrastructure w/private participation ($ millions)	..	..
Disaster risk reduction progress score (1–5 scale; 5 = best)	3.5	
Ease of doing business (ranking 1–183; 1 = best)	87	
Public sector mgmt & institutions avg. (1–6 scale; 6 = best)	..	
Primary completion rate, total (% of relevant age group)	104	97
Ratio of girls to boys in primary & secondary school (%)	99	100
GHG Emissions and Energy Use		
CO_2 emissions per capita (metric tons)	7.4	11.9
CO_2 emissions per units of GDP (kg/$1,000 of 2005 PPP $)	264.1	354.4
CO_2 emissions, total (MtCO$_2$)	445.1	13,285
GHG net emissions/removals by LUCF (2009, MtCO$_2$e)	-94.7	
Methane (CH_4) emissions, total (MtCO$_2$e)	40.8	1,539
Nitrous oxide (N_2O) emissions, total (MtCO$_2$e)	28.6	813
Other GHG emissions, total (MtCO$_2$e)	14.0	460
Energy use per capita (kilograms of oil equivalent)	2,814	4,944
Energy use per units of GDP (kg oil eq./$1,000 of 2005 PPP $)	105.2	147.0

National-Level Actions

Latest UNFCCC national communication	3/17/2010 (5th)
Annex-I emissions reduction target (base year: 1990)	20% / 30% (EU)
NAMA submission	n/a
NAPA submission	n/a
Renewable energy target	Yes

Carbon Markets

Hosted Clean Development Mechanism (CDM) projects	n/a
Issued Certified Emission Reductions (CERs) from CDM (thousands)	n/a
Hosted Joint Implementation (JI) projects	..
Issued Emission Reduction Units (ERUs) from JI (thousands)	..

Jamaica

Population (millions)	2.7	GDP ($ billions)	14.0
Pop. growth (avg. ann. %, 1990-2010)	0.6	GNI per capita (Atlas $)	4,770

Climate

Average daily min/max temperature (1961-90, Celsius)	21 / 29
Projected annual temperature change (2045-65, Celsius)	1.3 to 1.8
Average annual precipitation (1961-90, mm)	2,051
Projected annual precipitation change (2045-65, mm)	-102 to 28
Projected change in annual hot days/warm nights	14 / 24
Projected change in annual cool days/cold nights	-3 / -3

	Country data	Latin America & the Carib.	Upper middle income
Exposure to Impacts			
Land area below 5m (% of land area)	7.1	1.5	1.8
Population below 5m (% of total)	5.8	3.8	6.5
Population in urban agglomerations > 1 million (%)	..	35	22
Urban pop. growth (avg. annual %, 1990-2010)	1.0	2.0	2.3
Droughts, floods, extreme temps (% pop. avg., 1990-2009)	1.1		
Annual freshwater withdrawals (% of internal resources)	6.2	2.0	5.6
Agricultural land under irrigation (% of total ag. land)	..	..	..
Population living below $1.25 a day (% of total)	<2	8.1	..
Nationally terrestrial protected areas (% of total land area)	18.9	20.8	13.6
Under-five mortality rate (per 1,000)	24	23	20
Child malnutrition, underweight (% of under age five)	2.2	3.8	4.1
Malaria incidence rate (per 100,000 people)	..	206	80
Resilience			
Access to improved sanitation (% of total pop.)	83	79	68
Access to improved water source (% of total pop.)	94	93	92
Cereal yield (kg. per hectare)	1,262	3,337	3,690
Access to electricity (% of total population)	92.0	93.4	98.0
Paved roads (% of total roads)	73.3	28.1	50.5
Health workers (per 1,000 people)	2.5	6.9	4.5
Foreign direct investment, net inflows (% of GDP)	1.6	2.3	2.7
Invest. in infrastructure w/private participation ($ millions)	170	33,064	26,166
Disaster risk reduction progress score (1-5 scale; 5 = best)	3.8		
Ease of doing business (ranking 1-183; 1 = best)	88		
Public sector mgmt & institutions avg. (1-6 scale; 6 = best)	..		
Primary completion rate, total (% of relevant age group)	89	102	98
Ratio of girls to boys in primary & secondary school (%)	100	102	103
GHG Emissions and Energy Use			
CO_2 emissions per capita (metric tons)	4.5	2.8	5.3
CO_2 emissions per units of GDP (kg/$1,000 of 2005 PPP $)	618.4	285.6	659.4
CO_2 emissions, total (MtCO_2)	12.2	1,584	12,860
GHG net emissions/removals by LUCF (1994, MtCO_2e)	-0.2		
Methane (CH_4) emissions, total (MtCO_2e)	1.3	1,009	3,455
Nitrous oxide (N_2O) emissions, total (MtCO_2e)	0.6	442	1,144
Other GHG emissions, total (MtCO_2e)	0.1	21	243
Energy use per capita (kilograms of oil equivalent)	1,208	1,245	1,848
Energy use per units of GDP (kg oil eq./$1,000 of 2005 PPP $)	169.3	130.6	227.1

National-Level Actions

Latest UNFCCC national communication	11/21/2000 (1st)
Annex-I emissions reduction target	n/a
NAMA submission	..
NAPA submission	n/a
Renewable energy target	Yes

Carbon Markets

Hosted Clean Development Mechanism (CDM) projects	1
Issued Certified Emission Reductions (CERs) from CDM (thousands)	211
Hosted Joint Implementation (JI) projects	n/a
Issued Emission Reduction Units (ERUs) from JI (thousands)	n/a

Japan

Population (millions)	127.5	GDP ($ billions)	5,497.8
Pop. growth (avg. ann. %, 1990–2010)	0.2	GNI per capita (Atlas $)	42,130

Climate

Average daily min/max temperature (1961–90, Celsius)	7 / 15
Projected annual temperature change (2045–65, Celsius)	1.8 to 2.3
Average annual precipitation (1961–90, mm)	1,668
Projected annual precipitation change (2045–65, mm)	-47 to 80
Projected change in annual hot days/warm nights	3 / 6
Projected change in annual cool days/cold nights	-2 / -2

	Country data	High income
Exposure to Impacts		
Land area below 5m (% of land area)	5.9	2.2
Population below 5m (% of total)	16.2	7.7
Population in urban agglomerations > 1 million (%)	49	..
Urban pop. growth (avg. annual %, 1990–2010)	0.4	1.0
Droughts, floods, extreme temps (% pop. avg., 1990–2009)	0.0	
Annual freshwater withdrawals (% of internal resources)	20.6	10.4
Agricultural land under irrigation (% of total ag. land)	35.2	..
Population living below $1.25 a day (% of total)	..	..
Nationally terrestrial protected areas (% of total land area)	16.3	13.4
Under-five mortality rate (per 1,000)	3	6
Child malnutrition, underweight (% of under age five)	..	..
Malaria incidence rate (per 100,000 people)	..	..
Resilience		
Access to improved sanitation (% of total pop.)	100	100
Access to improved water source (% of total pop.)	100	100
Cereal yield (kg. per hectare)	5,920	5,445
Access to electricity (% of total population)	..	
Paved roads (% of total roads)	79.6	87.3
Health workers (per 1,000 people)	6.2	10.7
Foreign direct investment, net inflows (% of GDP)	-0.0	1.8
Invest. in infrastructure w/private participation ($ millions)	..	..
Disaster risk reduction progress score (1–5 scale; 5 = best)	4.5	
Ease of doing business (ranking 1–183; 1 = best)	20	
Public sector mgmt & institutions avg. (1–6 scale; 6 = best)	..	
Primary completion rate, total (% of relevant age group)	102	97
Ratio of girls to boys in primary & secondary school (%)	100	100
GHG Emissions and Energy Use		
CO_2 emissions per capita (metric tons)	9.5	11.9
CO_2 emissions per units of GDP (kg/$1,000 of 2005 PPP $)	302.2	354.4
CO_2 emissions, total (MtCO_2)	1,208.2	13,285
GHG net emissions/removals by LUCF (2009, MtCO_2e)	-71.5	
Methane (CH_4) emissions, total (MtCO_2e)	42.8	1,539
Nitrous oxide (N_2O) emissions, total (MtCO_2e)	29.8	813
Other GHG emissions, total (MtCO_2e)	53.8	460
Energy use per capita (kilograms of oil equivalent)	3,883	4,944
Energy use per units of GDP (kg oil eq./$1,000 of 2005 PPP $)	125.7	147.0

National-Level Actions

Latest UNFCCC national communication	12/21/2009 (5th)
Annex-I emissions reduction target (base year: 1990)	25%
NAMA submission	n/a
NAPA submission	n/a
Renewable energy target	Yes

Carbon Markets

Hosted Clean Development Mechanism (CDM) projects	n/a
Issued Certified Emission Reductions (CERs) from CDM (thousands)	n/a
Hosted Joint Implementation (JI) projects	..
Issued Emission Reduction Units (ERUs) from JI (thousands)	..

Jordan

Population (millions)	6.0	GDP ($ billions) 27.6
Pop. growth (avg. ann. %, 1990–2010)	3.2	GNI per capita (Atlas $) 4,390

Climate

Average daily min/max temperature (1961-90, Celsius)	11 / 25
Projected annual temperature change (2045-65, Celsius)	2.1 to 2.9
Average annual precipitation (1961-90, mm)	111
Projected annual precipitation change (2045-65, mm)	-28 to -3
Projected change in annual hot days/warm nights	4 / 7
Projected change in annual cool days/cold nights	-1 / -2

	Country data	Middle East & N. Africa	Upper middle income
Exposure to Impacts			
Land area below 5m (% of land area)	2.0	1.4	1.8
Population below 5m (% of total)	4.2	9.7	6.5
Population in urban agglomerations > 1 million (%)	18	20	22
Urban pop. growth (avg. annual %, 1990-2010)	3.6	2.5	2.3
Droughts, floods, extreme temps (% pop. avg., 1990-2009)	0.4		
Annual freshwater withdrawals (% of internal resources)	136.5	121.9	5.6
Agricultural land under irrigation (% of total ag. land)	9.2	..	..
Population living below $1.25 a day (% of total)	<2	3.6	..
Nationally terrestrial protected areas (% of total land area)	9.4	4.0	13.6
Under-five mortality rate (per 1,000)	22	34	20
Child malnutrition, underweight (% of under age five)	1.9	6.8	4.1
Malaria incidence rate (per 100,000 people)	..	..	80
Resilience			
Access to improved sanitation (% of total pop.)	98	84	68
Access to improved water source (% of total pop.)	96	87	92
Cereal yield (kg. per hectare)	1,044	2,512	3,690
Access to electricity (% of total population)	99.9	92.9	98.0
Paved roads (% of total roads)	100.0	74.3	50.5
Health workers (per 1,000 people)	6.5	3.6	4.5
Foreign direct investment, net inflows (% of GDP)	6.2	2.9	2.7
Invest. in infrastructure w/private participation ($ millions)	301	5,854	26,166
Disaster risk reduction progress score (1-5 scale; 5 = best)	..		
Ease of doing business (ranking 1-183; 1 = best)	96		
Public sector mgmt & institutions avg. (1-6 scale; 6 = best)	..		
Primary completion rate, total (% of relevant age group)	99	88	98
Ratio of girls to boys in primary & secondary school (%)	102	93	103
GHG Emissions and Energy Use			
CO$_2$ emissions per capita (metric tons)	3.7	3.8	5.3
CO$_2$ emissions per units of GDP (kg/$1,000 of 2005 PPP $)	723.4	604.6	659.4
CO$_2$ emissions, total (MtCO$_2$)	21.4	1,230	12,860
GHG net emissions/removals by LUCF (2000, MtCO$_2$e)	0.7		
Methane (CH$_4$) emissions, total (MtCO$_2$e)	1.8	287	3,455
Nitrous oxide (N$_2$O) emissions, total (MtCO$_2$e)	0.7	74	1,144
Other GHG emissions, total (MtCO$_2$e)	0.1	7	243
Energy use per capita (kilograms of oil equivalent)	1,260	1,399	1,848
Energy use per units of GDP (kg oil eq./$1,000 of 2005 PPP $)	246.3	213.9	227.1

National-Level Actions

Latest UNFCCC national communication	11/8/2009 (2nd)
Annex-I emissions reduction target	n/a
NAMA submission	Yes
NAPA submission	n/a
Renewable energy target	Yes

Carbon Markets

Hosted Clean Development Mechanism (CDM) projects	2
Issued Certified Emission Reductions (CERs) from CDM (thousands)	986
Hosted Joint Implementation (JI) projects	n/a
Issued Emission Reduction Units (ERUs) from JI (thousands)	n/a

Kazakhstan

Population (millions)	16.3	GDP ($ billions)	143.0
Pop. growth (avg. ann. %, 1990–2010)	-0.0	GNI per capita (Atlas $)	7,440

Climate

Average daily min/max temperature (1961-90, Celsius)	1 / 12
Projected annual temperature change (2045-65, Celsius)	2.2 to 3.1
Average annual precipitation (1961-90, mm)	250
Projected annual precipitation change (2045-65, mm)	-1 to 37
Projected change in annual hot days/warm nights	2 / 5
Projected change in annual cool days/cold nights	-1 / -1

	Country data	Europe & Central Asia	Upper middle income
Exposure to Impacts			
Land area below 5m (% of land area)	6.7	2.5	1.8
Population below 5m (% of total)	3.9	3.0	6.5
Population in urban agglomerations > 1 million (%)	8	18	22
Urban pop. growth (avg. annual %, 1990-2010)	0.2	0.3	2.3
Droughts, floods, extreme temps (% pop. avg., 1990-2009)	0.2		
Annual freshwater withdrawals (% of internal resources)	42.1	6.5	5.6
Agricultural land under irrigation (% of total ag. land)	..	..	..
Population living below $1.25 a day (% of total)	<2	3.7	..
Nationally terrestrial protected areas (% of total land area)	2.5	7.5	13.6
Under-five mortality rate (per 1,000)	33	23	20
Child malnutrition, underweight (% of under age five)	4.9	..	4.1
Malaria incidence rate (per 100,000 people)	..	..	80
Resilience			
Access to improved sanitation (% of total pop.)	97	89	68
Access to improved water source (% of total pop.)	95	95	92
Cereal yield (kg. per hectare)	1,254	2,475	3,690
Access to electricity (% of total population)	..	..	98.0
Paved roads (% of total roads)	89.9	85.8	50.5
Health workers (per 1,000 people)	3.8	9.9	4.5
Foreign direct investment, net inflows (% of GDP)	7.0	2.8	2.7
Invest. in infrastructure w/private participation ($ millions)	596	22,652	26,166
Disaster risk reduction progress score (1-5 scale; 5 = best)	..		
Ease of doing business (ranking 1-183; 1 = best)	47		
Public sector mgmt & institutions avg. (1-6 scale; 6 = best)	..		
Primary completion rate, total (% of relevant age group)	108	95	98
Ratio of girls to boys in primary & secondary school (%)	99	97	103
GHG Emissions and Energy Use			
CO_2 emissions per capita (metric tons)	15.1	7.7	5.3
CO_2 emissions per units of GDP (kg/$1,000 of 2005 PPP $)	1,444.1	708.0	659.4
CO_2 emissions, total (MtCO_2)	237.0	3,110	12,860
GHG net emissions/removals by LUCF (MtCO_2e)	..		
Methane (CH_4) emissions, total (MtCO_2e)	47.1	937	3,455
Nitrous oxide (N_2O) emissions, total (MtCO_2e)	17.6	214	1,144
Other GHG emissions, total (MtCO_2e)	0.3	76	243
Energy use per capita (kilograms of oil equivalent)	4,134	2,833	1,848
Energy use per units of GDP (kg oil eq./$1,000 of 2005 PPP $)	396.5	276.8	227.1

National-Level Actions

Latest UNFCCC national communication	6/4/2009 (2nd)
Annex-I emissions reduction target (base year: 1992)	15%
NAMA submission	..
NAPA submission	n/a
Renewable energy target	..

Carbon Markets

Hosted Clean Development Mechanism (CDM) projects	..
Issued Certified Emission Reductions (CERs) from CDM (thousands)	..
Hosted Joint Implementation (JI) projects	n/a
Issued Emission Reduction Units (ERUs) from JI (thousands)	n/a

Kenya

Population (millions)	40.5
Pop. growth (avg. ann. %, 1990-2010)	2.7
GDP ($ billions)	31.4
GNI per capita (Atlas $)	790

Climate

Average daily min/max temperature (1961-90, Celsius)	19 / 31
Projected annual temperature change (2045-65, Celsius)	1.9 to 2.1
Average annual precipitation (1961-90, mm)	692
Projected annual precipitation change (2045-65, mm)	0 to 144
Projected change in annual hot days/warm nights	8 / 25
Projected change in annual cool days/cold nights	-2 / -3

	Country data	Sub-Saharan Africa	Low income
Exposure to Impacts			
Land area below 5m (% of land area)	0.2	0.4	0.7
Population below 5m (% of total)	1.4	2.0	5.1
Population in urban agglomerations > 1 million (%)	9	14	11
Urban pop. growth (avg. annual %, 1990-2010)	3.7	4.0	3.7
Droughts, floods, extreme temps (% pop. avg., 1990-2009)	6.5		
Annual freshwater withdrawals (% of internal resources)	13.2	3.2	3.7
Agricultural land under irrigation (% of total ag. land)	0.0	..	..
Population living below $1.25 a day (% of total)	19.7	50.9	..
Nationally terrestrial protected areas (% of total land area)	11.6	11.7	10.6
Under-five mortality rate (per 1,000)	85	121	108
Child malnutrition, underweight (% of under age five)	16.4	24.6	28.3
Malaria incidence rate (per 100,000 people)	30,307	26,113	16,659
Resilience			
Access to improved sanitation (% of total pop.)	31	31	35
Access to improved water source (% of total pop.)	59	60	63
Cereal yield (kg. per hectare)	1,204	1,297	2,047
Access to electricity (% of total population)	16.1	32.5	23.0
Paved roads (% of total roads)	14.1	18.3	14.1
Health workers (per 1,000 people)	0.1	1.2	0.7
Foreign direct investment, net inflows (% of GDP)	0.4	3.6	3.2
Invest. in infrastructure w/private participation ($ millions)	492	11,957	4,471
Disaster risk reduction progress score (1-5 scale; 5 = best)	4.0		
Ease of doing business (ranking 1-183; 1 = best)	109		
Public sector mgmt & institutions avg. (1-6 scale; 6 = best)	3.3		
Primary completion rate, total (% of relevant age group)	90	67	65
Ratio of girls to boys in primary & secondary school (%)	95	89	91
GHG Emissions and Energy Use			
CO_2 emissions per capita (metric tons)	0.3	0.8	0.3
CO_2 emissions per units of GDP (kg/$1,000 of 2005 PPP $)	187.6	428.6	270.2
CO_2 emissions, total (MtCO$_2$)	10.4	685	219
GHG net emissions/removals by LUCF (1994, MtCO$_2$e)	-28.0		
Methane (CH$_4$) emissions, total (MtCO$_2$e)	22.1	590	436
Nitrous oxide (N$_2$O) emissions, total (MtCO$_2$e)	10.5	334	209
Other GHG emissions, total (MtCO$_2$e)	0.0	..	..
Energy use per capita (kilograms of oil equivalent)	474	689	365
Energy use per units of GDP (kg oil eq./$1,000 of 2005 PPP $)	329.4	308.4	303.9

National-Level Actions

Latest UNFCCC national communication	10/22/2002 (1st)
Annex-I emissions reduction target	n/a
NAMA submission	..
NAPA submission	n/a
Renewable energy target	..

Carbon Markets

Hosted Clean Development Mechanism (CDM) projects	5
Issued Certified Emission Reductions (CERs) from CDM (thousands)	0
Hosted Joint Implementation (JI) projects	n/a
Issued Emission Reduction Units (ERUs) from JI (thousands)	n/a

Kiribati

Population (thousands)	99.5	GDP ($ millions)	151.2
Pop. growth (avg. ann. %, 1990–2010)	1.6	GNI per capita (Atlas $)	2,010

Climate

Average daily min/max temperature (1961–90, Celsius)	25 / 31
Projected annual temperature change (2045–65, Celsius)	1.6 to 2.0
Average annual precipitation (1961–90, mm)	1,942
Projected annual precipitation change (2045–65, mm)	81 to 385
Projected change in annual hot days/warm nights	14 / 24
Projected change in annual cool days/cold nights	-2 / -2

	Country data	East Asia & Pacific	Lower middle income
Exposure to Impacts			
Land area below 5m (% of land area)	96.7	2.5	1.7
Population below 5m (% of total)	95.2	10.3	6.5
Population in urban agglomerations > 1 million (%)	..	..	14
Urban pop. growth (avg. annual %, 1990–2010)	2.8	3.3	2.8
Droughts, floods, extreme temps (% pop. avg., 1990–2009)	5.0		
Annual freshwater withdrawals (% of internal resources)	..	10.8	18.7
Agricultural land under irrigation (% of total ag. land)	..	..	..
Population living below $1.25 a day (% of total)	..	16.8	..
Nationally terrestrial protected areas (% of total land area)	22.0	14.9	9.5
Under-five mortality rate (per 1,000)	49	24	69
Child malnutrition, underweight (% of under age five)	..	9.0	31.7
Malaria incidence rate (per 100,000 people)	..	525	4,874
Resilience			
Access to improved sanitation (% of total pop.)	31	59	45
Access to improved water source (% of total pop.)	61	88	84
Cereal yield (kg. per hectare)	..	4,860	2,754
Access to electricity (% of total population)	..	90.8	67.3
Paved roads (% of total roads)	..	15.9	29.3
Health workers (per 1,000 people)	0.3	2.8	2.6
Foreign direct investment, net inflows (% of GDP)	2.4	3.0	2.4
Invest. in infrastructure w/private participation ($ millions)	..	14,638	81,789
Disaster risk reduction progress score (1–5 scale; 5 = best)	..		
Ease of doing business (ranking 1–183; 1 = best)	115		
Public sector mgmt & institutions avg. (1–6 scale; 6 = best)	3.1		
Primary completion rate, total (% of relevant age group)	118	97	88
Ratio of girls to boys in primary & secondary school (%)	107	103	93
GHG Emissions and Energy Use			
CO_2 emissions per capita (metric tons)	0.3	4.3	1.6
CO_2 emissions per units of GDP (kg/$1,000 of 2005 PPP $)	134.6	827.1	523.9
CO_2 emissions, total (MtCO_2)	0.0	8,259	3,744
GHG net emissions/removals by LUCF (MtCO_2e)	..		
Methane (CH_4) emissions, total (MtCO_2e)	..	1,928	1,705
Nitrous oxide (N_2O) emissions, total (MtCO_2e)	..	707	687
Other GHG emissions, total (MtCO_2e)	..	..	17
Energy use per capita (kilograms of oil equivalent)	116	1,436	680
Energy use per units of GDP (kg oil eq./$1,000 of 2005 PPP $)	49.9	259.5	217.9

National-Level Actions

Latest UNFCCC national communication	10/30/1999 (1st)
Annex-I emissions reduction target	n/a
NAMA submission	..
NAPA submission	Yes
Renewable energy target	..

Carbon Markets

Hosted Clean Development Mechanism (CDM) projects	..
Issued Certified Emission Reductions (CERs) from CDM (thousands)	..
Hosted Joint Implementation (JI) projects	n/a
Issued Emission Reduction Units (ERUs) from JI (thousands)	n/a

Korea, Dem. Rep.

Population (millions)	24.3	GDP ($ millions)	..
Pop. growth (avg. ann. %, 1990-2010)	0.9	GNI per capita (Atlas $)	..

Climate

Average daily min/max temperature (1961-90, Celsius)	0 / 11
Projected annual temperature change (2045-65, Celsius)	2.1 to 2.7
Average annual precipitation (1961-90, mm)	1,062
Projected annual precipitation change (2045-65, mm)	-9 to 129
Projected change in annual hot days/warm nights	3 / 5
Projected change in annual cool days/cold nights	-1 / -2

	Country data	East Asia & Pacific	Low income
Exposure to Impacts			
Land area below 5m (% of land area)	2.4	2.5	0.7
Population below 5m (% of total)	5.3	10.3	5.1
Population in urban agglomerations > 1 million (%)	12	..	11
Urban pop. growth (avg. annual %, 1990-2010)	1.4	3.3	3.7
Droughts, floods, extreme temps (% pop. avg., 1990-2009)	2.5		
Annual freshwater withdrawals (% of internal resources)	10.3	10.8	3.7
Agricultural land under irrigation (% of total ag. land)	..		
Population living below $1.25 a day (% of total)	..	16.8	..
Nationally terrestrial protected areas (% of total land area)	4.0	14.9	10.6
Under-five mortality rate (per 1,000)	33	24	108
Child malnutrition, underweight (% of under age five)	20.6	9.0	28.3
Malaria incidence rate (per 100,000 people)	284	525	16,659
Resilience			
Access to improved sanitation (% of total pop.)	59	59	35
Access to improved water source (% of total pop.)	100	88	63
Cereal yield (kg. per hectare)	3,513	4,860	2,047
Access to electricity (% of total population)	26.0	90.8	23.0
Paved roads (% of total roads)	2.8	15.9	14.1
Health workers (per 1,000 people)	7.4	2.8	0.7
Foreign direct investment, net inflows (% of GDP)	..	3.0	3.2
Invest. in infrastructure w/private participation ($ millions)	47	14,638	4,471
Disaster risk reduction progress score (1-5 scale; 5 = best)	..		
Ease of doing business (ranking 1-183; 1 = best)	..		
Public sector mgmt & institutions avg. (1-6 scale; 6 = best)	..		
Primary completion rate, total (% of relevant age group)	..	97	65
Ratio of girls to boys in primary & secondary school (%)	..	103	91
GHG Emissions and Energy Use			
CO$_2$ emissions per capita (metric tons)	3.2	4.3	0.3
CO$_2$ emissions per units of GDP (kg/$1,000 of 2005 PPP $)	..	827.1	270.2
CO$_2$ emissions, total (MtCO$_2$)	78.4	8,259	219
GHG net emissions/removals by LUCF (1990, MtCO$_2$e)	-14.6		
Methane (CH$_4$) emissions, total (MtCO$_2$e)	18.2	1,928	436
Nitrous oxide (N$_2$O) emissions, total (MtCO$_2$e)	3.4	707	209
Other GHG emissions, total (MtCO$_2$e)	2.8	..	..
Energy use per capita (kilograms of oil equivalent)	795	1,436	365
Energy use per units of GDP (kg oil eq./$1,000 of 2005 PPP $)	..	259.5	303.9

National-Level Actions

Latest UNFCCC national communication	5/7/2004 (1st)
Annex-I emissions reduction target	n/a
NAMA submission	..
NAPA submission	n/a
Renewable energy target	..

Carbon Markets

Hosted Clean Development Mechanism (CDM) projects	0
Issued Certified Emission Reductions (CERs) from CDM (thousands)	0
Hosted Joint Implementation (JI) projects	n/a
Issued Emission Reduction Units (ERUs) from JI (thousands)	n/a

Korea, Rep.

Population (millions)	48.9	GDP ($ billions)	1,014.5
Pop. growth (avg. ann. %, 1990–2010)	0.7	GNI per capita (Atlas $)	19,890

Climate

Average daily min/max temperature (1961–90, Celsius)	7 / 17
Projected annual temperature change (2045–65, Celsius)	1.8 to 2.3
Average annual precipitation (1961–90, mm)	1,404
Projected annual precipitation change (2045–65, mm)	0 to 181
Projected change in annual hot days/warm nights	3 / 5
Projected change in annual cool days/cold nights	-1 / -2

	Country data	High Income
Exposure to Impacts		
Land area below 5m (% of land area)	4.3	2.2
Population below 5m (% of total)	5.0	7.7
Population in urban agglomerations > 1 million (%)	48	..
Urban pop. growth (avg. annual %, 1990–2010)	1.2	1.0
Droughts, floods, extreme temps (% pop. avg., 1990–2009)	0.1	
Annual freshwater withdrawals (% of internal resources)	39.3	10.4
Agricultural land under irrigation (% of total ag. land)	51.6	..
Population living below $1.25 a day (% of total)	..	..
Nationally terrestrial protected areas (% of total land area)	2.4	13.4
Under-five mortality rate (per 1,000)	5	6
Child malnutrition, underweight (% of under age five)	..	..
Malaria incidence rate (per 100,000 people)	8	..
Resilience		
Access to improved sanitation (% of total pop.)	100	100
Access to improved water source (% of total pop.)	98	100
Cereal yield (kg. per hectare)	7,238	5,445
Access to electricity (% of total population)	..	
Paved roads (% of total roads)	78.5	87.3
Health workers (per 1,000 people)	7.3	10.7
Foreign direct investment, net inflows (% of GDP)	-0.0	1.8
Invest. in infrastructure w/private participation ($ millions)	..	..
Disaster risk reduction progress score (1–5 scale; 5 = best)	..	
Ease of doing business (ranking 1–183; 1 = best)	8	
Public sector mgmt & institutions avg. (1–6 scale; 6 = best)	..	
Primary completion rate, total (% of relevant age group)	101	97
Ratio of girls to boys in primary & secondary school (%)	97	100
GHG Emissions and Energy Use		
CO_2 emissions per capita (metric tons)	10.5	11.9
CO_2 emissions per units of GDP (kg/$1,000 of 2005 PPP $)	410.5	354.4
CO_2 emissions, total (MtCO_2)	509.2	13,285
GHG net emissions/removals by LUCF (2001, MtCO_2e)	-34.6	
Methane (CH_4) emissions, total (MtCO_2e)	32.1	1,539
Nitrous oxide (N_2O) emissions, total (MtCO_2e)	13.5	813
Other GHG emissions, total (MtCO_2e)	10.2	460
Energy use per capita (kilograms of oil equivalent)	5,044	4,944
Energy use per units of GDP (kg oil eq./$1,000 of 2005 PPP $)	186.6	147.0

National-Level Actions

Latest UNFCCC national communication	12/1/2003 (2nd)
Annex-I emissions reduction target	n/a
NAMA submission	Yes, with Goal
NAPA submission	n/a
Renewable energy target	Yes

Carbon Markets

Hosted Clean Development Mechanism (CDM) projects	64
Issued Certified Emission Reductions (CERs) from CDM (thousands)	77,317
Hosted Joint Implementation (JI) projects	n/a
Issued Emission Reduction Units (ERUs) from JI (thousands)	n/a

KOSOVO

Population (millions)	1.8	GDP ($ billions)	5.6
Pop. growth (avg. ann. %, 1990–2010)	-0.1	GNI per capita (Atlas $)	3,300

Climate

Average daily min/max temperature (1961–90, Celsius)	..
Projected annual temperature change (2045–65, Celsius)	2.0 to 3.1
Average annual precipitation (1961–90, mm)	..
Projected annual precipitation change (2045–65, mm)	-148 to -34
Projected change in annual hot days/warm nights	3 / 6
Projected change in annual cool days/cold nights	-1 / -1

	Country data	Europe & Central Asia	Lower middle income
Exposure to Impacts			
Land area below 5m (% of land area)	..	2.5	1.7
Population below 5m (% of total)	..	3.0	6.5
Population in urban agglomerations > 1 million (%)	..	18	14
Urban pop. growth (avg. annual %, 1990–2010)	..	0.3	2.8
Droughts, floods, extreme temps (% pop. avg., 1990–2009)	..		
Annual freshwater withdrawals (% of internal resources)	..	6.5	18.7
Agricultural land under irrigation (% of total ag. land)	..	..	..
Population living below $1.25 a day (% of total)	..	3.7	..
Nationally terrestrial protected areas (% of total land area)	..	7.5	9.5
Under-five mortality rate (per 1,000)	..	23	69
Child malnutrition, underweight (% of under age five)	..	..	31.7
Malaria incidence rate (per 100,000 people)	..	..	4,874
Resilience			
Access to improved sanitation (% of total pop.)	..	89	45
Access to improved water source (% of total pop.)	..	95	84
Cereal yield (kg. per hectare)	..	2,475	2,754
Access to electricity (% of total population)	..	..	67.3
Paved roads (% of total roads)	..	85.8	29.3
Health workers (per 1,000 people)	..	9.9	2.6
Foreign direct investment, net inflows (% of GDP)	7.4	2.8	2.4
Invest. in infrastructure w/private participation ($ millions)	5	22,652	81,789
Disaster risk reduction progress score (1–5 scale; 5 = best)	..		
Ease of doing business (ranking 1–183; 1 = best)	117		
Public sector mgmt & institutions avg. (1–6 scale; 6 = best)	3.2		
Primary completion rate, total (% of relevant age group)	..	95	88
Ratio of girls to boys in primary & secondary school (%)	..	97	93
GHG Emissions and Energy Use			
CO_2 emissions per capita (metric tons)	..	7.7	1.6
CO_2 emissions per units of GDP (kg/$1,000 of 2005 PPP $)	..	708.0	523.9
CO_2 emissions, total (MtCO$_2$)	..	3,110	3,744
GHG net emissions/removals by LUCF (MtCO$_2$e)	..		
Methane (CH_4) emissions, total (MtCO$_2$e)	..	937	1,705
Nitrous oxide (N_2O) emissions, total (MtCO$_2$e)	..	214	687
Other GHG emissions, total (MtCO$_2$e)	..	76	17
Energy use per capita (kilograms of oil equivalent)	..	2,833	680
Energy use per units of GDP (kg oil eq./$1,000 of 2005 PPP $)	..	276.8	217.9
National-Level Actions			
Latest UNFCCC national communication			n/a
Annex-I emissions reduction target			n/a
NAMA submission			n/a
NAPA submission			n/a
Renewable energy target			..
Carbon Markets			
Hosted Clean Development Mechanism (CDM) projects			n/a
Issued Certified Emission Reductions (CERs) from CDM (thousands)			n/a
Hosted Joint Implementation (JI) projects			n/a
Issued Emission Reduction Units (ERUs) from JI (thousands)			n/a

Kuwait

Population (millions)	2.7	GDP ($ billions)	109.5
Pop. growth (avg. ann. %, 1990–2010)	1.4	GNI per capita (Atlas $)	47,790

Climate

Average daily min/max temperature (1961–90, Celsius)	19 / 32
Projected annual temperature change (2045–65, Celsius)	2.2 to 3.1
Average annual precipitation (1961–90, mm)	121
Projected annual precipitation change (2045–65, mm)	-19 to 4
Projected change in annual hot days/warm nights	4 / 7
Projected change in annual cool days/cold nights	-2 / -2

	Country data	High income
Exposure to Impacts		
Land area below 5m (% of land area)	8.9	2.2
Population below 5m (% of total)	22.8	7.7
Population in urban agglomerations > 1 million (%)	84	..
Urban pop. growth (avg. annual %, 1990–2010)	1.4	1.0
Droughts, floods, extreme temps (% pop. avg., 1990–2009)	0.0	
Annual freshwater withdrawals (% of internal resources)	..	10.4
Agricultural land under irrigation (% of total ag. land)	..	..
Population living below $1.25 a day (% of total)	..	..
Nationally terrestrial protected areas (% of total land area)	1.6	13.4
Under-five mortality rate (per 1,000)	11	6
Child malnutrition, underweight (% of under age five)	1.7	..
Malaria incidence rate (per 100,000 people)	..	
Resilience		
Access to improved sanitation (% of total pop.)	100	100
Access to improved water source (% of total pop.)	99	100
Cereal yield (kg. per hectare)	3,084	5,445
Access to electricity (% of total population)	100.0	..
Paved roads (% of total roads)	85.0	87.3
Health workers (per 1,000 people)	6.3	10.7
Foreign direct investment, net inflows (% of GDP)	1.0	1.8
Invest. in infrastructure w/private participation ($ millions)	..	
Disaster risk reduction progress score (1–5 scale; 5 = best)	..	
Ease of doing business (ranking 1–183; 1 = best)	67	
Public sector mgmt & institutions avg. (1–6 scale; 6 = best)	..	
Primary completion rate, total (% of relevant age group)	93	97
Ratio of girls to boys in primary & secondary school (%)	101	100
GHG Emissions and Energy Use		
CO$_2$ emissions per capita (metric tons)	30.1	11.9
CO$_2$ emissions per units of GDP (kg/$1,000 of 2005 PPP $)	602.0	354.4
CO$_2$ emissions, total (MtCO$_2$)	76.7	13,285
GHG net emissions/removals by LUCF (MtCO$_2$e)		
Methane (CH$_4$) emissions, total (MtCO$_2$e)	14.4	1,539
Nitrous oxide (N$_2$O) emissions, total (MtCO$_2$e)	0.6	813
Other GHG emissions, total (MtCO$_2$e)	0.9	460
Energy use per capita (kilograms of oil equivalent)	11,402	4,944
Energy use per units of GDP (kg oil eq./$1,000 of 2005 PPP $)	217.6	147.0

National-Level Actions

Latest UNFCCC national communication	..
Annex-I emissions reduction target	n/a
NAMA submission	..
NAPA submission	n/a
Renewable energy target	Yes

Carbon Markets

Hosted Clean Development Mechanism (CDM) projects	..
Issued Certified Emission Reductions (CERs) from CDM (thousands)	..
Hosted Joint Implementation (JI) projects	n/a
Issued Emission Reduction Units (ERUs) from JI (thousands)	n/a

Kyrgyz Republic

Population (millions)	5.4	GDP ($ billions)	4.6
Pop. growth (avg. ann. %, 1990-2010)	1.0	GNI per capita (Atlas $)	880

Climate

Average daily min/max temperature (1961-90, Celsius)	-5 / 8
Projected annual temperature change (2045-65, Celsius)	2.3 to 3.2
Average annual precipitation (1961-90, mm)	381
Projected annual precipitation change (2045-65, mm)	-32 to 35
Projected change in annual hot days/warm nights	3 / 7
Projected change in annual cool days/cold nights	-1 / -1

	Country data	Europe & Central Asia	Low income
Exposure to Impacts			
Land area below 5m (% of land area)	0.0	2.5	0.7
Population below 5m (% of total)	0.0	3.0	5.1
Population in urban agglomerations > 1 million (%)	..	18	11
Urban pop. growth (avg. annual %, 1990-2010)	0.8	0.3	3.7
Droughts, floods, extreme temps (% pop. avg., 1990-2009)	2.1		
Annual freshwater withdrawals (% of internal resources)	20.6	6.5	3.7
Agricultural land under irrigation (% of total ag. land)	9.4	..	..
Population living below $1.25 a day (% of total)	<2	3.7	..
Nationally terrestrial protected areas (% of total land area)	6.9	7.5	10.6
Under-five mortality rate (per 1,000)	38	23	108
Child malnutrition, underweight (% of under age five)	2.7	..	28.3
Malaria incidence rate (per 100,000 people)	0	..	16,659
Resilience			
Access to improved sanitation (% of total pop.)	93	89	35
Access to improved water source (% of total pop.)	90	95	63
Cereal yield (kg. per hectare)	3,034	2,475	2,047
Access to electricity (% of total population)	..	..	23.0
Paved roads (% of total roads)	91.1	85.8	14.1
Health workers (per 1,000 people)	8.0	9.9	0.7
Foreign direct investment, net inflows (% of GDP)	5.1	2.8	3.2
Invest. in infrastructure w/private participation ($ millions)	14	22,652	4,471
Disaster risk reduction progress score (1-5 scale; 5 = best)	..		
Ease of doing business (ranking 1-183; 1 = best)	70		
Public sector mgmt & institutions avg. (1-6 scale; 6 = best)	3.0		
Primary completion rate, total (% of relevant age group)	94	95	65
Ratio of girls to boys in primary & secondary school (%)	101	97	91
GHG Emissions and Energy Use			
CO_2 emissions per capita (metric tons)	1.2	7.7	0.3
CO_2 emissions per units of GDP (kg/$1,000 of 2005 PPP $)	575.9	708.0	270.2
CO_2 emissions, total (MtCO_2)	6.2	3,110	219
GHG net emissions/removals by LUCF (2005, MtCO_2e)	-0.7		
Methane (CH_4) emissions, total (MtCO_2e)	3.6	937	436
Nitrous oxide (N_2O) emissions, total (MtCO_2e)	1.5	214	209
Other GHG emissions, total (MtCO_2e)	0.0	76	..
Energy use per capita (kilograms of oil equivalent)	566	2,833	365
Energy use per units of GDP (kg oil eq./$1,000 of 2005 PPP $)	271.4	276.8	303.9

National-Level Actions

Latest UNFCCC national communication	6/4/2009 (2nd)
Annex-I emissions reduction target	n/a
NAMA submission	..
NAPA submission	n/a
Renewable energy target	..

Carbon Markets

Hosted Clean Development Mechanism (CDM) projects	0
Issued Certified Emission Reductions (CERs) from CDM (thousands)	0
Hosted Joint Implementation (JI) projects	n/a
Issued Emission Reduction Units (ERUs) from JI (thousands)	n/a

Lao PDR

Population (millions)	6.2	GDP ($ billions)	7.5
Pop. growth (avg. ann. %, 1990–2010)	2.0	GNI per capita (Atlas $)	1,040

Climate

Average daily min/max temperature (1961–90, Celsius)	18 / 27
Projected annual temperature change (2045–65, Celsius)	1.6 to 2.4
Average annual precipitation (1961–90, mm)	1,834
Projected annual precipitation change (2045–65, mm)	-95 to 70
Projected change in annual hot days/warm nights	3 / 13
Projected change in annual cool days/cold nights	-1 / -1

	Country data	East Asia & Pacific	Lower middle income
Exposure to Impacts			
Land area below 5m (% of land area)	0.0	2.5	1.7
Population below 5m (% of total)	0.0	10.3	6.5
Population in urban agglomerations > 1 million (%)	..	..	14
Urban pop. growth (avg. annual %, 1990–2010)	5.8	3.3	2.8
Droughts, floods, extreme temps (% pop. avg., 1990–2009)	2.7		
Annual freshwater withdrawals (% of internal resources)	1.6	10.8	18.7
Agricultural land under irrigation (% of total ag. land)	..	..	..
Population living below $1.25 a day (% of total)	33.9	16.8	..
Nationally terrestrial protected areas (% of total land area)	16.3	14.9	9.5
Under-five mortality rate (per 1,000)	54	24	69
Child malnutrition, underweight (% of under age five)	31.6	9.0	31.7
Malaria incidence rate (per 100,000 people)	327	525	4,874
Resilience			
Access to improved sanitation (% of total pop.)	53	59	45
Access to improved water source (% of total pop.)	57	88	84
Cereal yield (kg. per hectare)	3,808	4,860	2,754
Access to electricity (% of total population)	55.0	90.8	67.3
Paved roads (% of total roads)	13.5	15.9	29.3
Health workers (per 1,000 people)	1.2	2.8	2.6
Foreign direct investment, net inflows (% of GDP)	4.7	3.0	2.4
Invest. in infrastructure w/private participation ($ millions)	3,860	14,638	81,789
Disaster risk reduction progress score (1–5 scale; 5 = best)	2.3		
Ease of doing business (ranking 1–183; 1 = best)	165		
Public sector mgmt & institutions avg. (1–6 scale; 6 = best)	3.1		
Primary completion rate, total (% of relevant age group)	75	97	88
Ratio of girls to boys in primary & secondary school (%)	87	103	93
GHG Emissions and Energy Use			
CO_2 emissions per capita (metric tons)	0.3	4.3	1.6
CO_2 emissions per units of GDP (kg/$1,000 of 2005 PPP $)	125.3	827.1	523.9
CO_2 emissions, total (MtCO_2)	1.5	8,259	3,744
GHG net emissions/removals by LUCF (1990, MtCO_2e)	-104.3		
Methane (CH_4) emissions, total (MtCO_2e)	..	1,928	1,705
Nitrous oxide (N_2O) emissions, total (MtCO_2e)	..	707	687
Other GHG emissions, total (MtCO_2e)	..	..	17
Energy use per capita (kilograms of oil equivalent)	..	1,436	680
Energy use per units of GDP (kg oil eq./$1,000 of 2005 PPP $)	..	259.5	217.9

National-Level Actions

Latest UNFCCC national communication	11/2/2000 (1st)
Annex-I emissions reduction target	n/a
NAMA submission	..
NAPA submission	Yes
Renewable energy target	..

Carbon Markets

Hosted Clean Development Mechanism (CDM) projects	1
Issued Certified Emission Reductions (CERs) from CDM (thousands)	2
Hosted Joint Implementation (JI) projects	n/a
Issued Emission Reduction Units (ERUs) from JI (thousands)	n/a

Latvia

Population (millions)	2.2	GDP ($ billions)	24.0
Pop. growth (avg. ann. %, 1990-2010)	-0.9	GNI per capita (Atlas $)	11,620

Climate

Average daily min/max temperature (1961-90, Celsius)	2 / 9
Projected annual temperature change (2045-65, Celsius)	2.1 to 3.1
Average annual precipitation (1961-90, mm)	641
Projected annual precipitation change (2045-65, mm)	31 to 89
Projected change in annual hot days/warm nights	2 / 5
Projected change in annual cool days/cold nights	-2 / -2

	Country data	Europe & Central Asia	Upper middle income
Exposure to Impacts			
Land area below 5m (% of land area)	3.0	2.5	1.8
Population below 5m (% of total)	23.9	3.0	6.5
Population in urban agglomerations > 1 million (%)	..	18	22
Urban pop. growth (avg. annual %, 1990-2010)	-1.0	0.3	2.3
Droughts, floods, extreme temps (% pop. avg., 1990-2009)	0.0		
Annual freshwater withdrawals (% of internal resources)	2.4	6.5	5.6
Agricultural land under irrigation (% of total ag. land)	0.0		
Population living below $1.25 a day (% of total)	<2	3.7	..
Nationally terrestrial protected areas (% of total land area)	17.8	7.5	13.6
Under-five mortality rate (per 1,000)	10	23	20
Child malnutrition, underweight (% of under age five)	..	..	4.1
Malaria incidence rate (per 100,000 people)	..	..	80
Resilience			
Access to improved sanitation (% of total pop.)	78	89	68
Access to improved water source (% of total pop.)	99	95	92
Cereal yield (kg. per hectare)	3,075	2,475	3,690
Access to electricity (% of total population)	..		98.0
Paved roads (% of total roads)	100.0	85.8	50.5
Health workers (per 1,000 people)	7.8	9.9	4.5
Foreign direct investment, net inflows (% of GDP)	1.4	2.8	2.7
Invest. in infrastructure w/private participation ($ millions)	122	22,652	26,166
Disaster risk reduction progress score (1-5 scale; 5 = best)	..		
Ease of doing business (ranking 1-183; 1 = best)	21		
Public sector mgmt & institutions avg. (1-6 scale; 6 = best)	..		
Primary completion rate, total (% of relevant age group)	93	95	98
Ratio of girls to boys in primary & secondary school (%)	100	97	103
GHG Emissions and Energy Use			
CO_2 emissions per capita (metric tons)	3.3	7.7	5.3
CO_2 emissions per units of GDP (kg/$1,000 of 2005 PPP $)	213.9	708.0	659.4
CO_2 emissions, total (MtCO_2)	7.6	3,110	12,860
GHG net emissions/removals by LUCF (2009, MtCO_2e)	-20.5		
Methane (CH_4) emissions, total (MtCO_2e)	3.1	937	3,455
Nitrous oxide (N_2O) emissions, total (MtCO_2e)	1.3	214	1,144
Other GHG emissions, total (MtCO_2e)	0.9	76	243
Energy use per capita (kilograms of oil equivalent)	1,871	2,833	1,848
Energy use per units of GDP (kg oil eq./$1,000 of 2005 PPP $)	144.9	276.8	227.1

National-Level Actions

Latest UNFCCC national communication	3/16/2010 (5th)
Annex-I emissions reduction target (base year: 1990)	20% / 30% (EU)
NAMA submission	n/a
NAPA submission	n/a
Renewable energy target	Yes

Carbon Markets

Hosted Clean Development Mechanism (CDM) projects	n/a
Issued Certified Emission Reductions (CERs) from CDM (thousands)	n/a
Hosted Joint Implementation (JI) projects	0
Issued Emission Reduction Units (ERUs) from JI (thousands)	0

Lebanon

| Population (millions) | 4.2 | GDP ($ billions) | 39.2 |
| Pop. growth (avg. ann. %, 1990–2010) | 1.8 | GNI per capita (Atlas $) | 9,080 |

Climate

Average daily min/max temperature (1961–90, Celsius)	11 / 22
Projected annual temperature change (2045–65, Celsius)	2.0 to 2.9
Average annual precipitation (1961-90, mm)	661
Projected annual precipitation change (2045–65, mm)	–75 to -27
Projected change in annual hot days/warm nights	4 / 7
Projected change in annual cool days/cold nights	-2 / -2

	Country data	Middle East & N. Africa	Upper middle income
Exposure to Impacts			
Land area below 5m (% of land area)	1.7	1.4	1.8
Population below 5m (% of total)	9.1	9.7	6.5
Population in urban agglomerations > 1 million (%)	46	20	22
Urban pop. growth (avg. annual %, 1990–2010)	2.0	2.5	2.3
Droughts, floods, extreme temps (% pop. avg., 1990–2009)	0.0		
Annual freshwater withdrawals (% of internal resources)	26.3	121.9	5.6
Agricultural land under irrigation (% of total ag. land)	19.9	..	..
Population living below $1.25 a day (% of total)	..	3.6	..
Nationally terrestrial protected areas (% of total land area)	0.5	4.0	13.6
Under-five mortality rate (per 1,000)	22	34	20
Child malnutrition, underweight (% of under age five)	4.2	6.8	4.1
Malaria incidence rate (per 100,000 people)	..	..	80
Resilience			
Access to improved sanitation (% of total pop.)	98	84	68
Access to improved water source (% of total pop.)	100	87	92
Cereal yield (kg. per hectare)	2,832	2,512	3,690
Access to electricity (% of total population)	99.9	92.9	98.0
Paved roads (% of total roads)	..	74.3	50.5
Health workers (per 1,000 people)	5.8	3.6	4.5
Foreign direct investment, net inflows (% of GDP)	12.7	2.9	2.7
Invest. in infrastructure w/private participation ($ millions)	3	5,854	26,166
Disaster risk reduction progress score (1-5 scale; 5 = best)	3.0		
Ease of doing business (ranking 1-183; 1 = best)	104		
Public sector mgmt & institutions avg. (1-6 scale; 6 = best)	..		
Primary completion rate, total (% of relevant age group)	85	88	98
Ratio of girls to boys in primary & secondary school (%)	104	93	103
GHG Emissions and Energy Use			
CO$_2$ emissions per capita (metric tons)	4.1	3.8	5.3
CO$_2$ emissions per units of GDP (kg/$1,000 of 2005 PPP $)	372.5	604.6	659.4
CO$_2$ emissions, total (MtCO$_2$)	17.1	1,230	12,860
GHG net emissions/removals by LUCF (2000, MtCO$_2$e)	-0.1		
Methane (CH$_4$) emissions, total (MtCO$_2$e)	1.0	287	3,455
Nitrous oxide (N$_2$O) emissions, total (MtCO$_2$e)	0.7	74	1,144
Other GHG emissions, total (MtCO$_2$e)	0.0	7	243
Energy use per capita (kilograms of oil equivalent)	1,580	1,399	1,848
Energy use per units of GDP (kg oil eq./$1,000 of 2005 PPP $)	133.2	213.9	227.1

National-Level Actions

Latest UNFCCC national communication	3/31/2011 (2nd)
Annex-I emissions reduction target	n/a
NAMA submission	..
NAPA submission	n/a
Renewable energy target	Yes

Carbon Markets

Hosted Clean Development Mechanism (CDM) projects	0
Issued Certified Emission Reductions (CERs) from CDM (thousands)	0
Hosted Joint Implementation (JI) projects	n/a
Issued Emission Reduction Units (ERUs) from JI (thousands)	n/a

Lesotho

Population (millions)	2.2	GDP ($ billions)	2.1
Pop. growth (avg. ann. %, 1990–2010)	1.4	GNI per capita (Atlas $)	1,040

Climate

Average daily min/max temperature (1961–90, Celsius)	5 / 19
Projected annual temperature change (2045–65, Celsius)	2.0 to 2.5
Average annual precipitation (1961–90, mm)	789
Projected annual precipitation change (2045–65, mm)	-66 to 89
Projected change in annual hot days/warm nights	4 / 10
Projected change in annual cool days/cold nights	-2 / -2

	Country data	Sub-Saharan Africa	Lower middle income
Exposure to Impacts			
Land area below 5m (% of land area)	0.0	0.4	1.7
Population below 5m (% of total)	0.0	2.0	6.5
Population in urban agglomerations > 1 million (%)	..	14	14
Urban pop. growth (avg. annual %, 1990–2010)	4.7	4.0	2.8
Droughts, floods, extreme temps (% pop. avg., 1990–2009)	3.4		
Annual freshwater withdrawals (% of internal resources)	1.0	3.2	18.7
Agricultural land under irrigation (% of total ag. land)	..	..	
Population living below $1.25 a day (% of total)	43.4	50.9	..
Nationally terrestrial protected areas (% of total land area)	0.5	11.7	9.5
Under-five mortality rate (per 1,000)	85	121	69
Child malnutrition, underweight (% of under age five)	16.6	24.6	31.7
Malaria incidence rate (per 100,000 people)	..	26,113	4,874
Resilience			
Access to improved sanitation (% of total pop.)	29	31	45
Access to improved water source (% of total pop.)	85	60	84
Cereal yield (kg. per hectare)	421	1,297	2,754
Access to electricity (% of total population)	16.0	32.5	67.3
Paved roads (% of total roads)	18.3	18.3	29.3
Health workers (per 1,000 people)	0.7	1.2	2.6
Foreign direct investment, net inflows (% of GDP)	5.5	3.6	2.4
Invest. in infrastructure w/private participation ($ millions)	11	11,957	81,789
Disaster risk reduction progress score (1-5 scale; 5 = best)	2.5		
Ease of doing business (ranking 1-183; 1 = best)	143		
Public sector mgmt & institutions avg. (1-6 scale; 6 = best)	3.5		
Primary completion rate, total (% of relevant age group)	69	67	88
Ratio of girls to boys in primary & secondary school (%)	107	89	93
GHG Emissions and Energy Use			
CO$_2$ emissions per capita (metric tons)	..	0.8	1.6
CO$_2$ emissions per units of GDP (kg/$1,000 of 2005 PPP $)	..	428.6	523.9
CO$_2$ emissions, total (MtCO$_2$)	..	685	3,744
GHG net emissions/removals by LUCF (1994, MtCO$_2$e)	1.3		
Methane (CH$_4$) emissions, total (MtCO$_2$e)	..	590	1,705
Nitrous oxide (N$_2$O) emissions, total (MtCO$_2$e)	..	334	687
Other GHG emissions, total (MtCO$_2$e)	..	..	17
Energy use per capita (kilograms of oil equivalent)	9	689	680
Energy use per units of GDP (kg oil eq./$1,000 of 2005 PPP $)	7.0	308.4	217.9

National-Level Actions

Latest UNFCCC national communication	4/17/2000 (1st)
Annex-I emissions reduction target	n/a
NAMA submission	..
NAPA submission	Yes
Renewable energy target	..

Carbon Markets

Hosted Clean Development Mechanism (CDM) projects	0
Issued Certified Emission Reductions (CERs) from CDM (thousands)	0
Hosted Joint Implementation (JI) projects	n/a
Issued Emission Reduction Units (ERUs) from JI (thousands)	n/a

Liberia

Population (millions)	4.0	GDP ($ millions)	986.2
Pop. growth (avg. ann. %, 1990–2010)	3.2	GNI per capita (Atlas $)	200

Climate

Average daily min/max temperature (1961–90, Celsius)	20 / 31
Projected annual temperature change (2045–65, Celsius)	1.7 to 2.2
Average annual precipitation (1961–90, mm)	2,391
Projected annual precipitation change (2045–65, mm)	-115 to 81
Projected change in annual hot days/warm nights	10 / 25
Projected change in annual cool days/cold nights	-3 / -3

	Country data	Sub-Saharan Africa	Low income
Exposure to Impacts			
Land area below 5m (% of land area)	0.4	0.4	0.7
Population below 5m (% of total)	3.3	2.0	5.1
Population in urban agglomerations > 1 million (%)	30	14	11
Urban pop. growth (avg. annual %, 1990–2010)	4.7	4.0	3.7
Droughts, floods, extreme temps (% pop. avg., 1990–2009)	1.9		
Annual freshwater withdrawals (% of internal resources)	0.1	3.2	3.7
Agricultural land under irrigation (% of total ag. land)	..	..	..
Population living below $1.25 a day (% of total)	83.7	50.9	..
Nationally terrestrial protected areas (% of total land area)	18.1	11.7	10.6
Under-five mortality rate (per 1,000)	103	121	108
Child malnutrition, underweight (% of under age five)	20.4	24.6	28.3
Malaria incidence rate (per 100,000 people)	29,994	26,113	16,659
Resilience			
Access to improved sanitation (% of total pop.)	17	31	35
Access to improved water source (% of total pop.)	68	60	63
Cereal yield (kg. per hectare)	1,610	1,297	2,047
Access to electricity (% of total population)	..	32.5	23.0
Paved roads (% of total roads)	6.2	18.3	14.1
Health workers (per 1,000 people)	0.3	1.2	0.7
Foreign direct investment, net inflows (% of GDP)	25.1	3.6	3.2
Invest. in infrastructure w/private participation ($ millions)	135	11,957	4,471
Disaster risk reduction progress score (1–5 scale; 5 = best)	..		
Ease of doing business (ranking 1–183; 1 = best)	151		
Public sector mgmt & institutions avg. (1–6 scale; 6 = best)	2.8		
Primary completion rate, total (% of relevant age group)	58	67	65
Ratio of girls to boys in primary & secondary school (%)	72	89	91
GHG Emissions and Energy Use			
CO_2 emissions per capita (metric tons)	0.2	0.8	0.3
CO_2 emissions per units of GDP (kg/$1,000 of 2005 PPP $)	447.7	428.6	270.2
CO_2 emissions, total (MtCO2)	0.6	685	219
GHG net emissions/removals by LUCF (MtCO2e)	..		
Methane (CH_4) emissions, total (MtCO2e)	..	590	436
Nitrous oxide (N_2O) emissions, total (MtCO2e)	..	334	209
Other GHG emissions, total (MtCO2e)	..	..	..
Energy use per capita (kilograms of oil equivalent)	..	689	365
Energy use per units of GDP (kg oil eq./$1,000 of 2005 PPP $)	..	308.4	303.9

National-Level Actions

Latest UNFCCC national communication	..
Annex-I emissions reduction target	n/a
NAMA submission	..
NAPA submission	Yes
Renewable energy target	..

Carbon Markets

Hosted Clean Development Mechanism (CDM) projects	1
Issued Certified Emission Reductions (CERs) from CDM (thousands)	0
Hosted Joint Implementation (JI) projects	n/a
Issued Emission Reduction Units (ERUs) from JI (thousands)	n/a

Libya

Population (millions)	6.4	GDP ($ billions)	62.4
Pop. growth (avg. ann. %, 1990-2010)	1.9	GNI per capita (Atlas $)	12,320

Climate
Average daily min/max temperature (1961-90, Celsius)	14 / 29
Projected annual temperature change (2045-65, Celsius)	2.0 to 2.4
Average annual precipitation (1961-90, mm)	57
Projected annual precipitation change (2045-65, mm)	-18 to 5
Projected change in annual hot days/warm nights	4 / 8
Projected change in annual cool days/cold nights	-2 / -2

	Country data	Middle East & N. Africa	Upper middle income
Exposure to Impacts			
Land area below 5m (% of land area)	0.8	1.4	1.8
Population below 5m (% of total)	4.7	9.7	6.5
Population in urban agglomerations > 1 million (%)	17	20	22
Urban pop. growth (avg. annual %, 1990-2010)	2.1	2.5	2.3
Droughts, floods, extreme temps (% pop. avg., 1990-2009)	0.0		
Annual freshwater withdrawals (% of internal resources)	718.0	121.9	5.6
Agricultural land under irrigation (% of total ag. land)	..	..	
Population living below $1.25 a day (% of total)	..	3.6	..
Nationally terrestrial protected areas (% of total land area)	0.1	4.0	13.6
Under-five mortality rate (per 1,000)	17	34	20
Child malnutrition, underweight (% of under age five)	5.6	6.8	4.1
Malaria incidence rate (per 100,000 people)	..	..	80
Resilience			
Access to improved sanitation (% of total pop.)	97	84	68
Access to improved water source (% of total pop.)	54	87	92
Cereal yield (kg. per hectare)	569	2,512	3,690
Access to electricity (% of total population)	99.8	92.9	98.0
Paved roads (% of total roads)	57.2	74.3	50.5
Health workers (per 1,000 people)	8.7	3.6	4.5
Foreign direct investment, net inflows (% of GDP)	2.7	2.9	2.7
Invest. in infrastructure w/private participation ($ millions)	..	5,854	26,166
Disaster risk reduction progress score (1-5 scale; 5 = best)	..		
Ease of doing business (ranking 1-183; 1 = best)	..		
Public sector mgmt & institutions avg. (1-6 scale; 6 = best)	..		
Primary completion rate, total (% of relevant age group)	..	88	98
Ratio of girls to boys in primary & secondary school (%)	105	93	103
GHG Emissions and Energy Use			
CO_2 emissions per capita (metric tons)	9.5	3.8	5.3
CO_2 emissions per units of GDP (kg/$1,000 of 2005 PPP $)	619.1	604.6	659.4
CO_2 emissions, total (MtCO$_2$)	58.3	1,230	12,860
GHG net emissions/removals by LUCF (MtCO$_2$e)			
Methane (CH_4) emissions, total (MtCO$_2$e)	14.7	287	3,455
Nitrous oxide (N_2O) emissions, total (MtCO$_2$e)	1.3	74	1,144
Other GHG emissions, total (MtCO$_2$e)	0.3	7	243
Energy use per capita (kilograms of oil equivalent)	3,258	1,399	1,848
Energy use per units of GDP (kg oil eq./$1,000 of 2005 PPP $)	212.1	213.9	227.1

National-Level Actions
Latest UNFCCC national communication	..
Annex-I emissions reduction target	n/a
NAMA submission	..
NAPA submission	n/a
Renewable energy target	Yes

Carbon Markets
Hosted Clean Development Mechanism (CDM) projects	0
Issued Certified Emission Reductions (CERs) from CDM (thousands)	0
Hosted Joint Implementation (JI) projects	n/a
Issued Emission Reduction Units (ERUs) from JI (thousands)	n/a

Liechtenstein

Population (thousands)	36.0	GDP ($ billions)	4.8
Pop. growth (avg. ann. %, 1990–2010)	1.1	GNI per capita (Atlas $)	137,070

Climate

Average daily min/max temperature (1961–90, Celsius)	2 / 9
Projected annual temperature change (2045–65, Celsius)	1.7 to 2.8
Average annual precipitation (1961–90, mm)	1,539
Projected annual precipitation change (2045–65, mm)	-66 to 32
Projected change in annual hot days/warm nights	3 / 5
Projected change in annual cool days/cold nights	-1 / -1

	Country data	High income
Exposure to Impacts		
Land area below 5m (% of land area)	0.0	2.2
Population below 5m (% of total)	0.0	7.7
Population in urban agglomerations > 1 million (%)	..	..
Urban pop. growth (avg. annual %, 1990–2010)	0.2	1.0
Droughts, floods, extreme temps (% pop. avg., 1990–2009)	..	
Annual freshwater withdrawals (% of internal resources)	..	10.4
Agricultural land under irrigation (% of total ag. land)	..	..
Population living below $1.25 a day (% of total)	..	..
Nationally terrestrial protected areas (% of total land area)	42.4	13.4
Under-five mortality rate (per 1,000)	2	6
Child malnutrition, underweight (% of under age five)	..	..
Malaria incidence rate (per 100,000 people)	..	..
Resilience		
Access to improved sanitation (% of total pop.)	..	100
Access to improved water source (% of total pop.)	..	100
Cereal yield (kg. per hectare)	..	5,445
Access to electricity (% of total population)	..	
Paved roads (% of total roads)	..	87.3
Health workers (per 1,000 people)	..	10.7
Foreign direct investment, net inflows (% of GDP)	..	1.8
Invest. in infrastructure w/private participation ($ millions)	..	..
Disaster risk reduction progress score (1–5 scale; 5 = best)	..	
Ease of doing business (ranking 1–183; 1 = best)	..	
Public sector mgmt & institutions avg. (1–6 scale; 6 = best)	..	
Primary completion rate, total (% of relevant age group)	107	97
Ratio of girls to boys in primary & secondary school (%)	93	100
GHG Emissions and Energy Use		
CO$_2$ emissions per capita (metric tons)	..	11.9
CO$_2$ emissions per units of GDP (kg/$1,000 of 2005 PPP $)	..	354.4
CO$_2$ emissions, total (MtCO$_2$)	..	13,285
GHG net emissions/removals by LUCF (2009, MtCO$_2$e)	0.0	
Methane (CH$_4$) emissions, total (MtCO$_2$e)	..	1,539
Nitrous oxide (N$_2$O) emissions, total (MtCO$_2$e)	..	813
Other GHG emissions, total (MtCO$_2$e)	..	460
Energy use per capita (kilograms of oil equivalent)	..	4,944
Energy use per units of GDP (kg oil eq./$1,000 of 2005 PPP $)	..	147.0

National-Level Actions

Latest UNFCCC national communication	1/25/2010 (5th)
Annex-I emissions reduction target (base year: 1990)	20% / 30%
NAMA submission	n/a
NAPA submission	n/a
Renewable energy target	..

Carbon Markets

Hosted Clean Development Mechanism (CDM) projects	n/a
Issued Certified Emission Reductions (CERs) from CDM (thousands)	n/a
Hosted Joint Implementation (JI) projects	..
Issued Emission Reduction Units (ERUs) from JI (thousands)	..

Lithuania

Population (millions)	3.3	GDP ($ billions)	36.3
Pop. growth (avg. ann. %, 1990–2010)	–0.5	GNI per capita (Atlas $)	11,390

Climate

Average daily min/max temperature (1961–90, Celsius)	2 / 10
Projected annual temperature change (2045–65, Celsius)	2.0 to 3.0
Average annual precipitation (1961–90, mm)	656
Projected annual precipitation change (2045–65, mm)	22 to 83
Projected change in annual hot days/warm nights	2 / 5
Projected change in annual cool days/cold nights	-2 / -2

	Country data	Europe & Central Asia	Upper middle income
Exposure to Impacts			
Land area below 5m (% of land area)	1.9	2.5	1.8
Population below 5m (% of total)	4.0	3.0	6.5
Population in urban agglomerations > 1 million (%)	..	18	22
Urban pop. growth (avg. annual %, 1990–2010)	-0.6	0.3	2.3
Droughts, floods, extreme temps (% pop. avg., 1990–2009)	0.0		
Annual freshwater withdrawals (% of internal resources)	17.7	6.5	5.6
Agricultural land under irrigation (% of total ag. land)	..	..	..
Population living below $1.25 a day (% of total)	<2	3.7	..
Nationally terrestrial protected areas (% of total land area)	4.5	7.5	13.6
Under-five mortality rate (per 1,000)	7	23	20
Child malnutrition, underweight (% of under age five)	..	..	4.1
Malaria incidence rate (per 100,000 people)	..	..	80
Resilience			
Access to improved sanitation (% of total pop.)	..	89	68
Access to improved water source (% of total pop.)	..	95	92
Cereal yield (kg. per hectare)	3,450	2,475	3,690
Access to electricity (% of total population)	..	..	98.0
Paved roads (% of total roads)	28.6	85.8	50.5
Health workers (per 1,000 people)	11.0	9.9	4.5
Foreign direct investment, net inflows (% of GDP)	1.7	2.8	2.7
Invest. in infrastructure w/private participation ($ millions)	104	22,652	26,166
Disaster risk reduction progress score (1–5 scale; 5 = best)	..		
Ease of doing business (ranking 1–183; 1 = best)	27		
Public sector mgmt & institutions avg. (1–6 scale; 6 = best)	..		
Primary completion rate, total (% of relevant age group)	96	95	98
Ratio of girls to boys in primary & secondary school (%)	99	97	103
GHG Emissions and Energy Use			
CO_2 emissions per capita (metric tons)	4.5	7.7	5.3
CO_2 emissions per units of GDP (kg/$1,000 of 2005 PPP $)	255.8	708.0	659.4
CO_2 emissions, total (MtCO_2)	15.1	3,110	12,860
GHG net emissions/removals by LUCF (2009, MtCO_2e)	-3.7		
Methane (CH_4) emissions, total (MtCO_2e)	5.5	937	3,455
Nitrous oxide (N_2O) emissions, total (MtCO_2e)	2.5	214	1,144
Other GHG emissions, total (MtCO_2e)	0.7	76	243
Energy use per capita (kilograms of oil equivalent)	2,512	2,833	1,848
Energy use per units of GDP (kg oil eq./$1,000 of 2005 PPP $)	166.3	276.8	227.1

National-Level Actions

Latest UNFCCC national communication	2/22/2010 (5th)
Annex-I emissions reduction target (base year: 1990)	20% / 30% (EU)
NAMA submission	n/a
NAPA submission	n/a
Renewable energy target	Yes

Carbon Markets

Hosted Clean Development Mechanism (CDM) projects	n/a
Issued Certified Emission Reductions (CERs) from CDM (thousands)	n/a
Hosted Joint Implementation (JI) projects	12
Issued Emission Reduction Units (ERUs) from JI (thousands)	2,408

Luxembourg

Population (thousands)	505.8	GDP ($ billions)	55.1
Pop. growth (avg. ann. %, 1990–2010)	1.4	GNI per capita (Atlas $)	79,630

Climate

Average daily min/max temperature (1961–90, Celsius)	4 / 13
Projected annual temperature change (2045–65, Celsius)	1.5 to 2.5
Average annual precipitation (1961–90, mm)	934
Projected annual precipitation change (2045–65, mm)	–86 to 26
Projected change in annual hot days/warm nights	3 / 5
Projected change in annual cool days/cold nights	–1 / –1

	Country data	High Income
Exposure to Impacts		
Land area below 5m (% of land area)	0.0	2.2
Population below 5m (% of total)	0.0	7.7
Population in urban agglomerations > 1 million (%)	..	..
Urban pop. growth (avg. annual %, 1990–2010)	1.5	1.0
Droughts, floods, extreme temps (% pop. avg., 1990–2009)	0.0	
Annual freshwater withdrawals (% of internal resources)	..	10.4
Agricultural land under irrigation (% of total ag. land)	..	..
Population living below $1.25 a day (% of total)	..	..
Nationally terrestrial protected areas (% of total land area)	19.8	13.4
Under-five mortality rate (per 1,000)	3	6
Child malnutrition, underweight (% of under age five)	..	..
Malaria incidence rate (per 100,000 people)	..	
Resilience		
Access to improved sanitation (% of total pop.)	100	100
Access to improved water source (% of total pop.)	100	100
Cereal yield (kg. per hectare)	6,202	5,445
Access to electricity (% of total population)	..	
Paved roads (% of total roads)	100.0	87.3
Health workers (per 1,000 people)	2.9	10.7
Foreign direct investment, net inflows (% of GDP)	279.2	1.8
Invest. in infrastructure w/private participation ($ millions)	..	..
Disaster risk reduction progress score (1–5 scale; 5 = best)	..	
Ease of doing business (ranking 1–183; 1 = best)	50	
Public sector mgmt & institutions avg. (1–6 scale; 6 = best)	..	
Primary completion rate, total (% of relevant age group)	84	97
Ratio of girls to boys in primary & secondary school (%)	102	100
GHG Emissions and Energy Use		
CO_2 emissions per capita (metric tons)	21.5	11.9
CO_2 emissions per units of GDP (kg/$1,000 of 2005 PPP $)	291.0	354.4
CO_2 emissions, total (MtCO$_2$)	10.5	13,285
GHG net emissions/removals by LUCF (2009, MtCO$_2$e)	–0.3	
Methane (CH_4) emissions, total (MtCO$_2$e)	1.1	1,539
Nitrous oxide (N_2O) emissions, total (MtCO$_2$e)	0.5	813
Other GHG emissions, total (MtCO$_2$e)	0.1	460
Energy use per capita (kilograms of oil equivalent)	8,313	4,944
Energy use per units of GDP (kg oil eq./$1,000 of 2005 PPP $)	116.8	147.0

National-Level Actions

Latest UNFCCC national communication	2/14/2010 (5th)
Annex-I emissions reduction target (base year: 1990)	20% / 30% (EU)
NAMA submission	n/a
NAPA submission	n/a
Renewable energy target	Yes

Carbon Markets

Hosted Clean Development Mechanism (CDM) projects	n/a
Issued Certified Emission Reductions (CERs) from CDM (thousands)	n/a
Hosted Joint Implementation (JI) projects	..
Issued Emission Reduction Units (ERUs) from JI (thousands)	..

Macao SAR, China

Population (thousands)	543.7	GDP ($ billions)	21.7
Pop. growth (avg. ann. %, 1990-2010)	2.1	GNI per capita (Atlas $)	40,030

Climate

Average daily min/max temperature (1961-90, Celsius)	20 / 26
Projected annual temperature change (2045-65, Celsius)	1.4 to 1.9
Average annual precipitation (1961-90, mm)	2,219
Projected annual precipitation change (2045-65, mm)	-83 to 73
Projected change in annual hot days/warm nights	7 / 10
Projected change in annual cool days/cold nights	-1 / -1

	Country data	High income
Exposure to Impacts		
Land area below 5m (% of land area)	35.4	2.2
Population below 5m (% of total)	79.9	7.7
Population in urban agglomerations > 1 million (%)	..	..
Urban pop. growth (avg. annual %, 1990-2010)	2.1	1.0
Droughts, floods, extreme temps (% pop. avg., 1990-2009)	..	
Annual freshwater withdrawals (% of internal resources)		10.4
Agricultural land under irrigation (% of total ag. land)	..	
Population living below $1.25 a day (% of total)		..
Nationally terrestrial protected areas (% of total land area)	..	13.4
Under-five mortality rate (per 1,000)	..	6
Child malnutrition, underweight (% of under age five)	..	
Malaria incidence rate (per 100,000 people)	..	..
Resilience		
Access to improved sanitation (% of total pop.)	..	100
Access to improved water source (% of total pop.)	..	100
Cereal yield (kg. per hectare)	..	5,445
Access to electricity (% of total population)	..	..
Paved roads (% of total roads)	100.0	87.3
Health workers (per 1,000 people)	..	10.7
Foreign direct investment, net inflows (% of GDP)	8.3	1.8
Invest. in infrastructure w/private participation ($ millions)	..	..
Disaster risk reduction progress score (1-5 scale; 5 = best)	..	
Ease of doing business (ranking 1-183; 1 = best)	..	
Public sector mgmt & institutions avg. (1-6 scale; 6 = best)	..	
Primary completion rate, total (% of relevant age group)	99	97
Ratio of girls to boys in primary & secondary school (%)	95	100
GHG Emissions and Energy Use		
CO_2 emissions per capita (metric tons)	2.6	11.9
CO_2 emissions per units of GDP (kg/$1,000 of 2005 PPP $)	46.0	354.4
CO_2 emissions, total (MtCO_2)	1.3	13,285
GHG net emissions/removals by LUCF (MtCO_2e)	..	
Methane (CH_4) emissions, total (MtCO_2e)	..	1,539
Nitrous oxide (N_2O) emissions, total (MtCO_2e)	..	813
Other GHG emissions, total (MtCO_2e)	..	460
Energy use per capita (kilograms of oil equivalent)	..	4,944
Energy use per units of GDP (kg oil eq./$1,000 of 2005 PPP $)	..	147.0
National-Level Actions		
Latest UNFCCC national communication		n/a
Annex-I emissions reduction target		n/a
NAMA submission		n/a
NAPA submission		n/a
Renewable energy target		..
Carbon Markets		
Hosted Clean Development Mechanism (CDM) projects		n/a
Issued Certified Emission Reductions (CERs) from CDM (thousands)		n/a
Hosted Joint Implementation (JI) projects		n/a
Issued Emission Reduction Units (ERUs) from JI (thousands)		n/a

Macedonia, FYR

Population (millions)	2.1	GDP ($ billions)	9.1
Pop. growth (avg. ann. %, 1990–2010)	0.4	GNI per capita (Atlas $)	4,520

Climate

Average daily min/max temperature (1961–90, Celsius)	5 / 15
Projected annual temperature change (2045–65, Celsius)	1.9 to 3.0
Average annual precipitation (1961–90, mm)	619
Projected annual precipitation change (2045–65, mm)	-150 to -43
Projected change in annual hot days/warm nights	3 / 6
Projected change in annual cool days/cold nights	-1 / -1

	Country data	Europe & Central Asia	Upper middle income
Exposure to Impacts			
Land area below 5m (% of land area)	0.0	2.5	1.8
Population below 5m (% of total)	0.0	3.0	6.5
Population in urban agglomerations > 1 million (%)	..	18	22
Urban pop. growth (avg. annual %, 1990–2010)	1.2	0.3	2.3
Droughts, floods, extreme temps (% pop. avg., 1990–2009)	0.3		
Annual freshwater withdrawals (% of internal resources)	28.8	6.5	5.6
Agricultural land under irrigation (% of total ag. land)	7.3	..	..
Population living below $1.25 a day (% of total)	<2	3.7	..
Nationally terrestrial protected areas (% of total land area)	4.8	7.5	13.6
Under-five mortality rate (per 1,000)	12	23	20
Child malnutrition, underweight (% of under age five)	1.8	..	4.1
Malaria incidence rate (per 100,000 people)	..	..	80
Resilience			
Access to improved sanitation (% of total pop.)	89	89	68
Access to improved water source (% of total pop.)	100	95	92
Cereal yield (kg. per hectare)	3,373	2,475	3,690
Access to electricity (% of total population)	..	..	98.0
Paved roads (% of total roads)	56.5	85.8	50.5
Health workers (per 1,000 people)	6.9	9.9	4.5
Foreign direct investment, net inflows (% of GDP)	3.2	2.8	2.7
Invest. in infrastructure w/private participation ($ millions)	86	22,652	26,166
Disaster risk reduction progress score (1–5 scale; 5 = best)	3.3		
Ease of doing business (ranking 1–183; 1 = best)	22		
Public sector mgmt & institutions avg. (1–6 scale; 6 = best)	..		
Primary completion rate, total (% of relevant age group)	92	95	98
Ratio of girls to boys in primary & secondary school (%)	99	97	103
GHG Emissions and Energy Use			
CO_2 emissions per capita (metric tons)	5.8	7.7	5.3
CO_2 emissions per units of GDP (kg/$1,000 of 2005 PPP $)	655.2	708.0	659.4
CO_2 emissions, total (MtCO_2)	11.8	3,110	12,860
GHG net emissions/removals by LUCF (2002, MtCO_2e)	-2.6		
Methane (CH_4) emissions, total (MtCO_2e)	1.4	937	3,455
Nitrous oxide (N_2O) emissions, total (MtCO_2e)	0.6	214	1,144
Other GHG emissions, total (MtCO_2e)	0.1	76	243
Energy use per capita (kilograms of oil equivalent)	1,352	2,833	1,848
Energy use per units of GDP (kg oil eq./$1,000 of 2005 PPP $)	155.6	276.8	227.1

National-Level Actions

Latest UNFCCC national communication	1/15/2009 (2nd)
Annex-I emissions reduction target	n/a
NAMA submission	Yes
NAPA submission	n/a
Renewable energy target	..

Carbon Markets

Hosted Clean Development Mechanism (CDM) projects	1
Issued Certified Emission Reductions (CERs) from CDM (thousands)	0
Hosted Joint Implementation (JI) projects	n/a
Issued Emission Reduction Units (ERUs) from JI (thousands)	n/a

Madagascar

Population (millions)	20.7	GDP ($ billions)	8.7
Pop. growth (avg. ann. %, 1990-2010)	3.0	GNI per capita (Atlas $)	430

Climate

Average daily min/max temperature (1961-90, Celsius)	18 / 27
Projected annual temperature change (2045-65, Celsius)	1.7 to 2.1
Average annual precipitation (1961-90, mm)	1,513
Projected annual precipitation change (2045-65, mm)	-104 to 56
Projected change in annual hot days/warm nights	8 / 16
Projected change in annual cool days/cold nights	-3 / -3

	Country data	Sub-Saharan Africa	Low Income
Exposure to Impacts			
Land area below 5m (% of land area)	1.3	0.4	0.7
Population below 5m (% of total)	2.0	2.0	5.1
Population in urban agglomerations > 1 million (%)	9	14	11
Urban pop. growth (avg. annual %, 1990-2010)	4.3	4.0	3.7
Droughts, floods, extreme temps (% pop. avg., 1990-2009)	0.9		
Annual freshwater withdrawals (% of internal resources)	4.4	3.2	3.7
Agricultural land under irrigation (% of total ag. land)	2.2	..	..
Population living below $1.25 a day (% of total)	67.8	50.9	..
Nationally terrestrial protected areas (% of total land area)	2.9	11.7	10.6
Under-five mortality rate (per 1,000)	62	121	108
Child malnutrition, underweight (% of under age five)	36.8	24.6	28.3
Malaria incidence rate (per 100,000 people)	3,735	26,113	16,659
Resilience			
Access to improved sanitation (% of total pop.)	11	31	35
Access to improved water source (% of total pop.)	41	60	63
Cereal yield (kg. per hectare)	2,582	1,297	2,047
Access to electricity (% of total population)	19.0	32.5	23.0
Paved roads (% of total roads)	11.6	18.3	14.1
Health workers (per 1,000 people)	0.2	1.2	0.7
Foreign direct investment, net inflows (% of GDP)	9.9	3.6	3.2
Invest. in infrastructure w/private participation ($ millions)	132	11,957	4,471
Disaster risk reduction progress score (1-5 scale; 5 = best)	3.8		
Ease of doing business (ranking 1-183; 1 = best)	137		
Public sector mgmt & institutions avg. (1-6 scale; 6 = best)	3.0		
Primary completion rate, total (% of relevant age group)	79	67	65
Ratio of girls to boys in primary & secondary school (%)	97	89	91
GHG Emissions and Energy Use			
CO_2 emissions per capita (metric tons)	0.1	0.8	0.3
CO_2 emissions per units of GDP (kg/$1,000 of 2005 PPP $)	102.9	428.6	270.2
CO_2 emissions, total (MtCO_2)	1.9	685	219
GHG net emissions/removals by LUCF (2000, MtCO_2e)	-233.3		
Methane (CH_4) emissions, total (MtCO_2e)	..	590	436
Nitrous oxide (N_2O) emissions, total (MtCO_2e)	..	334	209
Other GHG emissions, total (MtCO_2e)	..	..	..
Energy use per capita (kilograms of oil equivalent)	..	689	365
Energy use per units of GDP (kg oil eq./$1,000 of 2005 PPP $)	..	308.4	303.9

National-Level Actions

Latest UNFCCC national communication	12/7/2010 (2nd)
Annex-I emissions reduction target	n/a
NAMA submission	Yes
NAPA submission	Yes
Renewable energy target	Yes

Carbon Markets

Hosted Clean Development Mechanism (CDM) projects	1
Issued Certified Emission Reductions (CERs) from CDM (thousands)	0
Hosted Joint Implementation (JI) projects	n/a
Issued Emission Reduction Units (ERUs) from JI (thousands)	n/a

Maldives

Population (thousands)	315.9	GDP ($ billions)	1.5
Pop. growth (avg. ann. %, 1990–2010)	1.8	GNI per capita (Atlas $)	4,240

Climate

Average daily min/max temperature (1961–90, Celsius)	25 / 31
Projected annual temperature change (2045–65, Celsius)	1.5 to 1.8
Average annual precipitation (1961–90, mm)	1,972
Projected annual precipitation change (2045–65, mm)	-2 to 319
Projected change in annual hot days/warm nights	22 / 27
Projected change in annual cool days/cold nights	-3 / -3

	Country data	South Asia	Upper middle income
Exposure to Impacts			
Land area below 5m (% of land area)	100.0	1.5	1.8
Population below 5m (% of total)	100.0	4.4	6.5
Population in urban agglomerations > 1 million (%)	..	13	22
Urban pop. growth (avg. annual %, 1990–2010)	4.1	2.7	2.3
Droughts, floods, extreme temps (% pop. avg., 1990–2009)	0.0		
Annual freshwater withdrawals (% of internal resources)	..	50.6	5.6
Agricultural land under irrigation (% of total ag. land)	..	..	..
Population living below $1.25 a day (% of total)	<2	40.3	..
Nationally terrestrial protected areas (% of total land area)	..	6.1	13.6
Under-five mortality rate (per 1,000)	15	67	20
Child malnutrition, underweight (% of under age five)	25.7	42.5	4.1
Malaria incidence rate (per 100,000 people)	..	1,127	80
Resilience			
Access to improved sanitation (% of total pop.)	98	36	68
Access to improved water source (% of total pop.)	91	87	92
Cereal yield (kg. per hectare)	2,042	2,728	3,690
Access to electricity (% of total population)	..	62.1	98.0
Paved roads (% of total roads)	100.0	58.9	50.5
Health workers (per 1,000 people)	6.0	1.7	4.5
Foreign direct investment, net inflows (% of GDP)	11.1	1.3	2.7
Invest. in infrastructure w/private participation ($ millions)	490	73,548	26,166
Disaster risk reduction progress score (1–5 scale; 5 = best)	2.3		
Ease of doing business (ranking 1–183; 1 = best)	79		
Public sector mgmt & institutions avg. (1–6 scale; 6 = best)	3.5		
Primary completion rate, total (% of relevant age group)	119	86	98
Ratio of girls to boys in primary & secondary school (%)	98	92	103
GHG Emissions and Energy Use			
CO_2 emissions per capita (metric tons)	3.0	1.3	5.3
CO_2 emissions per units of GDP (kg/$1,000 of 2005 PPP $)	580.8	504.6	659.4
CO_2 emissions, total (MtCO$_2$)	0.9	1,970	12,860
GHG net emissions/removals by LUCF (MtCO$_2$e)	..		
Methane (CH$_4$) emissions, total (MtCO$_2$e)	..	846	3,455
Nitrous oxide (N$_2$O) emissions, total (MtCO$_2$e)	..	268	1,144
Other GHG emissions, total (MtCO$_2$e)	..	9	243
Energy use per capita (kilograms of oil equivalent)	985	532	1,848
Energy use per units of GDP (kg oil eq./$1,000 of 2005 PPP $)	200.3	193.5	227.1

National-Level Actions

Latest UNFCCC national communication	11/5/2001 (1st)
Annex-I emissions reduction target	n/a
NAMA submission	Yes, with Goal
NAPA submission	Yes
Renewable energy target	..

Carbon Markets

Hosted Clean Development Mechanism (CDM) projects	..
Issued Certified Emission Reductions (CERs) from CDM (thousands)	..
Hosted Joint Implementation (JI) projects	n/a
Issued Emission Reduction Units (ERUs) from JI (thousands)	n/a

Mali

Population (millions)	15.4	GDP ($ billions)	9.3
Pop. growth (avg. ann. %, 1990-2010)	2.9	GNI per capita (Atlas $)	600

Climate

Average daily min/max temperature (1961-90, Celsius)	21 / 36
Projected annual temperature change (2045-65, Celsius)	2.5 to 3.1
Average annual precipitation (1961-90, mm)	282
Projected annual precipitation change (2045-65, mm)	-142 to 43
Projected change in annual hot days/warm nights	5 / 13
Projected change in annual cool days/cold nights	-2 / -2

	Country data	Sub-Saharan Africa	Low income
Exposure to Impacts			
Land area below 5m (% of land area)	0.0	0.4	0.7
Population below 5m (% of total)	0.0	2.0	5.1
Population in urban agglomerations > 1 million (%)	11	14	11
Urban pop. growth (avg. annual %, 1990-2010)	4.6	4.0	3.7
Droughts, floods, extreme temps (% pop. avg., 1990-2009)	0.7		
Annual freshwater withdrawals (% of internal resources)	10.9	3.2	3.7
Agricultural land under irrigation (% of total ag. land)	..	..	..
Population living below $1.25 a day (% of total)	51.4	50.9	..
Nationally terrestrial protected areas (% of total land area)	2.4	11.7	10.6
Under-five mortality rate (per 1,000)	178	121	108
Child malnutrition, underweight (% of under age five)	27.9	24.6	28.3
Malaria incidence rate (per 100,000 people)	25,366	26,113	16,659
Resilience			
Access to improved sanitation (% of total pop.)	36	31	35
Access to improved water source (% of total pop.)	56	60	63
Cereal yield (kg. per hectare)	1,588	1,297	2,047
Access to electricity (% of total population)	..	32.5	23.0
Paved roads (% of total roads)	19.0	18.3	14.1
Health workers (per 1,000 people)	0.3	1.2	0.7
Foreign direct investment, net inflows (% of GDP)	1.6	3.6	3.2
Invest. in infrastructure w/private participation ($ millions)	254	11,957	4,471
Disaster risk reduction progress score (1-5 scale; 5 = best)	..		
Ease of doing business (ranking 1-183; 1 = best)	146		
Public sector mgmt & institutions avg. (1-6 scale; 6 = best)	3.4		
Primary completion rate, total (% of relevant age group)	64	67	65
Ratio of girls to boys in primary & secondary school (%)	80	89	91
GHG Emissions and Energy Use			
CO_2 emissions per capita (metric tons)	0.0	0.8	0.3
CO_2 emissions per units of GDP (kg/$1,000 of 2005 PPP $)	44.2	428.6	270.2
CO_2 emissions, total (MtCO$_2$)	0.6	685	219
GHG net emissions/removals by LUCF (1995, MtCO$_2$e)	-9.7		
Methane (CH_4) emissions, total (MtCO$_2$e)	..	590	436
Nitrous oxide (N_2O) emissions, total (MtCO$_2$e)	..	334	209
Other GHG emissions, total (MtCO$_2$e)	..	..	..
Energy use per capita (kilograms of oil equivalent)	..	689	365
Energy use per units of GDP (kg oil eq./$1,000 of 2005 PPP $)	..	308.4	303.9

National-Level Actions

Latest UNFCCC national communication	11/13/2000 (1st)
Annex-I emissions reduction target	n/a
NAMA submission	..
NAPA submission	Yes
Renewable energy target	Yes

Carbon Markets

Hosted Clean Development Mechanism (CDM) projects	1
Issued Certified Emission Reductions (CERs) from CDM (thousands)	0
Hosted Joint Implementation (JI) projects	n/a
Issued Emission Reduction Units (ERUs) from JI (thousands)	n/a

Malta

| Population (thousands) | 413.0 | GDP ($ billions) | 8.0 |
| Pop. growth (avg. ann. %, 1990–2010) | 0.7 | GNI per capita (Atlas $) | 18,430 |

Climate
Average daily min/max temperature (1961–90, Celsius)	15 / 23
Projected annual temperature change (2045–65, Celsius)	1.7 to 2.1
Average annual precipitation (1961–90, mm)	383
Projected annual precipitation change (2045–65, mm)	-67 to -28
Projected change in annual hot days/warm nights	5 / 7
Projected change in annual cool days/cold nights	-2 / -2

	Country data	High income
Exposure to Impacts		
Land area below 5m (% of land area)	19.4	2.2
Population below 5m (% of total)	21.8	7.7
Population in urban agglomerations > 1 million (%)	..	..
Urban pop. growth (avg. annual %, 1990–2010)	0.9	1.0
Droughts, floods, extreme temps (% pop. avg., 1990–2009)	..	
Annual freshwater withdrawals (% of internal resources)	53.5	10.4
Agricultural land under irrigation (% of total ag. land)	22.2	..
Population living below $1.25 a day (% of total)	..	..
Nationally terrestrial protected areas (% of total land area)	17.2	13.4
Under-five mortality rate (per 1,000)	6	6
Child malnutrition, underweight (% of under age five)	..	..
Malaria incidence rate (per 100,000 people)	..	..
Resilience		
Access to improved sanitation (% of total pop.)	100	100
Access to improved water source (% of total pop.)	100	100
Cereal yield (kg. per hectare)	4,431	5,445
Access to electricity (% of total population)	..	..
Paved roads (% of total roads)	87.5	87.3
Health workers (per 1,000 people)	9.7	10.7
Foreign direct investment, net inflows (% of GDP)	9.4	1.8
Invest. in infrastructure w/private participation ($ millions)	..	
Disaster risk reduction progress score (1–5 scale; 5 = best)	..	
Ease of doing business (ranking 1–183; 1 = best)	..	
Public sector mgmt & institutions avg. (1–6 scale; 6 = best)	..	
Primary completion rate, total (% of relevant age group)	100	97
Ratio of girls to boys in primary & secondary school (%)	99	100
GHG Emissions and Energy Use		
CO_2 emissions per capita (metric tons)	6.2	11.9
CO_2 emissions per units of GDP (kg/$1,000 of 2005 PPP $)	274.3	354.4
CO_2 emissions, total (MtCO$_2$)	2.6	13,285
GHG net emissions/removals by LUCF (2009, MtCO$_2$e)	-0.1	
Methane (CH$_4$) emissions, total (MtCO$_2$e)	0.2	1,539
Nitrous oxide (N$_2$O) emissions, total (MtCO$_2$e)	0.1	813
Other GHG emissions, total (MtCO$_2$e)	0.1	460
Energy use per capita (kilograms of oil equivalent)	1,935	4,944
Energy use per units of GDP (kg oil eq./$1,000 of 2005 PPP $)	87.5	147.0

National-Level Actions
Latest UNFCCC national communication	7/27/2010 (2nd)
Annex-I emissions reduction target (base year: 1990)	20% / 30% (EU)
NAMA submission	n/a
NAPA submission	n/a
Renewable energy target	Yes

Carbon Markets
Hosted Clean Development Mechanism (CDM) projects	n/a
Issued Certified Emission Reductions (CERs) from CDM (thousands)	n/a
Hosted Joint Implementation (JI) projects	..
Issued Emission Reduction Units (ERUs) from JI (thousands)	..

Marshall Islands

Population (thousands)	54.0	GDP ($ millions)	155.8
Pop. growth (avg. ann. %, 1990–2010)	0.7	GNI per capita (Atlas $)	3,450

Climate

Average daily min/max temperature (1961-90, Celsius)	25 / 30
Projected annual temperature change (2045-65, Celsius)	1.4 to 1.8
Average annual precipitation (1961-90, mm)	2,705
Projected annual precipitation change (2045-65, mm)	8 to 240
Projected change in annual hot days/warm nights	21 / 27
Projected change in annual cool days/cold nights	-3 / -3

	Country data	East Asia & Pacific	Lower middle income
Exposure to Impacts			
Land area below 5m (% of land area)	99.0	2.5	1.7
Population below 5m (% of total)	99.4	10.3	6.5
Population in urban agglomerations > 1 million (%)	..		14
Urban pop. growth (avg. annual %, 1990-2010)	1.2	3.3	2.8
Droughts, floods, extreme temps (% pop. avg., 1990-2009)	0.1		
Annual freshwater withdrawals (% of internal resources)	..	10.8	18.7
Agricultural land under irrigation (% of total ag. land)	..		
Population living below $1.25 a day (% of total)	..	16.8	..
Nationally terrestrial protected areas (% of total land area)	3.1	14.9	9.5
Under-five mortality rate (per 1,000)	26	24	69
Child malnutrition, underweight (% of under age five)	..	9.0	31.7
Malaria incidence rate (per 100,000 people)	..	525	4,874
Resilience			
Access to improved sanitation (% of total pop.)	73	59	45
Access to improved water source (% of total pop.)	94	88	84
Cereal yield (kg. per hectare)	..	4,860	2,754
Access to electricity (% of total population)	..	90.8	67.3
Paved roads (% of total roads)	..	15.9	29.3
Health workers (per 1,000 people)	3.1	2.8	2.6
Foreign direct investment, net inflows (% of GDP)	5.6	3.0	2.4
Invest. in infrastructure w/private participation ($ millions)	..	14,638	81,789
Disaster risk reduction progress score (1-5 scale; 5 = best)	1.8		
Ease of doing business (ranking 1-183; 1 = best)	106		
Public sector mgmt & institutions avg. (1-6 scale; 6 = best)	..		
Primary completion rate, total (% of relevant age group)	94	97	88
Ratio of girls to boys in primary & secondary school (%)	101	103	93
GHG Emissions and Energy Use			
CO_2 emissions per capita (metric tons)	1.9	4.3	1.6
CO_2 emissions per units of GDP (kg/$1,000 of 2005 PPP $)	..	827.1	523.9
CO_2 emissions, total (MtCO_2)	0.1	8,259	3,744
GHG net emissions/removals by LUCF (MtCO_2e)	..		
Methane (CH_4) emissions, total (MtCO_2e)	..	1,928	1,705
Nitrous oxide (N_2O) emissions, total (MtCO_2e)	..	707	687
Other GHG emissions, total (MtCO_2e)	..	..	17
Energy use per capita (kilograms of oil equivalent)	610	1,436	680
Energy use per units of GDP (kg oil eq./$1,000 of 2005 PPP $)	..	259.5	217.9

National-Level Actions

Latest UNFCCC national communication	11/24/2000 (1st)
Annex-I emissions reduction target	n/a
NAMA submission	Yes, with Goal
NAPA submission	n/a
Renewable energy target	..

Carbon Markets

Hosted Clean Development Mechanism (CDM) projects	..
Issued Certified Emission Reductions (CERs) from CDM (thousands)	..
Hosted Joint Implementation (JI) projects	n/a
Issued Emission Reduction Units (ERUs) from JI (thousands)	n/a

Mauritania

Population (millions)	3.5	GDP ($ billions)	3.6
Pop. growth (avg. ann. %, 1990-2010)	2.8	GNI per capita (Atlas $)	1,030

Climate

Average daily min/max temperature (1961-90, Celsius)	20 / 35
Projected annual temperature change (2045-65, Celsius)	2.4 to 3.1
Average annual precipitation (1961-90, mm)	92
Projected annual precipitation change (2045-65, mm)	-113 to 9
Projected change in annual hot days/warm nights	5 / 11
Projected change in annual cool days/cold nights	-2 / -2

	Country data	Sub-Saharan Africa	Lower middle income
Exposure to Impacts			
Land area below 5m (% of land area)	1.0	0.4	1.7
Population below 5m (% of total)	20.4	2.0	6.5
Population in urban agglomerations > 1 million (%)	..	14	14
Urban pop. growth (avg. annual %, 1990-2010)	3.0	4.0	2.8
Droughts, floods, extreme temps (% pop. avg., 1990-2009)	3.1		
Annual freshwater withdrawals (% of internal resources)	399.8	3.2	18.7
Agricultural land under irrigation (% of total ag. land)	..	..	..
Population living below $1.25 a day (% of total)	21.2	50.9	..
Nationally terrestrial protected areas (% of total land area)	0.5	11.7	9.5
Under-five mortality rate (per 1,000)	111	121	69
Child malnutrition, underweight (% of under age five)	16.7	24.6	31.7
Malaria incidence rate (per 100,000 people)	17,325	26,113	4,874
Resilience			
Access to improved sanitation (% of total pop.)	26	31	45
Access to improved water source (% of total pop.)	49	60	84
Cereal yield (kg. per hectare)	876	1,297	2,754
Access to electricity (% of total population)	..	32.5	67.3
Paved roads (% of total roads)	26.8	18.3	29.3
Health workers (per 1,000 people)	0.8	1.2	2.6
Foreign direct investment, net inflows (% of GDP)	0.4	3.6	2.4
Invest. in infrastructure w/private participation ($ millions)	133	11,957	81,789
Disaster risk reduction progress score (1-5 scale; 5 = best)	..		
Ease of doing business (ranking 1-183; 1 = best)	159		
Public sector mgmt & institutions avg. (1-6 scale; 6 = best)	3.0		
Primary completion rate, total (% of relevant age group)	64	67	88
Ratio of girls to boys in primary & secondary school (%)	103	89	93
GHG Emissions and Energy Use			
CO$_2$ emissions per capita (metric tons)	0.6	0.8	1.6
CO$_2$ emissions per units of GDP (kg/$1,000 of 2005 PPP $)	343.6	428.6	523.9
CO$_2$ emissions, total (MtCO$_2$)	2.0	685	3,744
GHG net emissions/removals by LUCF (2000, MtCO$_2$e)	-1.3		
Methane (CH$_4$) emissions, total (MtCO$_2$e)	..	590	1,705
Nitrous oxide (N$_2$O) emissions, total (MtCO$_2$e)	..	334	687
Other GHG emissions, total (MtCO$_2$e)	..	..	17
Energy use per capita (kilograms of oil equivalent)	..	689	680
Energy use per units of GDP (kg oil eq./$1,000 of 2005 PPP $)	..	308.4	217.9

National-Level Actions

Latest UNFCCC national communication	12/6/2008 (2nd)
Annex-I emissions reduction target	n/a
NAMA submission	Yes
NAPA submission	Yes
Renewable energy target	..

Carbon Markets

Hosted Clean Development Mechanism (CDM) projects	..
Issued Certified Emission Reductions (CERs) from CDM (thousands)	..
Hosted Joint Implementation (JI) projects	n/a
Issued Emission Reduction Units (ERUs) from JI (thousands)	n/a

Mauritius

Population (millions)	1.3	GDP ($ billions)	9.7
Pop. growth (avg. ann. %, 1990–2010)	1.0	GNI per capita (Atlas $)	7,750

Climate

Average daily min/max temperature (1961–90, Celsius)	19 / 26
Projected annual temperature change (2045–65, Celsius)	1.3 to 1.7
Average annual precipitation (1961–90, mm)	2,041
Projected annual precipitation change (2045–65, mm)	-165 to 67
Projected change in annual hot days/warm nights	8 / 14
Projected change in annual cool days/cold nights	-3 / -3

	Country data	Sub-Saharan Africa	Upper middle income
Exposure to Impacts			
Land area below 5m (% of land area)	7.1	0.4	1.8
Population below 5m (% of total)	5.6	2.0	6.5
Population in urban agglomerations > 1 million (%)	..	14	22
Urban pop. growth (avg. annual %, 1990–2010)	0.8	4.0	2.3
Droughts, floods, extreme temps (% pop. avg., 1990–2009)	0.0		
Annual freshwater withdrawals (% of internal resources)	26.4	3.2	5.6
Agricultural land under irrigation (% of total ag. land)	21.4	..	..
Population living below $1.25 a day (% of total)	..	50.9	..
Nationally terrestrial protected areas (% of total land area)	4.5	11.7	13.6
Under-five mortality rate (per 1,000)	15	121	20
Child malnutrition, underweight (% of under age five)	..	24.6	4.1
Malaria incidence rate (per 100,000 people)	..	26,113	80
Resilience			
Access to improved sanitation (% of total pop.)	91	31	68
Access to improved water source (% of total pop.)	99	60	92
Cereal yield (kg. per hectare)	8,307	1,297	3,690
Access to electricity (% of total population)	99.4	32.5	98.0
Paved roads (% of total roads)	98.0	18.3	50.5
Health workers (per 1,000 people)	4.8	1.2	4.5
Foreign direct investment, net inflows (% of GDP)	4.4	3.6	2.7
Invest. in infrastructure w/private participation ($ millions)	26	11,957	26,166
Disaster risk reduction progress score (1–5 scale; 5 = best)	3.5		
Ease of doing business (ranking 1–183; 1 = best)	23		
Public sector mgmt & institutions avg. (1–6 scale; 6 = best)	..		
Primary completion rate, total (% of relevant age group)	89	67	98
Ratio of girls to boys in primary & secondary school (%)	101	89	103
GHG Emissions and Energy Use			
CO_2 emissions per capita (metric tons)	3.1	0.8	5.3
CO_2 emissions per units of GDP (kg/$1,000 of 2005 PPP $)	269.6	428.6	659.4
CO_2 emissions, total (MtCO$_2$)	4.0	685	12,860
GHG net emissions/removals by LUCF (1995, MtCO$_2$e)	-0.2		
Methane (CH$_4$) emissions, total (MtCO$_2$e)	..	590	3,455
Nitrous oxide (N$_2$O) emissions, total (MtCO$_2$e)	..	334	1,144
Other GHG emissions, total (MtCO$_2$e)	..	..	243
Energy use per capita (kilograms of oil equivalent)	947	689	1,848
Energy use per units of GDP (kg oil eq./$1,000 of 2005 PPP $)	85.9	308.4	227.1

National-Level Actions

Latest UNFCCC national communication	5/28/1999 (1st)
Annex-I emissions reduction target	n/a
NAMA submission	Yes
NAPA submission	n/a
Renewable energy target	Yes

Carbon Markets

Hosted Clean Development Mechanism (CDM) projects	0
Issued Certified Emission Reductions (CERs) from CDM (thousands)	0
Hosted Joint Implementation (JI) projects	n/a
Issued Emission Reduction Units (ERUs) from JI (thousands)	n/a

Mayotte

Population (thousands)	204.1	GDP ($ millions)		..
Pop. growth (avg. ann. %, 1990–2010)	4.0	GNI per capita (Atlas $)		..

Climate
Average daily min/max temperature (1961–90, Celsius)	..
Projected annual temperature change (2045–65, Celsius)	1.5 to 1.8
Average annual precipitation (1961–90, mm)	
Projected annual precipitation change (2045–65, mm)	-24 to 112
Projected change in annual hot days/warm nights	13 / 20
Projected change in annual cool days/cold nights	-3 / -3

	Country data	Sub-Saharan Africa	Upper middle income
Exposure to Impacts			
Land area below 5m (% of land area)	21.6	0.4	1.8
Population below 5m (% of total)	21.6	2.0	6.5
Population in urban agglomerations > 1 million (%)	..	14	22
Urban pop. growth (avg. annual %, 1990–2010)	..	4.0	2.3
Droughts, floods, extreme temps (% pop. avg., 1990–2009)	..		
Annual freshwater withdrawals (% of internal resources)	..	3.2	5.6
Agricultural land under irrigation (% of total ag. land)	..		..
Population living below $1.25 a day (% of total)	..	50.9	..
Nationally terrestrial protected areas (% of total land area)	2.2	11.7	13.6
Under-five mortality rate (per 1,000)	..	121	20
Child malnutrition, underweight (% of under age five)	..	24.6	4.1
Malaria incidence rate (per 100,000 people)	..	26,113	80
Resilience			
Access to improved sanitation (% of total pop.)	..	31	68
Access to improved water source (% of total pop.)	..	60	92
Cereal yield (kg. per hectare)	..	1,297	3,690
Access to electricity (% of total population)	..	32.5	98.0
Paved roads (% of total roads)	..	18.3	50.5
Health workers (per 1,000 people)	..	1.2	4.5
Foreign direct investment, net inflows (% of GDP)	..	3.6	2.7
Invest. in infrastructure w/private participation ($ millions)	..	11,957	26,166
Disaster risk reduction progress score (1-5 scale; 5 = best)	..		
Ease of doing business (ranking 1-183; 1 = best)	..		
Public sector mgmt & institutions avg. (1-6 scale; 6 = best)	..		
Primary completion rate, total (% of relevant age group)	..	67	98
Ratio of girls to boys in primary & secondary school (%)	..	89	103
GHG Emissions and Energy Use			
CO_2 emissions per capita (metric tons)	..	0.8	5.3
CO_2 emissions per units of GDP (kg/$1,000 of 2005 PPP $)	..	428.6	659.4
CO_2 emissions, total (MtCO_2)	..	685	12,860
GHG net emissions/removals by LUCF (MtCO_2e)	..		
Methane (CH_4) emissions, total (MtCO_2e)	..	590	3,455
Nitrous oxide (N_2O) emissions, total (MtCO_2e)	..	334	1,144
Other GHG emissions, total (MtCO_2e)	..	..	243
Energy use per capita (kilograms of oil equivalent)	..	689	1,848
Energy use per units of GDP (kg oil eq./$1,000 of 2005 PPP $)	..	308.4	227.1

National-Level Actions
Latest UNFCCC national communication	n/a
Annex-I emissions reduction target	n/a
NAMA submission	n/a
NAPA submission	n/a
Renewable energy target	..

Carbon Markets
Hosted Clean Development Mechanism (CDM) projects	n/a
Issued Certified Emission Reductions (CERs) from CDM (thousands)	n/a
Hosted Joint Implementation (JI) projects	n/a
Issued Emission Reduction Units (ERUs) from JI (thousands)	n/a

Mexico

Population (millions)	113.4	GDP ($ billions)	1,039.7
Pop. growth (avg. ann. %, 1990-2010)	1.5	GNI per capita (Atlas $)	8,930

Climate

Average daily min/max temperature (1961-90, Celsius)	14 / 29
Projected annual temperature change (2045-65, Celsius)	1.7 to 2.8
Average annual precipitation (1961-90, mm)	752
Projected annual precipitation change (2045-65, mm)	-178 to 10
Projected change in annual hot days/warm nights	6 / 12
Projected change in annual cool days/cold nights	-2 / -2

	Country data	Latin America & the Carib.	Upper middle income
Exposure to Impacts			
Land area below 5m (% of land area)	2.9	1.5	1.8
Population below 5m (% of total)	2.7	3.8	6.5
Population in urban agglomerations > 1 million (%)	35	35	22
Urban pop. growth (avg. annual %, 1990-2010)	1.9	2.0	2.3
Droughts, floods, extreme temps (% pop. avg., 1990-2009)	0.1		
Annual freshwater withdrawals (% of internal resources)	19.3	2.0	5.6
Agricultural land under irrigation (% of total ag. land)	5.5	..	..
Population living below $1.25 a day (% of total)	<2	8.1	..
Nationally terrestrial protected areas (% of total land area)	11.1	20.8	13.6
Under-five mortality rate (per 1,000)	17	23	20
Child malnutrition, underweight (% of under age five)	3.4	3.8	4.1
Malaria incidence rate (per 100,000 people)	3	206	80
Resilience			
Access to improved sanitation (% of total pop.)	85	79	68
Access to improved water source (% of total pop.)	94	93	92
Cereal yield (kg. per hectare)	3,434	3,337	3,690
Access to electricity (% of total population)	..	93.4	98.0
Paved roads (% of total roads)	35.3	28.1	50.5
Health workers (per 1,000 people)	6.9	6.9	4.5
Foreign direct investment, net inflows (% of GDP)	1.8	2.3	2.7
Invest. in infrastructure w/private participation ($ millions)	6,360	33,064	26,166
Disaster risk reduction progress score (1-5 scale; 5 = best)	4.3		
Ease of doing business (ranking 1-183; 1 = best)	53		
Public sector mgmt & institutions avg. (1-6 scale; 6 = best)	..		
Primary completion rate, total (% of relevant age group)	104	102	98
Ratio of girls to boys in primary & secondary school (%)	102	102	103
GHG Emissions and Energy Use			
CO_2 emissions per capita (metric tons)	4.3	2.8	5.3
CO_2 emissions per units of GDP (kg/$1,000 of 2005 PPP $)	332.6	285.6	659.4
CO_2 emissions, total (MtCO_2)	475.8	1,584	12,860
GHG net emissions/removals by LUCF (2006, MtCO_2e)	70.2		
Methane (CH_4) emissions, total (MtCO_2e)	128.2	1,009	3,455
Nitrous oxide (N_2O) emissions, total (MtCO_2e)	42.5	442	1,144
Other GHG emissions, total (MtCO_2e)	4.6	21	243
Energy use per capita (kilograms of oil equivalent)	1,497	1,245	1,848
Energy use per units of GDP (kg oil eq./$1,000 of 2005 PPP $)	119.8	130.6	227.1

National-Level Actions

Latest UNFCCC national communication	4/20/2010 (4th)
Annex-I emissions reduction target	n/a
NAMA submission	Yes, with Goal
NAPA submission	n/a
Renewable energy target	..

Carbon Markets

Hosted Clean Development Mechanism (CDM) projects	132
Issued Certified Emission Reductions (CERs) from CDM (thousands)	10,122
Hosted Joint Implementation (JI) projects	n/a
Issued Emission Reduction Units (ERUs) from JI (thousands)	n/a

Micronesia, Fed. Sts.

Population (thousands)	111.1	GDP ($ millions)	287.4
Pop. growth (avg. ann. %, 1990–2010)	0.7	GNI per capita (Atlas $)	2,700

Climate

Average daily min/max temperature (1961–90, Celsius)	..
Projected annual temperature change (2045–65, Celsius)	1.4 to 1.7
Average annual precipitation (1961–90, mm)	..
Projected annual precipitation change (2045–65, mm)	−85 to 411
Projected change in annual hot days/warm nights	26 / 27
Projected change in annual cool days/cold nights	−3 / −3

	Country data	East Asia & Pacific	Lower middle income
Exposure to Impacts			
Land area below 5m (% of land area)	33.4	2.5	1.7
Population below 5m (% of total)	54.9	10.3	6.5
Population in urban agglomerations > 1 million (%)	..	..	14
Urban pop. growth (avg. annual %, 1990–2010)	0.1	3.3	2.8
Droughts, floods, extreme temps (% pop. avg., 1990–2009)	1.3		
Annual freshwater withdrawals (% of internal resources)	..	10.8	18.7
Agricultural land under irrigation (% of total ag. land)	..	..	..
Population living below $1.25 a day (% of total)	31.2	16.8	..
Nationally terrestrial protected areas (% of total land area)	4.0	14.9	9.5
Under-five mortality rate (per 1,000)	42	24	69
Child malnutrition, underweight (% of under age five)	..	9.0	31.7
Malaria incidence rate (per 100,000 people)	..	525	4,874
Resilience			
Access to improved sanitation (% of total pop.)	27	59	45
Access to improved water source (% of total pop.)	94	88	84
Cereal yield (kg. per hectare)	1,450	4,860	2,754
Access to electricity (% of total population)	..	90.8	67.3
Paved roads (% of total roads)	17.5	15.9	29.3
Health workers (per 1,000 people)	2.8	2.8	2.6
Foreign direct investment, net inflows (% of GDP)	3.5	3.0	2.4
Invest. in infrastructure w/private participation ($ millions)	..	14,638	81,789
Disaster risk reduction progress score (1–5 scale; 5 = best)	..		
Ease of doing business (ranking 1–183; 1 = best)	140		
Public sector mgmt & institutions avg. (1–6 scale; 6 = best)	..		
Primary completion rate, total (% of relevant age group)	..	97	88
Ratio of girls to boys in primary & secondary school (%)	102	103	93
GHG Emissions and Energy Use			
CO_2 emissions per capita (metric tons)	0.6	4.3	1.6
CO_2 emissions per units of GDP (kg/$1,000 of 2005 PPP $)	196.8	827.1	523.9
CO_2 emissions, total (MtCO$_2$)	0.1	8,259	3,744
GHG net emissions/removals by LUCF (MtCO$_2$e)	..		
Methane (CH$_4$) emissions, total (MtCO$_2$e)	..	1,928	1,705
Nitrous oxide (N$_2$O) emissions, total (MtCO$_2$e)	..	707	687
Other GHG emissions, total (MtCO$_2$e)	..	..	17
Energy use per capita (kilograms of oil equivalent)	..	1,436	680
Energy use per units of GDP (kg oil eq./$1,000 of 2005 PPP $)	..	259.5	217.9

National-Level Actions

Latest UNFCCC national communication	10/30/1999 (1st)
Annex-I emissions reduction target	n/a
NAMA submission	..
NAPA submission	n/a
Renewable energy target	..

Carbon Markets

Hosted Clean Development Mechanism (CDM) projects	..
Issued Certified Emission Reductions (CERs) from CDM (thousands)	..
Hosted Joint Implementation (JI) projects	n/a
Issued Emission Reduction Units (ERUs) from JI (thousands)	n/a

Moldova

Population (millions)	3.6	GDP ($ billions)	5.8
Pop. growth (avg. ann. %, 1990–2010)	-0.2	GNI per capita (Atlas $)	1,810

Climate

Average daily min/max temperature (1961-90, Celsius)	5 / 14
Projected annual temperature change (2045-65, Celsius)	2.0 to 3.3
Average annual precipitation (1961-90, mm)	553
Projected annual precipitation change (2045-65, mm)	-72 to 11
Projected change in annual hot days/warm nights	3 / 5
Projected change in annual cool days/cold nights	-1 / -2

	Country data	Europe & Central Asia	Lower middle income
Exposure to Impacts			
Land area below 5m (% of land area)	1.3	2.5	1.7
Population below 5m (% of total)	0.9	3.0	6.5
Population in urban agglomerations > 1 million (%)	..	18	14
Urban pop. growth (avg. annual %, 1990-2010)	-0.8	0.3	2.8
Droughts, floods, extreme temps (% pop. avg., 1990-2009)	0.3		
Annual freshwater withdrawals (% of internal resources)	191.5	6.5	18.7
Agricultural land under irrigation (% of total ag. land)	9.2	..	..
Population living below $1.25 a day (% of total)	<2	3.7	..
Nationally terrestrial protected areas (% of total land area)	1.4	7.5	9.5
Under-five mortality rate (per 1,000)	19	23	69
Child malnutrition, underweight (% of under age five)	3.2	..	31.7
Malaria incidence rate (per 100,000 people)	..	..	4,874
Resilience			
Access to improved sanitation (% of total pop.)	79	89	45
Access to improved water source (% of total pop.)	90	95	84
Cereal yield (kg. per hectare)	2,340	2,475	2,754
Access to electricity (% of total population)	..	..	67.3
Paved roads (% of total roads)	85.8	85.8	29.3
Health workers (per 1,000 people)	9.3	9.9	2.6
Foreign direct investment, net inflows (% of GDP)	3.3	2.8	2.4
Invest. in infrastructure w/private participation ($ millions)	35	22,652	81,789
Disaster risk reduction progress score (1-5 scale; 5 = best)	..		
Ease of doing business (ranking 1-183; 1 = best)	81		
Public sector mgmt & institutions avg. (1-6 scale; 6 = best)	3.4		
Primary completion rate, total (% of relevant age group)	93	95	88
Ratio of girls to boys in primary & secondary school (%)	101	97	93
GHG Emissions and Energy Use			
CO_2 emissions per capita (metric tons)	1.3	7.7	1.6
CO_2 emissions per units of GDP (kg/$1,000 of 2005 PPP $)	483.1	708.0	523.9
CO_2 emissions, total (MtCO_2)	4.8	3,110	3,744
GHG net emissions/removals by LUCF (2005, MtCO_2e)	-1.4		
Methane (CH_4) emissions, total (MtCO_2e)	3.4	937	1,705
Nitrous oxide (N_2O) emissions, total (MtCO_2e)	0.8	214	687
Other GHG emissions, total (MtCO_2e)	0.0	76	17
Energy use per capita (kilograms of oil equivalent)	687	2,833	680
Energy use per units of GDP (kg oil eq./$1,000 of 2005 PPP $)	263.6	276.8	217.9

National-Level Actions

Latest UNFCCC national communication	1/27/2010 (2nd)
Annex-I emissions reduction target	n/a
NAMA submission	Yes, with Goal
NAPA submission	n/a
Renewable energy target	Yes

Carbon Markets

Hosted Clean Development Mechanism (CDM) projects	4
Issued Certified Emission Reductions (CERs) from CDM (thousands)	0
Hosted Joint Implementation (JI) projects	n/a
Issued Emission Reduction Units (ERUs) from JI (thousands)	n/a

Monaco

Population (thousands)	35.4	GDP ($ billions)	6.1
Pop. growth (avg. ann. %, 1990–2010)	0.7	GNI per capita (Atlas $)	183,150

Climate
Average daily min/max temperature (1961–90, Celsius)	10 / 17
Projected annual temperature change (2045–65, Celsius)	1.8 to 2.7
Average annual precipitation (1961–90, mm)	894
Projected annual precipitation change (2045–65, mm)	-114 to 1
Projected change in annual hot days/warm nights	4 / 7
Projected change in annual cool days/cold nights	-2 / -2

	Country data	High income
Exposure to Impacts		
Land area below 5m (% of land area)		
Population below 5m (% of total)	100.0	2.2
Population in urban agglomerations > 1 million (%)	100.0	7.7
Urban pop. growth (avg. annual %, 1990–2010)	..	..
Droughts, floods, extreme temps (% pop. avg., 1990–2009)	0.7	1.0
Annual freshwater withdrawals (% of internal resources)	..	
Agricultural land under irrigation (% of total ag. land)	..	10.4
Population living below $1.25 a day (% of total)	..	..
Nationally terrestrial protected areas (% of total land area)	..	..
Under-five mortality rate (per 1,000)	23.7	13.4
Child malnutrition, underweight (% of under age five)	4	6
Malaria incidence rate (per 100,000 people)	..	..
	..	..
Resilience		
Access to improved sanitation (% of total pop.)	100	100
Access to improved water source (% of total pop.)	100	100
Cereal yield (kg. per hectare)	..	5,445
Access to electricity (% of total population)		
Paved roads (% of total roads)	100.0	87.3
Health workers (per 1,000 people)	..	10.7
Foreign direct investment, net inflows (% of GDP)	..	1.8
Invest. in infrastructure w/private participation ($ millions)	..	..
Disaster risk reduction progress score (1–5 scale; 5 = best)	..	
Ease of doing business (ranking 1–183; 1 = best)	..	
Public sector mgmt & institutions avg. (1–6 scale; 6 = best)	..	
Primary completion rate, total (% of relevant age group)	132	97
Ratio of girls to boys in primary & secondary school (%)	98	100

	Country data	High income
GHG Emissions and Energy Use		
CO_2 emissions per capita (metric tons)	..	11.9
CO_2 emissions per units of GDP (kg/$1,000 of 2005 PPP $)	..	354.4
CO_2 emissions, total (MtCO_2)	..	13,285
GHG net emissions/removals by LUCF (2009, MtCO_2e)	0.0	
Methane (CH_4) emissions, total (MtCO_2e)	..	1,539
Nitrous oxide (N_2O) emissions, total (MtCO_2e)	..	813
Other GHG emissions, total (MtCO_2e)	..	460
Energy use per capita (kilograms of oil equivalent)	..	4,944
Energy use per units of GDP (kg oil eq./$1,000 of 2005 PPP $)	..	147.0

National-Level Actions	
Latest UNFCCC national communication	3/25/2011 (5th)
Annex-I emissions reduction target (base year: 1990)	30%
NAMA submission	n/a
NAPA submission	n/a
Renewable energy target	..

Carbon Markets	
Hosted Clean Development Mechanism (CDM) projects	n/a
Issued Certified Emission Reductions (CERs) from CDM (thousands)	n/a
Hosted Joint Implementation (JI) projects	..
Issued Emission Reduction Units (ERUs) from JI (thousands)	..

Mongolia

Population (millions)	2.8	GDP ($ billions)	6.1
Pop. growth (avg. ann. %, 1990–2010)	1.1	GNI per capita (Atlas $)	1,850

Climate

Average daily min/max temperature (1961-90, Celsius)	-8 / 6
Projected annual temperature change (2045-65, Celsius)	2.3 to 3.1
Average annual precipitation (1961-90, mm)	241
Projected annual precipitation change (2045-65, mm)	1 to 50
Projected change in annual hot days/warm nights	2 / 4
Projected change in annual cool days/cold nights	-1 / -1

	Country data	East Asia & Pacific	Lower middle income
Exposure to Impacts			
Land area below 5m (% of land area)	0.0	2.5	1.7
Population below 5m (% of total)	0.0	10.3	6.5
Population in urban agglomerations > 1 million (%)	..	..	14
Urban pop. growth (avg. annual %, 1990-2010)	1.2	3.3	2.8
Droughts, floods, extreme temps (% pop. avg., 1990-2009)	2.6		
Annual freshwater withdrawals (% of internal resources)	1.4	10.8	18.7
Agricultural land under irrigation (% of total ag. land)	..		..
Population living below $1.25 a day (% of total)	22.4	16.8	..
Nationally terrestrial protected areas (% of total land area)	13.4	14.9	9.5
Under-five mortality rate (per 1,000)	32	24	69
Child malnutrition, underweight (% of under age five)	5.3	9.0	31.7
Malaria incidence rate (per 100,000 people)	..	525	4,874
Resilience			
Access to improved sanitation (% of total pop.)	50	59	45
Access to improved water source (% of total pop.)	76	88	84
Cereal yield (kg. per hectare)	1,552	4,860	2,754
Access to electricity (% of total population)	67.0	90.8	67.3
Paved roads (% of total roads)	3.5	15.9	29.3
Health workers (per 1,000 people)	6.3	2.8	2.6
Foreign direct investment, net inflows (% of GDP)	23.9	3.0	2.4
Invest. in infrastructure w/private participation ($ millions)	2	14,638	81,789
Disaster risk reduction progress score (1-5 scale; 5 = best)	2.8		
Ease of doing business (ranking 1-183; 1 = best)	86		
Public sector mgmt & institutions avg. (1-6 scale; 6 = best)	3.4		
Primary completion rate, total (% of relevant age group)	93	97	88
Ratio of girls to boys in primary & secondary school (%)	103	103	93
GHG Emissions and Energy Use			
CO_2 emissions per capita (metric tons)	4.1	4.3	1.6
CO_2 emissions per units of GDP (kg/$1,000 of 2005 PPP $)	1,146.7	827.1	523.9
CO_2 emissions, total (MtCO_2)	10.9	8,259	3,744
GHG net emissions/removals by LUCF (2006, MtCO_2e)	-2.1		
Methane (CH_4) emissions, total (MtCO_2e)	6.1	1,928	1,705
Nitrous oxide (N_2O) emissions, total (MtCO_2e)	3.5	707	687
Other GHG emissions, total (MtCO_2e)	0.0	..	17
Energy use per capita (kilograms of oil equivalent)	1,194	1,436	680
Energy use per units of GDP (kg oil eq./$1,000 of 2005 PPP $)	345.1	259.5	217.9

National-Level Actions

Latest UNFCCC national communication	12/10/2010 (2nd)
Annex-I emissions reduction target	n/a
NAMA submission	Yes
NAPA submission	n/a
Renewable energy target	Yes

Carbon Markets

Hosted Clean Development Mechanism (CDM) projects	3
Issued Certified Emission Reductions (CERs) from CDM (thousands)	15
Hosted Joint Implementation (JI) projects	n/a
Issued Emission Reduction Units (ERUs) from JI (thousands)	n/a

Montenegro

Population (thousands)	631.5	GDP ($ billions)	4.0
Pop. growth (avg. ann. %, 1990–2010)	0.2	GNI per capita (Atlas $)	6,620

Climate
Average daily min/max temperature (1961–90, Celsius)	..
Projected annual temperature change (2045–65, Celsius)	1.9 to 2.9
Average annual precipitation (1961–90, mm)	..
Projected annual precipitation change (2045–65, mm)	-138 to -27
Projected change in annual hot days/warm nights	3 / 6
Projected change in annual cool days/cold nights	-2 / -1

	Country data	Europe & Central Asia	Upper middle income
Exposure to Impacts			
Land area below 5m (% of land area)	..	2.5	1.8
Population below 5m (% of total)	..	3.0	6.5
Population in urban agglomerations > 1 million (%)	..	18	22
Urban pop. growth (avg. annual %, 1990–2010)	1.3	0.3	2.3
Droughts, floods, extreme temps (% pop. avg., 1990–2009)	0.0		
Annual freshwater withdrawals (% of internal resources)	..	6.5	5.6
Agricultural land under irrigation (% of total ag. land)	..	..	..
Population living below $1.25 a day (% of total)	<2	3.7	..
Nationally terrestrial protected areas (% of total land area)	13.3	7.5	13.6
Under-five mortality rate (per 1,000)	8	23	20
Child malnutrition, underweight (% of under age five)	2.2	..	4.1
Malaria incidence rate (per 100,000 people)	..	..	80
Resilience			
Access to improved sanitation (% of total pop.)	92	89	68
Access to improved water source (% of total pop.)	98	95	92
Cereal yield (kg. per hectare)	3,464	2,475	3,690
Access to electricity (% of total population)	..	..	98.0
Paved roads (% of total roads)	..	85.8	50.5
Health workers (per 1,000 people)	7.5	9.9	4.5
Foreign direct investment, net inflows (% of GDP)	19.0	2.8	2.7
Invest. in infrastructure w/private participation ($ millions)	6	22,652	26,166
Disaster risk reduction progress score (1–5 scale; 5 = best)	..		
Ease of doing business (ranking 1–183; 1 = best)	56		
Public sector mgmt & institutions avg. (1–6 scale; 6 = best)	..		
Primary completion rate, total (% of relevant age group)	..	95	98
Ratio of girls to boys in primary & secondary school (%)	100	97	103
GHG Emissions and Energy Use			
CO_2 emissions per capita (metric tons)	3.1	7.7	5.3
CO_2 emissions per units of GDP (kg/$1,000 of 2005 PPP $)	293.7	708.0	659.4
CO_2 emissions, total (MtCO$_2$)	2.0	3,110	12,860
GHG net emissions/removals by LUCF (2003, MtCO$_2$e)	-0.9		
Methane (CH_4) emissions, total (MtCO$_2$e)	..	937	3,455
Nitrous oxide (N_2O) emissions, total (MtCO$_2$e)	..	214	1,144
Other GHG emissions, total (MtCO$_2$e)	..	76	243
Energy use per capita (kilograms of oil equivalent)	1,384	2,833	1,848
Energy use per units of GDP (kg oil eq./$1,000 of 2005 PPP $)	139.9	276.8	227.1

National-Level Actions
Latest UNFCCC national communication	10/12/2010 (1st)
Annex-I emissions reduction target	n/a
NAMA submission	
NAPA submission	n/a
Renewable energy target	..

Carbon Markets
Hosted Clean Development Mechanism (CDM) projects	..
Issued Certified Emission Reductions (CERs) from CDM (thousands)	..
Hosted Joint Implementation (JI) projects	n/a
Issued Emission Reduction Units (ERUs) from JI (thousands)	n/a

Morocco

Population (millions)	32.0	GDP ($ billions) 91.2
Pop. growth (avg. ann. %, 1990-2010)	1.3	GNI per capita (Atlas $) 2,900

Climate

Average daily min/max temperature (1961-90, Celsius)	11 / 23
Projected annual temperature change (2045-65, Celsius)	2.1 to 3.0
Average annual precipitation (1961-90, mm)	346
Projected annual precipitation change (2045-65, mm)	-62 to -5
Projected change in annual hot days/warm nights	4 / 8
Projected change in annual cool days/cold nights	-2 / -2

	Country data	Middle East & N. Africa	Lower middle income
Exposure to Impacts			
Land area below 5m (% of land area)	0.7	1.4	1.7
Population below 5m (% of total)	3.8	9.7	6.5
Population in urban agglomerations > 1 million (%)	19	20	14
Urban pop. growth (avg. annual %, 1990-2010)	2.1	2.5	2.8
Droughts, floods, extreme temps (% pop. avg., 1990-2009)	0.1		
Annual freshwater withdrawals (% of internal resources)	43.4	121.9	18.7
Agricultural land under irrigation (% of total ag. land)	4.6	..	..
Population living below $1.25 a day (% of total)	2.5	3.6	..
Nationally terrestrial protected areas (% of total land area)	1.5	4.0	9.5
Under-five mortality rate (per 1,000)	36	34	69
Child malnutrition, underweight (% of under age five)	9.9	6.8	31.7
Malaria incidence rate (per 100,000 people)	..	..	4,874
Resilience			
Access to improved sanitation (% of total pop.)	69	84	45
Access to improved water source (% of total pop.)	81	87	84
Cereal yield (kg. per hectare)	1,911	2,512	2,754
Access to electricity (% of total population)	97.0	92.9	67.3
Paved roads (% of total roads)	67.8	74.3	29.3
Health workers (per 1,000 people)	1.5	3.6	2.6
Foreign direct investment, net inflows (% of GDP)	1.4	2.9	2.4
Invest. in infrastructure w/private participation ($ millions)	1,124	5,854	81,789
Disaster risk reduction progress score (1-5 scale; 5 = best)	3.0		
Ease of doing business (ranking 1-183; 1 = best)	94		
Public sector mgmt & institutions avg. (1-6 scale; 6 = best)	..		
Primary completion rate, total (% of relevant age group)	80	88	88
Ratio of girls to boys in primary & secondary school (%)	88	93	93
GHG Emissions and Energy Use			
CO_2 emissions per capita (metric tons)	1.5	3.8	1.6
CO_2 emissions per units of GDP (kg/$1,000 of 2005 PPP $)	379.0	604.6	523.9
CO_2 emissions, total (MtCO_2)	47.9	1,230	3,744
GHG net emissions/removals by LUCF (2000, MtCO_2e)	3.6		
Methane (CH_4) emissions, total (MtCO_2e)	10.6	287	1,705
Nitrous oxide (N_2O) emissions, total (MtCO_2e)	5.8	74	687
Other GHG emissions, total (MtCO_2e)	0.0	7	17
Energy use per capita (kilograms of oil equivalent)	477	1,399	680
Energy use per units of GDP (kg oil eq./$1,000 of 2005 PPP $)	113.7	213.9	217.9

National-Level Actions

Latest UNFCCC national communication	11/3/2010 (2nd)
Annex-I emissions reduction target	n/a
NAMA submission	Yes
NAPA submission	n/a
Renewable energy target	Yes

Carbon Markets

Hosted Clean Development Mechanism (CDM) projects	6
Issued Certified Emission Reductions (CERs) from CDM (thousands)	330
Hosted Joint Implementation (JI) projects	n/a
Issued Emission Reduction Units (ERUs) from JI (thousands)	n/a

Mozambique

Population (millions)	23.4	GDP ($ billions)	9.6
Pop. growth (avg. ann. %, 1990–2010)	2.7	GNI per capita (Atlas $)	440

Climate

Average daily min/max temperature (1961–90, Celsius)	19 / 29
Projected annual temperature change (2045–65, Celsius)	1.9 to 2.4
Average annual precipitation (1961–90, mm)	1,031
Projected annual precipitation change (2045–65, mm)	-69 to 61
Projected change in annual hot days/warm nights	5 / 15
Projected change in annual cool days/cold nights	-2 / -3

	Country data	Sub-Saharan Africa	Low income
Exposure to Impacts			
Land area below 5m (% of land area)	1.8	0.4	0.7
Population below 5m (% of total)	6.5	2.0	5.1
Population in urban agglomerations > 1 million (%)	7	14	11
Urban pop. growth (avg. annual %, 1990–2010)	5.7	4.0	3.7
Droughts, floods, extreme temps (% pop. avg., 1990–2009)	3.7		
Annual freshwater withdrawals (% of internal resources)	0.7	3.2	3.7
Agricultural land under irrigation (% of total ag. land)	..	..	..
Population living below $1.25 a day (% of total)	59.6	50.9	..
Nationally terrestrial protected areas (% of total land area)	15.8	11.7	10.6
Under-five mortality rate (per 1,000)	135	121	108
Child malnutrition, underweight (% of under age five)	21.2	24.6	28.3
Malaria incidence rate (per 100,000 people)	32,555	26,113	16,659
Resilience			
Access to improved sanitation (% of total pop.)	17	31	35
Access to improved water source (% of total pop.)	47	60	63
Cereal yield (kg. per hectare)	877	1,297	2,047
Access to electricity (% of total population)	11.7	32.5	23.0
Paved roads (% of total roads)	20.8	18.3	14.1
Health workers (per 1,000 people)	0.3	1.2	0.7
Foreign direct investment, net inflows (% of GDP)	8.2	3.6	3.2
Invest. in infrastructure w/private participation ($ millions)	80	11,957	4,471
Disaster risk reduction progress score (1–5 scale; 5 = best)	4.0		
Ease of doing business (ranking 1–183; 1 = best)	139		
Public sector mgmt & institutions avg. (1–6 scale; 6 = best)	3.4		
Primary completion rate, total (% of relevant age group)	61	67	65
Ratio of girls to boys in primary & secondary school (%)	89	89	91
GHG Emissions and Energy Use			
CO_2 emissions per capita (metric tons)	0.1	0.8	0.3
CO_2 emissions per units of GDP (kg/$1,000 of 2005 PPP $)	133.6	428.6	270.2
CO_2 emissions, total (MtCO_2)	2.3	685	219
GHG net emissions/removals by LUCF (1994, MtCO_2e)	7.7		
Methane (CH_4) emissions, total (MtCO_2e)	12.8	590	436
Nitrous oxide (N_2O) emissions, total (MtCO_2e)	9.5	334	209
Other GHG emissions, total (MtCO_2e)	0.3	..	..
Energy use per capita (kilograms of oil equivalent)	427	689	365
Energy use per units of GDP (kg oil eq./$1,000 of 2005 PPP $)	529.7	308.4	303.9

National-Level Actions

Latest UNFCCC national communication	6/2/2006 (1st)
Annex-I emissions reduction target	n/a
NAMA submission	..
NAPA submission	Yes
Renewable energy target	..

Carbon Markets

Hosted Clean Development Mechanism (CDM) projects	0
Issued Certified Emission Reductions (CERs) from CDM (thousands)	0
Hosted Joint Implementation (JI) projects	n/a
Issued Emission Reduction Units (ERUs) from JI (thousands)	n/a

Myanmar

Population (millions)	48.0	GDP ($ millions)	..
Pop. growth (avg. ann. %, 1990-2010)	1.0	GNI per capita (Atlas $)	..

Climate

Average daily min/max temperature (1961-90, Celsius)	18 / 8
Projected annual temperature change (2045-65, Celsius)	1.7 to 2.3
Average annual precipitation (1961-90, mm)	2,091
Projected annual precipitation change (2045-65, mm)	-84 to 97
Projected change in annual hot days/warm nights	4 / 14
Projected change in annual cool days/cold nights	-2 / -2

	Country data	East Asia & Pacific	Low income
Exposure to Impacts			
Land area below 5m (% of land area)	4.6	2.5	0.7
Population below 5m (% of total)	14.0	10.3	5.1
Population in urban agglomerations > 1 million (%)	11		11
Urban pop. growth (avg. annual %, 1990-2010)	2.5	3.3	3.7
Droughts, floods, extreme temps (% pop. avg., 1990-2009)	0.1		
Annual freshwater withdrawals (% of internal resources)	3.3	10.8	3.7
Agricultural land under irrigation (% of total ag. land)	24.8	..	..
Population living below $1.25 a day (% of total)	..	16.8	..
Nationally terrestrial protected areas (% of total land area)	6.3	14.9	10.6
Under-five mortality rate (per 1,000)	66	24	108
Child malnutrition, underweight (% of under age five)	29.6	9.0	28.3
Malaria incidence rate (per 100,000 people)	7,943	525	16,659
Resilience			
Access to improved sanitation (% of total pop.)	81	59	35
Access to improved water source (% of total pop.)	71	88	63
Cereal yield (kg. per hectare)	3,949	4,860	2,047
Access to electricity (% of total population)	13.0	90.8	23.0
Paved roads (% of total roads)	11.9	15.9	14.1
Health workers (per 1,000 people)	1.3	2.8	0.7
Foreign direct investment, net inflows (% of GDP)	..	3.0	3.2
Invest. in infrastructure w/private participation ($ millions)	556	14,638	4,471
Disaster risk reduction progress score (1-5 scale; 5 = best)	..		
Ease of doing business (ranking 1-183; 1 = best)	..		
Public sector mgmt & institutions avg. (1-6 scale; 6 = best)	..		
Primary completion rate, total (% of relevant age group)	99	97	65
Ratio of girls to boys in primary & secondary school (%)	100	103	91
GHG Emissions and Energy Use			
CO_2 emissions per capita (metric tons)	0.3	4.3	0.3
CO_2 emissions per units of GDP (kg/$1,000 of 2005 PPP $)	..	827.1	270.2
CO_2 emissions, total (MtCO_2)	12.8	8,259	219
GHG net emissions/removals by LUCF (MtCO_2e)	..		
Methane (CH_4) emissions, total (MtCO_2e)	77.2	1,928	436
Nitrous oxide (N_2O) emissions, total (MtCO_2e)	30.9	707	209
Other GHG emissions, total (MtCO_2e)	0.0	..	..
Energy use per capita (kilograms of oil equivalent)	316	1,436	365
Energy use per units of GDP (kg oil eq./$1,000 of 2005 PPP $)	..	259.5	303.9

National-Level Actions

Latest UNFCCC national communication	..
Annex-I emissions reduction target	n/a
NAMA submission	..
NAPA submission	..
Renewable energy target	..

Carbon Markets

Hosted Clean Development Mechanism (CDM) projects	0
Issued Certified Emission Reductions (CERs) from CDM (thousands)	0
Hosted Joint Implementation (JI) projects	n/a
Issued Emission Reduction Units (ERUs) from JI (thousands)	n/a

Namibia

Population (millions)	2.3	GDP ($ billions)	12.2
Pop. growth (avg. ann. %, 1990–2010)	2.4	GNI per capita (Atlas $)	4,500

Climate
Average daily min/max temperature (1961–90, Celsius)	13 / 27
Projected annual temperature change (2045–65, Celsius)	2.2 to 2.9
Average annual precipitation (1961–90, mm)	285
Projected annual precipitation change (2045–65, mm)	-67 to 23
Projected change in annual hot days/warm nights	6 / 13
Projected change in annual cool days/cold nights	-2 / -2

	Country data	Sub-Saharan Africa	Upper middle income
Exposure to Impacts			
Land area below 5m (% of land area)	0.3	0.4	1.8
Population below 5m (% of total)	2.9	2.0	6.5
Population in urban agglomerations > 1 million (%)	..	14	22
Urban pop. growth (avg. annual %, 1990–2010)	4.0	4.0	2.3
Droughts, floods, extreme temps (% pop. avg., 1990–2009)	3.4		
Annual freshwater withdrawals (% of internal resources)	4.9	3.2	5.6
Agricultural land under irrigation (% of total ag. land)	..	..	..
Population living below $1.25 a day (% of total)	49.1	50.9	..
Nationally terrestrial protected areas (% of total land area)	14.5	11.7	13.6
Under-five mortality rate (per 1,000)	40	121	20
Child malnutrition, underweight (% of under age five)	17.5	24.6	4.1
Malaria incidence rate (per 100,000 people)	4,589	26,113	80
Resilience			
Access to improved sanitation (% of total pop.)	33	31	68
Access to improved water source (% of total pop.)	92	60	92
Cereal yield (kg. per hectare)	365	1,297	3,690
Access to electricity (% of total population)	34.0	32.5	98.0
Paved roads (% of total roads)	12.8	18.3	50.5
Health workers (per 1,000 people)	3.2	1.2	4.5
Foreign direct investment, net inflows (% of GDP)	7.0	3.6	2.7
Invest. in infrastructure w/private participation ($ millions)	9	11,957	26,166
Disaster risk reduction progress score (1–5 scale; 5 = best)	..		
Ease of doing business (ranking 1-183; 1 = best)	78		
Public sector mgmt & institutions avg. (1–6 scale; 6 = best)	..		
Primary completion rate, total (% of relevant age group)	87	67	98
Ratio of girls to boys in primary & secondary school (%)	104	89	103
GHG Emissions and Energy Use			
CO_2 emissions per capita (metric tons)	1.8	0.8	5.3
CO_2 emissions per units of GDP (kg/$1,000 of 2005 PPP $)	311.4	428.6	659.4
CO_2 emissions, total (MtCO_2)	4.0	685	12,860
GHG net emissions/removals by LUCF (1994, MtCO_2e)	-5.7		
Methane (CH_4) emissions, total (MtCO_2e)	5.1	590	3,455
Nitrous oxide (N_2O) emissions, total (MtCO_2e)	3.8	334	1,144
Other GHG emissions, total (MtCO_2e)	0.0	..	243
Energy use per capita (kilograms of oil equivalent)	764	689	1,848
Energy use per units of GDP (kg oil eq./$1,000 of 2005 PPP $)	135.4	308.4	227.1

National-Level Actions
Latest UNFCCC national communication	10/7/2002 (1st)
Annex-I emissions reduction target	n/a
NAMA submission	..
NAPA submission	n/a
Renewable energy target	..

Carbon Markets
Hosted Clean Development Mechanism (CDM) projects	..
Issued Certified Emission Reductions (CERs) from CDM (thousands)	..
Hosted Joint Implementation (JI) projects	n/a
Issued Emission Reduction Units (ERUs) from JI (thousands)	n/a

Nauru

Population (thousands)	10.3	GDP ($ millions) ..
Pop. growth (avg. ann. %, 1990-2010)	0.6	GNI per capita (Atlas $) ..

Climate

Average daily min/max temperature (1961-90, Celsius)	25 / 31
Projected annual temperature change (2045-65, Celsius)	1.3 to 2.1
Average annual precipitation (1961-90, mm)	2,445
Projected annual precipitation change (2045-65, mm)	-60 to 565
Projected change in annual hot days/warm nights	18 / 26
Projected change in annual cool days/cold nights	-3 / -3

	Country data	East Asia & Pacific	Upper middle income
Exposure to Impacts			
Land area below 5m (% of land area)	40.4	2.5	1.8
Population below 5m (% of total)	40.4	10.3	6.5
Population in urban agglomerations > 1 million (%)	..	..	22
Urban pop. growth (avg. annual %, 1990-2010)	..	3.3	2.3
Droughts, floods, extreme temps (% pop. avg., 1990-2009)	..		
Annual freshwater withdrawals (% of internal resources)	..	10.8	5.6
Agricultural land under irrigation (% of total ag. land)	..	..	..
Population living below $1.25 a day (% of total)	..	16.8	..
Nationally terrestrial protected areas (% of total land area)	..	14.9	13.6
Under-five mortality rate (per 1,000)	40	24	20
Child malnutrition, underweight (% of under age five)	..	9.0	4.1
Malaria incidence rate (per 100,000 people)	..	525	80
Resilience			
Access to improved sanitation (% of total pop.)	50	59	68
Access to improved water source (% of total pop.)	90	88	92
Cereal yield (kg. per hectare)	..	4,860	3,690
Access to electricity (% of total population)	..	90.8	98.0
Paved roads (% of total roads)	..	15.9	50.5
Health workers (per 1,000 people)	5.6	2.8	4.5
Foreign direct investment, net inflows (% of GDP)	..	3.0	2.7
Invest. in infrastructure w/private participation ($ millions)	..	14,638	26,166
Disaster risk reduction progress score (1-5 scale; 5 = best)	..		
Ease of doing business (ranking 1-183; 1 = best)	..		
Public sector mgmt & institutions avg. (1-6 scale; 6 = best)	..		
Primary completion rate, total (% of relevant age group)	97	97	98
Ratio of girls to boys in primary & secondary school (%)	112	103	103
GHG Emissions and Energy Use			
CO$_2$ emissions per capita (metric tons)	13.9	4.3	5.3
CO$_2$ emissions per units of GDP (kg/$1,000 of 2005 PPP $)	..	827.1	659.4
CO$_2$ emissions, total (MtCO$_2$)	0.1	8,259	12,860
GHG net emissions/removals by LUCF (1994, MtCO$_2$e)	-0.0		
Methane (CH$_4$) emissions, total (MtCO$_2$e)	..	1,928	3,455
Nitrous oxide (N$_2$O) emissions, total (MtCO$_2$e)	..	707	1,144
Other GHG emissions, total (MtCO$_2$e)	..	..	243
Energy use per capita (kilograms of oil equivalent)	..	1,436	1,848
Energy use per units of GDP (kg oil eq./$1,000 of 2005 PPP $)	..	259.5	227.1

National-Level Actions

Latest UNFCCC national communication	10/30/1999 (1st)
Annex-I emissions reduction target	n/a
NAMA submission	..
NAPA submission	n/a
Renewable energy target	..

Carbon Markets

Hosted Clean Development Mechanism (CDM) projects	..
Issued Certified Emission Reductions (CERs) from CDM (thousands)	..
Hosted Joint Implementation (JI) projects	n/a
Issued Emission Reduction Units (ERUs) from JI (thousands)	n/a

Nepal

Population (millions)	30.0	GDP ($ billions)	15.7
Pop. growth (avg. ann. %, 1990–2010)	2.3	GNI per capita (Atlas $)	480

Climate

Average daily min/max temperature (1961–90, Celsius)	2 / 15
Projected annual temperature change (2045–65, Celsius)	2.2 to 3.4
Average annual precipitation (1961–90, mm)	1,321
Projected annual precipitation change (2045–65, mm)	-116 to 231
Projected change in annual hot days/warm nights	3 / 8
Projected change in annual cool days/cold nights	-2 / -2

	Country data	South Asia	Low income
Exposure to Impacts			
Land area below 5m (% of land area)	0.0	1.5	0.7
Population below 5m (% of total)	0.0	4.4	5.1
Population in urban agglomerations > 1 million (%)	..	13	11
Urban pop. growth (avg. annual %, 1990–2010)	5.8	2.7	3.7
Droughts, floods, extreme temps (% pop. avg., 1990–2009)	0.7		
Annual freshwater withdrawals (% of internal resources)	5.1	50.6	3.7
Agricultural land under irrigation (% of total ag. land)	27.7	..	..
Population living below $1.25 a day (% of total)	55.1	40.3	..
Nationally terrestrial protected areas (% of total land area)	17.0	6.1	10.6
Under-five mortality rate (per 1,000)	50	67	108
Child malnutrition, underweight (% of under age five)	38.8	42.5	28.3
Malaria incidence rate (per 100,000 people)	103	1,127	16,659
Resilience			
Access to improved sanitation (% of total pop.)	31	36	35
Access to improved water source (% of total pop.)	88	87	63
Cereal yield (kg. per hectare)	2,374	2,728	2,047
Access to electricity (% of total population)	43.6	62.1	23.0
Paved roads (% of total roads)	55.9	58.9	14.1
Health workers (per 1,000 people)	0.7	1.7	0.7
Foreign direct investment, net inflows (% of GDP)	0.6	1.3	3.2
Invest. in infrastructure w/private participation ($ millions)	34	73,548	4,471
Disaster risk reduction progress score (1–5 scale; 5 = best)	2.8		
Ease of doing business (ranking 1–183; 1 = best)	107		
Public sector mgmt & institutions avg. (1–6 scale; 6 = best)	2.8		
Primary completion rate, total (% of relevant age group)	70	86	65
Ratio of girls to boys in primary & secondary school (%)	82	92	91
GHG Emissions and Energy Use			
CO_2 emissions per capita (metric tons)	0.1	1.3	0.3
CO_2 emissions per units of GDP (kg/$1,000 of 2005 PPP $)	120.0	504.6	270.2
CO_2 emissions, total (MtCO_2)	3.5	1,970	219
GHG net emissions/removals by LUCF (1994, MtCO_2e)	8.1		
Methane (CH_4) emissions, total (MtCO_2e)	22.1	846	436
Nitrous oxide (N_2O) emissions, total (MtCO_2e)	4.5	268	209
Other GHG emissions, total (MtCO_2e)	0.0	9	..
Energy use per capita (kilograms of oil equivalent)	338	532	365
Energy use per units of GDP (kg oil eq./$1,000 of 2005 PPP $)	323.2	193.5	303.9

National-Level Actions

Latest UNFCCC national communication	9/1/2004 (1st)
Annex-I emissions reduction target	n/a
NAMA submission	
NAPA submission	Yes
Renewable energy target	..

Carbon Markets

Hosted Clean Development Mechanism (CDM) projects	4
Issued Certified Emission Reductions (CERs) from CDM (thousands)	92
Hosted Joint Implementation (JI) projects	n/a
Issued Emission Reduction Units (ERUs) from JI (thousands)	n/a

Netherlands

Population (millions)	16.6	GDP ($ billions)	783.4
Pop. growth (avg. ann. %, 1990-2010)	0.5	GNI per capita (Atlas $)	49,750

Climate

Average daily min/max temperature (1961-90, Celsius)	6 / 13
Projected annual temperature change (2045-65, Celsius)	1.4 to 2.3
Average annual precipitation (1961-90, mm)	778
Projected annual precipitation change (2045-65, mm)	-18 to 50
Projected change in annual hot days/warm nights	3 / 5
Projected change in annual cool days/cold nights	-2 / -2

	Country data	High income
Exposure to Impacts		
Land area below 5m (% of land area)	58.5	2.2
Population below 5m (% of total)	61.3	7.7
Population in urban agglomerations > 1 million (%)	12	..
Urban pop. growth (avg. annual %, 1990-2010)	1.5	1.0
Droughts, floods, extreme temps (% pop. avg., 1990-2009)	0.0	
Annual freshwater withdrawals (% of internal resources)	105.1	10.4
Agricultural land under irrigation (% of total ag. land)	10.6	..
Population living below $1.25 a day (% of total)	..	..
Nationally terrestrial protected areas (% of total land area)	12.4	13.4
Under-five mortality rate (per 1,000)	4	6
Child malnutrition, underweight (% of under age five)	..	..
Malaria incidence rate (per 100,000 people)	..	..
Resilience		
Access to improved sanitation (% of total pop.)	100	100
Access to improved water source (% of total pop.)	100	100
Cereal yield (kg. per hectare)	9,032	5,445
Access to electricity (% of total population)	..	..
Paved roads (% of total roads)	90.0	87.3
Health workers (per 1,000 people)	0.2	10.7
Foreign direct investment, net inflows (% of GDP)	-2.3	1.8
Invest. in infrastructure w/private participation ($ millions)	..	..
Disaster risk reduction progress score (1-5 scale; 5 = best)	..	
Ease of doing business (ranking 1-183; 1 = best)	31	
Public sector mgmt & institutions avg. (1-6 scale; 6 = best)	..	
Primary completion rate, total (% of relevant age group)	100	97
Ratio of girls to boys in primary & secondary school (%)	99	100
GHG Emissions and Energy Use		
CO_2 emissions per capita (metric tons)	10.6	11.9
CO_2 emissions per units of GDP (kg/$1,000 of 2005 PPP $)	277.0	354.4
CO_2 emissions, total (MtCO_2)	173.7	13,285
GHG net emissions/removals by LUCF (2009, MtCO_2e)	2.5	
Methane (CH_4) emissions, total (MtCO_2e)	21.3	1,539
Nitrous oxide (N_2O) emissions, total (MtCO_2e)	14.6	813
Other GHG emissions, total (MtCO_2e)	3.8	460
Energy use per capita (kilograms of oil equivalent)	5,016	4,944
Energy use per units of GDP (kg oil eq./$1,000 of 2005 PPP $)	135.9	147.0

National-Level Actions

Latest UNFCCC national communication	12/19/2009 (5th)
Annex-I emissions reduction target (base year: 1990)	20% / 30% (EU)
NAMA submission	n/a
NAPA submission	n/a
Renewable energy target	Yes

Carbon Markets

Hosted Clean Development Mechanism (CDM) projects	n/a
Issued Certified Emission Reductions (CERs) from CDM (thousands)	n/a
Hosted Joint Implementation (JI) projects	..
Issued Emission Reduction Units (ERUs) from JI (thousands)	..

New Caledonia

Population (thousands)	254.0	GDP ($ millions)	..
Pop. growth (avg. ann. %, 1990–2010)	2.1	GNI per capita (Atlas $)	..

Climate

Average daily min/max temperature (1961–90, Celsius)	19 / 25
Projected annual temperature change (2045–65, Celsius)	1.4 to 1.7
Average annual precipitation (1961–90, mm)	1,498
Projected annual precipitation change (2045–65, mm)	-122 to 118
Projected change in annual hot days/warm nights	7 / 12
Projected change in annual cool days/cold nights	-3 / -3

	Country data	High Income
Exposure to Impacts		
Land area below 5m (% of land area)	8.0	2.2
Population below 5m (% of total)	34.3	7.7
Population in urban agglomerations > 1 million (%)	..	
Urban pop. growth (avg. annual %, 1990–2010)	2.5	1.0
Droughts, floods, extreme temps (% pop. avg., 1990–2009)	..	
Annual freshwater withdrawals (% of internal resources)	..	10.4
Agricultural land under irrigation (% of total ag. land)	..	..
Population living below $1.25 a day (% of total)	..	..
Nationally terrestrial protected areas (% of total land area)	5.5	13.4
Under-five mortality rate (per 1,000)	..	6
Child malnutrition, underweight (% of under age five)	..	
Malaria incidence rate (per 100,000 people)	..	
Resilience		
Access to improved sanitation (% of total pop.)	..	100
Access to improved water source (% of total pop.)	..	100
Cereal yield (kg. per hectare)	3,391	5,445
Access to electricity (% of total population)	..	
Paved roads (% of total roads)	..	87.3
Health workers (per 1,000 people)	..	10.7
Foreign direct investment, net inflows (% of GDP)	..	1.8
Invest. in infrastructure w/private participation ($ millions)	..	..
Disaster risk reduction progress score (1–5 scale; 5 = best)	..	
Ease of doing business (ranking 1–183; 1 = best)	..	
Public sector mgmt & institutions avg. (1–6 scale; 6 = best)	..	
Primary completion rate, total (% of relevant age group)	..	97
Ratio of girls to boys in primary & secondary school (%)	..	100
GHG Emissions and Energy Use		
CO_2 emissions per capita (metric tons)	12.8	11.9
CO_2 emissions per units of GDP (kg/$1,000 of 2005 PPP $)	..	354.4
CO_2 emissions, total (MtCO_2)	3.1	13,285
GHG net emissions/removals by LUCF (MtCO_2e)	..	
Methane (CH_4) emissions, total (MtCO_2e)	..	1,539
Nitrous oxide (N_2O) emissions, total (MtCO_2e)	..	813
Other GHG emissions, total (MtCO_2e)	..	460
Energy use per capita (kilograms of oil equivalent)	..	4,944
Energy use per units of GDP (kg oil eq./$1,000 of 2005 PPP $)	..	147.0
National-Level Actions		
Latest UNFCCC national communication		n/a
Annex-I emissions reduction target		n/a
NAMA submission		n/a
NAPA submission		n/a
Renewable energy target		..
Carbon Markets		
Hosted Clean Development Mechanism (CDM) projects		n/a
Issued Certified Emission Reductions (CERs) from CDM (thousands)		n/a
Hosted Joint Implementation (JI) projects		n/a
Issued Emission Reduction Units (ERUs) from JI (thousands)		n/a

New Zealand

Population (millions)	4.4	GDP ($ billions)	126.7
Pop. growth (avg. ann. %, 1990–2010)	1.2	GNI per capita (Atlas $)	29,050

Climate

Average daily min/max temperature (1961–90, Celsius)	6 / 15
Projected annual temperature change (2045–65, Celsius)	1.1 to 1.7
Average annual precipitation (1961–90, mm)	1,732
Projected annual precipitation change (2045–65, mm)	-44 to 53
Projected change in annual hot days/warm nights	4 / 8
Projected change in annual cool days/cold nights	-2 / -2

	Country data	High income
Exposure to Impacts		
Land area below 5m (% of land area)	2.7	2.2
Population below 5m (% of total)	12.6	7.7
Population in urban agglomerations > 1 million (%)	32	..
Urban pop. growth (avg. annual %, 1990–2010)	1.3	1.0
Droughts, floods, extreme temps (% pop. avg., 1990–2009)	0.0	
Annual freshwater withdrawals (% of internal resources)	0.6	10.4
Agricultural land under irrigation (% of total ag. land)	3.2	..
Population living below $1.25 a day (% of total)	..	..
Nationally terrestrial protected areas (% of total land area)	25.8	13.4
Under-five mortality rate (per 1,000)	6	6
Child malnutrition, underweight (% of under age five)	..	..
Malaria incidence rate (per 100,000 people)	..	..
Resilience		
Access to improved sanitation (% of total pop.)	..	100
Access to improved water source (% of total pop.)	100	100
Cereal yield (kg. per hectare)	6,924	5,445
Access to electricity (% of total population)	..	
Paved roads (% of total roads)	65.9	87.3
Health workers (per 1,000 people)	13.3	10.7
Foreign direct investment, net inflows (% of GDP)	-1.0	1.8
Invest. in infrastructure w/private participation ($ millions)	..	..
Disaster risk reduction progress score (1–5 scale; 5 = best)	3.8	
Ease of doing business (ranking 1–183; 1 = best)	3	
Public sector mgmt & institutions avg. (1–6 scale; 6 = best)	..	
Primary completion rate, total (% of relevant age group)	..	97
Ratio of girls to boys in primary & secondary school (%)	102	100
GHG Emissions and Energy Use		
CO_2 emissions per capita (metric tons)	7.8	11.9
CO_2 emissions per units of GDP (kg/$1,000 of 2005 PPP $)	304.1	354.4
CO_2 emissions, total (MtCO$_2$)	33.1	13,285
GHG net emissions/removals by LUCF (2009, MtCO$_2$e)	-26.7	
Methane (CH_4) emissions, total (MtCO$_2$e)	27.6	1,539
Nitrous oxide (N_2O) emissions, total (MtCO$_2$e)	12.9	813
Other GHG emissions, total (MtCO$_2$e)	1.0	460
Energy use per capita (kilograms of oil equivalent)	4,193	4,944
Energy use per units of GDP (kg oil eq./$1,000 of 2005 PPP $)	162.9	147.0

National-Level Actions

Latest UNFCCC national communication	12/23/2009 (5th)
Annex-I emissions reduction target (base year: 1990)	10% / 20%
NAMA submission	n/a
NAPA submission	n/a
Renewable energy target	Yes

Carbon Markets

Hosted Clean Development Mechanism (CDM) projects	n/a
Issued Certified Emission Reductions (CERs) from CDM (thousands)	n/a
Hosted Joint Implementation (JI) projects	7
Issued Emission Reduction Units (ERUs) from JI (thousands)	1,898

Nicaragua

Population (millions)	5.8	GDP ($ billions)	6.6
Pop. growth (avg. ann. %, 1990–2010)	1.7	GNI per capita (Atlas $)	1,090

Climate

Average daily min/max temperature (1961–90, Celsius)	20 / 30
Projected annual temperature change (2045–65, Celsius)	1.6 to 2.4
Average annual precipitation (1961–90, mm)	2,391
Projected annual precipitation change (2045–65, mm)	-220 to 19
Projected change in annual hot days/warm nights	10 / 26
Projected change in annual cool days/cold nights	-3 / -3

	Country data	Latin America & the Carib.	Lower middle income
Exposure to Impacts			
Land area below 5m (% of land area)	3.6	1.5	1.7
Population below 5m (% of total)	1.5	3.8	6.5
Population in urban agglomerations > 1 million (%)	23	35	14
Urban pop. growth (avg. annual %, 1990–2010)	2.2	2.0	2.8
Droughts, floods, extreme temps (% pop. avg., 1990–2009)	0.8		
Annual freshwater withdrawals (% of internal resources)	0.7	2.0	18.7
Agricultural land under irrigation (% of total ag. land)	..	..	..
Population living below $1.25 a day (% of total)	15.8	8.1	..
Nationally terrestrial protected areas (% of total land area)	36.7	20.8	9.5
Under-five mortality rate (per 1,000)	27	23	69
Child malnutrition, underweight (% of under age five)	4.3	3.8	31.7
Malaria incidence rate (per 100,000 people)	26	206	4,874
Resilience			
Access to improved sanitation (% of total pop.)	52	79	45
Access to improved water source (% of total pop.)	85	93	84
Cereal yield (kg. per hectare)	2,077	3,337	2,754
Access to electricity (% of total population)	72.1	93.4	67.3
Paved roads (% of total roads)	12.0	28.1	29.3
Health workers (per 1,000 people)	1.4	6.9	2.6
Foreign direct investment, net inflows (% of GDP)	7.8	2.3	2.4
Invest. in infrastructure w/private participation ($ millions)	547	33,064	81,789
Disaster risk reduction progress score (1–5 scale; 5 = best)	3.8		
Ease of doing business (ranking 1–183; 1 = best)	118		
Public sector mgmt & institutions avg. (1–6 scale; 6 = best)	3.2		
Primary completion rate, total (% of relevant age group)	75	102	88
Ratio of girls to boys in primary & secondary school (%)	102	102	93
GHG Emissions and Energy Use			
CO_2 emissions per capita (metric tons)	0.8	2.8	1.6
CO_2 emissions per units of GDP (kg/$1,000 of 2005 PPP $)	308.2	285.6	523.9
CO_2 emissions, total (MtCO$_2$)	4.3	1,584	3,744
GHG net emissions/removals by LUCF (1994, MtCO$_2$e)	-13.1		
Methane (CH_4) emissions, total (MtCO$_2$e)	6.0	1,009	1,705
Nitrous oxide (N_2O) emissions, total (MtCO$_2$e)	3.3	442	687
Other GHG emissions, total (MtCO$_2$e)	0.0	21	17
Energy use per capita (kilograms of oil equivalent)	540	1,245	680
Energy use per units of GDP (kg oil eq./$1,000 of 2005 PPP $)	222.8	130.6	217.9

National-Level Actions

Latest UNFCCC national communication	6/22/2011 (2nd)
Annex-I emissions reduction target	n/a
NAMA submission	..
NAPA submission	n/a
Renewable energy target	Yes

Carbon Markets

Hosted Clean Development Mechanism (CDM) projects	5
Issued Certified Emission Reductions (CERs) from CDM (thousands)	602
Hosted Joint Implementation (JI) projects	n/a
Issued Emission Reduction Units (ERUs) from JI (thousands)	n/a

Niger

Population (millions)	15.5	GDP ($ billions)	5.5
Pop. growth (avg. ann. %, 1990-2010)	3.4	GNI per capita (Atlas $)	370

Climate

Average daily min/max temperature (1961-90, Celsius)	19 / 35
Projected annual temperature change (2045-65, Celsius)	2.4 to 2.8
Average annual precipitation (1961-90, mm)	151
Projected annual precipitation change (2045-65, mm)	-71 to 36
Projected change in annual hot days/warm nights	5 / 12
Projected change in annual cool days/cold nights	-2 / -2

	Country data	Sub-Saharan Africa	Low income
Exposure to Impacts			
Land area below 5m (% of land area)	0.0	0.4	0.7
Population below 5m (% of total)	0.0	2.0	5.1
Population in urban agglomerations > 1 million (%)	7	14	11
Urban pop. growth (avg. annual %, 1990-2010)	3.9	4.0	3.7
Droughts, floods, extreme temps (% pop. avg., 1990-2009)	7.5		
Annual freshwater withdrawals (% of internal resources)	67.5	3.2	3.7
Agricultural land under irrigation (% of total ag. land)	..	..	
Population living below $1.25 a day (% of total)	43.1	50.9	..
Nationally terrestrial protected areas (% of total land area)	6.8	11.7	10.6
Under-five mortality rate (per 1,000)	143	121	108
Child malnutrition, underweight (% of under age five)	39.9	24.6	28.3
Malaria incidence rate (per 100,000 people)	37,958	26,113	16,659
Resilience			
Access to improved sanitation (% of total pop.)	9	31	35
Access to improved water source (% of total pop.)	48	60	63
Cereal yield (kg. per hectare)	380	1,297	2,047
Access to electricity (% of total population)	..	32.5	23.0
Paved roads (% of total roads)	20.7	18.3	14.1
Health workers (per 1,000 people)	0.2	1.2	0.7
Foreign direct investment, net inflows (% of GDP)	17.1	3.6	3.2
Invest. in infrastructure w/private participation ($ millions)	107	11,957	4,471
Disaster risk reduction progress score (1-5 scale; 5 = best)	..		
Ease of doing business (ranking 1-183; 1 = best)	173		
Public sector mgmt & institutions avg. (1-6 scale; 6 = best)	3.2		
Primary completion rate, total (% of relevant age group)	41	67	65
Ratio of girls to boys in primary & secondary school (%)	78	89	91
GHG Emissions and Energy Use			
CO_2 emissions per capita (metric tons)	0.1	0.8	0.3
CO_2 emissions per units of GDP (kg/$1,000 of 2005 PPP $)	90.3	428.6	270.2
CO_2 emissions, total (MtCO$_2$)	0.9	685	219
GHG net emissions/removals by LUCF (2000, MtCO$_2$e)	-16.8		
Methane (CH_4) emissions, total (MtCO$_2$e)	..	590	436
Nitrous oxide (N_2O) emissions, total (MtCO$_2$e)	..	334	209
Other GHG emissions, total (MtCO$_2$e)	..	..	..
Energy use per capita (kilograms of oil equivalent)	..	689	365
Energy use per units of GDP (kg oil eq./$1,000 of 2005 PPP $)	..	308.4	303.9

National-Level Actions

Latest UNFCCC national communication	12/9/2009 (2nd)
Annex-I emissions reduction target	n/a
NAMA submission	..
NAPA submission	Yes
Renewable energy target	Yes

Carbon Markets

Hosted Clean Development Mechanism (CDM) projects	..
Issued Certified Emission Reductions (CERs) from CDM (thousands)	..
Hosted Joint Implementation (JI) projects	n/a
Issued Emission Reduction Units (ERUs) from JI (thousands)	n/a

Nigeria

Population (millions)	158.4	GDP ($ billions)	193.7
Pop. growth (avg. ann. %, 1990–2010)	2.4	GNI per capita (Atlas $)	1,180

Climate

Average daily min/max temperature (1961-90, Celsius)	21 / 33
Projected annual temperature change (2045-65, Celsius)	2.0 to 2.5
Average annual precipitation (1961-90, mm)	1,150
Projected annual precipitation change (2045-65, mm)	-128 to 89
Projected change in annual hot days/warm nights	6 / 19
Projected change in annual cool days/cold nights	-2 / -2

	Country data	Sub-Saharan Africa	Lower middle income
Exposure to Impacts			
Land area below 5m (% of land area)	0.5	0.4	1.7
Population below 5m (% of total)	3.0	2.0	6.5
Population in urban agglomerations > 1 million (%)	15	14	14
Urban pop. growth (avg. annual %, 1990-2010)	4.1	4.0	2.8
Droughts, floods, extreme temps (% pop. avg., 1990-2009)	0.1		
Annual freshwater withdrawals (% of internal resources)	4.7	3.2	18.7
Agricultural land under irrigation (% of total ag. land)	..	..	..
Population living below $1.25 a day (% of total)	64.4	50.9	..
Nationally terrestrial protected areas (% of total land area)	12.8	11.7	9.5
Under-five mortality rate (per 1,000)	143	121	69
Child malnutrition, underweight (% of under age five)	26.7	24.6	31.7
Malaria incidence rate (per 100,000 people)	38,259	26,113	4,874
Resilience			
Access to improved sanitation (% of total pop.)	32	31	45
Access to improved water source (% of total pop.)	58	60	84
Cereal yield (kg. per hectare)	1,528	1,297	2,754
Access to electricity (% of total population)	50.6	32.5	67.3
Paved roads (% of total roads)	15.0	18.3	29.3
Health workers (per 1,000 people)	2.0	1.2	2.6
Foreign direct investment, net inflows (% of GDP)	3.1	3.6	2.4
Invest. in infrastructure w/private participation ($ millions)	3,036	11,957	81,789
Disaster risk reduction progress score (1-5 scale; 5 = best)	4.0		
Ease of doing business (ranking 1-183; 1 = best)	133		
Public sector mgmt & institutions avg. (1-6 scale; 6 = best)	2.9		
Primary completion rate, total (% of relevant age group)	79	67	88
Ratio of girls to boys in primary & secondary school (%)	85	89	93
GHG Emissions and Energy Use			
CO_2 emissions per capita (metric tons)	0.6	0.8	1.6
CO_2 emissions per units of GDP (kg/$1,000 of 2005 PPP $)	326.6	428.6	523.9
CO_2 emissions, total (MtCO_2)	95.8	685	3,744
GHG net emissions/removals by LUCF (1994, MtCO_2e)	105.0		
Methane (CH_4) emissions, total (MtCO_2e)	130.3	590	1,705
Nitrous oxide (N_2O) emissions, total (MtCO_2e)	21.6	334	687
Other GHG emissions, total (MtCO_2e)	0.7	..	17
Energy use per capita (kilograms of oil equivalent)	701	689	680
Energy use per units of GDP (kg oil eq./$1,000 of 2005 PPP $)	345.1	308.4	217.9

National-Level Actions

Latest UNFCCC national communication	11/17/2003 (1st)
Annex-I emissions reduction target	n/a
NAMA submission	..
NAPA submission	n/a
Renewable energy target	Yes

Carbon Markets

Hosted Clean Development Mechanism (CDM) projects	5
Issued Certified Emission Reductions (CERs) from CDM (thousands)	312
Hosted Joint Implementation (JI) projects	n/a
Issued Emission Reduction Units (ERUs) from JI (thousands)	n/a

Niue

Population (thousands)	1.5	GDP ($ millions) ..
Pop. growth (avg. ann. %, 1990–2010)	-2.3	GNI per capita (Atlas $) ..

Climate

Average daily min/max temperature (1961–90, Celsius)	22 / 27
Projected annual temperature change (2045–65, Celsius)	1.3 to 1.7
Average annual precipitation (1961–90, mm)	2,210
Projected annual precipitation change (2045–65, mm)	-9 to 153
Projected change in annual hot days/warm nights	9 / 15
Projected change in annual cool days/cold nights	-3 / -3

	Country data	East Asia & Pacific	Upper middle income
Exposure to Impacts			
Land area below 5m (% of land area)	10.4	2.5	1.8
Population below 5m (% of total)	10.4	10.3	6.5
Population in urban agglomerations > 1 million (%)	..	..	22
Urban pop. growth (avg. annual %, 1990–2010)	..	3.3	2.3
Droughts, floods, extreme temps (% pop. avg., 1990–2009)	..		
Annual freshwater withdrawals (% of internal resources)	..	10.8	5.6
Agricultural land under irrigation (% of total ag. land)	..	..	..
Population living below $1.25 a day (% of total)	..	16.8	..
Nationally terrestrial protected areas (% of total land area)	22.2	14.9	13.6
Under-five mortality rate (per 1,000)	22	24	20
Child malnutrition, underweight (% of under age five)	..	9.0	4.1
Malaria incidence rate (per 100,000 people)	..	525	80

Resilience			
Access to improved sanitation (% of total pop.)	100	59	68
Access to improved water source (% of total pop.)	100	88	92
Cereal yield (kg. per hectare)	..	4,860	3,690
Access to electricity (% of total population)	..	90.8	98.0
Paved roads (% of total roads)	..	15.9	50.5
Health workers (per 1,000 people)	19.0	2.8	4.5
Foreign direct investment, net inflows (% of GDP)	..	3.0	2.7
Invest. in infrastructure w/private participation ($ millions)	..	14,638	26,166
Disaster risk reduction progress score (1–5 scale; 5 = best)	..		
Ease of doing business (ranking 1–183; 1 = best)	..		
Public sector mgmt & institutions avg. (1–6 scale; 6 = best)	..		
Primary completion rate, total (% of relevant age group)	126	97	98
Ratio of girls to boys in primary & secondary school (%)	129	103	103

GHG Emissions and Energy Use			
CO_2 emissions per capita (metric tons)	2.5	4.3	5.3
CO_2 emissions per units of GDP (kg/$1,000 of 2005 PPP $)	..	827.1	659.4
CO_2 emissions, total (MtCO₂)	0.0	8,259	12,860
GHG net emissions/removals by LUCF (1994, MtCO₂e)	0.1		
Methane (CH_4) emissions, total (MtCO₂e)	..	1,928	3,455
Nitrous oxide (N_2O) emissions, total (MtCO₂e)	..	707	1,144
Other GHG emissions, total (MtCO₂e)	..	..	243
Energy use per capita (kilograms of oil equivalent)	..	1,436	1,848
Energy use per units of GDP (kg oil eq./$1,000 of 2005 PPP $)	..	259.5	227.1

National-Level Actions

Latest UNFCCC national communication	10/2/2001 (1st)
Annex-I emissions reduction target	n/a
NAMA submission	..
NAPA submission	n/a
Renewable energy target	..

Carbon Markets

Hosted Clean Development Mechanism (CDM) projects	..
Issued Certified Emission Reductions (CERs) from CDM (thousands)	..
Hosted Joint Implementation (JI) projects	n/a
Issued Emission Reduction Units (ERUs) from JI (thousands)	n/a

Northern Mariana Islands

Population (thousands)	60.9	GDP ($ millions)	..
Pop. growth (avg. ann. %, 1990–2010)	1.6	GNI per capita (Atlas $)	..

Climate

Average daily min/max temperature (1961–90, Celsius)	24 / 30
Projected annual temperature change (2045–65, Celsius)	1.4 to 1.8
Average annual precipitation (1961–90, mm)	7,369
Projected annual precipitation change (2045–65, mm)	1 to 197
Projected change in annual hot days/warm nights	17 / 26
Projected change in annual cool days/cold nights	-3 / -3

	Country data	High income
Exposure to Impacts		
Land area below 5m (% of land area)	28.1	2.2
Population below 5m (% of total)	39.3	7.7
Population in urban agglomerations > 1 million (%)	..	..
Urban pop. growth (avg. annual %, 1990–2010)	1.7	1.0
Droughts, floods, extreme temps (% pop. avg., 1990–2009)	..	
Annual freshwater withdrawals (% of internal resources)	..	10.4
Agricultural land under irrigation (% of total ag. land)	..	..
Population living below $1.25 a day (% of total)	..	..
Nationally terrestrial protected areas (% of total land area)	1.1	13.4
Under-five mortality rate (per 1,000)	..	6
Child malnutrition, underweight (% of under age five)	..	..
Malaria incidence rate (per 100,000 people)	..	..
Resilience		
Access to improved sanitation (% of total pop.)	94	100
Access to improved water source (% of total pop.)	98	100
Cereal yield (kg. per hectare)	..	5,445
Access to electricity (% of total population)	..	
Paved roads (% of total roads)	..	87.3
Health workers (per 1,000 people)	..	10.7
Foreign direct investment, net inflows (% of GDP)	..	1.8
Invest. in infrastructure w/private participation ($ millions)	..	
Disaster risk reduction progress score (1–5 scale; 5 = best)	..	
Ease of doing business (ranking 1–183; 1 = best)	..	
Public sector mgmt & institutions avg. (1–6 scale; 6 = best)	..	
Primary completion rate, total (% of relevant age group)	..	97
Ratio of girls to boys in primary & secondary school (%)	..	100
GHG Emissions and Energy Use		
CO_2 emissions per capita (metric tons)	..	11.9
CO_2 emissions per units of GDP (kg/$1,000 of 2005 PPP $)	..	354.4
CO_2 emissions, total (MtCO_2)	..	13,285
GHG net emissions/removals by LUCF (MtCO_2e)	..	
Methane (CH_4) emissions, total (MtCO_2e)	..	1,539
Nitrous oxide (N_2O) emissions, total (MtCO_2e)	..	813
Other GHG emissions, total (MtCO_2e)	..	460
Energy use per capita (kilograms of oil equivalent)	..	4,944
Energy use per units of GDP (kg oil eq./$1,000 of 2005 PPP $)	..	147.0

National-Level Actions

Latest UNFCCC national communication	n/a
Annex-I emissions reduction target	n/a
NAMA submission	n/a
NAPA submission	n/a
Renewable energy target	..

Carbon Markets

Hosted Clean Development Mechanism (CDM) projects	n/a
Issued Certified Emission Reductions (CERs) from CDM (thousands)	n/a
Hosted Joint Implementation (JI) projects	n/a
Issued Emission Reduction Units (ERUs) from JI (thousands)	n/a

Norway

Population (millions)	4.9	GDP ($ billions)	414.5
Pop. growth (avg. ann. %, 1990-2010)	0.7	GNI per capita (Atlas $)	85,340

Climate

Average daily min/max temperature (1961-90, Celsius)	-2 / 5
Projected annual temperature change (2045-65, Celsius)	1.8 to 3.3
Average annual precipitation (1961-90, mm)	1,119
Projected annual precipitation change (2045-65, mm)	41 to 131
Projected change in annual hot days/warm nights	2 / 5
Projected change in annual cool days/cold nights	-2 / -2

	Country data	High income
Exposure to Impacts		
Land area below 5m (% of land area)	4.9	2.2
Population below 5m (% of total)	9.3	7.7
Population in urban agglomerations > 1 million (%)	..	..
Urban pop. growth (avg. annual %, 1990-2010)	1.1	1.0
Droughts, floods, extreme temps (% pop. avg., 1990-2009)	0.0	
Annual freshwater withdrawals (% of internal resources)	0.5	10.4
Agricultural land under irrigation (% of total ag. land)	5.4	..
Population living below $1.25 a day (% of total)	..	..
Nationally terrestrial protected areas (% of total land area)	14.4	13.4
Under-five mortality rate (per 1,000)	3	6
Child malnutrition, underweight (% of under age five)	..	..
Malaria incidence rate (per 100,000 people)	..	..
Resilience		
Access to improved sanitation (% of total pop.)	100	100
Access to improved water source (% of total pop.)	100	100
Cereal yield (kg. per hectare)	3,105	5,445
Access to electricity (% of total population)	..	..
Paved roads (% of total roads)	80.5	87.3
Health workers (per 1,000 people)	18.8	10.7
Foreign direct investment, net inflows (% of GDP)	2.8	1.8
Invest. in infrastructure w/private participation ($ millions)	..	..
Disaster risk reduction progress score (1-5 scale; 5 = best)	3.8	
Ease of doing business (ranking 1-183; 1 = best)	6	
Public sector mgmt & institutions avg. (1-6 scale; 6 = best)	..	
Primary completion rate, total (% of relevant age group)	100	97
Ratio of girls to boys in primary & secondary school (%)	99	100
GHG Emissions and Energy Use		
CO_2 emissions per capita (metric tons)	10.5	11.9
CO_2 emissions per units of GDP (kg/$1,000 of 2005 PPP $)	215.9	354.4
CO_2 emissions, total (MtCO_2)	50.0	13,285
GHG net emissions/removals by LUCF (2009, MtCO_2e)	-25.3	
Methane (CH_4) emissions, total (MtCO_2e)	16.9	1,539
Nitrous oxide (N_2O) emissions, total (MtCO_2e)	4.7	813
Other GHG emissions, total (MtCO_2e)	5.2	460
Energy use per capita (kilograms of oil equivalent)	6,332	4,944
Energy use per units of GDP (kg oil eq./$1,000 of 2005 PPP $)	134.9	147.0

National-Level Actions

Latest UNFCCC national communication	1/22/2010 (5th)
Annex-I emissions reduction target (base year: 1990)	30% / 40%
NAMA submission	n/a
NAPA submission	n/a
Renewable energy target	..

Carbon Markets

Hosted Clean Development Mechanism (CDM) projects	n/a
Issued Certified Emission Reductions (CERs) from CDM (thousands)	n/a
Hosted Joint Implementation (JI) projects	..
Issued Emission Reduction Units (ERUs) from JI (thousands)	..

Oman

Population (millions)	2.8	GDP ($ billions)	46.9
Pop. growth (avg. ann. %, 1990–2010)	2.0	GNI per capita (Atlas $)	18,260

Climate

Average daily min/max temperature (1961–90, Celsius)	21 / 30
Projected annual temperature change (2045–65, Celsius)	2.0 to 2.4
Average annual precipitation (1961–90, mm)	125
Projected annual precipitation change (2045–65, mm)	-16 to 31
Projected change in annual hot days/warm nights	4 / 12
Projected change in annual cool days/cold nights	-2 / -2

	Country data	High Income
Exposure to Impacts		
Land area below 5m (% of land area)	1.1	2.2
Population below 5m (% of total)	5.5	7.7
Population in urban agglomerations > 1 million (%)	..	
Urban pop. growth (avg. annual %, 1990–2010)	2.4	1.0
Droughts, floods, extreme temps (% pop. avg., 1990–2009)	..	
Annual freshwater withdrawals (% of internal resources)	94.7	10.4
Agricultural land under irrigation (% of total ag. land)	4.0	..
Population living below $1.25 a day (% of total)	..	..
Nationally terrestrial protected areas (% of total land area)	10.7	13.4
Under-five mortality rate (per 1,000)	9	6
Child malnutrition, underweight (% of under age five)	..	..
Malaria incidence rate (per 100,000 people)	..	..
Resilience		
Access to improved sanitation (% of total pop.)	87	100
Access to improved water source (% of total pop.)	88	100
Cereal yield (kg. per hectare)	3,473	5,445
Access to electricity (% of total population)	98.0	..
Paved roads (% of total roads)	43.5	87.3
Health workers (per 1,000 people)	6.0	10.7
Foreign direct investment, net inflows (% of GDP)	3.2	1.8
Invest. in infrastructure w/private participation ($ millions)	..	..
Disaster risk reduction progress score (1–5 scale; 5 = best)	..	
Ease of doing business (ranking 1–183; 1 = best)	49	
Public sector mgmt & institutions avg. (1–6 scale; 6 = best)	..	
Primary completion rate, total (% of relevant age group)	80	97
Ratio of girls to boys in primary & secondary school (%)	97	100
GHG Emissions and Energy Use		
CO_2 emissions per capita (metric tons)	17.3	11.9
CO_2 emissions per units of GDP (kg/$1,000 of 2005 PPP $)	703.9	354.4
CO_2 emissions, total (MtCO_2)	45.7	13,285
GHG net emissions/removals by LUCF (MtCO_2e)	..	
Methane (CH_4) emissions, total (MtCO_2e)	17.8	1,539
Nitrous oxide (N_2O) emissions, total (MtCO_2e)	0.6	813
Other GHG emissions, total (MtCO_2e)	0.2	460
Energy use per capita (kilograms of oil equivalent)	5,554	4,944
Energy use per units of GDP (kg oil eq./$1,000 of 2005 PPP $)	229.3	147.0

National-Level Actions

Latest UNFCCC national communication	..
Annex-I emissions reduction target	n/a
NAMA submission	..
NAPA submission	n/a
Renewable energy target	..

Carbon Markets

Hosted Clean Development Mechanism (CDM) projects	0
Issued Certified Emission Reductions (CERs) from CDM (thousands)	0
Hosted Joint Implementation (JI) projects	n/a
Issued Emission Reduction Units (ERUs) from JI (thousands)	n/a

Pakistan

Population (millions)	173.6	GDP ($ billions)	174.8
Pop. growth (avg. ann. %, 1990–2010)	2.2	GNI per capita (Atlas $)	1,050

Climate

Average daily min/max temperature (1961–90, Celsius)	13 / 27
Projected annual temperature change (2045–65, Celsius)	2.4 to 3.4
Average annual precipitation (1961–90, mm)	305
Projected annual precipitation change (2045–65, mm)	-60 to 36
Projected change in annual hot days/warm nights	3 / 8
Projected change in annual cool days/cold nights	-2 / -2

	Country data	South Asia	Lower middle income
Exposure to Impacts			
Land area below 5m (% of land area)	1.4	1.5	1.7
Population below 5m (% of total)	1.3	4.4	6.5
Population in urban agglomerations > 1 million (%)	18	13	14
Urban pop. growth (avg. annual %, 1990–2010)	3.1	2.7	2.8
Droughts, floods, extreme temps (% pop. avg., 1990–2009)	1.1		
Annual freshwater withdrawals (% of internal resources)	313.8	50.6	18.7
Agricultural land under irrigation (% of total ag. land)	73.9	..	..
Population living below $1.25 a day (% of total)	22.6	40.3	..
Nationally terrestrial protected areas (% of total land area)	10.3	6.1	9.5
Under-five mortality rate (per 1,000)	87	67	69
Child malnutrition, underweight (% of under age five)	31.3	42.5	31.7
Malaria incidence rate (per 100,000 people)	881	1,127	4,874
Resilience			
Access to improved sanitation (% of total pop.)	45	36	45
Access to improved water source (% of total pop.)	90	87	84
Cereal yield (kg. per hectare)	2,790	2,728	2,754
Access to electricity (% of total population)	62.4	62.1	67.3
Paved roads (% of total roads)	65.4	58.9	29.3
Health workers (per 1,000 people)	1.4	1.7	2.6
Foreign direct investment, net inflows (% of GDP)	1.2	1.3	2.4
Invest. in infrastructure w/private participation ($ millions)	437	73,548	81,789
Disaster risk reduction progress score (1–5 scale; 5 = best)	3.5		
Ease of doing business (ranking 1–183; 1 = best)	105		
Public sector mgmt & institutions avg. (1–6 scale; 6 = best)	3.1		
Primary completion rate, total (% of relevant age group)	61	86	88
Ratio of girls to boys in primary & secondary school (%)	82	92	93
GHG Emissions and Energy Use			
CO$_2$ emissions per capita (metric tons)	1.0	1.3	1.6
CO$_2$ emissions per units of GDP (kg/$1,000 of 2005 PPP $)	420.7	504.6	523.9
CO$_2$ emissions, total (MtCO$_2$)	163.2	1,970	3,744
GHG net emissions/removals by LUCF (1994, MtCO$_2$e)	6.5		
Methane (CH$_4$) emissions, total (MtCO$_2$e)	137.4	846	1,705
Nitrous oxide (N$_2$O) emissions, total (MtCO$_2$e)	26.8	268	687
Other GHG emissions, total (MtCO$_2$e)	0.8	9	17
Energy use per capita (kilograms of oil equivalent)	502	532	680
Energy use per units of GDP (kg oil eq./$1,000 of 2005 PPP $)	212.7	193.5	217.9

National-Level Actions

Latest UNFCCC national communication	11/15/2003 (1st)
Annex-I emissions reduction target	n/a
NAMA submission	..
NAPA submission	n/a
Renewable energy target	Yes

Carbon Markets

Hosted Clean Development Mechanism (CDM) projects	12
Issued Certified Emission Reductions (CERs) from CDM (thousands)	2,983
Hosted Joint Implementation (JI) projects	n/a
Issued Emission Reduction Units (ERUs) from JI (thousands)	n/a

Palau

Population (thousands)	20.5	GDP ($ millions)	169.7
Pop. growth (avg. ann. %, 1990–2010)	1.5	GNI per capita (Atlas $)	6,470

Climate

Average daily min/max temperature (1961–90, Celsius)	24 / 31
Projected annual temperature change (2045–65, Celsius)	1.4 to 1.7
Average annual precipitation (1961–90, mm)	3,259
Projected annual precipitation change (2045–65, mm)	−89 to 172
Projected change in annual hot days/warm nights	25 / 27
Projected change in annual cool days/cold nights	−3 / −3

	Country data	East Asia & Pacific	Upper middle income
Exposure to Impacts			
Land area below 5m (% of land area)	21.4	2.5	1.8
Population below 5m (% of total)	55.6	10.3	6.5
Population in urban agglomerations > 1 million (%)	..	..	22
Urban pop. growth (avg. annual %, 1990–2010)	2.4	3.3	2.3
Droughts, floods, extreme temps (% pop. avg., 1990–2009)	..		
Annual freshwater withdrawals (% of internal resources)	..	10.8	5.6
Agricultural land under irrigation (% of total ag. land)	..	..	..
Population living below $1.25 a day (% of total)	..	16.8	..
Nationally terrestrial protected areas (% of total land area)	2.0	14.9	13.6
Under-five mortality rate (per 1,000)	19	24	20
Child malnutrition, underweight (% of under age five)	..	9.0	4.1
Malaria incidence rate (per 100,000 people)	..	525	80
Resilience			
Access to improved sanitation (% of total pop.)	83	59	68
Access to improved water source (% of total pop.)	84	88	92
Cereal yield (kg. per hectare)	..	4,860	3,690
Access to electricity (% of total population)	..	90.8	98.0
Paved roads (% of total roads)	..	15.9	50.5
Health workers (per 1,000 people)	7.2	2.8	4.5
Foreign direct investment, net inflows (% of GDP)	1.4	3.0	2.7
Invest. in infrastructure w/private participation ($ millions)	..	14,638	26,166
Disaster risk reduction progress score (1–5 scale; 5 = best)	..		
Ease of doing business (ranking 1–183; 1 = best)	116		
Public sector mgmt & institutions avg. (1–6 scale; 6 = best)	..		
Primary completion rate, total (% of relevant age group)	104	97	98
Ratio of girls to boys in primary & secondary school (%)	100	103	103
GHG Emissions and Energy Use			
CO_2 emissions per capita (metric tons)	10.5	4.3	5.3
CO_2 emissions per units of GDP (kg/$1,000 of 2005 PPP $)	827.5	827.1	659.4
CO_2 emissions, total (MtCO_2)	0.2	8,259	12,860
GHG net emissions/removals by LUCF (MtCO_2e)	..		
Methane (CH_4) emissions, total (MtCO_2e)	..	1,928	3,455
Nitrous oxide (N_2O) emissions, total (MtCO_2e)	..	707	1,144
Other GHG emissions, total (MtCO_2e)	..	..	243
Energy use per capita (kilograms of oil equivalent)	..	1,436	1,848
Energy use per units of GDP (kg oil eq./$1,000 of 2005 PPP $)	..	259.5	227.1

National-Level Actions

Latest UNFCCC national communication	6/18/2003 (1st)
Annex-I emissions reduction target	n/a
NAMA submission	..
NAPA submission	n/a
Renewable energy target	..

Carbon Markets

Hosted Clean Development Mechanism (CDM) projects	..
Issued Certified Emission Reductions (CERs) from CDM (thousands)	..
Hosted Joint Implementation (JI) projects	n/a
Issued Emission Reduction Units (ERUs) from JI (thousands)	n/a

Panama

Population (millions)	3.5	GDP ($ billions)	26.8
Pop. growth (avg. ann. %, 1990–2010)	1.9	GNI per capita (Atlas $)	6,980

Climate

Average daily min/max temperature (1961–90, Celsius)	21 / 30
Projected annual temperature change (2045–65, Celsius)	1.6 to 2.2
Average annual precipitation (1961–90, mm)	2,692
Projected annual precipitation change (2045–65, mm)	-228 to 107
Projected change in annual hot days/warm nights	14 / 27
Projected change in annual cool days/cold nights	-3 / -3

	Country data	Latin America & the Carib.	Upper middle income
Exposure to Impacts			
Land area below 5m (% of land area)	3.7	1.5	1.8
Population below 5m (% of total)	4.0	3.8	6.5
Population in urban agglomerations > 1 million (%)	39	35	22
Urban pop. growth (avg. annual %, 1990–2010)	3.5	2.0	2.3
Droughts, floods, extreme temps (% pop. avg., 1990–2009)	0.2		
Annual freshwater withdrawals (% of internal resources)	0.3	2.0	5.6
Agricultural land under irrigation (% of total ag. land)	..	..	..
Population living below $1.25 a day (% of total)	2.4	8.1	..
Nationally terrestrial protected areas (% of total land area)	18.7	20.8	13.6
Under-five mortality rate (per 1,000)	20	23	20
Child malnutrition, underweight (% of under age five)	..	3.8	4.1
Malaria incidence rate (per 100,000 people)	35	206	80
Resilience			
Access to improved sanitation (% of total pop.)	69	79	68
Access to improved water source (% of total pop.)	93	93	92
Cereal yield (kg. per hectare)	2,019	3,337	3,690
Access to electricity (% of total population)	88.1	93.4	98.0
Paved roads (% of total roads)	38.1	28.1	50.5
Health workers (per 1,000 people)	4.3	6.9	4.5
Foreign direct investment, net inflows (% of GDP)	8.8	2.3	2.7
Invest. in infrastructure w/private participation ($ millions)	339	33,064	26,166
Disaster risk reduction progress score (1–5 scale; 5 = best)	3.0		
Ease of doing business (ranking 1–183; 1 = best)	61		
Public sector mgmt & institutions avg. (1–6 scale; 6 = best)	..		
Primary completion rate, total (% of relevant age group)	102	102	98
Ratio of girls to boys in primary & secondary school (%)	101	102	103
GHG Emissions and Energy Use			
CO_2 emissions per capita (metric tons)	2.0	2.8	5.3
CO_2 emissions per units of GDP (kg/$1,000 of 2005 PPP $)	173.8	285.6	659.4
CO_2 emissions, total (MtCO_2)	6.9	1,584	12,860
GHG net emissions/removals by LUCF (1994, MtCO_2e)	23.7		
Methane (CH_4) emissions, total (MtCO_2e)	3.2	1,009	3,455
Nitrous oxide (N_2O) emissions, total (MtCO_2e)	1.2	442	1,144
Other GHG emissions, total (MtCO_2e)	0.0	21	243
Energy use per capita (kilograms of oil equivalent)	896	1,245	1,848
Energy use per units of GDP (kg oil eq./$1,000 of 2005 PPP $)	75.5	130.6	227.1

National-Level Actions

Latest UNFCCC national communication	7/20/2001 (1st)
Annex-I emissions reduction target	n/a
NAMA submission	..
NAPA submission	n/a
Renewable energy target	..

Carbon Markets

Hosted Clean Development Mechanism (CDM) projects	7
Issued Certified Emission Reductions (CERs) from CDM (thousands)	138
Hosted Joint Implementation (JI) projects	n/a
Issued Emission Reduction Units (ERUs) from JI (thousands)	n/a

Papua New Guinea

Population (millions)	6.9	GDP ($ billions)	9.5
Pop. growth (avg. ann. %, 1990–2010)	2.5	GNI per capita (Atlas $)	1,300

Climate

Average daily min/max temperature (1961–90, Celsius)	20 / 30
Projected annual temperature change (2045–65, Celsius)	1.4 to 1.8
Average annual precipitation (1961–90, mm)	3,142
Projected annual precipitation change (2045–65, mm)	-163 to 421
Projected change in annual hot days/warm nights	16 / 26
Projected change in annual cool days/cold nights	-3 / -3

	Country data	East Asia & Pacific	Lower middle income
Exposure to Impacts			
Land area below 5m (% of land area)	1.8	2.5	1.7
Population below 5m (% of total)	2.0	10.3	6.5
Population in urban agglomerations > 1 million (%)	..	..	14
Urban pop. growth (avg. annual %, 1990–2010)	1.6	3.3	2.8
Droughts, floods, extreme temps (% pop. avg., 1990–2009)	0.7		
Annual freshwater withdrawals (% of internal resources)	0.0	10.8	18.7
Agricultural land under irrigation (% of total ag. land)	..	..	..
Population living below $1.25 a day (% of total)	35.8	16.8	..
Nationally terrestrial protected areas (% of total land area)	3.1	14.9	9.5
Under-five mortality rate (per 1,000)	61	24	69
Child malnutrition, underweight (% of under age five)	18.1	9.0	31.7
Malaria incidence rate (per 100,000 people)	18,012	525	4,874
Resilience			
Access to improved sanitation (% of total pop.)	45	59	45
Access to improved water source (% of total pop.)	40	88	84
Cereal yield (kg. per hectare)	4,415	4,860	2,754
Access to electricity (% of total population)	..	90.8	67.3
Paved roads (% of total roads)	3.5	15.9	29.3
Health workers (per 1,000 people)	0.6	2.8	2.6
Foreign direct investment, net inflows (% of GDP)	0.3	3.0	2.4
Invest. in infrastructure w/private participation ($ millions)	150	14,638	81,789
Disaster risk reduction progress score (1–5 scale; 5 = best)	..		
Ease of doing business (ranking 1–183; 1 = best)	101		
Public sector mgmt & institutions avg. (1–6 scale; 6 = best)	2.9		
Primary completion rate, total (% of relevant age group)	53	97	88
Ratio of girls to boys in primary & secondary school (%)	..	103	93
GHG Emissions and Energy Use			
CO_2 emissions per capita (metric tons)	0.3	4.3	1.6
CO_2 emissions per units of GDP (kg/$1,000 of 2005 PPP $)	158.0	827.1	523.9
CO_2 emissions, total (MtCO$_2$)	2.1	8,259	3,744
GHG net emissions/removals by LUCF (1994, MtCO$_2$e)	-0.4		
Methane (CH_4) emissions, total (MtCO$_2$e)	..	1,928	1,705
Nitrous oxide (N_2O) emissions, total (MtCO$_2$e)	..	707	687
Other GHG emissions, total (MtCO$_2$e)	..	..	17
Energy use per capita (kilograms of oil equivalent)	..	1,436	680
Energy use per units of GDP (kg oil eq./$1,000 of 2005 PPP $)	..	259.5	217.9

National-Level Actions

Latest UNFCCC national communication	2/27/2002 (1st)
Annex-I emissions reduction target	n/a
NAMA submission	Yes
NAPA submission	n/a
Renewable energy target	..

Carbon Markets

Hosted Clean Development Mechanism (CDM) projects	1
Issued Certified Emission Reductions (CERs) from CDM (thousands)	215
Hosted Joint Implementation (JI) projects	n/a
Issued Emission Reduction Units (ERUs) from JI (thousands)	n/a

Paraguay

Population (millions)	6.5	GDP ($ billions) 18.5
Pop. growth (avg. ann. %, 1990–2010)	2.1	GNI per capita (Atlas $) 2,940

Climate

Average daily min/max temperature (1961–90, Celsius)	18 / 29
Projected annual temperature change (2045–65, Celsius)	1.9 to 2.6
Average annual precipitation (1961–90, mm)	1,130
Projected annual precipitation change (2045–65, mm)	-48 to 112
Projected change in annual hot days/warm nights	3 / 12
Projected change in annual cool days/cold nights	-1 / -1

	Country data	Latin America & the Carib.	Lower middle income
Exposure to Impacts			
Land area below 5m (% of land area)	0.0	1.5	1.7
Population below 5m (% of total)	0.0	3.8	6.5
Population in urban agglomerations > 1 million (%)	31	35	14
Urban pop. growth (avg. annual %, 1990–2010)	3.3	2.0	2.8
Droughts, floods, extreme temps (% pop. avg., 1990–2009)	0.7		
Annual freshwater withdrawals (% of internal resources)	0.5	2.0	18.7
Agricultural land under irrigation (% of total ag. land)	..	..	..
Population living below $1.25 a day (% of total)	5.1	8.1	..
Nationally terrestrial protected areas (% of total land area)	5.4	20.8	9.5
Under-five mortality rate (per 1,000)	25	23	69
Child malnutrition, underweight (% of under age five)	..	3.8	31.7
Malaria incidence rate (per 100,000 people)	16	206	4,874
Resilience			
Access to improved sanitation (% of total pop.)	70	79	45
Access to improved water source (% of total pop.)	86	93	84
Cereal yield (kg. per hectare)	2,358	3,337	2,754
Access to electricity (% of total population)	96.7	93.4	67.3
Paved roads (% of total roads)	50.8	28.1	29.3
Health workers (per 1,000 people)	2.9	6.9	2.6
Foreign direct investment, net inflows (% of GDP)	2.3	2.3	2.4
Invest. in infrastructure w/private participation ($ millions)	45	33,064	81,789
Disaster risk reduction progress score (1–5 scale; 5 = best)	3.8		
Ease of doing business (ranking 1–183; 1 = best)	102		
Public sector mgmt & institutions avg. (1–6 scale; 6 = best)	..		
Primary completion rate, total (% of relevant age group)	93	102	88
Ratio of girls to boys in primary & secondary school (%)	100	102	93
GHG Emissions and Energy Use			
CO_2 emissions per capita (metric tons)	0.7	2.8	1.6
CO_2 emissions per units of GDP (kg/$1,000 of 2005 PPP $)	151.9	285.6	523.9
CO_2 emissions, total (MtCO_2)	4.1	1,584	3,744
GHG net emissions/removals by LUCF (1994, MtCO_2e)	19.5		
Methane (CH_4) emissions, total (MtCO_2e)	15.4	1,009	1,705
Nitrous oxide (N_2O) emissions, total (MtCO_2e)	9.1	442	687
Other GHG emissions, total (MtCO_2e)	0.0	21	17
Energy use per capita (kilograms of oil equivalent)	749	1,245	680
Energy use per units of GDP (kg oil eq./$1,000 of 2005 PPP $)	182.3	130.6	217.9

National-Level Actions

Latest UNFCCC national communication	4/10/2002 (1st)
Annex-I emissions reduction target	n/a
NAMA submission	..
NAPA submission	n/a
Renewable energy target	..

Carbon Markets

Hosted Clean Development Mechanism (CDM) projects	2
Issued Certified Emission Reductions (CERs) from CDM (thousands)	0
Hosted Joint Implementation (JI) projects	n/a
Issued Emission Reduction Units (ERUs) from JI (thousands)	n/a

Peru

Population (millions)	29.1	GDP ($ billions)	153.8
Pop. growth (avg. ann. %, 1990–2010)	1.5	GNI per capita (Atlas $)	4,780

Climate
Average daily min/max temperature (1961–90, Celsius)	14 / 26
Projected annual temperature change (2045–65, Celsius)	2.1 to 2.7
Average annual precipitation (1961–90, mm)	1,493
Projected annual precipitation change (2045–65, mm)	-57 to 181
Projected change in annual hot days/warm nights	8 / 23
Projected change in annual cool days/cold nights	-3 / -3

	Country data	Latin America & the Carib.	Upper middle income
Exposure to Impacts			
Land area below 5m (% of land area)	0.4	1.5	1.8
Population below 5m (% of total)	1.7	3.8	6.5
Population in urban agglomerations > 1 million (%)	31	35	22
Urban pop. growth (avg. annual %, 1990–2010)	1.7	2.0	2.3
Droughts, floods, extreme temps (% pop. avg., 1990–2009)	2.0		
Annual freshwater withdrawals (% of internal resources)	1.2	2.0	5.6
Agricultural land under irrigation (% of total ag. land)	..		..
Population living below $1.25 a day (% of total)	5.9	8.1	..
Nationally terrestrial protected areas (% of total land area)	13.6	20.8	13.6
Under-five mortality rate (per 1,000)	19	23	20
Child malnutrition, underweight (% of under age five)	5.4	3.8	4.1
Malaria incidence rate (per 100,000 people)	478	206	80
Resilience			
Access to improved sanitation (% of total pop.)	68	79	68
Access to improved water source (% of total pop.)	82	93	92
Cereal yield (kg. per hectare)	3,910	3,337	3,690
Access to electricity (% of total population)	85.7	93.4	98.0
Paved roads (% of total roads)	13.9	28.1	50.5
Health workers (per 1,000 people)	2.2	6.9	4.5
Foreign direct investment, net inflows (% of GDP)	4.8	2.3	2.7
Invest. in infrastructure w/private participation ($ millions)	1,663	33,064	26,166
Disaster risk reduction progress score (1–5 scale; 5 = best)	3.0		
Ease of doing business (ranking 1–183; 1 = best)	41		
Public sector mgmt & institutions avg. (1–6 scale; 6 = best)	..		
Primary completion rate, total (% of relevant age group)	*101	102	98
Ratio of girls to boys in primary & secondary school (%)	99	102	103
GHG Emissions and Energy Use			
CO_2 emissions per capita (metric tons)	1.4	2.8	5.3
CO_2 emissions per units of GDP (kg/$1,000 of 2005 PPP $)	178.7	285.6	659.4
CO_2 emissions, total (MtCO_2)	40.5	1,584	12,860
GHG net emissions/removals by LUCF (2000, MtCO_2e)	56.8		
Methane (CH_4) emissions, total (MtCO_2e)	17.2	1,009	3,455
Nitrous oxide (N_2O) emissions, total (MtCO_2e)	7.6	442	1,144
Other GHG emissions, total (MtCO_2e)	0.3	21	243
Energy use per capita (kilograms of oil equivalent)	550	1,245	1,848
Energy use per units of GDP (kg oil eq./$1,000 of 2005 PPP $)	69.2	130.6	227.1

National-Level Actions
Latest UNFCCC national communication	9/28/2010 (2nd)
Annex-I emissions reduction target	n/a
NAMA submission	Yes, with Goal
NAPA submission	n/a
Renewable energy target	..

Carbon Markets
Hosted Clean Development Mechanism (CDM) projects	25
Issued Certified Emission Reductions (CERs) from CDM (thousands)	620
Hosted Joint Implementation (JI) projects	n/a
Issued Emission Reduction Units (ERUs) from JI (thousands)	n/a

Philippines

Population (millions)	93.3	GDP ($ billions)	199.6
Pop. growth (avg. ann. %, 1990-2010)	2.1	GNI per capita (Atlas $)	2,060

Climate

Average daily min/max temperature (1961-90, Celsius)	22 / 30
Projected annual temperature change (2045-65, Celsius)	1.4 to 1.8
Average annual precipitation (1961-90, mm)	2,348
Projected annual precipitation change (2045-65, mm)	-136 to 140
Projected change in annual hot days/warm nights	13 / 24
Projected change in annual cool days/cold nights	-2 / -3

	Country data	East Asia & Pacific	Lower middle income
Exposure to Impacts			
Land area below 5m (% of land area)	.	6.0	2.5	1.7
Population below 5m (% of total)	10.5	10.3	6.5
Population in urban agglomerations > 1 million (%)	14	..	14
Urban pop. growth (avg. annual %, 1990-2010)	3.6	3.3	2.8
Droughts, floods, extreme temps (% pop. avg., 1990-2009)	0.8		
Annual freshwater withdrawals (% of internal resources)	16.5	10.8	18.7
Agricultural land under irrigation (% of total ag. land)	..	..	..
Population living below $1.25 a day (% of total)	22.6	16.8	..
Nationally terrestrial protected areas (% of total land area)	10.9	14.9	9.5
Under-five mortality rate (per 1,000)	29	24	69
Child malnutrition, underweight (% of under age five)	20.7	9.0	31.7
Malaria incidence rate (per 100,000 people)	96	525	4,874
Resilience			
Access to improved sanitation (% of total pop.)	76	59	45
Access to improved water source (% of total pop.)	91	88	84
Cereal yield (kg. per hectare)	3,229	4,860	2,754
Access to electricity (% of total population)	89.7	90.8	67.3
Paved roads (% of total roads)	9.9	15.9	29.3
Health workers (per 1,000 people)	7.2	2.8	2.6
Foreign direct investment, net inflows (% of GDP)	0.9	3.0	2.4
Invest. in infrastructure w/private participation ($ millions)	2,817	14,638	81,789
Disaster risk reduction progress score (1-5 scale; 5 = best)	..		
Ease of doing business (ranking 1-183; 1 = best)	136		
Public sector mgmt & institutions avg. (1-6 scale; 6 = best)	..		
Primary completion rate, total (% of relevant age group)	94	97	88
Ratio of girls to boys in primary & secondary school (%)	102	103	93
GHG Emissions and Energy Use			
CO_2 emissions per capita (metric tons)	0.9	4.3	1.6
CO_2 emissions per units of GDP (kg/$1,000 of 2005 PPP $)	272.6	827.1	523.9
CO_2 emissions, total (MtCO_2)	83.2	8,259	3,744
GHG net emissions/removals by LUCF (1994, MtCO_2e)	-0.1		
Methane (CH_4) emissions, total (MtCO_2e)	51.9	1,928	1,705
Nitrous oxide (N_2O) emissions, total (MtCO_2e)	13.0	707	687
Other GHG emissions, total (MtCO_2e)	0.4	..	17
Energy use per capita (kilograms of oil equivalent)	424	1,436	680
Energy use per units of GDP (kg oil eq./$1,000 of 2005 PPP $)	125.9	259.5	217.9

National-Level Actions

Latest UNFCCC national communication	5/19/2000 (1st)
Annex-I emissions reduction target	n/a
NAMA submission	..
NAPA submission	n/a
Renewable energy target	Yes

Carbon Markets

Hosted Clean Development Mechanism (CDM) projects	57
Issued Certified Emission Reductions (CERs) from CDM (thousands)	245
Hosted Joint Implementation (JI) projects	n/a
Issued Emission Reduction Units (ERUs) from JI (thousands)	n/a

Poland

Population (millions)	38.2	GDP ($ billions)	468.6
Pop. growth (avg. ann. %, 1990–2010)	0.0	GNI per capita (Atlas $)	12,410

Climate

Average daily min/max temperature (1961–90, Celsius)	4 / 12
Projected annual temperature change (2045–65, Celsius)	1.9 to 2.8
Average annual precipitation (1961–90, mm)	600
Projected annual precipitation change (2045–65, mm)	-12 to 64
Projected change in annual hot days/warm nights	2 / 5
Projected change in annual cool days/cold nights	-2 / -2

	Country data	High income
Exposure to Impacts		
Land area below 5m (% of land area)	1.7	2.2
Population below 5m (% of total)	2.5	7.7
Population in urban agglomerations > 1 million (%)	4	..
Urban pop. growth (avg. annual %, 1990–2010)	0.0	1.0
Droughts, floods, extreme temps (% pop. avg., 1990–2009)	0.0	
Annual freshwater withdrawals (% of internal resources)	24.5	10.4
Agricultural land under irrigation (% of total ag. land)	0.4	..
Population living below $1.25 a day (% of total)	<2	..
Nationally terrestrial protected areas (% of total land area)	21.8	13.4
Under-five mortality rate (per 1,000)	6	6
Child malnutrition, underweight (% of under age five)	..	..
Malaria incidence rate (per 100,000 people)	..	..
Resilience		
Access to improved sanitation (% of total pop.)	90	100
Access to improved water source (% of total pop.)	100	100
Cereal yield (kg. per hectare)	3,475	5,445
Access to electricity (% of total population)	..	
Paved roads (% of total roads)	68.2	87.3
Health workers (per 1,000 people)	7.9	10.7
Foreign direct investment, net inflows (% of GDP)	1.9	1.8
Invest. in infrastructure w/private participation ($ millions)	4,638	..
Disaster risk reduction progress score (1–5 scale; 5 = best)	3.3	
Ease of doing business (ranking 1–183; 1 = best)	62	
Public sector mgmt & institutions avg. (1–6 scale; 6 = best)	..	
Primary completion rate, total (% of relevant age group)	95	97
Ratio of girls to boys in primary & secondary school (%)	100	100
GHG Emissions and Energy Use		
CO_2 emissions per capita (metric tons)	8.3	11.9
CO_2 emissions per units of GDP (kg/$1,000 of 2005 PPP $)	503.8	354.4
CO_2 emissions, total (MtCO$_2$)	316.1	13,285
GHG net emissions/removals by LUCF (2009, MtCO$_2$e)	-37.2	
Methane (CH_4) emissions, total (MtCO$_2$e)	70.0	1,539
Nitrous oxide (N_2O) emissions, total (MtCO$_2$e)	30.2	813
Other GHG emissions, total (MtCO$_2$e)	2.5	460
Energy use per capita (kilograms of oil equivalent)	2,663	4,944
Energy use per units of GDP (kg oil eq./$1,000 of 2005 PPP $)	153.6	147.0

National-Level Actions

Latest UNFCCC national communication	3/12/2010 (5th)
Annex-I emissions reduction target (base year: 1990)	20% / 30% (EU)
NAMA submission	n/a
NAPA submission	n/a
Renewable energy target	Yes

Carbon Markets

Hosted Clean Development Mechanism (CDM) projects	n/a
Issued Certified Emission Reductions (CERs) from CDM (thousands)	n/a
Hosted Joint Implementation (JI) projects	17
Issued Emission Reduction Units (ERUs) from JI (thousands)	0

Portugal

Population (millions)	10.6	GDP ($ billions)	228.5
Pop. growth (avg. ann. %, 1990–2010)	0.4	GNI per capita (Atlas $)	21,850

Climate

Average daily min/max temperature (1961–90, Celsius)	10 / 20
Projected annual temperature change (2045–65, Celsius)	1.3 to 2.3
Average annual precipitation (1961–90, mm)	855
Projected annual precipitation change (2045–65, mm)	-113 to -7
Projected change in annual hot days/warm nights	5 / 9
Projected change in annual cool days/cold nights	-2 / -2

	Country data	High income
Exposure to Impacts		
Land area below 5m (% of land area)	2.3	2.2
Population below 5m (% of total)	5.2	7.7
Population in urban agglomerations > 1 million (%)	39	..
Urban pop. growth (avg. annual %, 1990–2010)	1.5	1.0
Droughts, floods, extreme temps (% pop. avg., 1990–2009)	0.0	
Annual freshwater withdrawals (% of internal resources)	31.3	10.4
Agricultural land under irrigation (% of total ag. land)	11.4	..
Population living below $1.25 a day (% of total)	..	..
Nationally terrestrial protected areas (% of total land area)	5.9	13.4
Under-five mortality rate (per 1,000)	4	6
Child malnutrition, underweight (% of under age five)	..	..
Malaria incidence rate (per 100,000 people)	..	..
Resilience		
Access to improved sanitation (% of total pop.)	100	100
Access to improved water source (% of total pop.)	99	100
Cereal yield (kg. per hectare)	3,455	5,445
Access to electricity (% of total population)	..	..
Paved roads (% of total roads)	86.0	87.3
Health workers (per 1,000 people)	3.8	10.7
Foreign direct investment, net inflows (% of GDP)	0.6	1.8
Invest. in infrastructure w/private participation ($ millions)	..	..
Disaster risk reduction progress score (1-5 scale; 5 = best)	..	
Ease of doing business (ranking 1-183; 1 = best)	30	
Public sector mgmt & institutions avg. (1-6 scale; 6 = best)	..	
Primary completion rate, total (% of relevant age group)	103	97
Ratio of girls to boys in primary & secondary school (%)	101	100
GHG Emissions and Energy Use		
CO$_2$ emissions per capita (metric tons)	5.3	11.9
CO$_2$ emissions per units of GDP (kg/$1,000 of 2005 PPP $)	241.4	354.4
CO$_2$ emissions, total (MtCO$_2$)	56.3	13,285
GHG net emissions/removals by LUCF (2009, MtCO$_2$e)	-14.1	
Methane (CH$_4$) emissions, total (MtCO$_2$e)	12.2	1,539
Nitrous oxide (N$_2$O) emissions, total (MtCO$_2$e)	6.0	813
Other GHG emissions, total (MtCO$_2$e)	0.8	460
Energy use per capita (kilograms of oil equivalent)	2,210	4,944
Energy use per units of GDP (kg oil eq./$1,000 of 2005 PPP $)	102.0	147.0

National-Level Actions

Latest UNFCCC national communication	6/11/2010 (5th)
Annex-I emissions reduction target (base year: 1990)	20% / 30% (EU)
NAMA submission	n/a
NAPA submission	n/a
Renewable energy target	Yes

Carbon Markets

Hosted Clean Development Mechanism (CDM) projects	n/a
Issued Certified Emission Reductions (CERs) from CDM (thousands)	n/a
Hosted Joint Implementation (JI) projects	..
Issued Emission Reduction Units (ERUs) from JI (thousands)	..

Puerto Rico

Population (millions)	4.0	GDP ($ millions)	..
Pop. growth (avg. ann. %, 1990–2010)	0.6	GNI per capita (Atlas $)	..

Climate

Average daily min/max temperature (1961–90, Celsius)	21 / 29
Projected annual temperature change (2045–65, Celsius)	1.4 to 1.8
Average annual precipitation (1961–90, mm)	2,054
Projected annual precipitation change (2045–65, mm)	-133 to 37
Projected change in annual hot days/warm nights	13 / 24
Projected change in annual cool days/cold nights	-3 / -3

	Country data	High income
Exposure to Impacts		
Land area below 5m (% of land area)	7.7	2.2
Population below 5m (% of total)	11.3	7.7
Population in urban agglomerations > 1 million (%)	69	..
Urban pop. growth (avg. annual %, 1990–2010)	2.2	1.0
Droughts, floods, extreme temps (% pop. avg., 1990–2009)	0.0	
Annual freshwater withdrawals (% of internal resources)	14.0	10.4
Agricultural land under irrigation (% of total ag. land)	8.5	..
Population living below $1.25 a day (% of total)	..	..
Nationally terrestrial protected areas (% of total land area)	10.1	13.4
Under-five mortality rate (per 1,000)	..	6
Child malnutrition, underweight (% of under age five)	..	..
Malaria incidence rate (per 100,000 people)	..	..
Resilience		
Access to improved sanitation (% of total pop.)	..	100
Access to improved water source (% of total pop.)	..	100
Cereal yield (kg. per hectare)	1,878	5,445
Access to electricity (% of total population)	..	
Paved roads (% of total roads)	95.0	87.3
Health workers (per 1,000 people)	..	10.7
Foreign direct investment, net inflows (% of GDP)	..	1.8
Invest. in infrastructure w/private participation ($ millions)	..	
Disaster risk reduction progress score (1–5 scale; 5 = best)	..	
Ease of doing business (ranking 1–183; 1 = best)	43	
Public sector mgmt & institutions avg. (1–6 scale; 6 = best)	..	
Primary completion rate, total (% of relevant age group)	..	97
Ratio of girls to boys in primary & secondary school (%)	102	100
GHG Emissions and Energy Use		
CO_2 emissions per capita (metric tons)	..	11.9
CO_2 emissions per units of GDP (kg/$1,000 of 2005 PPP $)	..	354.4
CO_2 emissions, total (MtCO_2)	..	13,285
GHG net emissions/removals by LUCF (MtCO_2e)	..	
Methane (CH_4) emissions, total (MtCO_2e)	..	1,539
Nitrous oxide (N_2O) emissions, total (MtCO_2e)	..	813
Other GHG emissions, total (MtCO_2e)	..	460
Energy use per capita (kilograms of oil equivalent)	..	4,944
Energy use per units of GDP (kg oil eq./$1,000 of 2005 PPP $)	..	147.0
National-Level Actions		
Latest UNFCCC national communication		n/a
Annex-I emissions reduction target		n/a
NAMA submission		n/a
NAPA submission		n/a
Renewable energy target		..
Carbon Markets		
Hosted Clean Development Mechanism (CDM) projects		n/a
Issued Certified Emission Reductions (CERs) from CDM (thousands)		n/a
Hosted Joint Implementation (JI) projects		n/a
Issued Emission Reduction Units (ERUs) from JI (thousands)		n/a

Qatar

Population (millions)	1.8	GDP ($ billions)	98.3
Pop. growth (avg. ann. %, 1990–2010)	6.6	GNI per capita (Atlas $)	..

Climate
Average daily min/max temperature (1961–90, Celsius)	21 / 33
Projected annual temperature change (2045–65, Celsius)	2.3 to 2.9
Average annual precipitation (1961–90, mm)	74
Projected annual precipitation change (2045–65, mm)	-23 to 8
Projected change in annual hot days/warm nights	5 / 9
Projected change in annual cool days/cold nights	-2 / -2

	Country data	High income
Exposure to Impacts		
Land area below 5m (% of land area)	13.4	2.2
Population below 5m (% of total)	23.1	7.7
Population in urban agglomerations > 1 million (%)	..	..
Urban pop. growth (avg. annual %, 1990–2010)	6.8	1.0
Droughts, floods, extreme temps (% pop. avg., 1990–2009)	..	
Annual freshwater withdrawals (% of internal resources)	471.4	10.4
Agricultural land under irrigation (% of total ag. land)	..	..
Population living below $1.25 a day (% of total)	..	..
Nationally terrestrial protected areas (% of total land area)	0.7	13.4
Under-five mortality rate (per 1,000)	8	6
Child malnutrition, underweight (% of under age five)	..	..
Malaria incidence rate (per 100,000 people)	..	..
Resilience		
Access to improved sanitation (% of total pop.)	100	100
Access to improved water source (% of total pop.)	100	100
Cereal yield (kg. per hectare)	4,746	5,445
Access to electricity (% of total population)	98.7	
Paved roads (% of total roads)	90.0	87.3
Health workers (per 1,000 people)	10.1	10.7
Foreign direct investment, net inflows (% of GDP)	8.3	1.8
Invest. in infrastructure w/private participation ($ millions)	..	..
Disaster risk reduction progress score (1–5 scale; 5 = best)	..	
Ease of doing business (ranking 1–183; 1 = best)	36	
Public sector mgmt & institutions avg. (1–6 scale; 6 = best)	..	
Primary completion rate, total (% of relevant age group)	108	97
Ratio of girls to boys in primary & secondary school (%)	120	100
GHG Emissions and Energy Use		
CO_2 emissions per capita (metric tons)	49.1	11.9
CO_2 emissions per units of GDP (kg/$1,000 of 2005 PPP $)	636.1	354.4
CO_2 emissions, total (MtCO_2)	68.5	13,285
GHG net emissions/removals by LUCF (MtCO_2e)	..	
Methane (CH_4) emissions, total (MtCO_2e)	15.7	1,539
Nitrous oxide (N_2O) emissions, total (MtCO_2e)	0.2	813
Other GHG emissions, total (MtCO_2e)	0.0	460
Energy use per capita (kilograms of oil equivalent)	14,911	4,944
Energy use per units of GDP (kg oil eq./$1,000 of 2005 PPP $)	203.7	147.0

National-Level Actions
Latest UNFCCC national communication	6/20/2011 (1st)
Annex-I emissions reduction target	n/a
NAMA submission	..
NAPA submission	n/a
Renewable energy target	..

Carbon Markets
Hosted Clean Development Mechanism (CDM) projects	1
Issued Certified Emission Reductions (CERs) from CDM (thousands)	0
Hosted Joint Implementation (JI) projects	n/a
Issued Emission Reduction Units (ERUs) from JI (thousands)	n/a

Romania

Population (millions)	21.4	GDP ($ billions)	161.6
Pop. growth (avg. ann. %, 1990–2010)	-0.4	GNI per capita (Atlas $)	7,840

Climate
Average daily min/max temperature (1961-90, Celsius)	4 / 14
Projected annual temperature change (2045-65, Celsius)	2.0 to 3.1
Average annual precipitation (1961-90, mm)	637
Projected annual precipitation change (2045-65, mm)	-92 to 2
Projected change in annual hot days/warm nights	3 / 5
Projected change in annual cool days/cold nights	-1 / -2

	Country data	Europe & Central Asia	Upper middle Income
Exposure to Impacts			
Land area below 5m (% of land area)	2.9	2.5	1.8
Population below 5m (% of total)	2.9	3.0	6.5
Population in urban agglomerations > 1 million (%)	9	18	22
Urban pop. growth (avg. annual %, 1990-2010)	-0.3	0.3	2.3
Droughts, floods, extreme temps (% pop. avg., 1990-2009)	0.1		
Annual freshwater withdrawals (% of internal resources)	21.7	6.5	5.6
Agricultural land under irrigation (% of total ag. land)	2.2	..	..
Population living below $1.25 a day (% of total)	<2	3.7	..
Nationally terrestrial protected areas (% of total land area)	7.1	7.5	13.6
Under-five mortality rate (per 1,000)	14	23	20
Child malnutrition, underweight (% of under age five)	3.5	..	4.1
Malaria incidence rate (per 100,000 people)	..	..	80
Resilience			
Access to improved sanitation (% of total pop.)	72	89	68
Access to improved water source (% of total pop.)	..	95	92
Cereal yield (kg. per hectare)	2,825	2,475	3,690
Access to electricity (% of total population)	..	..	98.0
Paved roads (% of total roads)	30.2	85.8	50.5
Health workers (per 1,000 people)	6.1	9.9	4.5
Foreign direct investment, net inflows (% of GDP)	2.1	2.8	2.7
Invest. in infrastructure w/private participation ($ millions)	680	22,652	26,166
Disaster risk reduction progress score (1-5 scale; 5 = best)	3.3		
Ease of doing business (ranking 1-183; 1 = best)	72		
Public sector mgmt & institutions avg. (1-6 scale; 6 = best)	..		
Primary completion rate, total (% of relevant age group)	96	95	98
Ratio of girls to boys in primary & secondary school (%)	99	97	103
GHG Emissions and Energy Use			
CO_2 emissions per capita (metric tons)	4.4	7.7	5.3
CO_2 emissions per units of GDP (kg/$1,000 of 2005 PPP $)	373.1	708.0	659.4
CO_2 emissions, total (MtCO$_2$)	94.7	3,110	12,860
GHG net emissions/removals by LUCF (2009, MtCO$_2$e)	-36.5		
Methane (CH$_4$) emissions, total (MtCO$_2$e)	24.3	937	3,455
Nitrous oxide (N$_2$O) emissions, total (MtCO$_2$e)	11.5	214	1,144
Other GHG emissions, total (MtCO$_2$e)	0.7	76	243
Energy use per capita (kilograms of oil equivalent)	1,602	2,833	1,848
Energy use per units of GDP (kg oil eq./$1,000 of 2005 PPP $)	148.2	276.8	227.1

National-Level Actions
Latest UNFCCC national communication	2/15/2010 (5th)
Annex-I emissions reduction target (base year: 1990)	20% / 30% (EU)
NAMA submission	n/a
NAPA submission	n/a
Renewable energy target	Yes

Carbon Markets
Hosted Clean Development Mechanism (CDM) projects	n/a
Issued Certified Emission Reductions (CERs) from CDM (thousands)	n/a
Hosted Joint Implementation (JI) projects	15
Issued Emission Reduction Units (ERUs) from JI (thousands)	2,405

Russian Federation

Population (millions)	141.8	GDP ($ billions)	1,479.8
Pop. growth (avg. ann. %, 1990-2010)	-0.2	GNI per capita (Atlas $)	9,910

Climate

Average daily min/max temperature (1961-90, Celsius)	-10 / 0
Projected annual temperature change (2045-65, Celsius)	2.6 to 3.7
Average annual precipitation (1961-90, mm)	460
Projected annual precipitation change (2045-65, mm)	24 to 79
Projected change in annual hot days/warm nights	2 / 4
Projected change in annual cool days/cold nights	-2 / -2

	Country data	Europe & Central Asia	Upper middle income
Exposure to Impacts			
Land area below 5m (% of land area)	1.9	2.5	1.8
Population below 5m (% of total)	2.9	3.0	6.5
Population in urban agglomerations > 1 million (%)	18	18	22
Urban pop. growth (avg. annual %, 1990-2010)	-0.3	0.3	2.3
Droughts, floods, extreme temps (% pop. avg., 1990-2009)	0.1		
Annual freshwater withdrawals (% of internal resources)	1.5	6.5	5.6
Agricultural land under irrigation (% of total ag. land)	2.0	..	..
Population living below $1.25 a day (% of total)	<2	3.7	..
Nationally terrestrial protected areas (% of total land area)	9.0	7.5	13.6
Under-five mortality rate (per 1,000)	12	23	20
Child malnutrition, underweight (% of under age five)	..	..	4.1
Malaria incidence rate (per 100,000 people)	..	..	80
Resilience			
Access to improved sanitation (% of total pop.)	87	89	68
Access to improved water source (% of total pop.)	96	95	92
Cereal yield (kg. per hectare)	2,281	2,475	3,690
Access to electricity (% of total population)	..	..	98.0
Paved roads (% of total roads)	80.1	85.8	50.5
Health workers (per 1,000 people)	12.8	9.9	4.5
Foreign direct investment, net inflows (% of GDP)	2.9	2.8	2.7
Invest. in infrastructure w/private participation ($ millions)	16,097	22,652	26,166
Disaster risk reduction progress score (1-5 scale; 5 = best)	..		
Ease of doing business (ranking 1-183; 1 = best)	120		
Public sector mgmt & institutions avg. (1-6 scale; 6 = best)	..		
Primary completion rate, total (% of relevant age group)	95	95	98
Ratio of girls to boys in primary & secondary school (%)	98	97	103
GHG Emissions and Energy Use			
CO_2 emissions per capita (metric tons)	12.0	7.7	5.3
CO_2 emissions per units of GDP (kg/$1,000 of 2005 PPP $)	815.1	708.0	659.4
CO_2 emissions, total (MtCO_2)	1,708.7	3,110	12,860
GHG net emissions/removals by LUCF (2009, MtCO_2e)	-656.5		
Methane (CH_4) emissions, total (MtCO_2e)	562.8	937	3,455
Nitrous oxide (N_2O) emissions, total (MtCO_2e)	76.1	214	1,144
Other GHG emissions, total (MtCO_2e)	59.7	76	243
Energy use per capita (kilograms of oil equivalent)	4,561	2,833	1,848
Energy use per units of GDP (kg oil eq./$1,000 of 2005 PPP $)	334.8	276.8	227.1

National-Level Actions

Latest UNFCCC national communication	3/16/2010 (5th)
Annex-I emissions reduction target (base year: 1990)	15% / 25%
NAMA submission	n/a
NAPA submission	n/a
Renewable energy target	Yes

Carbon Markets

Hosted Clean Development Mechanism (CDM) projects	n/a
Issued Certified Emission Reductions (CERs) from CDM (thousands)	n/a
Hosted Joint Implementation (JI) projects	25
Issued Emission Reduction Units (ERUs) from JI (thousands)	7,211

Rwanda

Population (millions)	10.6	GDP ($ billions)	5.6
Pop. growth (avg. ann. %, 1990–2010)	2.0	GNI per capita (Atlas $)	520

Climate

Average daily min/max temperature (1961-90, Celsius)	12 / 24
Projected annual temperature change (2045-65, Celsius)	2.1 to 2.4
Average annual precipitation (1961-90, mm)	1,212
Projected annual precipitation change (2045-65, mm)	-12 to 211
Projected change in annual hot days/warm nights	8 / 26
Projected change in annual cool days/cold nights	-2 / -3

	Country data	Sub-Saharan Africa	Low income
Exposure to Impacts			
Land area below 5m (% of land area)	0.0	0.4	0.7
Population below 5m (% of total)	0.0	2.0	5.1
Population in urban agglomerations > 1 million (%)	..	14	11
Urban pop. growth (avg. annual %, 1990-2010)	8.3	4.0	3.7
Droughts, floods, extreme temps (% pop. avg., 1990-2009)	1.3		
Annual freshwater withdrawals (% of internal resources)	1.6	3.2	3.7
Agricultural land under irrigation (% of total ag. land)	..	..	..
Population living below $1.25 a day (% of total)	76.8	50.9	..
Nationally terrestrial protected areas (% of total land area)	10.0	11.7	10.6
Under-five mortality rate (per 1,000)	91	121	108
Child malnutrition, underweight (% of under age five)	18.0	24.6	28.3
Malaria incidence rate (per 100,000 people)	11,429	26,113	16,659
Resilience			
Access to improved sanitation (% of total pop.)	54	31	35
Access to improved water source (% of total pop.)	65	60	63
Cereal yield (kg. per hectare)	1,829	1,297	2,047
Access to electricity (% of total population)	..	32.5	23.0
Paved roads (% of total roads)	19.0	18.3	14.1
Health workers (per 1,000 people)	0.5	1.2	0.7
Foreign direct investment, net inflows (% of GDP)	0.8	3.6	3.2
Invest. in infrastructure w/private participation ($ millions)	63	11,957	4,471
Disaster risk reduction progress score (1-5 scale; 5 = best)	..		
Ease of doing business (ranking 1-183; 1 = best)	45		
Public sector mgmt & institutions avg. (1-6 scale; 6 = best)	3.7		
Primary completion rate, total (% of relevant age group)	54	67	65
Ratio of girls to boys in primary & secondary school (%)	100	89	91
GHG Emissions and Energy Use			
CO_2 emissions per capita (metric tons)	0.1	0.8	0.3
CO_2 emissions per units of GDP (kg/$1,000 of 2005 PPP $)	71.1	428.6	270.2
CO_2 emissions, total (MtCO$_2$)	0.7	685	219
GHG net emissions/removals by LUCF (2002, MtCO$_2$e)	-7.0		
Methane (CH$_4$) emissions, total (MtCO$_2$e)	..	590	436
Nitrous oxide (N$_2$O) emissions, total (MtCO$_2$e)	..	334	209
Other GHG emissions, total (MtCO$_2$e)	..	..	..
Energy use per capita (kilograms of oil equivalent)	..	689	365
Energy use per units of GDP (kg oil eq./$1,000 of 2005 PPP $)	..	308.4	303.9

National-Level Actions

Latest UNFCCC national communication	9/6/2005 (1st)
Annex-I emissions reduction target	n/a
NAMA submission	..
NAPA submission	Yes
Renewable energy target	Yes

Carbon Markets

Hosted Clean Development Mechanism (CDM) projects	3
Issued Certified Emission Reductions (CERs) from CDM (thousands)	0
Hosted Joint Implementation (JI) projects	n/a
Issued Emission Reduction Units (ERUs) from JI (thousands)	n/a

Samoa

Population (thousands)	183.1	GDP ($ millions)	565.2
Pop. growth (avg. ann. %, 1990-2010)	0.6	GNI per capita (Atlas $)	2,860

Climate

Average daily min/max temperature (1961-90, Celsius)	24 / 30
Projected annual temperature change (2045-65, Celsius)	1.3 to 1.6
Average annual precipitation (1961-90, mm)	2,991
Projected annual precipitation change (2045-65, mm)	-41 to 196
Projected change in annual hot days/warm nights	16 / 25
Projected change in annual cool days/cold nights	-3 / -3

	Country data	East Asia & Pacific	Lower middle income
Exposure to Impacts			
Land area below 5m (% of land area)	7.3	2.5	1.7
Population below 5m (% of total)	15.6	10.3	6.5
Population in urban agglomerations > 1 million (%)	..	..	14
Urban pop. growth (avg. annual %, 1990-2010)	1.1	3.3	2.8
Droughts, floods, extreme temps (% pop. avg., 1990-2009)	0.0		
Annual freshwater withdrawals (% of internal resources)	..	10.8	18.7
Agricultural land under irrigation (% of total ag. land)	..	..	..
Population living below $1.25 a day (% of total)	..	16.8	..
Nationally terrestrial protected areas (% of total land area)	3.4	14.9	9.5
Under-five mortality rate (per 1,000)	20	24	69
Child malnutrition, underweight (% of under age five)	..	9.0	31.7
Malaria incidence rate (per 100,000 people)	..	525	4,874
Resilience			
Access to improved sanitation (% of total pop.)	100	59	45
Access to improved water source (% of total pop.)	88	88	84
Cereal yield (kg. per hectare)	..	4,860	2,754
Access to electricity (% of total population)	..	90.8	67.3
Paved roads (% of total roads)	14.2	15.9	29.3
Health workers (per 1,000 people)	1.2	2.8	2.6
Foreign direct investment, net inflows (% of GDP)	0.4	3.0	2.4
Invest. in infrastructure w/private participation ($ millions)	..	14,638	81,789
Disaster risk reduction progress score (1-5 scale; 5 = best)	3.5		
Ease of doing business (ranking 1-183; 1 = best)	60		
Public sector mgmt & institutions avg. (1-6 scale; 6 = best)	4.0		
Primary completion rate, total (% of relevant age group)	93	97	88
Ratio of girls to boys in primary & secondary school (%)	105	103	93
GHG Emissions and Energy Use			
CO$_2$ emissions per capita (metric tons)	0.9	4.3	1.6
CO$_2$ emissions per units of GDP (kg/$1,000 of 2005 PPP $)	213.0	827.1	523.9
CO$_2$ emissions, total (MtCO$_2$)	0.2	8,259	3,744
GHG net emissions/removals by LUCF (1994, MtCO$_2$e)	-0.1		
Methane (CH$_4$) emissions, total (MtCO$_2$e)	..	1,928	1,705
Nitrous oxide (N$_2$O) emissions, total (MtCO$_2$e)	..	707	687
Other GHG emissions, total (MtCO$_2$e)	..	..	17
Energy use per capita (kilograms of oil equivalent)	320	1,436	680
Energy use per units of GDP (kg oil eq./$1,000 of 2005 PPP $)	80.4	259.5	217.9

National-Level Actions

Latest UNFCCC national communication	6/14/2010 (2nd)
Annex-I emissions reduction target	n/a
NAMA submission	..
NAPA submission	Yes
Renewable energy target	..

Carbon Markets

Hosted Clean Development Mechanism (CDM) projects	..
Issued Certified Emission Reductions (CERs) from CDM (thousands)	..
Hosted Joint Implementation (JI) projects	n/a
Issued Emission Reduction Units (ERUs) from JI (thousands)	n/a

San Marino

Population (thousands)	31.5	GDP ($ billions)	1.9
Pop. growth (avg. ann. %, 1990–2010)	1.3	GNI per capita (Atlas $)	50,400

Climate

Average daily min/max temperature (1961–90, Celsius)	8 / 16
Projected annual temperature change (2045–65, Celsius)	1.9 to 3.0
Average annual precipitation (1961–90, mm)	840
Projected annual precipitation change (2045–65, mm)	-111 to 3
Projected change in annual hot days/warm nights	4 / 6
Projected change in annual cool days/cold nights	-1 / -1

	Country data	High income
Exposure to Impacts		
Land area below 5m (% of land area)	0.0	2.2
Population below 5m (% of total)	0.0	7.7
Population in urban agglomerations > 1 million (%)	..	..
Urban pop. growth (avg. annual %, 1990–2010)	1.5	1.0
Droughts, floods, extreme temps (% pop. avg., 1990–2009)	..	
Annual freshwater withdrawals (% of internal resources)	..	10.4
Agricultural land under irrigation (% of total ag. land)	..	..
Population living below $1.25 a day (% of total)	..	..
Nationally terrestrial protected areas (% of total land area)	..	13.4
Under-five mortality rate (per 1,000)	2	6
Child malnutrition, underweight (% of under age five)	..	..
Malaria incidence rate (per 100,000 people)	..	..
Resilience		
Access to improved sanitation (% of total pop.)	..	100
Access to improved water source (% of total pop.)	..	100
Cereal yield (kg. per hectare)	..	5,445
Access to electricity (% of total population)	..	
Paved roads (% of total roads)	..	87.3
Health workers (per 1,000 people)	..	10.7
Foreign direct investment, net inflows (% of GDP)	..	1.8
Invest. in infrastructure w/private participation ($ millions)	..	..
Disaster risk reduction progress score (1–5 scale; 5 = best)	..	
Ease of doing business (ranking 1–183; 1 = best)	..	
Public sector mgmt & institutions avg. (1–6 scale; 6 = best)	..	
Primary completion rate, total (% of relevant age group)	92	97
Ratio of girls to boys in primary & secondary school (%)	103	100
GHG Emissions and Energy Use		
CO_2 emissions per capita (metric tons)	..	11.9
CO_2 emissions per units of GDP (kg/$1,000 of 2005 PPP $)	..	354.4
CO_2 emissions, total (MtCO_2)	..	13,285
GHG net emissions/removals by LUCF (2007, MtCO_2e)	0.0	
Methane (CH_4) emissions, total (MtCO_2e)	..	1,539
Nitrous oxide (N_2O) emissions, total (MtCO_2e)	..	813
Other GHG emissions, total (MtCO_2e)	..	460
Energy use per capita (kilograms of oil equivalent)	..	4,944
Energy use per units of GDP (kg oil eq./$1,000 of 2005 PPP $)	..	147.0
National-Level Actions		
Latest UNFCCC national communication		8/24/2009 (1st)
Annex-I emissions reduction target		n/a
NAMA submission		Yes
NAPA submission		n/a
Renewable energy target		..
Carbon Markets		
Hosted Clean Development Mechanism (CDM) projects		..
Issued Certified Emission Reductions (CERs) from CDM (thousands)		..
Hosted Joint Implementation (JI) projects		n/a
Issued Emission Reduction Units (ERUs) from JI (thousands)		n/a

São Tomé and Príncipe

Population (thousands)	165.4	GDP ($ millions)	196.8
Pop. growth (avg. ann. %, 1990-2010)	1.8	GNI per capita (Atlas $)	1,200

Climate

Average daily min/max temperature (1961-90, Celsius)	21 / 27
Projected annual temperature change (2045-65, Celsius)	1.5 to 2.0
Average annual precipitation (1961-90, mm)	2,169
Projected annual precipitation change (2045-65, mm)	-42 to 137
Projected change in annual hot days/warm nights	20 / 27
Projected change in annual cool days/cold nights	-3 / -3

	Country data	Sub-Saharan Africa	Lower middle income
Exposure to Impacts			
Land area below 5m (% of land area)	14.7	0.4	1.7
Population below 5m (% of total)	11.1	2.0	6.5
Population in urban agglomerations > 1 million (%)	..	14	14
Urban pop. growth (avg. annual %, 1990-2010)	3.5	4.0	2.8
Droughts, floods, extreme temps (% pop. avg., 1990-2009)	..		
Annual freshwater withdrawals (% of internal resources)	0.3	3.2	18.7
Agricultural land under irrigation (% of total ag. land)	..	..	..
Population living below $1.25 a day (% of total)	29.7	50.9	..
Nationally terrestrial protected areas (% of total land area)	..	11.7	9.5
Under-five mortality rate (per 1,000)	80	121	69
Child malnutrition, underweight (% of under age five)	13.1	24.6	31.7
Malaria incidence rate (per 100,000 people)	1,961	26,113	4,874
Resilience			
Access to improved sanitation (% of total pop.)	26	31	45
Access to improved water source (% of total pop.)	89	60	84
Cereal yield (kg. per hectare)	4,056	1,297	2,754
Access to electricity (% of total population)	..	32.5	67.3
Paved roads (% of total roads)	68.1	18.3	29.3
Health workers (per 1,000 people)	2.4	1.2	2.6
Foreign direct investment, net inflows (% of GDP)	1.5	3.6	2.4
Invest. in infrastructure w/private participation ($ millions)	50	11,957	81,789
Disaster risk reduction progress score (1-5 scale; 5 = best)	..		
Ease of doing business (ranking 1-183; 1 = best)	163		
Public sector mgmt & institutions avg. (1-6 scale; 6 = best)	3.1		
Primary completion rate, total (% of relevant age group)	85	67	88
Ratio of girls to boys in primary & secondary school (%)	100	89	93
GHG Emissions and Energy Use			
CO_2 emissions per capita (metric tons)	0.8	0.8	1.6
CO_2 emissions per units of GDP (kg/$1,000 of 2005 PPP $)	496.2	428.6	523.9
CO_2 emissions, total (MtCO_2)	0.1	685	3,744
GHG net emissions/removals by LUCF (1998, MtCO_2e)	-1.5		
Methane (CH_4) emissions, total (MtCO_2e)	..	590	1,705
Nitrous oxide (N_2O) emissions, total (MtCO_2e)	..	334	687
Other GHG emissions, total (MtCO_2e)	..	..	17
Energy use per capita (kilograms of oil equivalent)	280	689	680
Energy use per units of GDP (kg oil eq./$1,000 of 2005 PPP $)	180.0	308.4	217.9

National-Level Actions

Latest UNFCCC national communication	5/19/2005 (1st)
Annex-I emissions reduction target	n/a
NAMA submission	..
NAPA submission	Yes
Renewable energy target	..

Carbon Markets

Hosted Clean Development Mechanism (CDM) projects	..
Issued Certified Emission Reductions (CERs) from CDM (thousands)	..
Hosted Joint Implementation (JI) projects	n/a
Issued Emission Reduction Units (ERUs) from JI (thousands)	n/a

Saudi Arabia

Population (millions)	27.4	GDP ($ billions)	434.7
Pop. growth (avg. ann. %, 1990–2010)	2.7	GNI per capita (Atlas $)	16,190

Climate
Average daily min/max temperature (1961–90, Celsius)	18 / 31
Projected annual temperature change (2045–65, Celsius)	2.3 to 2.9
Average annual precipitation (1961–90, mm)	..
Projected annual precipitation change (2045–65, mm)	-27 to 9
Projected change in annual hot days/warm nights	5 / 9
Projected change in annual cool days/cold nights	-1 / -2

	Country data	High income
Exposure to Impacts		
Land area below 5m (% of land area)	0.5	2.2
Population below 5m (% of total)	1.0	7.7
Population in urban agglomerations > 1 million (%)	39	..
Urban pop. growth (avg. annual %, 1990–2010)	3.1	1.0
Droughts, floods, extreme temps (% pop. avg., 1990–2009)	0.0	
Annual freshwater withdrawals (% of internal resources)	943.3	10.4
Agricultural land under irrigation (% of total ag. land)	..	..
Population living below $1.25 a day (% of total)	..	..
Nationally terrestrial protected areas (% of total land area)	31.3	13.4
Under-five mortality rate (per 1,000)	18	6
Child malnutrition, underweight (% of under age five)	5.3	..
Malaria incidence rate (per 100,000 people)	7	..
Resilience		
Access to improved sanitation (% of total pop.)	99	100
Access to improved water source (% of total pop.)	96	100
Cereal yield (kg. per hectare)	4,161	5,445
Access to electricity (% of total population)	99.0	..
Paved roads (% of total roads)	21.5	87.3
Health workers (per 1,000 people)	3.0	10.7
Foreign direct investment, net inflows (% of GDP)	5.0	1.8
Invest. in infrastructure w/private participation ($ millions)	..	..
Disaster risk reduction progress score (1–5 scale; 5 = best)	..	
Ease of doing business (ranking 1–183; 1 = best)	12	
Public sector mgmt & institutions avg. (1–6 scale; 6 = best)	..	
Primary completion rate, total (% of relevant age group)	88	97
Ratio of girls to boys in primary & secondary school (%)	91	100
GHG Emissions and Energy Use		
CO_2 emissions per capita (metric tons)	16.6	11.9
CO_2 emissions per units of GDP (kg/$1,000 of 2005 PPP $)	805.7	354.4
CO_2 emissions, total (MtCO$_2$)	433.6	13,285
GHG net emissions/removals by LUCF (1990, MtCO$_2$e)	-15.2	
Methane (CH$_4$) emissions, total (MtCO$_2$e)	48.2	1,539
Nitrous oxide (N$_2$O) emissions, total (MtCO$_2$e)	6.5	813
Other GHG emissions, total (MtCO$_2$e)	2.2	460
Energy use per capita (kilograms of oil equivalent)	5,888	4,944
Energy use per units of GDP (kg oil eq./$1,000 of 2005 PPP $)	292.9	147.0

National-Level Actions
Latest UNFCCC national communication	11/29/2005 (1st)
Annex-I emissions reduction target	n/a
NAMA submission	..
NAPA submission	n/a
Renewable energy target	..

Carbon Markets
Hosted Clean Development Mechanism (CDM) projects	0
Issued Certified Emission Reductions (CERs) from CDM (thousands)	0
Hosted Joint Implementation (JI) projects	n/a
Issued Emission Reduction Units (ERUs) from JI (thousands)	n/a

Senegal

Population (millions)	12.4	GDP ($ billions)	13.0
Pop. growth (avg. ann. %, 1990-2010)	2.7	GNI per capita (Atlas $)	1,090

Climate

Average daily min/max temperature (1961-90, Celsius)	21 / 35
Projected annual temperature change (2045-65, Celsius)	2.0 to 2.7
Average annual precipitation (1961-90, mm)	687
Projected annual precipitation change (2045-65, mm)	-124 to 37
Projected change in annual hot days/warm nights	7 / 17
Projected change in annual cool days/cold nights	-2 / -3

	Country data	Sub-Saharan Africa	Lower middle income
Exposure to Impacts			
Land area below 5m (% of land area)	4.5	0.4	1.7
Population below 5m (% of total)	14.8	2.0	6.5
Population in urban agglomerations > 1 million (%)	23	14	14
Urban pop. growth (avg. annual %, 1990-2010)	3.2	4.0	2.8
Droughts, floods, extreme temps (% pop. avg., 1990-2009)	0.6		
Annual freshwater withdrawals (% of internal resources)	8.6	3.2	18.7
Agricultural land under irrigation (% of total ag. land)	0.7	..	..
Population living below $1.25 a day (% of total)	33.5	50.9	..
Nationally terrestrial protected areas (% of total land area)	24.1	11.7	9.5
Under-five mortality rate (per 1,000)	75	121	69
Child malnutrition, underweight (% of under age five)	14.5	24.6	31.7
Malaria incidence rate (per 100,000 people)	7,077	26,113	4,874
Resilience			
Access to improved sanitation (% of total pop.)	51	31	45
Access to improved water source (% of total pop.)	69	60	84
Cereal yield (kg. per hectare)	1,135	1,297	2,754
Access to electricity (% of total population)	42.0	32.5	67.3
Paved roads (% of total roads)	29.3	18.3	29.3
Health workers (per 1,000 people)	0.5	1.2	2.6
Foreign direct investment, net inflows (% of GDP)	1.8	3.6	2.4
Invest. in infrastructure w/private participation ($ millions)	258	11,957	81,789
Disaster risk reduction progress score (1-5 scale; 5 = best)	2.8		
Ease of doing business (ranking 1-183; 1 = best)	154		
Public sector mgmt & institutions avg. (1-6 scale; 6 = best)	3.5		
Primary completion rate, total (% of relevant age group)	57	67	88
Ratio of girls to boys in primary & secondary school (%)	95	89	93
GHG Emissions and Energy Use			
CO_2 emissions per capita (metric tons)	0.4	0.8	1.6
CO_2 emissions per units of GDP (kg/$1,000 of 2005 PPP $)	246.0	428.6	523.9
CO_2 emissions, total (MtCO_2)	5.0	685	3,744
GHG net emissions/removals by LUCF (2000, MtCO_2e)	-10.5		
Methane (CH_4) emissions, total (MtCO_2e)	7.1	590	1,705
Nitrous oxide (N_2O) emissions, total (MtCO_2e)	4.1	334	687
Other GHG emissions, total (MtCO_2e)	0.0	..	17
Energy use per capita (kilograms of oil equivalent)	243	689	680
Energy use per units of GDP (kg oil eq./$1,000 of 2005 PPP $)	142.2	308.4	217.9

National-Level Actions

Latest UNFCCC national communication	9/16/2010 (2nd)
Annex-I emissions reduction target	n/a
NAMA submission	..
NAPA submission	Yes
Renewable energy target	Yes

Carbon Markets

Hosted Clean Development Mechanism (CDM) projects	1
Issued Certified Emission Reductions (CERs) from CDM (thousands)	0
Hosted Joint Implementation (JI) projects	n/a
Issued Emission Reduction Units (ERUs) from JI (thousands)	n/a

Serbia

Population (millions)	7.3	GDP ($ billions)	39.1
Pop. growth (avg. ann. %, 1990–2010)	-0.2	GNI per capita (Atlas $)	5,810

Climate

Average daily min/max temperature (1961–90, Celsius)	..
Projected annual temperature change (2045–65, Celsius)	2.0 to 3.1
Average annual precipitation (1961–90, mm)	..
Projected annual precipitation change (2045–65, mm)	-125 to -15
Projected change in annual hot days/warm nights	3 / 6
Projected change in annual cool days/cold nights	-1 / -1

	Country data	Europe & Central Asia	Upper middle income
Exposure to Impacts			
Land area below 5m (% of land area)	0.2	2.5	1.8
Population below 5m (% of total)	0.1	3.0	6.5
Population in urban agglomerations > 1 million (%)	15	18	22
Urban pop. growth (avg. annual %, 1990–2010)	0.0	0.3	2.3
Droughts, floods, extreme temps (% pop. avg., 1990–2009)	0.0		
Annual freshwater withdrawals (% of internal resources)	..	6.5	5.6
Agricultural land under irrigation (% of total ag. land)	0.6	..	..
Population living below $1.25 a day (% of total)	<2	3.7	..
Nationally terrestrial protected areas (% of total land area)	6.0	7.5	13.6
Under-five mortality rate (per 1,000)	7	23	20
Child malnutrition, underweight (% of under age five)	1.8	..	4.1
Malaria incidence rate (per 100,000 people)	..	..	80
Resilience			
Access to improved sanitation (% of total pop.)	92	89	68
Access to improved water source (% of total pop.)	99	95	92
Cereal yield (kg. per hectare)	4,623	2,475	3,690
Access to electricity (% of total population)	..	..	98.0
Paved roads (% of total roads)	47.7	85.8	50.5
Health workers (per 1,000 people)	6.5	9.9	4.5
Foreign direct investment, net inflows (% of GDP)	3.4	2.8	2.7
Invest. in infrastructure w/private participation ($ millions)	107	22,652	26,166
Disaster risk reduction progress score (1–5 scale; 5 = best)	..		
Ease of doing business (ranking 1–183; 1 = best)	92		
Public sector mgmt & institutions avg. (1–6 scale; 6 = best)	2.9		
Primary completion rate, total (% of relevant age group)	96	95	98
Ratio of girls to boys in primary & secondary school (%)	101	97	103
GHG Emissions and Energy Use			
CO_2 emissions per capita (metric tons)	6.8	7.7	5.3
CO_2 emissions per units of GDP (kg/$1,000 of 2005 PPP $)	663.2	708.0	659.4
CO_2 emissions, total (MtCO$_2$)	49.9	3,110	12,860
GHG net emissions/removals by LUCF (1998, MtCO$_2$e)	-8.7		
Methane (CH_4) emissions, total (MtCO$_2$e)	7.8	937	3,455
Nitrous oxide (N_2O) emissions, total (MtCO$_2$e)	4.6	214	1,144
Other GHG emissions, total (MtCO$_2$e)	4.5	76	243
Energy use per capita (kilograms of oil equivalent)	1,974	2,833	1,848
Energy use per units of GDP (kg oil eq./$1,000 of 2005 PPP $)	198.1	276.8	227.1

National-Level Actions

Latest UNFCCC national communication	11/29/2010 (1st)
Annex-I emissions reduction target	n/a
NAMA submission	..
NAPA submission	n/a
Renewable energy target	..

Carbon Markets

Hosted Clean Development Mechanism (CDM) projects	0
Issued Certified Emission Reductions (CERs) from CDM (thousands)	0
Hosted Joint Implementation (JI) projects	n/a
Issued Emission Reduction Units (ERUs) from JI (thousands)	n/a

Seychelles

Population (thousands)	86.5	GDP ($ millions)	936.6
Pop. growth (avg. ann. %, 1990–2010)	1.1	GNI per capita (Atlas $)	9,760

Climate

Average daily min/max temperature (1961–90, Celsius)	25 / 30
Projected annual temperature change (2045–65, Celsius)	1.5 to 1.8
Average annual precipitation (1961–90, mm)	1,970
Projected annual precipitation change (2045–65, mm)	-75 to 226
Projected change in annual hot days/warm nights	18 / 25
Projected change in annual cool days/cold nights	-3 / -3

	Country data	Sub-Saharan Africa	Upper middle income
Exposure to Impacts			
Land area below 5m (% of land area)	43.9	0.4	1.8
Population below 5m (% of total)	41.3	2.0	6.5
Population in urban agglomerations > 1 million (%)	..	14	22
Urban pop. growth (avg. annual %, 1990–2010)	1.6	4.0	2.3
Droughts, floods, extreme temps (% pop. avg., 1990–2009)	0.1		
Annual freshwater withdrawals (% of internal resources)	..	3.2	5.6
Agricultural land under irrigation (% of total ag. land)	..	..	..
Population living below $1.25 a day (% of total)	<2	50.9	..
Nationally terrestrial protected areas (% of total land area)	42.0	11.7	13.6
Under-five mortality rate (per 1,000)	14	121	20
Child malnutrition, underweight (% of under age five)	..	24.6	4.1
Malaria incidence rate (per 100,000 people)	..	26,113	80
Resilience			
Access to improved sanitation (% of total pop.)	..	31	68
Access to improved water source (% of total pop.)	..	60	92
Cereal yield (kg. per hectare)	..	1,297	3,690
Access to electricity (% of total population)	..	32.5	98.0
Paved roads (% of total roads)	96.5	18.3	50.5
Health workers (per 1,000 people)	9.4	1.2	4.5
Foreign direct investment, net inflows (% of GDP)	39.4	3.6	2.7
Invest. in infrastructure w/private participation ($ millions)	15	11,957	26,166
Disaster risk reduction progress score (1-5 scale; 5 = best)	..		
Ease of doing business (ranking 1-183; 1 = best)	103		
Public sector mgmt & institutions avg. (1-6 scale; 6 = best)	..		
Primary completion rate, total (% of relevant age group)	105	67	98
Ratio of girls to boys in primary & secondary school (%)	103	89	103
GHG Emissions and Energy Use			
CO_2 emissions per capita (metric tons)	7.8	0.8	5.3
CO_2 emissions per units of GDP (kg/$1,000 of 2005 PPP $)	404.4	428.6	659.4
CO_2 emissions, total (MtCO_2)	0.7	685	12,860
GHG net emissions/removals by LUCF (1995, MtCO_2e)	-0.8		
Methane (CH_4) emissions, total (MtCO_2e)	..	590	3,455
Nitrous oxide (N_2O) emissions, total (MtCO_2e)	..	334	1,144
Other GHG emissions, total (MtCO_2e)	..	..	243
Energy use per capita (kilograms of oil equivalent)	2,411	689	1,848
Energy use per units of GDP (kg oil eq./$1,000 of 2005 PPP $)	120.0	308.4	227.1

National-Level Actions

Latest UNFCCC national communication	11/15/2020 (1st)
Annex-I emissions reduction target	n/a
NAMA submission	..
NAPA submission	n/a
Renewable energy target	..

Carbon Markets

Hosted Clean Development Mechanism (CDM) projects	..
Issued Certified Emission Reductions (CERs) from CDM (thousands)	..
Hosted Joint Implementation (JI) projects	n/a
Issued Emission Reduction Units (ERUs) from JI (thousands)	n/a

Sierra Leone

Population (millions)	5.9	GDP ($ billions)	1.9
Pop. growth (avg. ann. %, 1990–2010)	1.9	GNI per capita (Atlas $)	340

Climate

Average daily min/max temperature (1961–90, Celsius)	21 / 31
Projected annual temperature change (2045–65, Celsius)	1.8 to 2.3
Average annual precipitation (1961–90, mm)	2,526
Projected annual precipitation change (2045–65, mm)	-96 to 128
Projected change in annual hot days/warm nights	9 / 24
Projected change in annual cool days/cold nights	-3 / -3

	Country data	Sub-Saharan Africa	Low income
Exposure to Impacts			
Land area below 5m (% of land area)	3.0	0.4	0.7
Population below 5m (% of total)	5.1	2.0	5.1
Population in urban agglomerations > 1 million (%)	..	14	11
Urban pop. growth (avg. annual %, 1990–2010)	2.7	4.0	3.7
Droughts, floods, extreme temps (% pop. avg., 1990–2009)	0.2		
Annual freshwater withdrawals (% of internal resources)	0.3	3.2	3.7
Agricultural land under irrigation (% of total ag. land)	..	..	..
Population living below $1.25 a day (% of total)	53.4	50.9	..
Nationally terrestrial protected areas (% of total land area)	5.0	11.7	10.6
Under-five mortality rate (per 1,000)	174	121	108
Child malnutrition, underweight (% of under age five)	21.3	24.6	28.3
Malaria incidence rate (per 100,000 people)	36,141	26,113	16,659
Resilience			
Access to improved sanitation (% of total pop.)	13	31	35
Access to improved water source (% of total pop.)	49	60	63
Cereal yield (kg. per hectare)	1,402	1,297	2,047
Access to electricity (% of total population)	..	32.5	23.0
Paved roads (% of total roads)	8.0	18.3	14.1
Health workers (per 1,000 people)	0.2	1.2	0.7
Foreign direct investment, net inflows (% of GDP)	4.5	3.6	3.2
Invest. in infrastructure w/private participation ($ millions)	168	11,957	4,471
Disaster risk reduction progress score (1–5 scale; 5 = best)	3.0		
Ease of doing business (ranking 1–183; 1 = best)	141		
Public sector mgmt & institutions avg. (1–6 scale; 6 = best)	3.0		
Primary completion rate, total (% of relevant age group)	..	67	65
Ratio of girls to boys in primary & secondary school (%)	68	89	91
GHG Emissions and Energy Use			
CO_2 emissions per capita (metric tons)	0.2	0.8	0.3
CO_2 emissions per units of GDP (kg/$1,000 of 2005 PPP $)	332.2	428.6	270.2
CO_2 emissions, total (MtCO_2)	1.3	685	219
GHG net emissions/removals by LUCF (MtCO_2e)	..		
Methane (CH_4) emissions, total (MtCO_2e)	..	590	436
Nitrous oxide (N_2O) emissions, total (MtCO_2e)	..	334	209
Other GHG emissions, total (MtCO_2e)	..	..	..
Energy use per capita (kilograms of oil equivalent)	..	689	365
Energy use per units of GDP (kg oil eq./$1,000 of 2005 PPP $)	..	308.4	303.9

National-Level Actions

Latest UNFCCC national communication	1/8/2007 (1st)
Annex-I emissions reduction target	n/a
NAMA submission	Yes
NAPA submission	Yes
Renewable energy target	..

Carbon Markets

Hosted Clean Development Mechanism (CDM) projects	0
Issued Certified Emission Reductions (CERs) from CDM (thousands)	0
Hosted Joint Implementation (JI) projects	n/a
Issued Emission Reduction Units (ERUs) from JI (thousands)	n/a

Singapore

Population (millions)	5.1	GDP ($ billions)	222.7
Pop. growth (avg. ann. %, 1990-2010)	2.6	GNI per capita (Atlas $)	41,430

Climate

Average daily min/max temperature (1961-90, Celsius)	23 / 30
Projected annual temperature change (2045-65, Celsius)	1.5 to 1.8
Average annual precipitation (1961-90, mm)	2,497
Projected annual precipitation change (2045-65, mm)	-134 to 49
Projected change in annual hot days/warm nights	12 / 26
Projected change in annual cool days/cold nights	-3 / -3

	Country data	High income
Exposure to Impacts		
Land area below 5m (% of land area)	8.1	2.2
Population below 5m (% of total)	12.1	7.7
Population in urban agglomerations > 1 million (%)	95	..
Urban pop. growth (avg. annual %, 1990-2010)	2.6	1.0
Droughts, floods, extreme temps (% pop. avg., 1990-2009)	..	
Annual freshwater withdrawals (% of internal resources)	..	10.4
Agricultural land under irrigation (% of total ag. land)	..	..
Population living below $1.25 a day (% of total)	..	..
Nationally terrestrial protected areas (% of total land area)	5.4	13.4
Under-five mortality rate (per 1,000)	3	6
Child malnutrition, underweight (% of under age five)	3.3	..
Malaria incidence rate (per 100,000 people)	..	..
Resilience		
Access to improved sanitation (% of total pop.)	100	100
Access to improved water source (% of total pop.)	100	100
Cereal yield (kg. per hectare)	..	5,445
Access to electricity (% of total population)	100.0	..
Paved roads (% of total roads)	100.0	87.3
Health workers (per 1,000 people)	7.7	10.7
Foreign direct investment, net inflows (% of GDP)	17.3	1.8
Invest. in infrastructure w/private participation ($ millions)	..	..
Disaster risk reduction progress score (1-5 scale; 5 = best)	..	
Ease of doing business (ranking 1-183; 1 = best)	1	
Public sector mgmt & institutions avg. (1-6 scale; 6 = best)	..	
Primary completion rate, total (% of relevant age group)	..	97
Ratio of girls to boys in primary & secondary school (%)	..	100
GHG Emissions and Energy Use		
CO_2 emissions per capita (metric tons)	6.7	11.9
CO_2 emissions per units of GDP (kg/$1,000 of 2005 PPP $)	139.0	354.4
CO_2 emissions, total (MtCO_2)	32.3	13,285
GHG net emissions/removals by LUCF (MtCO_2e)	..	
Methane (CH_4) emissions, total (MtCO_2e)	2.2	1,539
Nitrous oxide (N_2O) emissions, total (MtCO_2e)	1.1	813
Other GHG emissions, total (MtCO_2e)	2.5	460
Energy use per capita (kilograms of oil equivalent)	3,704	4,944
Energy use per units of GDP (kg oil eq./$1,000 of 2005 PPP $)	80.2	147.0

National-Level Actions

Latest UNFCCC national communication	11/12/2010 (2nd)
Annex-I emissions reduction target	n/a
NAMA submission	Yes, with Goal
NAPA submission	n/a
Renewable energy target	..

Carbon Markets

Hosted Clean Development Mechanism (CDM) projects	2
Issued Certified Emission Reductions (CERs) from CDM (thousands)	0
Hosted Joint Implementation (JI) projects	n/a
Issued Emission Reduction Units (ERUs) from JI (thousands)	n/a

Sint Maarten (Dutch part)

Population (thousands)	37.9	GDP ($ millions)	..
Pop. growth (avg. ann. %, 1990–2010)	1.6	GNI per capita (Atlas $)	..

Climate

Average daily min/max temperature (1961–90, Celsius)	..
Projected annual temperature change (2045–65, Celsius)	..
Average annual precipitation (1961–90, mm)	..
Projected annual precipitation change (2045–65, mm)	..
Projected change in annual hot days/warm nights	..
Projected change in annual cool days/cold nights	..

	Country data	High income
Exposure to Impacts		
Land area below 5m (% of land area)	..	2.2
Population below 5m (% of total)	..	7.7
Population in urban agglomerations > 1 million (%)	..	
Urban pop. growth (avg. annual %, 1990–2010)	..	1.0
Droughts, floods, extreme temps (% pop. avg., 1990–2009)	..	
Annual freshwater withdrawals (% of internal resources)	..	10.4
Agricultural land under irrigation (% of total ag. land)	..	
Population living below $1.25 a day (% of total)	..	..
Nationally terrestrial protected areas (% of total land area)	..	13.4
Under-five mortality rate (per 1,000)	..	6
Child malnutrition, underweight (% of under age five)	..	
Malaria incidence rate (per 100,000 people)	..	..
Resilience		
Access to improved sanitation (% of total pop.)	..	100
Access to improved water source (% of total pop.)	..	100
Cereal yield (kg. per hectare)	..	5,445
Access to electricity (% of total population)	..	
Paved roads (% of total roads)	..	87.3
Health workers (per 1,000 people)	..	10.7
Foreign direct investment, net inflows (% of GDP)	..	1.8
Invest. in infrastructure w/private participation ($ millions)	..	
Disaster risk reduction progress score (1–5 scale; 5 = best)	..	
Ease of doing business (ranking 1-183; 1 = best)	..	
Public sector mgmt & institutions avg. (1–6 scale; 6 = best)	..	
Primary completion rate, total (% of relevant age group)	..	97
Ratio of girls to boys in primary & secondary school (%)	..	100
GHG Emissions and Energy Use		
CO_2 emissions per capita (metric tons)	..	11.9
CO_2 emissions per units of GDP (kg/$1,000 of 2005 PPP $)	..	354.4
CO_2 emissions, total (MtCO_2)	..	13,285
GHG net emissions/removals by LUCF (MtCO_2e)	..	
Methane (CH_4) emissions, total (MtCO_2e)	..	1,539
Nitrous oxide (N_2O) emissions, total (MtCO_2e)	..	813
Other GHG emissions, total (MtCO_2e)	..	460
Energy use per capita (kilograms of oil equivalent)	..	4,944
Energy use per units of GDP (kg oil eq./$1,000 of 2005 PPP $)	..	147.0
National-Level Actions		
Latest UNFCCC national communication		n/a
Annex-I emissions reduction target		n/a
NAMA submission		n/a
NAPA submission		n/a
Renewable energy target		..
Carbon Markets		
Hosted Clean Development Mechanism (CDM) projects		n/a
Issued Certified Emission Reductions (CERs) from CDM (thousands)		n/a
Hosted Joint Implementation (JI) projects		n/a
Issued Emission Reduction Units (ERUs) from JI (thousands)		n/a

Slovak Republic

Population (millions)	5.4	GDP ($ billions)	89.0
Pop. growth (avg. ann. %, 1990–2010)	0.1	GNI per capita (Atlas $)	16,210

Climate

Average daily min/max temperature (1961–90, Celsius)	2 / 12
Projected annual temperature change (2045–65, Celsius)	2.0 to 2.9
Average annual precipitation (1961–90, mm)	824
Projected annual precipitation change (2045–65, mm)	-44 to 45
Projected change in annual hot days/warm nights	3 / 5
Projected change in annual cool days/cold nights	-1 / -2

	Country data	High income
Exposure to Impacts		
Land area below 5m (% of land area)	0.0	2.2
Population below 5m (% of total)	0.0	7.7
Population in urban agglomerations > 1 million (%)	..	..
Urban pop. growth (avg. annual %, 1990–2010)	0.2	1.0
Droughts, floods, extreme temps (% pop. avg., 1990–2009)	0.0	
Annual freshwater withdrawals (% of internal resources)	..	10.4
Agricultural land under irrigation (% of total ag. land)	1.0	..
Population living below $1.25 a day (% of total)	<2	..
Nationally terrestrial protected areas (% of total land area)	23.5	13.4
Under-five mortality rate (per 1,000)	8	6
Child malnutrition, underweight (% of under age five)	..	..
Malaria incidence rate (per 100,000 people)	..	..
Resilience		
Access to improved sanitation (% of total pop.)	100	100
Access to improved water source (% of total pop.)	100	100
Cereal yield (kg. per hectare)	4,327	5,445
Access to electricity (% of total population)	..	..
Paved roads (% of total roads)	87.0	87.3
Health workers (per 1,000 people)	6.6	10.7
Foreign direct investment, net inflows (% of GDP)	0.6	1.8
Invest. in infrastructure w/private participation ($ millions)		..
Disaster risk reduction progress score (1–5 scale; 5 = best)	..	
Ease of doing business (ranking 1–183; 1 = best)	48	
Public sector mgmt & institutions avg. (1–6 scale; 6 = best)	..	
Primary completion rate, total (% of relevant age group)	97	97
Ratio of girls to boys in primary & secondary school (%)	101	100
GHG Emissions and Energy Use		
CO_2 emissions per capita (metric tons)	6.9	11.9
CO_2 emissions per units of GDP (kg/$1,000 of 2005 PPP $)	338.6	354.4
CO_2 emissions, total (MtCO$_2$)	37.6	13,285
GHG net emissions/removals by LUCF (2009, MtCO$_2$e)	-3.4	
Methane (CH_4) emissions, total (MtCO$_2$e)	3.9	1,539
Nitrous oxide (N_2O) emissions, total (MtCO$_2$e)	3.4	813
Other GHG emissions, total (MtCO$_2$e)	0.4	460
Energy use per capita (kilograms of oil equivalent)	3,178	4,944
Energy use per units of GDP (kg oil eq./$1,000 of 2005 PPP $)	165.1	147.0

National-Level Actions

Latest UNFCCC national communication	2/15/2010 (5th)
Annex-I emissions reduction target (base year: 1990)	20% / 30% (EU)
NAMA submission	n/a
NAPA submission	n/a
Renewable energy target	Yes

Carbon Markets

Hosted Clean Development Mechanism (CDM) projects	n/a
Issued Certified Emission Reductions (CERs) from CDM (thousands)	n/a
Hosted Joint Implementation (JI) projects	0
Issued Emission Reduction Units (ERUs) from JI (thousands)	0

Slovenia

Population (millions)	2.1	GDP ($ billions)	47.8
Pop. growth (avg. ann. %, 1990–2010)	0.1	GNI per capita (Atlas $)	24,000

Climate
Average daily min/max temperature (1961–90, Celsius)	4 / 14
Projected annual temperature change (2045–65, Celsius)	2.0 to 3.0
Average annual precipitation (1961–90, mm)	1,161
Projected annual precipitation change (2045–65, mm)	-93 to 5
Projected change in annual hot days/warm nights	3 / 6
Projected change in annual cool days/cold nights	-1 / -1

	Country data	High income
Exposure to Impacts		
Land area below 5m (% of land area)	0.2	2.2
Population below 5m (% of total)	1.3	7.7
Population in urban agglomerations > 1 million (%)	..	..
Urban pop. growth (avg. annual %, 1990–2010)	-0.1	1.0
Droughts, floods, extreme temps (% pop. avg., 1990–2009)	0.0	
Annual freshwater withdrawals (% of internal resources)	..	10.4
Agricultural land under irrigation (% of total ag. land)	0.9	..
Population living below $1.25 a day (% of total)	<2	..
Nationally terrestrial protected areas (% of total land area)	12.1	13.4
Under-five mortality rate (per 1,000)	3	6
Child malnutrition, underweight (% of under age five)	..	..
Malaria incidence rate (per 100,000 people)	..	..
Resilience		
Access to improved sanitation (% of total pop.)	100	100
Access to improved water source (% of total pop.)	99	100
Cereal yield (kg. per hectare)	5,257	5,445
Access to electricity (% of total population)	..	
Paved roads (% of total roads)	100.0	87.3
Health workers (per 1,000 people)	10.6	10.7
Foreign direct investment, net inflows (% of GDP)	0.8	1.8
Invest. in infrastructure w/private participation ($ millions)	..	..
Disaster risk reduction progress score (1–5 scale; 5 = best)	..	
Ease of doing business (ranking 1–183; 1 = best)	37	
Public sector mgmt & institutions avg. (1–6 scale; 6 = best)	..	
Primary completion rate, total (% of relevant age group)	96	97
Ratio of girls to boys in primary & secondary school (%)	99	100
GHG Emissions and Energy Use		
CO_2 emissions per capita (metric tons)	8.5	11.9
CO_2 emissions per units of GDP (kg/$1,000 of 2005 PPP $)	312.1	354.4
CO_2 emissions, total (MtCO$_2$)	17.2	13,285
GHG net emissions/removals by LUCF (2009, MtCO$_2$e)	-8.5	
Methane (CH_4) emissions, total (MtCO$_2$e)	3.5	1,539
Nitrous oxide (N_2O) emissions, total (MtCO$_2$e)	1.2	813
Other GHG emissions, total (MtCO$_2$e)	0.5	460
Energy use per capita (kilograms of oil equivalent)	3,455	4,944
Energy use per units of GDP (kg oil eq./$1,000 of 2005 PPP $)	138.3	147.0

National-Level Actions
Latest UNFCCC national communication	4/6/2010 (5th)
Annex-I emissions reduction target (base year: 1990)	20% / 30% (EU)
NAMA submission	n/a
NAPA submission	n/a
Renewable energy target	Yes

Carbon Markets
Hosted Clean Development Mechanism (CDM) projects	n/a
Issued Certified Emission Reductions (CERs) from CDM (thousands)	n/a
Hosted Joint Implementation (JI) projects	..
Issued Emission Reduction Units (ERUs) from JI (thousands)	..

Solomon Islands

Population (thousands)	538.1	GDP ($ millions)	678.6
Pop. growth (avg. ann. %, 1990–2010)	2.8	GNI per capita (Atlas $)	1,030

Climate

Average daily min/max temperature (1961–90, Celsius)	22 / 30
Projected annual temperature change (2045–65, Celsius)	1.4 to 1.7
Average annual precipitation (1961–90, mm)	3,028
Projected annual precipitation change (2045–65, mm)	-107 to 314
Projected change in annual hot days/warm nights	22 / 27
Projected change in annual cool days/cold nights	-3 / -3

	Country data	East Asia & Pacific	Lower middle income
Exposure to Impacts			
Land area below 5m (% of land area)	11.5	2.5	1.7
Population below 5m (% of total)	13.4	10.3	6.5
Population in urban agglomerations > 1 million (%)	..	..	14
Urban pop. growth (avg. annual %, 1990–2010)	4.3	3.3	2.8
Droughts, floods, extreme temps (% pop. avg., 1990–2009)	0.1		
Annual freshwater withdrawals (% of internal resources)	..	10.8	18.7
Agricultural land under irrigation (% of total ag. land)	..	..	..
Population living below $1.25 a day (% of total)	..	16.8	..
Nationally terrestrial protected areas (% of total land area)	0.1	14.9	9.5
Under-five mortality rate (per 1,000)	27	24	69
Child malnutrition, underweight (% of under age five)	11.5	9.0	31.7
Malaria incidence rate (per 100,000 people)	13,718	525	4,874
Resilience			
Access to improved sanitation (% of total pop.)	29	59	45
Access to improved water source (% of total pop.)	69	88	84
Cereal yield (kg. per hectare)	3,265	4,860	2,754
Access to electricity (% of total population)	..	90.8	67.3
Paved roads (% of total roads)	2.4	15.9	29.3
Health workers (per 1,000 people)	1.6	2.8	2.6
Foreign direct investment, net inflows (% of GDP)	35.0	3.0	2.4
Invest. in infrastructure w/private participation ($ millions)	5	14,638	81,789
Disaster risk reduction progress score (1–5 scale; 5 = best)	2.0		
Ease of doing business (ranking 1–183; 1 = best)	74		
Public sector mgmt & institutions avg. (1–6 scale; 6 = best)	2.7		
Primary completion rate, total (% of relevant age group)	..	97	88
Ratio of girls to boys in primary & secondary school (%)	94	103	93
GHG Emissions and Energy Use			
CO_2 emissions per capita (metric tons)	0.4	4.3	1.6
CO_2 emissions per units of GDP (kg/$1,000 of 2005 PPP $)	160.1	827.1	523.9
CO_2 emissions, total (MtCO$_2$)	0.2	8,259	3,744
GHG net emissions/removals by LUCF (MtCO$_2$e)	..		
Methane (CH$_4$) emissions, total (MtCO$_2$e)	..	1,928	1,705
Nitrous oxide (N$_2$O) emissions, total (MtCO$_2$e)	..	707	687
Other GHG emissions, total (MtCO$_2$e)	..	..	17
Energy use per capita (kilograms of oil equivalent)	129	1,436	680
Energy use per units of GDP (kg oil eq./$1,000 of 2005 PPP $)	55.5	259.5	217.9

National-Level Actions

Latest UNFCCC national communication	9/29/2004 (1st)
Annex-I emissions reduction target	n/a
NAMA submission	..
NAPA submission	Yes
Renewable energy target	..

Carbon Markets

Hosted Clean Development Mechanism (CDM) projects	..
Issued Certified Emission Reductions (CERs) from CDM (thousands)	..
Hosted Joint Implementation (JI) projects	n/a
Issued Emission Reduction Units (ERUs) from JI (thousands)	n/a

Somalia

Population (millions)	9.3	GDP ($ millions)	..
Pop. growth (avg. ann. %, 1990–2010)	1.7	GNI per capita (Atlas $)	..

Climate

Average daily min/max temperature (1961–90, Celsius)	21 / 33
Projected annual temperature change (2045–65, Celsius)	1.9 to 2.2
Average annual precipitation (1961–90, mm)	282
Projected annual precipitation change (2045–65, mm)	-4 to 111
Projected change in annual hot days/warm nights	9 / 21
Projected change in annual cool days/cold nights	-2 / -3

	Country data	Sub-Saharan Africa	Low income
Exposure to Impacts			
Land area below 5m (% of land area)	0.6	0.4	0.7
Population below 5m (% of total)	2.2	2.0	5.1
Population in urban agglomerations > 1 million (%)	16	14	11
Urban pop. growth (avg. annual %, 1990–2010)	2.9	4.0	3.7
Droughts, floods, extreme temps (% pop. avg., 1990–2009)	4.6		
Annual freshwater withdrawals (% of internal resources)	55.0	3.2	3.7
Agricultural land under irrigation (% of total ag. land)	..	..	..
Population living below $1.25 a day (% of total)	..	50.9	..
Nationally terrestrial protected areas (% of total land area)	0.6	11.7	10.6
Under-five mortality rate (per 1,000)	180	121	108
Child malnutrition, underweight (% of under age five)	32.8	24.6	28.3
Malaria incidence rate (per 100,000 people)	8,711	26,113	16,659
Resilience			
Access to improved sanitation (% of total pop.)	23	31	35
Access to improved water source (% of total pop.)	30	60	63
Cereal yield (kg. per hectare)	371	1,297	2,047
Access to electricity (% of total population)	..	32.5	23.0
Paved roads (% of total roads)	11.8	18.3	14.1
Health workers (per 1,000 people)	0.1	1.2	0.7
Foreign direct investment, net inflows (% of GDP)	..	3.6	3.2
Invest. in infrastructure w/private participation ($ millions)	1	11,957	4,471
Disaster risk reduction progress score (1–5 scale; 5 = best)	..		
Ease of doing business (ranking 1–183; 1 = best)	..		
Public sector mgmt & institutions avg. (1–6 scale; 6 = best)	..		
Primary completion rate, total (% of relevant age group)	..	67	65
Ratio of girls to boys in primary & secondary school (%)	53	89	91
GHG Emissions and Energy Use			
CO_2 emissions per capita (metric tons)	0.1	0.8	0.3
CO_2 emissions per units of GDP (kg/$1,000 of 2005 PPP $)	..	428.6	270.2
CO_2 emissions, total (MtCO_2)	0.6	685	219
GHG net emissions/removals by LUCF (MtCO_2e)	..		
Methane (CH_4) emissions, total (MtCO_2e)	..	590	436
Nitrous oxide (N_2O) emissions, total (MtCO_2e)	..	334	209
Other GHG emissions, total (MtCO_2e)	..	..	..
Energy use per capita (kilograms of oil equivalent)	..	689	365
Energy use per units of GDP (kg oil eq./$1,000 of 2005 PPP $)	..	308.4	303.9

National-Level Actions

Latest UNFCCC national communication	..
Annex-I emissions reduction target	n/a
NAMA submission	..
NAPA submission	..
Renewable energy target	..

Carbon Markets

Hosted Clean Development Mechanism (CDM) projects	..
Issued Certified Emission Reductions (CERs) from CDM (thousands)	..
Hosted Joint Implementation (JI) projects	n/a
Issued Emission Reduction Units (ERUs) from JI (thousands)	n/a

South Africa

Population (millions)	50.0	GDP ($ billions)	363.7
Pop. growth (avg. ann. %, 1990–2010)	1.8	GNI per capita (Atlas $)	6,090

Climate

Average daily min/max temperature (1961-90, Celsius)	11 / 25
Projected annual temperature change (2045-65, Celsius)	1.9 to 2.7
Average annual precipitation (1961-90, mm)	495
Projected annual precipitation change (2045-65, mm)	-78 to 33
Projected change in annual hot days/warm nights	4 / 10
Projected change in annual cool days/cold nights	-2 / -2

	Country data	Sub-Saharan Africa	Upper middle income
Exposure to Impacts			
Land area below 5m (% of land area)	0.1	0.4	1.8
Population below 5m (% of total)	0.5	2.0	6.5
Population in urban agglomerations > 1 million (%)	34	14	22
Urban pop. growth (avg. annual %, 1990-2010)	2.6	4.0	2.3
Droughts, floods, extreme temps (% pop. avg., 1990-2009)	1.8		
Annual freshwater withdrawals (% of internal resources)	27.9	3.2	5.6
Agricultural land under irrigation (% of total ag. land)	..	..	..
Population living below $1.25 a day (% of total)	17.4	50.9	..
Nationally terrestrial protected areas (% of total land area)	6.9	11.7	13.6
Under-five mortality rate (per 1,000)	57	121	20
Child malnutrition, underweight (% of under age five)	..	24.6	4.1
Malaria incidence rate (per 100,000 people)	80	26,113	80
Resilience			
Access to improved sanitation (% of total pop.)	77	31	68
Access to improved water source (% of total pop.)	91	60	92
Cereal yield (kg. per hectare)	4,414	1,297	3,690
Access to electricity (% of total population)	75.0	32.5	98.0
Paved roads (% of total roads)	17.3	18.3	50.5
Health workers (per 1,000 people)	4.9	1.2	4.5
Foreign direct investment, net inflows (% of GDP)	0.4	3.6	2.7
Invest. in infrastructure w/private participation ($ millions)	2,107	11,957	26,166
Disaster risk reduction progress score (1-5 scale; 5 = best)	..		
Ease of doing business (ranking 1-183; 1 = best)	35		
Public sector mgmt & institutions avg. (1-6 scale; 6 = best)	..		
Primary completion rate, total (% of relevant age group)	93	67	98
Ratio of girls to boys in primary & secondary school (%)	99	89	103
GHG Emissions and Energy Use			
CO_2 emissions per capita (metric tons)	8.9	0.8	5.3
CO_2 emissions per units of GDP (kg/$1,000 of 2005 PPP $)	930.3	428.6	659.4
CO_2 emissions, total (MtCO$_2$)	435.9	685	12,860
GHG net emissions/removals by LUCF (1994, MtCO$_2$e)	-18.6		
Methane (CH_4) emissions, total (MtCO$_2$e)	63.8	590	3,455
Nitrous oxide (N_2O) emissions, total (MtCO$_2$e)	24.0	334	1,144
Other GHG emissions, total (MtCO$_2$e)	2.6	..	243
Energy use per capita (kilograms of oil equivalent)	2,921	689	1,848
Energy use per units of GDP (kg oil eq./$1,000 of 2005 PPP $)	312.7	308.4	227.1

National-Level Actions

Latest UNFCCC national communication	12/11/2003 (1st)
Annex-I emissions reduction target	n/a
NAMA submission	Yes, with Goal
NAPA submission	n/a
Renewable energy target	Yes

Carbon Markets

Hosted Clean Development Mechanism (CDM) projects	20
Issued Certified Emission Reductions (CERs) from CDM (thousands)	1,900
Hosted Joint Implementation (JI) projects	n/a
Issued Emission Reduction Units (ERUs) from JI (thousands)	n/a

Spain

Population (millions)	46.1	GDP ($ billions)	1,407.4
Pop. growth (avg. ann. %, 1990–2010)	0.9	GNI per capita (Atlas $)	31,750

Climate

Average daily min/max temperature (1961–90, Celsius)	8 / 19
Projected annual temperature change (2045–65, Celsius)	1.5 to 2.6
Average annual precipitation (1961–90, mm)	636
Projected annual precipitation change (2045–65, mm)	–112 to -18
Projected change in annual hot days/warm nights	4 / 8
Projected change in annual cool days/cold nights	-2 / -2

	Country data	High income
Exposure to Impacts		
Land area below 5m (% of land area)	1.3	2.2
Population below 5m (% of total)	6.6	7.7
Population in urban agglomerations > 1 million (%)	24	..
Urban pop. growth (avg. annual %, 1990–2010)	1.0	1.0
Droughts, floods, extreme temps (% pop. avg., 1990–2009)	0.7	
Annual freshwater withdrawals (% of internal resources)	33.4	10.4
Agricultural land under irrigation (% of total ag. land)	11.9	..
Population living below $1.25 a day (% of total)	..	..
Nationally terrestrial protected areas (% of total land area)	8.6	13.4
Under-five mortality rate (per 1,000)	5	6
Child malnutrition, underweight (% of under age five)	..	..
Malaria incidence rate (per 100,000 people)	..	..
Resilience		
Access to improved sanitation (% of total pop.)	100	100
Access to improved water source (% of total pop.)	100	100
Cereal yield (kg. per hectare)	2,940	5,445
Access to electricity (% of total population)	..	
Paved roads (% of total roads)	99.0	87.3
Health workers (per 1,000 people)	8.9	10.7
Foreign direct investment, net inflows (% of GDP)	1.8	1.8
Invest. in infrastructure w/private participation ($ millions)	..	..
Disaster risk reduction progress score (1-5 scale; 5 = best)	..	
Ease of doing business (ranking 1-183; 1 = best)	44	
Public sector mgmt & institutions avg. (1-6 scale; 6 = best)	..	
Primary completion rate, total (% of relevant age group)	103	97
Ratio of girls to boys in primary & secondary school (%)	102	100
GHG Emissions and Energy Use		
CO_2 emissions per capita (metric tons)	7.2	11.9
CO_2 emissions per units of GDP (kg/$1,000 of 2005 PPP $)	255.1	354.4
CO_2 emissions, total (MtCO_2)	329.3	13,285
GHG net emissions/removals by LUCF (2009, MtCO_2e)	-28.6	
Methane (CH_4) emissions, total (MtCO_2e)	36.3	1,539
Nitrous oxide (N_2O) emissions, total (MtCO_2e)	26.5	813
Other GHG emissions, total (MtCO_2e)	9.1	460
Energy use per capita (kilograms of oil equivalent)	2,781	4,944
Energy use per units of GDP (kg oil eq./$1,000 of 2005 PPP $)	103.2	147.0

National-Level Actions

Latest UNFCCC national communication	12/18/2009 (5th)
Annex-I emissions reduction target (base year: 1990)	20% / 30% (EU)
NAMA submission	n/a
NAPA submission	n/a
Renewable energy target	Yes

Carbon Markets

Hosted Clean Development Mechanism (CDM) projects	n/a
Issued Certified Emission Reductions (CERs) from CDM (thousands)	n/a
Hosted Joint Implementation (JI) projects	3
Issued Emission Reduction Units (ERUs) from JI (thousands)	0

Sri Lanka

Population (millions)	20.9	GDP ($ billions)	49.6
Pop. growth (avg. ann. %, 1990-2010)	0.9	GNI per capita (Atlas $)	2,240

Climate

Average daily min/max temperature (1961-90, Celsius)	23 / 31
Projected annual temperature change (2045-65, Celsius)	1.5 to 1.8
Average annual precipitation (1961-90, mm)	1,712
Projected annual precipitation change (2045-65, mm)	11 to 196
Projected change in annual hot days/warm nights	8 / 24
Projected change in annual cool days/cold nights	-3 / -3

	Country data	South Asia	Lower middle income
Exposure to Impacts			
Land area below 5m (% of land area)	3.9	1.5	1.7
Population below 5m (% of total)	5.4	4.4	6.5
Population in urban agglomerations > 1 million (%)	..	13	14
Urban pop. growth (avg. annual %, 1990-2010)	0.3	2.7	2.8
Droughts, floods, extreme temps (% pop. avg., 1990-2009)	2.2		
Annual freshwater withdrawals (% of internal resources)	24.5	50.6	18.7
Agricultural land under irrigation (% of total ag. land)	..	..	..
Population living below $1.25 a day (% of total)	7.0	40.3	..
Nationally terrestrial protected areas (% of total land area)	20.8	6.1	9.5
Under-five mortality rate (per 1,000)	17	67	69
Child malnutrition, underweight (% of under age five)	21.6	42.5	31.7
Malaria incidence rate (per 100,000 people)	21	1,127	4,874
Resilience			
Access to improved sanitation (% of total pop.)	91	36	45
Access to improved water source (% of total pop.)	90	87	84
Cereal yield (kg. per hectare)	3,664	2,728	2,754
Access to electricity (% of total population)	76.6	62.1	67.3
Paved roads (% of total roads)	81.0	58.9	29.3
Health workers (per 1,000 people)	1.9	1.7	2.6
Foreign direct investment, net inflows (% of GDP)	1.0	1.3	2.4
Invest. in infrastructure w/private participation ($ millions)	72	73,548	81,789
Disaster risk reduction progress score (1-5 scale; 5 = best)	3.5		
Ease of doing business (ranking 1-183; 1 = best)	89		
Public sector mgmt & institutions avg. (1-6 scale; 6 = best)	3.4		
Primary completion rate, total (% of relevant age group)	97	86	88
Ratio of girls to boys in primary & secondary school (%)	104	92	93
GHG Emissions and Energy Use			
CO_2 emissions per capita (metric tons)	0.6	1.3	1.6
CO_2 emissions per units of GDP (kg/$1,000 of 2005 PPP $)	138.5	504.6	523.9
CO_2 emissions, total (MtCO$_2$)	11.8	1,970	3,744
GHG net emissions/removals by LUCF (1995, MtCO$_2$e)	379.1		
Methane (CH_4) emissions, total (MtCO$_2$e)	10.2	846	1,705
Nitrous oxide (N_2O) emissions, total (MtCO$_2$e)	2.1	268	687
Other GHG emissions, total (MtCO$_2$e)	0.0	9	17
Energy use per capita (kilograms of oil equivalent)	449	532	680
Energy use per units of GDP (kg oil eq./$1,000 of 2005 PPP $)	105.5	193.5	217.9

National-Level Actions

Latest UNFCCC national communication	11/6/2000 (1st)
Annex-I emissions reduction target	n/a
NAMA submission	..
NAPA submission	n/a
Renewable energy target	Yes

Carbon Markets

Hosted Clean Development Mechanism (CDM) projects	7
Issued Certified Emission Reductions (CERs) from CDM (thousands)	238
Hosted Joint Implementation (JI) projects	n/a
Issued Emission Reduction Units (ERUs) from JI (thousands)	n/a

St. Kitts and Nevis

Population (thousands)	52.4	GDP ($ millions)	526.0
Pop. growth (avg. ann. %, 1990–2010)	1.1	GNI per capita (Atlas $)	9,520

Climate

Average daily min/max temperature (1961–90, Celsius)	21 / 28
Projected annual temperature change (2045–65, Celsius)	1.3 to 1.8
Average annual precipitation (1961–90, mm)	2,133
Projected annual precipitation change (2045–65, mm)	-102 to 32
Projected change in annual hot days/warm nights	12 / 23
Projected change in annual cool days/cold nights	-3 / -3

	Country data	Latin America & the Carib.	Upper middle Income
Exposure to Impacts			
Land area below 5m (% of land area)	19.0	1.5	1.8
Population below 5m (% of total)	22.1	3.8	6.5
Population in urban agglomerations > 1 million (%)	..	35	22
Urban pop. growth (avg. annual %, 1990–2010)	0.8	2.0	2.3
Droughts, floods, extreme temps (% pop. avg., 1990–2009)	..		
Annual freshwater withdrawals (% of internal resources)	..	2.0	5.6
Agricultural land under irrigation (% of total ag. land)	0.0	..	..
Population living below $1.25 a day (% of total)	..	8.1	..
Nationally terrestrial protected areas (% of total land area)	3.6	20.8	13.6
Under-five mortality rate (per 1,000)	8	23	20
Under nutrition, underweight (% of under age five)	..	3.8	4.1
Malaria incidence rate (per 100,000 people)	..	206	80
Resilience			
Access to improved sanitation (% of total pop.)	96	79	68
Access to improved water source (% of total pop.)	99	93	92
Cereal yield (kg. per hectare)	..	3,337	3,690
Access to electricity (% of total population)	..	93.4	98.0
Paved roads (% of total roads)	..	28.1	50.5
Health workers (per 1,000 people)	5.8	6.9	4.5
Foreign direct investment, net inflows (% of GDP)	24.3	2.3	2.7
Invest. in infrastructure w/private participation ($ millions)	13	33,064	26,166
Disaster risk reduction progress score (1–5 scale; 5 = best)	3.5		
Ease of doing business (ranking 1–183; 1 = best)	95		
Public sector mgmt & institutions avg. (1–6 scale; 6 = best)	..		
Primary completion rate, total (% of relevant age group)	96	102	98
Ratio of girls to boys in primary & secondary school (%)	104	102	103
GHG Emissions and Energy Use			
CO_2 emissions per capita (metric tons)	4.9	2.8	5.3
CO_2 emissions per units of GDP (kg/$1,000 of 2005 PPP $)	350.5	285.6	659.4
CO_2 emissions, total (MtCO$_2$)	0.2	1,584	12,860
GHG net emissions/removals by LUCF (1994, MtCO$_2$e)	-0.1		
Methane (CH$_4$) emissions, total (MtCO$_2$e)	..	1,009	3,455
Nitrous oxide (N$_2$O) emissions, total (MtCO$_2$e)	..	442	1,144
Other GHG emissions, total (MtCO$_2$e)	..	21	243
Energy use per capita (kilograms of oil equivalent)	1,645	1,245	1,848
Energy use per units of GDP (kg oil eq./$1,000 of 2005 PPP $)	122.1	130.6	227.1

National-Level Actions

Latest UNFCCC national communication	11/30/2001 (1st)
Annex-I emissions reduction target	n/a
NAMA submission	..
NAPA submission	n/a
Renewable energy target	..

Carbon Markets

Hosted Clean Development Mechanism (CDM) projects	..
Issued Certified Emission Reductions (CERs) from CDM (thousands)	..
Hosted Joint Implementation (JI) projects	n/a
Issued Emission Reduction Units (ERUs) from JI (thousands)	n/a

St. Lucia

Population (thousands)	174.0	GDP ($ millions)	932.0
Pop. growth (avg. ann. %, 1990-2010)	1.3	GNI per capita (Atlas $)	4,970

Climate
Average daily min/max temperature (1961-90, Celsius)	22 / 29
Projected annual temperature change (2045-65, Celsius)	1.4 to 1.7
Average annual precipitation (1961-90, mm)	2,301
Projected annual precipitation change (2045-65, mm)	-159 to 14
Projected change in annual hot days/warm nights	14 / 24
Projected change in annual cool days/cold nights	-3 / -3

	Country data	Latin America & the Carib.	Upper middle income
Exposure to Impacts			
Land area below 5m (% of land area)	8.0	1.5	1.8
Population below 5m (% of total)	8.0	3.8	6.5
Population in urban agglomerations > 1 million (%)	..	35	22
Urban pop. growth (avg. annual %, 1990-2010)	1.1	2.0	2.3
Droughts, floods, extreme temps (% pop. avg., 1990-2009)	..		
Annual freshwater withdrawals (% of internal resources)	..	2.0	5.6
Agricultural land under irrigation (% of total ag. land)	..	..	..
Population living below $1.25 a day (% of total)	20.9	8.1	..
Nationally terrestrial protected areas (% of total land area)	14.3	20.8	13.6
Under-five mortality rate (per 1,000)	16	23	20
Child malnutrition, underweight (% of under age five)	..	3.8	4.1
Malaria incidence rate (per 100,000 people)	..	206	80
Resilience			
Access to improved sanitation (% of total pop.)	89	79	68
Access to improved water source (% of total pop.)	98	93	92
Cereal yield (kg. per hectare)	..	3,337	3,690
Access to electricity (% of total population)	..	93.4	98.0
Paved roads (% of total roads)	..	28.1	50.5
Health workers (per 1,000 people)	2.6	6.9	4.5
Foreign direct investment, net inflows (% of GDP)	13.0	2.3	2.7
Invest. in infrastructure w/private participation ($ millions)	11	33,064	26,166
Disaster risk reduction progress score (1-5 scale; 5 = best)	3.3		
Ease of doing business (ranking 1-183; 1 = best)	52		
Public sector mgmt & institutions avg. (1-6 scale; 6 = best)	4.0		
Primary completion rate, total (% of relevant age group)	96	102	98
Ratio of girls to boys in primary & secondary school (%)	99	102	103
GHG Emissions and Energy Use			
CO_2 emissions per capita (metric tons)	2.3	2.8	5.3
CO_2 emissions per units of GDP (kg/$1,000 of 2005 PPP $)	253.7	285.6	659.4
CO_2 emissions, total (MtCO_2)	0.4	1,584	12,860
GHG net emissions/removals by LUCF (1994, MtCO_2e)	-0.3		
Methane (CH_4) emissions, total (MtCO_2e)	..	1,009	3,455
Nitrous oxide (N_2O) emissions, total (MtCO_2e)	..	442	1,144
Other GHG emissions, total (MtCO_2e)	..	21	243
Energy use per capita (kilograms of oil equivalent)	760	1,245	1,848
Energy use per units of GDP (kg oil eq./$1,000 of 2005 PPP $)	82.7	130.6	227.1

National-Level Actions
Latest UNFCCC national communication	11/30/2001 (1st)
Annex-I emissions reduction target	n/a
NAMA submission	..
NAPA submission	n/a
Renewable energy target	..

Carbon Markets
Hosted Clean Development Mechanism (CDM) projects	..
Issued Certified Emission Reductions (CERs) from CDM (thousands)	..
Hosted Joint Implementation (JI) projects	n/a
Issued Emission Reduction Units (ERUs) from JI (thousands)	n/a

St. Martin (French part)

Population (thousands)	30.2	GDP ($ millions)	..
Pop. growth (avg. ann. %, 1990–2010)	0.0	GNI per capita (Atlas $)	..

Climate

Average daily min/max temperature (1961–90, Celsius)	..
Projected annual temperature change (2045–65, Celsius)	..
Average annual precipitation (1961–90, mm)	..
Projected annual precipitation change (2045–65, mm)	..
Projected change in annual hot days/warm nights	..
Projected change in annual cool days/cold nights	..

	Country data	High Income
Exposure to Impacts		
Land area below 5m (% of land area)	..	2.2
Population below 5m (% of total)	..	7.7
Population in urban agglomerations > 1 million (%)	..	..
Urban pop. growth (avg. annual %, 1990–2010)	..	1.0
Droughts, floods, extreme temps (% pop. avg., 1990–2009)	..	
Annual freshwater withdrawals (% of internal resources)	..	10.4
Agricultural land under irrigation (% of total ag. land)	..	..
Population living below $1.25 a day (% of total)	..	..
Nationally terrestrial protected areas (% of total land area)	..	13.4
Under-five mortality rate (per 1,000)	..	6
Child malnutrition, underweight (% of under age five)	..	..
Malaria incidence rate (per 100,000 people)	..	..
Resilience		
Access to improved sanitation (% of total pop.)	..	100
Access to improved water source (% of total pop.)	..	100
Cereal yield (kg. per hectare)	..	5,445
Access to electricity (% of total population)	..	..
Paved roads (% of total roads)	..	87.3
Health workers (per 1,000 people)	..	10.7
Foreign direct investment, net inflows (% of GDP)	..	1.8
Invest. in infrastructure w/private participation ($ millions)	..	..
Disaster risk reduction progress score (1–5 scale; 5 = best)	..	
Ease of doing business (ranking 1–183; 1 = best)	..	
Public sector mgmt & institutions avg. (1–6 scale; 6 = best)	..	
Primary completion rate, total (% of relevant age group)	..	97
Ratio of girls to boys in primary & secondary school (%)	..	100
GHG Emissions and Energy Use		
CO_2 emissions per capita (metric tons)	..	11.9
CO_2 emissions per units of GDP (kg/$1,000 of 2005 PPP $)	..	354.4
CO_2 emissions, total (MtCO$_2$)	..	13,285
GHG net emissions/removals by LUCF (MtCO$_2$e)	..	
Methane (CH$_4$) emissions, total (MtCO$_2$e)	..	1,539
Nitrous oxide (N$_2$O) emissions, total (MtCO$_2$e)	..	813
Other GHG emissions, total (MtCO$_2$e)	..	460
Energy use per capita (kilograms of oil equivalent)	..	4,944
Energy use per units of GDP (kg oil eq./$1,000 of 2005 PPP $)	..	147.0
National-Level Actions		
Latest UNFCCC national communication		n/a
Annex-I emissions reduction target		n/a
NAMA submission		n/a
NAPA submission		n/a
Renewable energy target		..
Carbon Markets		
Hosted Clean Development Mechanism (CDM) projects		n/a
Issued Certified Emission Reductions (CERs) from CDM (thousands)		n/a
Hosted Joint Implementation (JI) projects		n/a
Issued Emission Reduction Units (ERUs) from JI (thousands)		n/a

St. Vincent & the Grenadines

Population (thousands)	109.3	GDP ($ millions)	561.6
Pop. growth (avg. ann. %, 1990-2010)	0.1	GNI per capita (Atlas $)	4,850

Climate

Average daily min/max temperature (1961-90, Celsius)	23 / 30
Projected annual temperature change (2045-65, Celsius)	1.4 to 1.7
Average annual precipitation (1961-90, mm)	1,583
Projected annual precipitation change (2045-65, mm)	-165 to 15
Projected change in annual hot days/warm nights	15 / 25
Projected change in annual cool days/cold nights	-3 / -3

	Country data	Latin America & the Carib.	Upper middle income
Exposure to Impacts			
Land area below 5m (% of land area)	22.0	1.5	1.8
Population below 5m (% of total)	22.0	3.8	6.5
Population in urban agglomerations > 1 million (%)	..	35	22
Urban pop. growth (avg. annual %, 1990-2010)	0.9	2.0	2.3
Droughts, floods, extreme temps (% pop. avg., 1990-2009)	0.0		
Annual freshwater withdrawals (% of internal resources)	..	2.0	5.6
Agricultural land under irrigation (% of total ag. land)	..	..	..
Population living below $1.25 a day (% of total)	..	8.1	..
Nationally terrestrial protected areas (% of total land area)	10.9	20.8	13.6
Under-five mortality rate (per 1,000)	21	23	20
Child malnutrition, underweight (% of under age five)	..	3.8	4.1
Malaria incidence rate (per 100,000 people)	..	206	80
Resilience			
Access to improved sanitation (% of total pop.)	..	79	68
Access to improved water source (% of total pop.)	..	93	92
Cereal yield (kg. per hectare)	3,387	3,337	3,690
Access to electricity (% of total population)	..	93.4	98.0
Paved roads (% of total roads)	70.0	28.1	50.5
Health workers (per 1,000 people)	4.5	6.9	4.5
Foreign direct investment, net inflows (% of GDP)	17.8	2.3	2.7
Invest. in infrastructure w/private participation ($ millions)	35	33,064	26,166
Disaster risk reduction progress score (1-5 scale; 5 = best)	..		
Ease of doing business (ranking 1-183; 1 = best)	75		
Public sector mgmt & institutions avg. (1-6 scale; 6 = best)	3.8		
Primary completion rate, total (% of relevant age group)	109	102	98
Ratio of girls to boys in primary & secondary school (%)	98	102	103
GHG Emissions and Energy Use			
CO$_2$ emissions per capita (metric tons)	1.8	2.8	5.3
CO$_2$ emissions per units of GDP (kg/$1,000 of 2005 PPP $)	215.2	285.6	659.4
CO$_2$ emissions, total (MtCO$_2$)	0.2	1,584	12,860
GHG net emissions/removals by LUCF (1997, MtCO$_2$e)	-0.1		
Methane (CH$_4$) emissions, total (MtCO$_2$e)	..	1,009	3,455
Nitrous oxide (N$_2$O) emissions, total (MtCO$_2$e)	..	442	1,144
Other GHG emissions, total (MtCO$_2$e)	..	21	243
Energy use per capita (kilograms of oil equivalent)	642	1,245	1,848
Energy use per units of GDP (kg oil eq./$1,000 of 2005 PPP $)	75.7	130.6	227.1

National-Level Actions

Latest UNFCCC national communication	11/21/2000 (1st)
Annex-I emissions reduction target	n/a
NAMA submission	..
NAPA submission	n/a
Renewable energy target	..

Carbon Markets

Hosted Clean Development Mechanism (CDM) projects	..
Issued Certified Emission Reductions (CERs) from CDM (thousands)	..
Hosted Joint Implementation (JI) projects	n/a
Issued Emission Reduction Units (ERUs) from JI (thousands)	n/a

Sudan

Population (millions)	43.6	GDP ($ billions)	62.0
Pop. growth (avg. ann. %, 1990–2010)	2.5	GNI per capita (Atlas $)	1,270

Climate

Average daily min/max temperature (1961–90, Celsius)	19 / 34
Projected annual temperature change (2045–65, Celsius)	2.1 to 2.6
Average annual precipitation (1961–90, mm)	417
Projected annual precipitation change (2045–65, mm)	-69 to 44
Projected change in annual hot days/warm nights	5 / 17
Projected change in annual cool days/cold nights	-2 / -2

	Country data	Sub-Saharan Africa	Lower middle income
Exposure to Impacts			
Land area below 5m (% of land area)	0.1	0.4	1.7
Population below 5m (% of total)	0.2	2.0	6.5
Population in urban agglomerations > 1 million (%)	12	14	14
Urban pop. growth (avg. annual %, 1990–2010)	5.1	4.0	2.8
Droughts, floods, extreme temps (% pop. avg., 1990–2009)	2.8		
Annual freshwater withdrawals (% of internal resources)	123.8	3.2	18.7
Agricultural land under irrigation (% of total ag. land)	1.0		..
Population living below $1.25 a day (% of total)	..	50.9	..
Nationally terrestrial protected areas (% of total land area)	4.9	11.7	9.5
Under-five mortality rate (per 1,000)	103	121	69
Child malnutrition, underweight (% of under age five)	31.7	24.6	31.7
Malaria incidence rate (per 100,000 people)	12,805	26,113	4,874
Resilience			
Access to improved sanitation (% of total pop.)	34	31	45
Access to improved water source (% of total pop.)	57	60	84
Cereal yield (kg. per hectare)	587	1,297	2,754
Access to electricity (% of total population)	35.9	32.5	67.3
Paved roads (% of total roads)	36.3	18.3	29.3
Health workers (per 1,000 people)	1.1	1.2	2.6
Foreign direct investment, net inflows (% of GDP)	4.7	3.6	2.4
Invest. in infrastructure w/private participation ($ millions)	478	11,957	81,789
Disaster risk reduction progress score (1–5 scale; 5 = best)	..		
Ease of doing business (ranking 1–183; 1 = best)	135		
Public sector mgmt & institutions avg. (1–6 scale; 6 = best)	2.2		
Primary completion rate, total (% of relevant age group)	57	67	88
Ratio of girls to boys in primary & secondary school (%)	89	89	93
GHG Emissions and Energy Use			
CO$_2$ emissions per capita (metric tons)	0.3	0.8	1.6
CO$_2$ emissions per units of GDP (kg/$1,000 of 2005 PPP $)	173.2	428.6	523.9
CO$_2$ emissions, total (MtCO$_2$)	14.1	685	3,744
GHG net emissions/removals by LUCF (1995, MtCO$_2$e)	17.8		
Methane (CH$_4$) emissions, total (MtCO$_2$e)	67.4	590	1,705
Nitrous oxide (N$_2$O) emissions, total (MtCO$_2$e)	49.5	334	687
Other GHG emissions, total (MtCO$_2$e)	0.0	..	17
Energy use per capita (kilograms of oil equivalent)	372	689	680
Energy use per units of GDP (kg oil eq./$1,000 of 2005 PPP $)	187.5	308.4	217.9

National-Level Actions

Latest UNFCCC national communication	6/7/2003 (1st)
Annex-I emissions reduction target	n/a
NAMA submission	..
NAPA submission	Yes
Renewable energy target	..

Carbon Markets

Hosted Clean Development Mechanism (CDM) projects	0
Issued Certified Emission Reductions (CERs) from CDM (thousands)	0
Hosted Joint Implementation (JI) projects	n/a
Issued Emission Reduction Units (ERUs) from JI (thousands)	n/a

Suriname

Population (thousands)	524.6	GDP ($ billions)	3.3
Pop. growth (avg. ann. %, 1990-2010)	1.3	GNI per capita (Atlas $)	5,920

Climate

Average daily min/max temperature (1961-90, Celsius)	21 / 30
Projected annual temperature change (2045-65, Celsius)	1.9 to 2.9
Average annual precipitation (1961-90, mm)	2,331
Projected annual precipitation change (2045-65, mm)	-138 to 107
Projected change in annual hot days/warm nights	10 / 27
Projected change in annual cool days/cold nights	-2 / -3

	Country data	Latin America & the Carib.	Upper middle income
Exposure to Impacts			
Land area below 5m (% of land area)	3.4	1.5	1.8
Population below 5m (% of total)	68.2	3.8	6.5
Population in urban agglomerations > 1 million (%)	..	35	22
Urban pop. growth (avg. annual %, 1990-2010)	1.8	2.0	2.3
Droughts, floods, extreme temps (% pop. avg., 1990-2009)	0.3		
Annual freshwater withdrawals (% of internal resources)	0.8	2.0	5.6
Agricultural land under irrigation (% of total ag. land)	..	..	..
Population living below $1.25 a day (% of total)	15.5	8.1	..
Nationally terrestrial protected areas (% of total land area)	11.4	20.8	13.6
Under-five mortality rate (per 1,000)	31	23	20
Child malnutrition, underweight (% of under age five)	7.5	3.8	4.1
Malaria incidence rate (per 100,000 people)	681	206	80
Resilience			
Access to improved sanitation (% of total pop.)	84	79	68
Access to improved water source (% of total pop.)	93	93	92
Cereal yield (kg. per hectare)	3,750	3,337	3,690
Access to electricity (% of total population)	..	93.4	98.0
Paved roads (% of total roads)	26.3	28.1	50.5
Health workers (per 1,000 people)	2.1	6.9	4.5
Foreign direct investment, net inflows (% of GDP)	-2.9	2.3	2.7
Invest. in infrastructure w/private participation ($ millions)	60	33,064	26,166
Disaster risk reduction progress score (1-5 scale; 5 = best)	..		
Ease of doing business (ranking 1-183; 1 = best)	158		
Public sector mgmt & institutions avg. (1-6 scale; 6 = best)	..		
Primary completion rate, total (% of relevant age group)	88	102	98
Ratio of girls to boys in primary & secondary school (%)	107	102	103
GHG Emissions and Energy Use			
CO_2 emissions per capita (metric tons)	4.7	2.8	5.3
CO_2 emissions per units of GDP (kg/$1,000 of 2005 PPP $)	697.7	285.6	659.4
CO_2 emissions, total ($MtCO_2$)	2.4	1,584	12,860
GHG net emissions/removals by LUCF (2003, $MtCO_2e$)	1.5		
Methane (CH_4) emissions, total ($MtCO_2e$)	..	1,009	3,455
Nitrous oxide (N_2O) emissions, total ($MtCO_2e$)	..	442	1,144
Other GHG emissions, total ($MtCO_2e$)	..	21	243
Energy use per capita (kilograms of oil equivalent)	1,400	1,245	1,848
Energy use per units of GDP (kg oil eq./$1,000 of 2005 PPP $)	213.8	130.6	227.1

National-Level Actions

Latest UNFCCC national communication	3/27/2006 (1st)
Annex-I emissions reduction target	n/a
NAMA submission	..
NAPA submission	n/a
Renewable energy target	..

Carbon Markets

Hosted Clean Development Mechanism (CDM) projects	..
Issued Certified Emission Reductions (CERs) from CDM (thousands)	..
Hosted Joint Implementation (JI) projects	n/a
Issued Emission Reduction Units (ERUs) from JI (thousands)	n/a

Swaziland

Population (millions)	1.2	GDP ($ billions)	3.6
Pop. growth (avg. ann. %, 1990–2010)	1.6	GNI per capita (Atlas $)	2,630

Climate

Average daily min/max temperature (1961-90, Celsius)	16 / 27
Projected annual temperature change (2045-65, Celsius)	2.0 to 2.4
Average annual precipitation (1961-90, mm)	788
Projected annual precipitation change (2045-65, mm)	-82 to 34
Projected change in annual hot days/warm nights	4 / 11
Projected change in annual cool days/cold nights	-2 / -2

	Country data	Sub-Saharan Africa	Lower middle income
Exposure to Impacts			
Land area below 5m (% of land area)	0.0	0.4	1.7
Population below 5m (% of total)	0.0	2.0	6.5
Population in urban agglomerations > 1 million (%)	..	14	14
Urban pop. growth (avg. annual %, 1990-2010)	2.1	4.0	2.8
Droughts, floods, extreme temps (% pop. avg., 1990-2009)	9.2		
Annual freshwater withdrawals (% of internal resources)	39.5	3.2	18.7
Agricultural land under irrigation (% of total ag. land)	..		..
Population living below $1.25 a day (% of total)	62.9	50.9	..
Nationally terrestrial protected areas (% of total land area)	3.0	11.7	9.5
Under-five mortality rate (per 1,000)	78	121	69
Child malnutrition, underweight (% of under age five)	6.1	24.6	31.7
Malaria incidence rate (per 100,000 people)	57	26,113	4,874
Resilience			
Access to improved sanitation (% of total pop.)	55	31	45
Access to improved water source (% of total pop.)	69	60	84
Cereal yield (kg. per hectare)	1,148	1,297	2,754
Access to electricity (% of total population)	..	32.5	67.3
Paved roads (% of total roads)	30.0	18.3	29.3
Health workers (per 1,000 people)	6.5	1.2	2.6
Foreign direct investment, net inflows (% of GDP)	2.5	3.6	2.4
Invest. in infrastructure w/private participation ($ millions)	15	11,957	81,789
Disaster risk reduction progress score (1-5 scale; 5 = best)	..		
Ease of doing business (ranking 1-183; 1 = best)	124		
Public sector mgmt & institutions avg. (1-6 scale; 6 = best)	..		
Primary completion rate, total (% of relevant age group)	72	67	88
Ratio of girls to boys in primary & secondary school (%)	92	89	93
GHG Emissions and Energy Use			
CO_2 emissions per capita (metric tons)	0.9	0.8	1.6
CO_2 emissions per units of GDP (kg/$1,000 of 2005 PPP $)	205.6	428.6	523.9
CO_2 emissions, total (MtCO_2)	1.1	685	3,744
GHG net emissions/removals by LUCF (1994, MtCO_2e)	-3.3		
Methane (CH_4) emissions, total (MtCO_2e)	..	590	1,705
Nitrous oxide (N_2O) emissions, total (MtCO_2e)	..	334	687
Other GHG emissions, total (MtCO_2e)	..	..	17
Energy use per capita (kilograms of oil equivalent)	373	689	680
Energy use per units of GDP (kg oil eq./$1,000 of 2005 PPP $)	81.5	308.4	217.9

National-Level Actions

Latest UNFCCC national communication	5/21/2002 (1st)
Annex-I emissions reduction target	n/a
NAMA submission	..
NAPA submission	n/a
Renewable energy target	..

Carbon Markets

Hosted Clean Development Mechanism (CDM) projects	0
Issued Certified Emission Reductions (CERs) from CDM (thousands)	0
Hosted Joint Implementation (JI) projects	n/a
Issued Emission Reduction Units (ERUs) from JI (thousands)	n/a

Sweden

Population (millions)	9.4	GDP ($ billions)	458.0
Pop. growth (avg. ann. %, 1990–2010)	0.5	GNI per capita (Atlas $)	50,000

Climate

Average daily min/max temperature (1961–90, Celsius)	-2 / 6
Projected annual temperature change (2045-65, Celsius)	2.1 to 3.1
Average annual precipitation (1961–90, mm)	624
Projected annual precipitation change (2045-65, mm)	35 to 107
Projected change in annual hot days/warm nights	2 / 4
Projected change in annual cool days/cold nights	-2 / -2

	Country data	High income
Exposure to Impacts		
Land area below 5m (% of land area)	1.5	2.2
Population below 5m (% of total)	6.3	7.7
Population in urban agglomerations > 1 million (%)	14	..
Urban pop. growth (avg. annual %, 1990–2010)	0.6	1.0
Droughts, floods, extreme temps (% pop. avg., 1990–2009)	0.0	
Annual freshwater withdrawals (% of internal resources)	1.6	10.4
Agricultural land under irrigation (% of total ag. land)	..	..
Population living below $1.25 a day (% of total)	..	..
Nationally terrestrial protected areas (% of total land area)	11.3	13.4
Under-five mortality rate (per 1,000)	3	6
Child malnutrition, underweight (% of under age five)	..	..
Malaria incidence rate (per 100,000 people)	..	..
Resilience		
Access to improved sanitation (% of total pop.)	100	100
Access to improved water source (% of total pop.)	100	100
Cereal yield (kg. per hectare)	5,086	5,445
Access to electricity (% of total population)	..	
Paved roads (% of total roads)	23.6	87.3
Health workers (per 1,000 people)	15.2	10.7
Foreign direct investment, net inflows (% of GDP)	1.2	1.8
Invest. in infrastructure w/private participation ($ millions)	..	..
Disaster risk reduction progress score (1-5 scale; 5 = best)	3.8	
Ease of doing business (ranking 1-183; 1 = best)	14	
Public sector mgmt & institutions avg. (1-6 scale; 6 = best)	..	
Primary completion rate, total (% of relevant age group)	95	97
Ratio of girls to boys in primary & secondary school (%)	99	100
GHG Emissions and Energy Use		
CO_2 emissions per capita (metric tons)	5.3	11.9
CO_2 emissions per units of GDP (kg/$1,000 of 2005 PPP $)	155.1	354.4
CO_2 emissions, total (MtCO$_2$)	49.0	13,285
GHG net emissions/removals by LUCF (2009, MtCO$_2$e)	-41.6	
Methane (CH_4) emissions, total (MtCO$_2$e)	11.3	1,539
Nitrous oxide (N_2O) emissions, total (MtCO$_2$e)	5.9	813
Other GHG emissions, total (MtCO$_2$e)	2.1	460
Energy use per capita (kilograms of oil equivalent)	5,414	4,944
Energy use per units of GDP (kg oil eq./$1,000 of 2005 PPP $)	160.7	147.0

National-Level Actions

Latest UNFCCC national communication	2/4/2010 (5th)
Annex-I emissions reduction target (base year: 1990)	20% / 30% (EU)
NAMA submission	n/a
NAPA submission	n/a
Renewable energy target	Yes

Carbon Markets

Hosted Clean Development Mechanism (CDM) projects	n/a
Issued Certified Emission Reductions (CERs) from CDM (thousands)	n/a
Hosted Joint Implementation (JI) projects	0
Issued Emission Reduction Units (ERUs) from JI (thousands)	0

Switzerland

Population (millions)	7.8	GDP ($ billions)	523.8
Pop. growth (avg. ann. %, 1990–2010)	0.8	GNI per capita (Atlas $)	70,030

Climate

Average daily min/max temperature (1961–90, Celsius)	2 / 9
Projected annual temperature change (2045–65, Celsius)	1.7 to 2.8
Average annual precipitation (1961–90, mm)	1,537
Projected annual precipitation change (2045–65, mm)	-89 to 11
Projected change in annual hot days/warm nights	3 / 6
Projected change in annual cool days/cold nights	-1 / -1

	Country data	High income
Exposure to Impacts		
Land area below 5m (% of land area)	0.0	2.2
Population below 5m (% of total)	0.0	7.7
Population in urban agglomerations > 1 million (%)	15	..
Urban pop. growth (avg. annual %, 1990–2010)	0.8	1.0
Droughts, floods, extreme temps (% pop. avg., 1990–2009)	0.0	
Annual freshwater withdrawals (% of internal resources)	6.5	10.4
Agricultural land under irrigation (% of total ag. land)	..	
Population living below $1.25 a day (% of total)	..	..
Nationally terrestrial protected areas (% of total land area)	22.8	13.4
Under-five mortality rate (per 1,000)	5	6
Child malnutrition, underweight (% of under age five)	..	
Malaria incidence rate (per 100,000 people)	..	..
Resilience		
Access to improved sanitation (% of total pop.)	100	100
Access to improved water source (% of total pop.)	100	100
Cereal yield (kg. per hectare)	6,579	5,445
Access to electricity (% of total population)	..	
Paved roads (% of total roads)	100.0	87.3
Health workers (per 1,000 people)	4.1	10.7
Foreign direct investment, net inflows (% of GDP)	-1.2	1.8
Invest. in infrastructure w/private participation ($ millions)	..	
Disaster risk reduction progress score (1–5 scale; 5 = best)	4.8	
Ease of doing business (ranking 1–183; 1 = best)	26	
Public sector mgmt & institutions avg. (1–6 scale; 6 = best)	..	
Primary completion rate, total (% of relevant age group)	96	97
Ratio of girls to boys in primary & secondary school (%)	98	100
GHG Emissions and Energy Use		
CO_2 emissions per capita (metric tons)	5.3	11.9
CO_2 emissions per units of GDP (kg/$1,000 of 2005 PPP $)	138.7	354.4
CO_2 emissions, total (MtCO$_2$)	40.4	13,285
GHG net emissions/removals by LUCF (2009, MtCO$_2$e)	0.1	
Methane (CH_4) emissions, total (MtCO$_2$e)	4.7	1,539
Nitrous oxide (N_2O) emissions, total (MtCO$_2$e)	2.4	813
Other GHG emissions, total (MtCO$_2$e)	2.1	460
Energy use per capita (kilograms of oil equivalent)	3,362	4,944
Energy use per units of GDP (kg oil eq./$1,000 of 2005 PPP $)	89.8	147.0

National-Level Actions

Latest UNFCCC national communication	12/14/2009 (5th)
Annex-I emissions reduction target (base year: 1990)	20% / 30%
NAMA submission	n/a
NAPA submission	n/a
Renewable energy target	Yes

Carbon Markets

Hosted Clean Development Mechanism (CDM) projects	n/a
Issued Certified Emission Reductions (CERs) from CDM (thousands)	n/a
Hosted Joint Implementation (JI) projects	..
Issued Emission Reduction Units (ERUs) from JI (thousands)	..

Syrian Arab Republic

Population (millions)	20.4	GDP ($ billions)	59.1
Pop. growth (avg. ann. %, 1990–2010)	2.5	GNI per capita (Atlas $)	2,790

Climate

Average daily min/max temperature (1961–90, Celsius)	11 / 25
Projected annual temperature change (2045–65, Celsius)	2.2 to 3.1
Average annual precipitation (1961–90, mm)	318
Projected annual precipitation change (2045–65, mm)	-57 to -13
Projected change in annual hot days/warm nights	3 / 7
Projected change in annual cool days/cold nights	-2 / -1

	Country data	Middle East & N. Africa	Lower middle income
Exposure to Impacts			
Land area below 5m (% of land area)	0.1	1.4	1.7
Population below 5m (% of total)	0.3	9.7	6.5
Population in urban agglomerations > 1 million (%)	34	20	14
Urban pop. growth (avg. annual %, 1990–2010)	3.1	2.5	2.8
Droughts, floods, extreme temps (% pop. avg., 1990–2009)	0.5		
Annual freshwater withdrawals (% of internal resources)	235.0	121.9	18.7
Agricultural land under irrigation (% of total ag. land)	8.9	..	..
Population living below $1.25 a day (% of total)	<2	3.6	..
Nationally terrestrial protected areas (% of total land area)	0.6	4.0	9.5
Under-five mortality rate (per 1,000)	16	34	69
Child malnutrition, underweight (% of under age five)	10.0	6.8	31.7
Malaria incidence rate (per 100,000 people)	..	..	4,874
Resilience			
Access to improved sanitation (% of total pop.)	96	84	45
Access to improved water source (% of total pop.)	89	87	84
Cereal yield (kg. per hectare)	1,708	2,512	2,754
Access to electricity (% of total population)	92.7	92.9	67.3
Paved roads (% of total roads)	91.0	74.3	29.3
Health workers (per 1,000 people)	3.4	3.6	2.6
Foreign direct investment, net inflows (% of GDP)	2.3	2.9	2.4
Invest. in infrastructure w/private participation ($ millions)	65	5,854	81,789
Disaster risk reduction progress score (1–5 scale; 5 = best)	3.5		
Ease of doing business (ranking 1–183; 1 = best)	134		
Public sector mgmt & institutions avg. (1–6 scale; 6 = best)	..		
Primary completion rate, total (% of relevant age group)	112	88	88
Ratio of girls to boys in primary & secondary school (%)	97	93	93
GHG Emissions and Energy Use			
CO_2 emissions per capita (metric tons)	3.6	3.8	1.6
CO_2 emissions per units of GDP (kg/$1,000 of 2005 PPP $)	808.0	604.6	523.9
CO_2 emissions, total (MtCO_2)	71.6	1,230	3,744
GHG net emissions/removals by LUCF (MtCO_2e)	..		
Methane (CH_4) emissions, total (MtCO_2e)	12.5	287	1,705
Nitrous oxide (N_2O) emissions, total (MtCO_2e)	5.5	74	687
Other GHG emissions, total (MtCO_2e)	0.0	7	17
Energy use per capita (kilograms of oil equivalent)	1,123	1,399	680
Energy use per units of GDP (kg oil eq./$1,000 of 2005 PPP $)	239.5	213.9	217.9

National-Level Actions

Latest UNFCCC national communication	12/29/2010 (1st)
Annex-I emissions reduction target	n/a
NAMA submission	..
NAPA submission	n/a
Renewable energy target	Yes

Carbon Markets

Hosted Clean Development Mechanism (CDM) projects	3
Issued Certified Emission Reductions (CERs) from CDM (thousands)	0
Hosted Joint Implementation (JI) projects	n/a
Issued Emission Reduction Units (ERUs) from JI (thousands)	n/a

Tajikistan

Population (millions)	6.9	GDP ($ billions)	5.6
Pop. growth (avg. ann. %, 1990–2010)	1.3	GNI per capita (Atlas $)	800

Climate
Average daily min/max temperature (1961–90, Celsius)	-4 / 8
Projected annual temperature change (2045–65, Celsius)	2.3 to 3.4
Average annual precipitation (1961–90, mm)	491
Projected annual precipitation change (2045–65, mm)	-46 to 27
Projected change in annual hot days/warm nights	3 / 7
Projected change in annual cool days/cold nights	-1 / -1

	Country data	Europe & Central Asia	Low income
Exposure to Impacts			
Land area below 5m (% of land area)	0.0	2.5	0.7
Population below 5m (% of total)	0.0	3.0	5.1
Population in urban agglomerations > 1 million (%)	..	18	11
Urban pop. growth (avg. annual %, 1990–2010)	0.4	0.3	3.7
Droughts, floods, extreme temps (% pop. avg., 1990–2009)	5.4		
Annual freshwater withdrawals (% of internal resources)	18.0	6.5	3.7
Agricultural land under irrigation (% of total ag. land)	14.8	..	..
Population living below $1.25 a day (% of total)	21.5	3.7	..
Nationally terrestrial protected areas (% of total land area)	4.1	7.5	10.6
Under-five mortality rate (per 1,000)	63	23	108
Child malnutrition, underweight (% of under age five)	14.9	..	28.3
Malaria incidence rate (per 100,000 people)	9	..	16,659
Resilience			
Access to improved sanitation (% of total pop.)	94	89	35
Access to improved water source (% of total pop.)	70	95	63
Cereal yield (kg. per hectare)	2,731	2,475	2,047
Access to electricity (% of total population)	..	..	23.0
Paved roads (% of total roads)	..	85.8	14.1
Health workers (per 1,000 people)	7.0	9.9	0.7
Foreign direct investment, net inflows (% of GDP)	0.3	2.8	3.2
Invest. in infrastructure w/private participation ($ millions)	56	22,652	4,471
Disaster risk reduction progress score (1–5 scale; 5 = best)	..		
Ease of doing business (ranking 1–183; 1 = best)	147		
Public sector mgmt & institutions avg. (1–6 scale; 6 = best)	2.8		
Primary completion rate, total (% of relevant age group)	98	95	65
Ratio of girls to boys in primary & secondary school (%)	91	97	91
GHG Emissions and Energy Use			
CO_2 emissions per capita (metric tons)	0.5	7.7	0.3
CO_2 emissions per units of GDP (kg/$1,000 of 2005 PPP $)	264.0	708.0	270.2
CO_2 emissions, total (MtCO$_2$)	3.1	3,110	219
GHG net emissions/removals by LUCF (2003, MtCO$_2$e)	-1.9		
Methane (CH_4) emissions, total (MtCO$_2$e)	3.9	937	436
Nitrous oxide (N_2O) emissions, total (MtCO$_2$e)	1.4	214	209
Other GHG emissions, total (MtCO$_2$e)	0.4	76	..
Energy use per capita (kilograms of oil equivalent)	342	2,833	365
Energy use per units of GDP (kg oil eq./$1,000 of 2005 PPP $)	180.3	276.8	303.9

National-Level Actions
Latest UNFCCC national communication	12/31/2008 (2nd)
Annex-I emissions reduction target	n/a
NAMA submission	
NAPA submission	Yes
Renewable energy target	n/a
	..

Carbon Markets
Hosted Clean Development Mechanism (CDM) projects	0
Issued Certified Emission Reductions (CERs) from CDM (thousands)	0
Hosted Joint Implementation (JI) projects	n/a
Issued Emission Reduction Units (ERUs) from JI (thousands)	n/a

Tanzania

Population (millions)	44.8	GDP ($ billions)	23.1
Pop. growth (avg. ann. %, 1990-2010)	2.8	GNI per capita (Atlas $)	530

Climate

Average daily min/max temperature (1961-90, Celsius)	17 / 28
Projected annual temperature change (2045-65, Celsius)	1.9 to 2.2
Average annual precipitation (1961-90, mm)	1,071
Projected annual precipitation change (2045-65, mm)	-9 to 167
Projected change in annual hot days/warm nights	6 / 22
Projected change in annual cool days/cold nights	-2 / -3

	Country data	Sub-Saharan Africa	Low income
Exposure to Impacts			
Land area below 5m (% of land area)	0.2	0.4	0.7
Population below 5m (% of total)	1.3	2.0	5.1
Population in urban agglomerations > 1 million (%)	7	14	11
Urban pop. growth (avg. annual %, 1990-2010)	4.5	4.0	3.7
Droughts, floods, extreme temps (% pop. avg., 1990-2009)	1.5		
Annual freshwater withdrawals (% of internal resources)	6.2	3.2	3.7
Agricultural land under irrigation (% of total ag. land)	..	..	..
Population living below $1.25 a day (% of total)	67.9	50.9	..
Nationally terrestrial protected areas (% of total land area)	27.7	11.7	10.6
Under-five mortality rate (per 1,000)	76	121	108
Child malnutrition, underweight (% of under age five)	16.7	24.6	28.3
Malaria incidence rate (per 100,000 people)	24,088	26,113	16,659
Resilience			
Access to improved sanitation (% of total pop.)	24	31	35
Access to improved water source (% of total pop.)	54	60	63
Cereal yield (kg. per hectare)	1,110	1,297	2,047
Access to electricity (% of total population)	13.9	32.5	23.0
Paved roads (% of total roads)	7.4	18.3	14.1
Health workers (per 1,000 people)	0.2	1.2	0.7
Foreign direct investment, net inflows (% of GDP)	1.9	3.6	3.2
Invest. in infrastructure w/private participation ($ millions)	625	11,957	4,471
Disaster risk reduction progress score (1-5 scale; 5 = best)	3.5		
Ease of doing business (ranking 1-183; 1 = best)	127		
Public sector mgmt & institutions avg. (1-6 scale; 6 = best)	3.3		
Primary completion rate, total (% of relevant age group)	102	67	65
Ratio of girls to boys in primary & secondary school (%)	96	89	91
GHG Emissions and Energy Use			
CO_2 emissions per capita (metric tons)	0.2	0.8	0.3
CO_2 emissions per units of GDP (kg/$1,000 of 2005 PPP $)	130.4	428.6	270.2
CO_2 emissions, total (MtCO_2)	6.5	685	219
GHG net emissions/removals by LUCF (1994, $MtCO_2e$)	913.6		
Methane (CH_4) emissions, total ($MtCO_2e$)	32.0	590	436
Nitrous oxide (N_2O) emissions, total ($MtCO_2e$)	21.6	334	209
Other GHG emissions, total ($MtCO_2e$)	0.0	..	..
Energy use per capita (kilograms of oil equivalent)	451	689	365
Energy use per units of GDP (kg oil eq./$1,000 of 2005 PPP $)	373.1	308.4	303.9

National-Level Actions

Latest UNFCCC national communication	7/4/2003 (1st)
Annex-I emissions reduction target	n/a
NAMA submission	..
NAPA submission	Yes
Renewable energy target	..

Carbon Markets

Hosted Clean Development Mechanism (CDM) projects	1
Issued Certified Emission Reductions (CERs) from CDM (thousands)	56
Hosted Joint Implementation (JI) projects	n/a
Issued Emission Reduction Units (ERUs) from JI (thousands)	n/a

Thailand

Population (millions)	69.1	GDP ($ billions)	318.8
Pop. growth (avg. ann. %, 1990–2010)	1.0	GNI per capita (Atlas $)	4,150

Climate

Average daily min/max temperature (1961–90, Celsius)	21 / 31
Projected annual temperature change (2045–65, Celsius)	1.7 to 2.1
Average annual precipitation (1961–90, mm)	1,622
Projected annual precipitation change (2045–65, mm)	-109 to 76
Projected change in annual hot days/warm nights	4 / 17
Projected change in annual cool days/cold nights	-2 / -2

	Country data	East Asia & Pacific	Upper middle income
Exposure to Impacts			
Land area below 5m (% of land area)	4.2	2.5	1.8
Population below 5m (% of total)	13.8	10.3	6.5
Population in urban agglomerations > 1 million (%)	10	..	22
Urban pop. growth (avg. annual %, 1990–2010)	1.7	3.3	2.3
Droughts, floods, extreme temps (% pop. avg., 1990–2009)	3.8		
Annual freshwater withdrawals (% of internal resources)	25.5	10.8	5.6
Agricultural land under irrigation (% of total ag. land)	..	..	..
Population living below $1.25 a day (% of total)	<2	16.8	..
Nationally terrestrial protected areas (% of total land area)	19.6	14.9	13.6
Under-five mortality rate (per 1,000)	13	24	20
Child malnutrition, underweight (% of under age five)	7.0	9.0	4.1
Malaria incidence rate (per 100,000 people)	322	525	80
Resilience			
Access to improved sanitation (% of total pop.)	96	59	68
Access to improved water source (% of total pop.)	98	88	92
Cereal yield (kg. per hectare)	2,951	4,860	3,690
Access to electricity (% of total population)	99.3	90.8	98.0
Paved roads (% of total roads)	98.5	15.9	50.5
Health workers (per 1,000 people)	1.8	2.8	4.5
Foreign direct investment, net inflows (% of GDP)	2.0	3.0	2.7
Invest. in infrastructure w/private participation ($ millions)	4,720	14,638	26,166
Disaster risk reduction progress score (1-5 scale; 5 = best)	3.8		
Ease of doing business (ranking 1-183; 1 = best)	17		
Public sector mgmt & institutions avg. (1-6 scale; 6 = best)	..		
Primary completion rate, total (% of relevant age group)	..	97	98
Ratio of girls to boys in primary & secondary school (%)	103	103	103
GHG Emissions and Energy Use			
CO_2 emissions per capita (metric tons)	4.2	4.3	5.3
CO_2 emissions per units of GDP (kg/$1,000 of 2005 PPP $)	567.3	827.1	659.4
CO_2 emissions, total (MtCO$_2$)	285.7	8,259	12,860
GHG net emissions/removals by LUCF (2000, MtCO$_2$e)	-7.9		
Methane (CH_4) emissions, total (MtCO$_2$e)	83.3	1,928	3,455
Nitrous oxide (N_2O) emissions, total (MtCO$_2$e)	22.3	707	1,144
Other GHG emissions, total (MtCO$_2$e)	1.1	..	243
Energy use per capita (kilograms of oil equivalent)	1,504	1,436	1,848
Energy use per units of GDP (kg oil eq./$1,000 of 2005 PPP $)	210.0	259.5	227.1

National-Level Actions

Latest UNFCCC national communication	3/24/2011 (2nd)
Annex-I emissions reduction target	n/a
NAMA submission	..
NAPA submission	n/a
Renewable energy target	Yes

Carbon Markets

Hosted Clean Development Mechanism (CDM) projects	55
Issued Certified Emission Reductions (CERs) from CDM (thousands)	902
Hosted Joint Implementation (JI) projects	n/a
Issued Emission Reduction Units (ERUs) from JI (thousands)	n/a

Timor-Leste

Population (millions)	1.1	GDP ($ millions)	701.0
Pop. growth (avg. ann. %, 1990–2010)	2.1	GNI per capita (Atlas $)	2,220

Climate

Average daily min/max temperature (1961–90, Celsius)	..
Projected annual temperature change (2045–65, Celsius)	1.3 to 1.7
Average annual precipitation (1961–90, mm)	..
Projected annual precipitation change (2045–65, mm)	-123 to 206
Projected change in annual hot days/warm nights	16 / 26
Projected change in annual cool days/cold nights	-3 / -3

	Country data	East Asia & Pacific	Lower middle income
Exposure to Impacts			
Land area below 5m (% of land area)	2.9	2.5	1.7
Population below 5m (% of total)	4.4	10.3	6.5
Population in urban agglomerations > 1 million (%)	..	..	14
Urban pop. growth (avg. annual %, 1990–2010)	3.6	3.3	2.8
Droughts, floods, extreme temps (% pop. avg., 1990–2009)	0.0		
Annual freshwater withdrawals (% of internal resources)	..	10.8	18.7
Agricultural land under irrigation (% of total ag. land)	..	..	..
Population living below $1.25 a day (% of total)	37.4	16.8	..
Nationally terrestrial protected areas (% of total land area)	6.0	14.9	9.5
Under-five mortality rate (per 1,000)	55	24	69
Child malnutrition, underweight (% of under age five)	41.5	9.0	31.7
Malaria incidence rate (per 100,000 people)	46,380	525	4,874
Resilience			
Access to improved sanitation (% of total pop.)	50	59	45
Access to improved water source (% of total pop.)	69	88	84
Cereal yield (kg. per hectare)	2,316	4,860	2,754
Access to electricity (% of total population)	22.0	90.8	67.3
Paved roads (% of total roads)	..	15.9	29.3
Health workers (per 1,000 people)	2.3	2.8	2.6
Foreign direct investment, net inflows (% of GDP)	39.9	3.0	2.4
Invest. in infrastructure w/private participation ($ millions)	..	14,638	81,789
Disaster risk reduction progress score (1–5 scale; 5 = best)	..		
Ease of doing business (ranking 1–183; 1 = best)	168		
Public sector mgmt & institutions avg. (1–6 scale; 6 = best)	2.7		
Primary completion rate, total (% of relevant age group)	80	97	88
Ratio of girls to boys in primary & secondary school (%)	95	103	93
GHG Emissions and Energy Use			
CO$_2$ emissions per capita (metric tons)	0.2	4.3	1.6
CO$_2$ emissions per units of GDP (kg/$1,000 of 2005 PPP $)	234.5	827.1	523.9
CO$_2$ emissions, total (MtCO$_2$)	0.2	8,259	3,744
GHG net emissions/removals by LUCF (MtCO$_2$e)	..		
Methane (CH$_4$) emissions, total (MtCO$_2$e)	..	1,928	1,705
Nitrous oxide (N$_2$O) emissions, total (MtCO$_2$e)	..	707	687
Other GHG emissions, total (MtCO$_2$e)	..	..	17
Energy use per capita (kilograms of oil equivalent)	58	1,436	680
Energy use per units of GDP (kg oil eq./$1,000 of 2005 PPP $)	84.9	259.5	217.9

National-Level Actions

Latest UNFCCC national communication	12/20/2001 (1st)
Annex-I emissions reduction target	n/a
NAMA submission	..
NAPA submission	Yes
Renewable energy target	..

Carbon Markets

Hosted Clean Development Mechanism (CDM) projects	..
Issued Certified Emission Reductions (CERs) from CDM (thousands)	..
Hosted Joint Implementation (JI) projects	n/a
Issued Emission Reduction Units (ERUs) from JI (thousands)	n/a

Togo

Population (millions)	6.0	GDP ($ billions)	3.2
Pop. growth (avg. ann. %, 1990–2010)	2.5	GNI per capita (Atlas $)	490

Climate
Average daily min/max temperature (1961–90, Celsius)	22 / 33
Projected annual temperature change (2045–65, Celsius)	1.9 to 2.5
Average annual precipitation (1961–90, mm)	1,168
Projected annual precipitation change (2045–65, mm)	-175 to 100
Projected change in annual hot days/warm nights	6 / 21
Projected change in annual cool days/cold nights	-2 / -2

	Country data	Sub-Saharan Africa	Low income
Exposure to Impacts			
Land area below 5m (% of land area)	0.6	0.4	0.7
Population below 5m (% of total)	6.1	2.0	5.1
Population in urban agglomerations > 1 million (%)	28	14	11
Urban pop. growth (avg. annual %, 1990–2010)	4.3	4.0	3.7
Droughts, floods, extreme temps (% pop. avg., 1990–2009)	0.5		
Annual freshwater withdrawals (% of internal resources)	1.5	3.2	3.7
Agricultural land under irrigation (% of total ag. land)	..	..	..
Population living below $1.25 a day (% of total)	38.7	50.9	..
Nationally terrestrial protected areas (% of total land area)	11.3	11.7	10.6
Under-five mortality rate (per 1,000)	103	121	108
Child malnutrition, underweight (% of under age five)	22.3	24.6	28.3
Malaria incidence rate (per 100,000 people)	30,388	26,113	16,659
Resilience			
Access to improved sanitation (% of total pop.)	12	31	35
Access to improved water source (% of total pop.)	60	60	63
Cereal yield (kg. per hectare)	1,398	1,297	2,047
Access to electricity (% of total population)	20.0	32.5	23.0
Paved roads (% of total roads)	21.0	18.3	14.1
Health workers (per 1,000 people)	0.3	1.2	0.7
Foreign direct investment, net inflows (% of GDP)	1.3	3.6	3.2
Invest. in infrastructure w/private participation ($ millions)	23	11,957	4,471
Disaster risk reduction progress score (1–5 scale; 5 = best)	..		
Ease of doing business (ranking 1–183; 1 = best)	162		
Public sector mgmt & institutions avg. (1–6 scale; 6 = best)	2.6		
Primary completion rate, total (% of relevant age group)	61	67	65
Ratio of girls to boys in primary & secondary school (%)	75	89	91
GHG Emissions and Energy Use			
CO_2 emissions per capita (metric tons)	0.2	0.8	0.3
CO_2 emissions per units of GDP (kg/$1,000 of 2005 PPP $)	280.6	428.6	270.2
CO_2 emissions, total (MtCO_2)	1.4	685	219
GHG net emissions/removals by LUCF (1998, MtCO_2e)	28.1		
Methane (CH_4) emissions, total (MtCO_2e)	2.9	590	436
Nitrous oxide (N_2O) emissions, total (MtCO_2e)	1.7	334	209
Other GHG emissions, total (MtCO_2e)	0.0	..	..
Energy use per capita (kilograms of oil equivalent)	445	689	365
Energy use per units of GDP (kg oil eq./$1,000 of 2005 PPP $)	503.1	308.4	303.9

National-Level Actions
Latest UNFCCC national communication	7/21/2005 (1st)
Annex-I emissions reduction target	n/a
NAMA submission	Yes
NAPA submission	Yes
Renewable energy target	..

Carbon Markets
Hosted Clean Development Mechanism (CDM) projects	0
Issued Certified Emission Reductions (CERs) from CDM (thousands)	0
Hosted Joint Implementation (JI) projects	n/a
Issued Emission Reduction Units (ERUs) from JI (thousands)	n/a

Tonga

Population (thousands)	104.1	GDP ($ millions)	357.5
Pop. growth (avg. ann. %, 1990–2010)	0.4	GNI per capita (Atlas $)	3,390

Climate

Average daily min/max temperature (1961–90, Celsius)	23 / 28
Projected annual temperature change (2045–65, Celsius)	1.3 to 1.7
Average annual precipitation (1961–90, mm)	1,966
Projected annual precipitation change (2045–65, mm)	-13 to 182
Projected change in annual hot days/warm nights	8 / 14
Projected change in annual cool days/cold nights	-3 / -3

	Country data	East Asia & Pacific	Lower middle income
Exposure to Impacts			
Land area below 5m (% of land area)	40.5	2.5	1.7
Population below 5m (% of total)	31.3	10.3	6.5
Population in urban agglomerations > 1 million (%)	..	..	14
Urban pop. growth (avg. annual %, 1990–2010)	1.0	3.3	2.8
Droughts, floods, extreme temps (% pop. avg., 1990–2009)	..		
Annual freshwater withdrawals (% of internal resources)	..	10.8	18.7
Agricultural land under irrigation (% of total ag. land)	..		
Population living below $1.25 a day (% of total)	..	16.8	..
Nationally terrestrial protected areas (% of total land area)	14.5	14.9	9.5
Under-five mortality rate (per 1,000)	16	24	69
Child malnutrition, underweight (% of under age five)	..	9.0	31.7
Malaria incidence rate (per 100,000 people)	..	525	4,874
Resilience			
Access to improved sanitation (% of total pop.)	96	59	45
Access to improved water source (% of total pop.)	100	88	84
Cereal yield (kg. per hectare)	..	4,860	2,754
Access to electricity (% of total population)	..	90.8	67.3
Paved roads (% of total roads)	27.0	15.9	29.3
Health workers (per 1,000 people)	2.9	2.8	2.6
Foreign direct investment, net inflows (% of GDP)	4.5	3.0	2.4
Invest. in infrastructure w/private participation ($ millions)	10	14,638	81,789
Disaster risk reduction progress score (1–5 scale; 5 = best)	..		
Ease of doing business (ranking 1–183; 1 = best)	58		
Public sector mgmt & institutions avg. (1–6 scale; 6 = best)	3.8		
Primary completion rate, total (% of relevant age group)	105	97	88
Ratio of girls to boys in primary & secondary school (%)	100	103	93
GHG Emissions and Energy Use			
CO_2 emissions per capita (metric tons)	1.7	4.3	1.6
CO_2 emissions per units of GDP (kg/$1,000 of 2005 PPP $)	413.9	827.1	523.9
CO_2 emissions, total (MtCO$_2$)	0.2	8,259	3,744
GHG net emissions/removals by LUCF (1994, MtCO$_2$e)	-0.3		
Methane (CH_4) emissions, total (MtCO$_2$e)	..	1,928	1,705
Nitrous oxide (N_2O) emissions, total (MtCO$_2$e)	..	707	687
Other GHG emissions, total (MtCO$_2$e)	..	..	17
Energy use per capita (kilograms of oil equivalent)	567	1,436	680
Energy use per units of GDP (kg oil eq./$1,000 of 2005 PPP $)	139.9	259.5	217.9

National-Level Actions

Latest UNFCCC national communication	11/30/2001 (1st)
Annex-I emissions reduction target	n/a
NAMA submission	..
NAPA submission	n/a
Renewable energy target	Yes

Carbon Markets

Hosted Clean Development Mechanism (CDM) projects	..
Issued Certified Emission Reductions (CERs) from CDM (thousands)	..
Hosted Joint Implementation (JI) projects	n/a
Issued Emission Reduction Units (ERUs) from JI (thousands)	n/a

Trinidad and Tobago

Population (millions)	1.3	GDP ($ billions)	20.4
Pop. growth (avg. ann. %, 1990–2010)	0.5	GNI per capita (Atlas $)	15,400

Climate

Average daily min/max temperature (1961–90, Celsius)	22 / 30
Projected annual temperature change (2045–65, Celsius)	1.5 to 2.1
Average annual precipitation (1961–90, mm)	1,787
Projected annual precipitation change (2045–65, mm)	-266 to 8
Projected change in annual hot days/warm nights	15 / 26
Projected change in annual cool days/cold nights	-3 / -3

	Country data	High Income
Exposure to Impacts		
Land area below 5m (% of land area)	8.0	2.2
Population below 5m (% of total)	7.5	7.7
Population in urban agglomerations > 1 million (%)	..	..
Urban pop. growth (avg. annual %, 1990–2010)	3.0	1.0
Droughts, floods, extreme temps (% pop. avg., 1990–2009)	0.0	
Annual freshwater withdrawals (% of internal resources)	6.0	10.4
Agricultural land under irrigation (% of total ag. land)	12.7	..
Population living below $1.25 a day (% of total)	4.2	..
Nationally terrestrial protected areas (% of total land area)	31.2	13.4
Under-five mortality rate (per 1,000)	27	6
Child malnutrition, underweight (% of under age five)	4.4	..
Malaria incidence rate (per 100,000 people)	..	
Resilience		
Access to improved sanitation (% of total pop.)	92	100
Access to improved water source (% of total pop.)	94	100
Cereal yield (kg. per hectare)	2,598	5,445
Access to electricity (% of total population)	99.0	..
Paved roads (% of total roads)	51.1	87.3
Health workers (per 1,000 people)	4.7	10.7
Foreign direct investment, net inflows (% of GDP)	2.7	1.8
Invest. in infrastructure w/private participation ($ millions)	..	..
Disaster risk reduction progress score (1–5 scale; 5 = best)	..	
Ease of doing business (ranking 1–183; 1 = best)	68	
Public sector mgmt & institutions avg. (1–6 scale; 6 = best)	..	
Primary completion rate, total (% of relevant age group)	93	97
Ratio of girls to boys in primary & secondary school (%)	101	100
GHG Emissions and Energy Use		
CO_2 emissions per capita (metric tons)	37.4	11.9
CO_2 emissions per units of GDP (kg/$1,000 of 2005 PPP $)	1,552.9	354.4
CO_2 emissions, total (MtCO_2)	49.8	13,285
GHG net emissions/removals by LUCF (1990, MtCO_2e)	-1.5	
Methane (CH_4) emissions, total (MtCO_2e)	10.1	1,539
Nitrous oxide (N_2O) emissions, total (MtCO_2e)	0.2	813
Other GHG emissions, total (MtCO_2e)	0.0	460
Energy use per capita (kilograms of oil equivalent)	15,158	4,944
Energy use per units of GDP (kg oil eq./$1,000 of 2005 PPP $)	654.9	147.0

National-Level Actions

Latest UNFCCC national communication	11/30/2001 (1st)
Annex-I emissions reduction target	n/a
NAMA submission	..
NAPA submission	n/a
Renewable energy target	..

Carbon Markets

Hosted Clean Development Mechanism (CDM) projects	..
Issued Certified Emission Reductions (CERs) from CDM (thousands)	..
Hosted Joint Implementation (JI) projects	n/a
Issued Emission Reduction Units (ERUs) from JI (thousands)	n/a

Tunisia

Population (millions)	10.5	GDP ($ billions)	44.3
Pop. growth (avg. ann. %, 1990-2010)	1.3	GNI per capita (Atlas $)	4,060

Climate
Average daily min/max temperature (1961-90, Celsius)	14 / 25
Projected annual temperature change (2045-65, Celsius)	1.9 to 2.6
Average annual precipitation (1961-90, mm)	313
Projected annual precipitation change (2045-65, mm)	-57 to -16
Projected change in annual hot days/warm nights	3 / 7
Projected change in annual cool days/cold nights	-2 / -2

	Country data	Middle East & N. Africa	Upper middle income
Exposure to Impacts			
Land area below 5m (% of land area)	2.8	1.4	1.8
Population below 5m (% of total)	9.5	9.7	6.5
Population in urban agglomerations > 1 million (%)	..	20	22
Urban pop. growth (avg. annual %, 1990-2010)	2.0	2.5	2.3
Droughts, floods, extreme temps (% pop. avg., 1990-2009)	0.1		
Annual freshwater withdrawals (% of internal resources)	67.6	121.9	5.6
Agricultural land under irrigation (% of total ag. land)	4.1	..	..
Population living below $1.25 a day (% of total)	2.6	3.6	..
Nationally terrestrial protected areas (% of total land area)	1.3	4.0	13.6
Under-five mortality rate (per 1,000)	16	34	20
Child malnutrition, underweight (% of under age five)	3.3	6.8	4.1
Malaria incidence rate (per 100,000 people)	..	..	80
Resilience			
Access to improved sanitation (% of total pop.)	85	84	68
Access to improved water source (% of total pop.)	94	87	92
Cereal yield (kg. per hectare)	1,813	2,512	3,690
Access to electricity (% of total population)	99.5	92.9	98.0
Paved roads (% of total roads)	75.2	74.3	50.5
Health workers (per 1,000 people)	4.5	3.6	4.5
Foreign direct investment, net inflows (% of GDP)	3.4	2.9	2.7
Invest. in infrastructure w/private participation ($ millions)	1,061	5,854	26,166
Disaster risk reduction progress score (1-5 scale; 5 = best)	..		
Ease of doing business (ranking 1-183; 1 = best)	46		
Public sector mgmt & institutions avg. (1-6 scale; 6 = best)	..		
Primary completion rate, total (% of relevant age group)	90	88	98
Ratio of girls to boys in primary & secondary school (%)	103	93	103
GHG Emissions and Energy Use			
CO_2 emissions per capita (metric tons)	2.4	3.8	5.3
CO_2 emissions per units of GDP (kg/$1,000 of 2005 PPP $)	329.2	604.6	659.4
CO_2 emissions, total (MtCO$_2$)	25.0	1,230	12,860
GHG net emissions/removals by LUCF (1994, MtCO$_2$e)	-1.8		
Methane (CH$_4$) emissions, total (MtCO$_2$e)	8.2	287	3,455
Nitrous oxide (N$_2$O) emissions, total (MtCO$_2$e)	2.4	74	1,144
Other GHG emissions, total (MtCO$_2$e)	0.0	7	243
Energy use per capita (kilograms of oil equivalent)	881	1,399	1,848
Energy use per units of GDP (kg oil eq./$1,000 of 2005 PPP $)	117.4	213.9	227.1

National-Level Actions
Latest UNFCCC national communication	10/27/2001 (1st)
Annex-I emissions reduction target	n/a
NAMA submission	Yes
NAPA submission	n/a
Renewable energy target	Yes

Carbon Markets
Hosted Clean Development Mechanism (CDM) projects	2
Issued Certified Emission Reductions (CERs) from CDM (thousands)	0
Hosted Joint Implementation (JI) projects	n/a
Issued Emission Reduction Units (ERUs) from JI (thousands)	n/a

Turkey

Population (millions)	72.8	GDP ($ billions)	735.3
Pop. growth (avg. ann. %, 1990–2010)	1.5	GNI per capita (Atlas $)	9,890

Climate

Average daily min/max temperature (1961–90, Celsius)	5 / 17
Projected annual temperature change (2045–65, Celsius)	1.9 to 2.9
Average annual precipitation (1961–90, mm)	593
Projected annual precipitation change (2045–65, mm)	-103 to -29
Projected change in annual hot days/warm nights	3 / 6
Projected change in annual cool days/cold nights	-1 / -1

	Country data	Europe & Central Asia	Upper middle income
Exposure to Impacts			
Land area below 5m (% of land area)	1.0	2.5	1.8
Population below 5m (% of total)	2.4	3.0	6.5
Population in urban agglomerations > 1 million (%)	29	18	22
Urban pop. growth (avg. annual %, 1990–2010)	2.3	0.3	2.3
Droughts, floods, extreme temps (% pop. avg., 1990–2009)	0.1		
Annual freshwater withdrawals (% of internal resources)	17.7	6.5	5.6
Agricultural land under irrigation (% of total ag. land)	13.4	..	..
Population living below $1.25 a day (% of total)	2.7	3.7	..
Nationally terrestrial protected areas (% of total land area)	1.9	7.5	13.6
Under-five mortality rate (per 1,000)	18	23	20
Child malnutrition, underweight (% of under age five)	3.5	..	4.1
Malaria incidence rate (per 100,000 people)	0	..	80
Resilience			
Access to improved sanitation (% of total pop.)	90	89	68
Access to improved water source (% of total pop.)	99	95	92
Cereal yield (kg. per hectare)	2,808	2,475	3,690
Access to electricity (% of total population)	..	..	98.0
Paved roads (% of total roads)	..	85.8	50.5
Health workers (per 1,000 people)	1.6	9.9	4.5
Foreign direct investment, net inflows (% of GDP)	1.3	2.8	2.7
Invest. in infrastructure w/private participation ($ millions)	6,606	22,652	26,166
Disaster risk reduction progress score (1–5 scale; 5 = best)	..		
Ease of doing business (ranking 1–183; 1 = best)	71		
Public sector mgmt & institutions avg. (1–6 scale; 6 = best)	..		
Primary completion rate, total (% of relevant age group)	93	95	98
Ratio of girls to boys in primary & secondary school (%)	93	97	103
GHG Emissions and Energy Use			
CO_2 emissions per capita (metric tons)	4.0	7.7	5.3
CO_2 emissions per units of GDP (kg/$1,000 of 2005 PPP $)	322.8	708.0	659.4
CO_2 emissions, total (MtCO_2)	284.0	3,110	12,860
GHG net emissions/removals by LUCF (2009, MtCO_2e)	-82.5		
Methane (CH_4) emissions, total (MtCO_2e)	64.3	937	3,455
Nitrous oxide (N_2O) emissions, total (MtCO_2e)	32.8	214	1,144
Other GHG emissions, total (MtCO_2e)	5.1	76	243
Energy use per capita (kilograms of oil equivalent)	1,440	2,833	1,848
Energy use per units of GDP (kg oil eq./$1,000 of 2005 PPP $)	114.9	276.8	227.1

National-Level Actions

Latest UNFCCC national communication	2/20/2007 (4th)
Annex-I emissions reduction target	
NAMA submission	n/a
NAPA submission	n/a
Renewable energy target	Yes

Carbon Markets

Hosted Clean Development Mechanism (CDM) projects	n/a
Issued Certified Emission Reductions (CERs) from CDM (thousands)	n/a
Hosted Joint Implementation (JI) projects	..
Issued Emission Reduction Units (ERUs) from JI (thousands)	..

Turkmenistan

Population (millions)	5.0	GDP ($ billions) 21.1
Pop. growth (avg. ann. %, 1990-2010)	1.6	GNI per capita (Atlas $) 3,800

Climate
Average daily min/max temperature (1961-90, Celsius)	9 / 22
Projected annual temperature change (2045-65, Celsius)	1.8 to 3.0
Average annual precipitation (1961-90, mm)	162
Projected annual precipitation change (2045-65, mm)	-32 to 12
Projected change in annual hot days/warm nights	3 / 6
Projected change in annual cool days/cold nights	-1 / -1

	Country data	Europe & Central Asia	Lower middle income
Exposure to Impacts			
Land area below 5m (% of land area)	5.3	2.5	1.7
Population below 5m (% of total)	5.6	3.0	6.5
Population in urban agglomerations > 1 million (%)	..	18	14
Urban pop. growth (avg. annual %, 1990-2010)	2.1	0.3	2.8
Droughts, floods, extreme temps (% pop. avg., 1990-2009)	0.0		
Annual freshwater withdrawals (% of internal resources)	1,831.6	6.5	18.7
Agricultural land under irrigation (% of total ag. land)	..	..	..
Population living below $1.25 a day (% of total)	24.8	3.7	..
Nationally terrestrial protected areas (% of total land area)	3.0	7.5	9.5
Under-five mortality rate (per 1,000)	56	23	69
Child malnutrition, underweight (% of under age five)	10.5	..	31.7
Malaria incidence rate (per 100,000 people)	0	..	4,874
Resilience			
Access to improved sanitation (% of total pop.)	98	89	45
Access to improved water source (% of total pop.)	83	95	84
Cereal yield (kg. per hectare)	3,203	2,475	2,754
Access to electricity (% of total population)	..	..	67.3
Paved roads (% of total roads)	81.2	85.8	29.3
Health workers (per 1,000 people)	7.0	9.9	2.6
Foreign direct investment, net inflows (% of GDP)	9.9	2.8	2.4
Invest. in infrastructure w/private participation ($ millions)	44	22,652	81,789
Disaster risk reduction progress score (1-5 scale; 5 = best)	..		
Ease of doing business (ranking 1-183; 1 = best)	..		
Public sector mgmt & institutions avg. (1-6 scale; 6 = best)	..		
Primary completion rate, total (% of relevant age group)	..	95	88
Ratio of girls to boys in primary & secondary school (%)	..	97	93
GHG Emissions and Energy Use			
CO_2 emissions per capita (metric tons)	9.7	7.7	1.6
CO_2 emissions per units of GDP (kg/$1,000 of 2005 PPP $)	1,537.5	708.0	523.9
CO_2 emissions, total (MtCO_2)	47.8	3,110	3,744
GHG net emissions/removals by LUCF (2004, MtCO_2e)	-0.8		
Methane (CH_4) emissions, total (MtCO_2e)	28.0	937	1,705
Nitrous oxide (N_2O) emissions, total (MtCO_2e)	4.3	214	687
Other GHG emissions, total (MtCO_2e)	0.1	76	17
Energy use per capita (kilograms of oil equivalent)	3,933	2,833	680
Energy use per units of GDP (kg oil eq./$1,000 of 2005 PPP $)	593.2	276.8	217.9

National-Level Actions
Latest UNFCCC national communication	11/29/2010 (2nd)
Annex-I emissions reduction target	n/a
NAMA submission	..
NAPA submission	n/a
Renewable energy target	..

Carbon Markets
Hosted Clean Development Mechanism (CDM) projects	..
Issued Certified Emission Reductions (CERs) from CDM (thousands)	..
Hosted Joint Implementation (JI) projects	n/a
Issued Emission Reduction Units (ERUs) from JI (thousands)	n/a

Turks and Caicos Islands

Population (thousands)	38.4	GDP ($ millions)	..
Pop. growth (avg. ann. %, 1990–2010)	6.0	GNI per capita (Atlas $)	..

Climate

Average daily min/max temperature (1961–90, Celsius)	25 / 31
Projected annual temperature change (2045–65, Celsius)	1.4 to 1.7
Average annual precipitation (1961–90, mm)	3,035
Projected annual precipitation change (2045–65, mm)	-87 to 52
Projected change in annual hot days/warm nights	11 / 18
Projected change in annual cool days/cold nights	-3 / -2

	Country data	High income
Exposure to Impacts		
Land area below 5m (% of land area)	53.3	2.2
Population below 5m (% of total)	53.3	7.7
Population in urban agglomerations > 1 million (%)	..	..
Urban pop. growth (avg. annual %, 1990–2010)	..	1.0
Droughts, floods, extreme temps (% pop. avg., 1990–2009)	..	
Annual freshwater withdrawals (% of internal resources)	..	10.4
Agricultural land under irrigation (% of total ag. land)	..	
Population living below $1.25 a day (% of total)	..	
Nationally terrestrial protected areas (% of total land area)	42.9	13.4
Under-five mortality rate (per 1,000)	..	6
Child malnutrition, underweight (% of under age five)	..	
Malaria incidence rate (per 100,000 people)	..	
Resilience		
Access to improved sanitation (% of total pop.)	96	100
Access to improved water source (% of total pop.)	100	100
Cereal yield (kg. per hectare)	..	5,445
Access to electricity (% of total population)	..	
Paved roads (% of total roads)	..	87.3
Health workers (per 1,000 people)	..	10.7
Foreign direct investment, net inflows (% of GDP)	..	1.8
Invest. in infrastructure w/private participation ($ millions)	..	
Disaster risk reduction progress score (1–5 scale; 5 = best)	2.3	
Ease of doing business (ranking 1–183; 1 = best)	..	
Public sector mgmt & institutions avg. (1–6 scale; 6 = best)	..	
Primary completion rate, total (% of relevant age group)	92	97
Ratio of girls to boys in primary & secondary school (%)	100	100
GHG Emissions and Energy Use		
CO_2 emissions per capita (metric tons)	4.4	11.9
CO_2 emissions per units of GDP (kg/$1,000 of 2005 PPP $)	..	354.4
CO_2 emissions, total (MtCO$_2$)	0.2	13,285
GHG net emissions/removals by LUCF (MtCO$_2$e)	..	
Methane (CH_4) emissions, total (MtCO$_2$e)	..	1,539
Nitrous oxide (N_2O) emissions, total (MtCO$_2$e)	..	813
Other GHG emissions, total (MtCO$_2$e)	..	460
Energy use per capita (kilograms of oil equivalent)	..	4,944
Energy use per units of GDP (kg oil eq./$1,000 of 2005 PPP $)	..	147.0

National-Level Actions

Latest UNFCCC national communication	n/a
Annex-I emissions reduction target	n/a
NAMA submission	n/a
NAPA submission	n/a
Renewable energy target	..

Carbon Markets

Hosted Clean Development Mechanism (CDM) projects	n/a
Issued Certified Emission Reductions (CERs) from CDM (thousands)	n/a
Hosted Joint Implementation (JI) projects	n/a
Issued Emission Reduction Units (ERUs) from JI (thousands)	n/a

Tuvalu

Population (thousands)	9.8	GDP ($ millions)	31.4
Pop. growth (avg. ann. %, 1990-2010)	0.4	GNI per capita (Atlas $)	4,530

Climate

Average daily min/max temperature (1961-90, Celsius)	25 / 31
Projected annual temperature change (2045-65, Celsius)	1.4 to 1.9
Average annual precipitation (1961-90, mm)	3,035
Projected annual precipitation change (2045-65, mm)	9 to 651
Projected change in annual hot days/warm nights	24 / 27
Projected change in annual cool days/cold nights	-3 / -3

	Country data	East Asia & Pacific	Lower middle income
Exposure to Impacts			
Land area below 5m (% of land area)	100.0	2.5	1.7
Population below 5m (% of total)	100.0	10.3	6.5
Population in urban agglomerations > 1 million (%)	..	..	14
Urban pop. growth (avg. annual %, 1990-2010)	..	3.3	2.8
Droughts, floods, extreme temps (% pop. avg., 1990-2009)	..		
Annual freshwater withdrawals (% of internal resources)	..	10.8	18.7
Agricultural land under irrigation (% of total ag. land)	..	..	..
Population living below $1.25 a day (% of total)	..	16.8	..
Nationally terrestrial protected areas (% of total land area)	0.4	14.9	9.5
Under-five mortality rate (per 1,000)	33	24	69
Child malnutrition, underweight (% of under age five)	1.6	9.0	31.7
Malaria incidence rate (per 100,000 people)	..	525	4,874
Resilience			
Access to improved sanitation (% of total pop.)	84	59	45
Access to improved water source (% of total pop.)	97	88	84
Cereal yield (kg. per hectare)	..	4,860	2,754
Access to electricity (% of total population)	..	90.8	67.3
Paved roads (% of total roads)	..	15.9	29.3
Health workers (per 1,000 people)	6.5	2.8	2.6
Foreign direct investment, net inflows (% of GDP)	4.8	3.0	2.4
Invest. in infrastructure w/private participation ($ millions)	..	14,638	81,789
Disaster risk reduction progress score (1-5 scale; 5 = best)	..		
Ease of doing business (ranking 1-183; 1 = best)	..		
Public sector mgmt & institutions avg. (1-6 scale; 6 = best)	..		
Primary completion rate, total (% of relevant age group)	99	97	88
Ratio of girls to boys in primary & secondary school (%)	112	103	93
GHG Emissions and Energy Use			
CO_2 emissions per capita (metric tons)	..	4.3	1.6
CO_2 emissions per units of GDP (kg/$1,000 of 2005 PPP $)	..	827.1	523.9
CO_2 emissions, total (MtCO_2)	..	8,259	3,744
GHG net emissions/removals by LUCF (MtCO_2e)	..		
Methane (CH_4) emissions, total (MtCO_2e)	..	1,928	1,705
Nitrous oxide (N_2O) emissions, total (MtCO_2e)	..	707	687
Other GHG emissions, total (MtCO_2e)	..	..	17
Energy use per capita (kilograms of oil equivalent)	..	1,436	680
Energy use per units of GDP (kg oil eq./$1,000 of 2005 PPP $)	..	259.5	217.9

National-Level Actions

Latest UNFCCC national communication	10/30/1999 (1st)
Annex-I emissions reduction target	n/a
NAMA submission	..
NAPA submission	Yes
Renewable energy target	..

Carbon Markets

Hosted Clean Development Mechanism (CDM) projects	..
Issued Certified Emission Reductions (CERs) from CDM (thousands)	..
Hosted Joint Implementation (JI) projects	n/a
Issued Emission Reduction Units (ERUs) from JI (thousands)	n/a

Uganda

Population (millions)	33.4	GDP ($ billions)	17.0
Pop. growth (avg. ann. %, 1990–2010)	3.2	GNI per capita (Atlas $)	500

Climate

Average daily min/max temperature (1961–90, Celsius)	17 / 29
Projected annual temperature change (2045–65, Celsius)	2.1 to 2.3
Average annual precipitation (1961–90, mm)	1,180
Projected annual precipitation change (2045–65, mm)	−13 to 224
Projected change in annual hot days/warm nights	6 / 26
Projected change in annual cool days/cold nights	−2 / −3

	Country data	Sub-Saharan Africa	Low income
Exposure to Impacts			
Land area below 5m (% of land area)	0.0	0.4	0.7
Population below 5m (% of total)	0.0	2.0	5.1
Population in urban agglomerations > 1 million (%)	5	14	11
Urban pop. growth (avg. annual %, 1990–2010)	4.1	4.0	3.7
Droughts, floods, extreme temps (% pop. avg., 1990–2009)	0.9		
Annual freshwater withdrawals (% of internal resources)	0.8	3.2	3.7
Agricultural land under irrigation (% of total ag. land)	..	..	..
Population living below $1.25 a day (% of total)	37.7	50.9	..
Nationally terrestrial protected areas (% of total land area)	9.7	11.7	10.6
Under-five mortality rate (per 1,000)	99	121	108
Child malnutrition, underweight (% of under age five)	16.4	24.6	28.3
Malaria incidence rate (per 100,000 people)	36,233	26,113	16,659
Resilience			
Access to improved sanitation (% of total pop.)	48	31	35
Access to improved water source (% of total pop.)	67	60	63
Cereal yield (kg. per hectare)	1,539	1,297	2,047
Access to electricity (% of total population)	9.0	32.5	23.0
Paved roads (% of total roads)	23.0	18.3	14.1
Health workers (per 1,000 people)	1.4	1.2	0.7
Foreign direct investment, net inflows (% of GDP)	4.8	3.6	3.2
Invest. in infrastructure w/private participation ($ millions)	257	11,957	4,471
Disaster risk reduction progress score (1–5 scale; 5 = best)	..		
Ease of doing business (ranking 1–183; 1 = best)	123		
Public sector mgmt & institutions avg. (1–6 scale; 6 = best)	3.2		
Primary completion rate, total (% of relevant age group)	73	67	65
Ratio of girls to boys in primary & secondary school (%)	99	89	91
GHG Emissions and Energy Use			
CO_2 emissions per capita (metric tons)	0.1	0.8	0.3
CO_2 emissions per units of GDP (kg/$1,000 of 2005 PPP $)	110.8	428.6	270.2
CO_2 emissions, total (MtCO_2)	3.7	685	219
GHG net emissions/removals by LUCF (1994, MtCO_2e)	8.3		
Methane (CH_4) emissions, total (MtCO_2e)	..	590	436
Nitrous oxide (N_2O) emissions, total (MtCO_2e)	..	334	209
Other GHG emissions, total (MtCO_2e)	..	..	..
Energy use per capita (kilograms of oil equivalent)	..	689	365
Energy use per units of GDP (kg oil eq./$1,000 of 2005 PPP $)	..	308.4	303.9

National-Level Actions

Latest UNFCCC national communication	10/26/2002 (1st)
Annex-I emissions reduction target	n/a
NAMA submission	..
NAPA submission	Yes
Renewable energy target	Yes

Carbon Markets

Hosted Clean Development Mechanism (CDM) projects	5
Issued Certified Emission Reductions (CERs) from CDM (thousands)	0
Hosted Joint Implementation (JI) projects	n/a
Issued Emission Reduction Units (ERUs) from JI (thousands)	n/a

Ukraine

Population (millions)	45.9	GDP ($ billions)	137.9
Pop. growth (avg. ann. %, 1990–2010)	-0.6	GNI per capita (Atlas $)	3,010

Climate
Average daily min/max temperature (1961–90, Celsius)	4 / 13
Projected annual temperature change (2045–65, Celsius)	2.1 to 3.0
Average annual precipitation (1961–90, mm)	565
Projected annual precipitation change (2045–65, mm)	-43 to 31
Projected change in annual hot days/warm nights	3 / 5
Projected change in annual cool days/cold nights	-1 / -2

	Country data	Europe & Central Asia	Lower middle income
Exposure to Impacts			
Land area below 5m (% of land area)	1.5	2.5	1.7
Population below 5m (% of total)	2.1	3.0	6.5
Population in urban agglomerations > 1 million (%)	14	18	14
Urban pop. growth (avg. annual %, 1990-2010)	-0.5	0.3	2.8
Droughts, floods, extreme temps (% pop. avg., 1990–2009)	0.3		
Annual freshwater withdrawals (% of internal resources)	72.5	6.5	18.7
Agricultural land under irrigation (% of total ag. land)	5.3	..	..
Population living below $1.25 a day (% of total)	<2	3.7	..
Nationally terrestrial protected areas (% of total land area)	3.5	7.5	9.5
Under-five mortality rate (per 1,000)	13	23	69
Child malnutrition, underweight (% of under age five)	0.9	..	31.7
Malaria incidence rate (per 100,000 people)	..	..	4,874
Resilience			
Access to improved sanitation (% of total pop.)	95	89	45
Access to improved water source (% of total pop.)	98	95	84
Cereal yield (kg. per hectare)	3,004	2,475	2,754
Access to electricity (% of total population)	..	..	67.3
Paved roads (% of total roads)	97.8	85.8	29.3
Health workers (per 1,000 people)	11.6	9.9	2.6
Foreign direct investment, net inflows (% of GDP)	4.7	2.8	2.4
Invest. in infrastructure w/private participation ($ millions)	423	22,652	81,789
Disaster risk reduction progress score (1-5 scale; 5 = best)	..		
Ease of doing business (ranking 1-183; 1 = best)	152		
Public sector mgmt & institutions avg. (1-6 scale; 6 = best)	..		
Primary completion rate, total (% of relevant age group)	95	95	88
Ratio of girls to boys in primary & secondary school (%)	99	97	93
GHG Emissions and Energy Use			
CO_2 emissions per capita (metric tons)	7.0	7.7	1.6
CO_2 emissions per units of GDP (kg/$1,000 of 2005 PPP $)	1,040.6	708.0	523.9
CO_2 emissions, total (MtCO_2)	323.5	3,110	3,744
GHG net emissions/removals by LUCF (2009, MtCO_2e)	-19.2		
Methane (CH_4) emissions, total (MtCO_2e)	70.4	937	1,705
Nitrous oxide (N_2O) emissions, total (MtCO_2e)	26.1	214	687
Other GHG emissions, total (MtCO_2e)	0.7	76	17
Energy use per capita (kilograms of oil equivalent)	2,507	2,833	680
Energy use per units of GDP (kg oil eq./$1,000 of 2005 PPP $)	435.9	276.8	217.9

National-Level Actions
Latest UNFCCC national communication	2/8/2010 (5th)
Annex-I emissions reduction target (base year: 1990)	20%
NAMA submission	n/a
NAPA submission	n/a
Renewable energy target	..

Carbon Markets
Hosted Clean Development Mechanism (CDM) projects	n/a
Issued Certified Emission Reductions (CERs) from CDM (thousands)	n/a
Hosted Joint Implementation (JI) projects	80
Issued Emission Reduction Units (ERUs) from JI (thousands)	39,780

United Arab Emirates

Population (millions)	7.5	GDP ($ billions)	230.3
Pop. growth (avg. ann. %, 1990–2010)	7.1	GNI per capita (Atlas $)	..

Climate

Average daily min/max temperature (1961–90, Celsius)	21 / 33
Projected annual temperature change (2045–65, Celsius)	2.2 to 2.8
Average annual precipitation (1961–90, mm)	78
Projected annual precipitation change (2045–65, mm)	-26 to 17
Projected change in annual hot days/warm nights	4 / 9
Projected change in annual cool days/cold nights	-2 / -2

	Country data	High income
Exposure to Impacts		
Land area below 5m (% of land area)	4.6	2.2
Population below 5m (% of total)	7.3	7.7
Population in urban agglomerations > 1 million (%)	21	..
Urban pop. growth (avg. annual %, 1990–2010)	7.0	1.0
Droughts, floods, extreme temps (% pop. avg., 1990–2009)	..	
Annual freshwater withdrawals (% of internal resources)	2,032.0	10.4
Agricultural land under irrigation (% of total ag. land)	..	
Population living below $1.25 a day (% of total)	..	
Nationally terrestrial protected areas (% of total land area)	5.6	13.4
Under-five mortality rate (per 1,000)	7	6
Child malnutrition, underweight (% of under age five)	..	
Malaria incidence rate (per 100,000 people)	..	..
Resilience		
Access to improved sanitation (% of total pop.)	97	100
Access to improved water source (% of total pop.)	100	100
Cereal yield (kg. per hectare)	3,000	5,445
Access to electricity (% of total population)	100.0	
Paved roads (% of total roads)	100.0	87.3
Health workers (per 1,000 people)	6.0	10.7
Foreign direct investment, net inflows (% of GDP)	1.7	1.8
Invest. in infrastructure w/private participation ($ millions)	..	
Disaster risk reduction progress score (1–5 scale; 5 = best)	..	
Ease of doing business (ranking 1-183; 1 = best)	33	
Public sector mgmt & institutions avg. (1–6 scale; 6 = best)	..	
Primary completion rate, total (% of relevant age group)	99	97
Ratio of girls to boys in primary & secondary school (%)	100	100
GHG Emissions and Energy Use		
CO_2 emissions per capita (metric tons)	25.0	11.9
CO_2 emissions per units of GDP (kg/$1,000 of 2005 PPP $)	638.6	354.4
CO_2 emissions, total (MtCO_2)	155.1	13,285
GHG net emissions/removals by LUCF (2000, MtCO_2e)	-9.7	
Methane (CH_4) emissions, total (MtCO_2e)	23.3	1,539
Nitrous oxide (N_2O) emissions, total (MtCO_2e)	1.2	813
Other GHG emissions, total (MtCO_2e)	1.1	460
Energy use per capita (kilograms of oil equivalent)	8,588	4,944
Energy use per units of GDP (kg oil eq./$1,000 of 2005 PPP $)	247.1	147.0

National-Level Actions

Latest UNFCCC national communication	4/7/2010 (2nd)
Annex-I emissions reduction target	n/a
NAMA submission	..
NAPA submission	n/a
Renewable energy target	..

Carbon Markets

Hosted Clean Development Mechanism (CDM) projects	5
Issued Certified Emission Reductions (CERs) from CDM (thousands)	80
Hosted Joint Implementation (JI) projects	n/a
Issued Emission Reduction Units (ERUs) from JI (thousands)	n/a

United Kingdom

Population (millions)	62.2	GDP ($ billions)	2,246.1
Pop. growth (avg. ann. %, 1990–2010)	0.4	GNI per capita (Atlas $)	38,560

Climate

Average daily min/max temperature (1961–90, Celsius)	5 / 12
Projected annual temperature change (2045–65, Celsius)	1.1 to 1.8
Average annual precipitation (1961–90, mm)	1,220
Projected annual precipitation change (2045–65, mm)	-10 to 66
Projected change in annual hot days/warm nights	3 / 5
Projected change in annual cool days/cold nights	-1 / -2

	Country data	High income
Exposure to Impacts		
Land area below 5m (% of land area)	7.6	2.2
Population below 5m (% of total)	8.6	7.7
Population in urban agglomerations > 1 million (%)	26	..
Urban pop. growth (avg. annual %, 1990–2010)	0.5	1.0
Droughts, floods, extreme temps (% pop. avg., 1990–2009)	0.0	
Annual freshwater withdrawals (% of internal resources)	10.0	10.4
Agricultural land under irrigation (% of total ag. land)	..	..
Population living below $1.25 a day (% of total)	..	
Nationally terrestrial protected areas (% of total land area)	24.4	13.4
Under-five mortality rate (per 1,000)	5	6
Child malnutrition, underweight (% of under age five)	..	..
Malaria incidence rate (per 100,000 people)	..	..
Resilience		
Access to improved sanitation (% of total pop.)	100	100
Access to improved water source (% of total pop.)	100	100
Cereal yield (kg. per hectare)	7,072	5,445
Access to electricity (% of total population)	..	..
Paved roads (% of total roads)	100.0	87.3
Health workers (per 1,000 people)	13.0	10.7
Foreign direct investment, net inflows (% of GDP)	2.1	1.8
Invest. in infrastructure w/private participation ($ millions)	..	..
Disaster risk reduction progress score (1–5 scale; 5 = best)	..	
Ease of doing business (ranking 1–183; 1 = best)	7	
Public sector mgmt & institutions avg. (1–6 scale; 6 = best)	..	
Primary completion rate, total (% of relevant age group)	..	97
Ratio of girls to boys in primary & secondary school (%)	101	100
GHG Emissions and Energy Use		
CO_2 emissions per capita (metric tons)	8.5	11.9
CO_2 emissions per units of GDP (kg/$1,000 of 2005 PPP $)	251.5	354.4
CO_2 emissions, total (MtCO$_2$)	522.9	13,285
GHG net emissions/removals by LUCF (2009, MtCO$_2$e)	-4.1	
Methane (CH$_4$) emissions, total (MtCO$_2$e)	65.8	1,539
Nitrous oxide (N$_2$O) emissions, total (MtCO$_2$e)	30.6	813
Other GHG emissions, total (MtCO$_2$e)	10.4	460
Energy use per capita (kilograms of oil equivalent)	3,283	4,944
Energy use per units of GDP (kg oil eq./$1,000 of 2005 PPP $)	102.0	147.0

National-Level Actions

Latest UNFCCC national communication	6/12/2009 (5th)
Annex-I emissions reduction target (base year: 1990)	20% / 30% (EU)
NAMA submission	n/a
NAPA submission	n/a
Renewable energy target	Yes

Carbon Markets

Hosted Clean Development Mechanism (CDM) projects	n/a
Issued Certified Emission Reductions (CERs) from CDM (thousands)	n/a
Hosted Joint Implementation (JI) projects	..
Issued Emission Reduction Units (ERUs) from JI (thousands)	..

United States

Population (millions)	309.1	GDP ($ billions)	14,582.4
Pop. growth (avg. ann. %, 1990–2010)	1.1	GNI per capita (Atlas $)	47,240

Climate

Average daily min/max temperature (1961–90, Celsius)	2 / 15
Projected annual temperature change (2045–65, Celsius)	2.0 to 3.0
Average annual precipitation (1961–90, mm)	736
Projected annual precipitation change (2045–65, mm)	-26 to 98
Projected change in annual hot days/warm nights	3 / 6
Projected change in annual cool days/cold nights	-1 / -1

	Country data	High income
Exposure to Impacts		
Land area below 5m (% of land area)	1.7	2.2
Population below 5m (% of total)	4.1	7.7
Population in urban agglomerations > 1 million (%)	45	
Urban pop. growth (avg. annual %, 1990–2010)	1.5	1.0
Droughts, floods, extreme temps (% pop. avg., 1990–2009)	0.2	
Annual freshwater withdrawals (% of internal resources)	17.0	10.4
Agricultural land under irrigation (% of total ag. land)	..	
Population living below $1.25 a day (% of total)	..	..
Nationally terrestrial protected areas (% of total land area)	14.8	13.4
Under-five mortality rate (per 1,000)	8	6
Child malnutrition, underweight (% of under age five)	1.3	
Malaria incidence rate (per 100,000 people)	..	..
Resilience		
Access to improved sanitation (% of total pop.)	100	100
Access to improved water source (% of total pop.)	99	100
Cereal yield (kg. per hectare)	7,238	5,445
Access to electricity (% of total population)	..	
Paved roads (% of total roads)	67.4	87.3
Health workers (per 1,000 people)	9.8	10.7
Foreign direct investment, net inflows (% of GDP)	1.6	1.8
Invest. in infrastructure w/private participation ($ millions)	..	..
Disaster risk reduction progress score (1–5 scale; 5 = best)	3.5	
Ease of doing business (ranking 1–183; 1 = best)	4	
Public sector mgmt & institutions avg. (1–6 scale; 6 = best)	..	
Primary completion rate, total (% of relevant age group)	96	97
Ratio of girls to boys in primary & secondary school (%)	101	100
GHG Emissions and Energy Use		
CO_2 emissions per capita (metric tons)	17.9	11.9
CO_2 emissions per units of GDP (kg/$1,000 of 2005 PPP $)	414.8	354.4
CO_2 emissions, total (MtCO$_2$)	5,461.0	13,285
GHG net emissions/removals by LUCF (2009, MtCO$_2$e)	-990.1	
Methane (CH$_4$) emissions, total (MtCO$_2$e)	548.1	1,539
Nitrous oxide (N$_2$O) emissions, total (MtCO$_2$e)	317.2	813
Other GHG emissions, total (MtCO$_2$e)	239.5	460
Energy use per capita (kilograms of oil equivalent)	7,232	4,944
Energy use per units of GDP (kg oil eq./$1,000 of 2005 PPP $)	169.6	147.0

National-Level Actions

Latest UNFCCC national communication	5/28/2010 (5th)
Annex-I emissions reduction target (base year: 2005)	17%
NAMA submission	n/a
NAPA submission	n/a
Renewable energy target	..

Carbon Markets

Hosted Clean Development Mechanism (CDM) projects	n/a
Issued Certified Emission Reductions (CERs) from CDM (thousands)	n/a
Hosted Joint Implementation (JI) projects	..
Issued Emission Reduction Units (ERUs) from JI (thousands)	..

Uruguay

Population (millions)	3.4	GDP ($ billions)	40.3
Pop. growth (avg. ann. %, 1990-2010)	0.4	GNI per capita (Atlas $)	10,590

Climate
Average daily min/max temperature (1961-90, Celsius)	12 / 23
Projected annual temperature change (2045-65, Celsius)	1.4 to 1.8
Average annual precipitation (1961-90, mm)	1,265
Projected annual precipitation change (2045-65, mm)	0 to 130
Projected change in annual hot days/warm nights	2 / 6
Projected change in annual cool days/cold nights	-1 / -1

	Country data	Latin America & the Carib.	Upper middle income
Exposure to Impacts			
Land area below 5m (% of land area)	1.9	1.5	1.8
Population below 5m (% of total)	4.7	3.8	6.5
Population in urban agglomerations > 1 million (%)	49	35	22
Urban pop. growth (avg. annual %, 1990-2010)	0.6	2.0	2.3
Droughts, floods, extreme temps (% pop. avg., 1990-2009)	0.3		
Annual freshwater withdrawals (% of internal resources)	5.3	2.0	5.6
Agricultural land under irrigation (% of total ag. land)	1.2	..	..
Population living below $1.25 a day (% of total)	<2	8.1	
Nationally terrestrial protected areas (% of total land area)	0.3	20.8	13.6
Under-five mortality rate (per 1,000)	11	23	20
Child malnutrition, underweight (% of under age five)	6.0	3.8	4.1
Malaria incidence rate (per 100,000 people)	..	206	80
Resilience			
Access to improved sanitation (% of total pop.)	100	79	68
Access to improved water source (% of total pop.)	100	93	92
Cereal yield (kg. per hectare)	4,045	3,337	3,690
Access to electricity (% of total population)	98.3	93.4	98.0
Paved roads (% of total roads)	..	28.1	50.5
Health workers (per 1,000 people)	9.3	6.9	4.5
Foreign direct investment, net inflows (% of GDP)	4.0	2.3	2.7
Invest. in infrastructure w/private participation ($ millions)	42	33,064	26,166
Disaster risk reduction progress score (1-5 scale; 5 = best)	..		
Ease of doing business (ranking 1-183; 1 = best)	90		
Public sector mgmt & institutions avg. (1-6 scale; 6 = best)	..		
Primary completion rate, total (% of relevant age group)	106	102	98
Ratio of girls to boys in primary & secondary school (%)	104	102	103
GHG Emissions and Energy Use			
CO_2 emissions per capita (metric tons)	2.5	2.8	5.3
CO_2 emissions per units of GDP (kg/$1,000 of 2005 PPP $)	214.0	285.6	659.4
CO_2 emissions, total (MtCO_2)	8.3	1,584	12,860
GHG net emissions/removals by LUCF (2004, MtCO_2e)	-10.3		
Methane (CH_4) emissions, total (MtCO_2e)	19.6	1,009	3,455
Nitrous oxide (N_2O) emissions, total (MtCO_2e)	7.0	442	1,144
Other GHG emissions, total (MtCO_2e)	0.1	21	243
Energy use per capita (kilograms of oil equivalent)	1,224	1,245	1,848
Energy use per units of GDP (kg oil eq./$1,000 of 2005 PPP $)	102.5	130.6	227.1

National-Level Actions
Latest UNFCCC national communication	11/18/2010 (3rd)
Annex-I emissions reduction target	n/a
NAMA submission	..
NAPA submission	n/a
Renewable energy target	..

Carbon Markets
Hosted Clean Development Mechanism (CDM) projects	6
Issued Certified Emission Reductions (CERs) from CDM (thousands)	41
Hosted Joint Implementation (JI) projects	n/a
Issued Emission Reduction Units (ERUs) from JI (thousands)	n/a

Uzbekistan

| Population (millions) | 28.2 | GDP ($ billions) | 39.0 |
| Pop. growth (avg. ann. %, 1990–2010) | 1.6 | GNI per capita (Atlas $) | 1,280 |

Climate
Average daily min/max temperature (1961–90, Celsius)	6 / 18
Projected annual temperature change (2045–65, Celsius)	2.0 to 3.0
Average annual precipitation (1961–90, mm)	206
Projected annual precipitation change (2045–65, mm)	-26 to 17
Projected change in annual hot days/warm nights	3 / 6
Projected change in annual cool days/cold nights	-1 / -1

	Country data	Europe & Central Asia	Lower middle income
Exposure to Impacts			
Land area below 5m (% of land area)	0.1	2.5	1.7
Population below 5m (% of total)	0.0	3.0	6.5
Population in urban agglomerations > 1 million (%)	8	18	14
Urban pop. growth (avg. annual %, 1990–2010)	1.2	0.3	2.8
Droughts, floods, extreme temps (% pop. avg., 1990–2009)	0.1		
Annual freshwater withdrawals (% of internal resources)	364.8	6.5	18.7
Agricultural land under irrigation (% of total ag. land)	..	..	..
Population living below $1.25 a day (% of total)	46.3	3.7	..
Nationally terrestrial protected areas (% of total land area)	2.3	7.5	9.5
Under-five mortality rate (per 1,000)	52	23	69
Child malnutrition, underweight (% of under age five)	4.4	..	31.7
Malaria incidence rate (per 100,000 people)	0	..	4,874
Resilience			
Access to improved sanitation (% of total pop.)	100	89	45
Access to improved water source (% of total pop.)	87	95	84
Cereal yield (kg. per hectare)	4,269	2,475	2,754
Access to electricity (% of total population)	..	..	67.3
Paved roads (% of total roads)	87.3	85.8	29.3
Health workers (per 1,000 people)	13.4	9.9	2.6
Foreign direct investment, net inflows (% of GDP)	2.1	2.8	2.4
Invest. in infrastructure w/private participation ($ millions)	644	22,652	81,789
Disaster risk reduction progress score (1–5 scale; 5 = best)	..		
Ease of doing business (ranking 1–183; 1 = best)	166		
Public sector mgmt & institutions avg. (1–6 scale; 6 = best)	2.8		
Primary completion rate, total (% of relevant age group)	92	95	88
Ratio of girls to boys in primary & secondary school (%)	99	97	93
GHG Emissions and Energy Use			
CO_2 emissions per capita (metric tons)	4.6	7.7	1.6
CO_2 emissions per units of GDP (kg/$1,000 of 2005 PPP $)	1,862.7	708.0	523.9
CO_2 emissions, total (MtCO_2)	124.9	3,110	3,744
GHG net emissions/removals by LUCF (2005, MtCO_2e)	0.4		
Methane (CH_4) emissions, total (MtCO_2e)	39.6	937	1,705
Nitrous oxide (N_2O) emissions, total (MtCO_2e)	10.0	214	687
Other GHG emissions, total (MtCO_2e)	0.6	76	17
Energy use per capita (kilograms of oil equivalent)	1,758	2,833	680
Energy use per units of GDP (kg oil eq./$1,000 of 2005 PPP $)	673.3	276.8	217.9

National-Level Actions
Latest UNFCCC national communication	12/3/2008 (2nd)
Annex-I emissions reduction target	n/a
NAMA submission	..
NAPA submission	n/a
Renewable energy target	..

Carbon Markets
Hosted Clean Development Mechanism (CDM) projects	11
Issued Certified Emission Reductions (CERs) from CDM (thousands)	0
Hosted Joint Implementation (JI) projects	n/a
Issued Emission Reduction Units (ERUs) from JI (thousands)	n/a

Vanuatu

Population (thousands)	239.7	GDP ($ millions)	729.0
Pop. growth (avg. ann. %, 1990–2010)	2.5	GNI per capita (Atlas $)	2,760

Climate

Average daily min/max temperature (1961–90, Celsius)	21 / 27
Projected annual temperature change (2045–65, Celsius)	1.3 to 1.7
Average annual precipitation (1961–90, mm)	2,876
Projected annual precipitation change (2045–65, mm)	-163 to 180
Projected change in annual hot days/warm nights	10 / 19
Projected change in annual cool days/cold nights	-3 / -3

	Country data	East Asia & Pacific	Lower middle income
Exposure to Impacts			
Land area below 5m (% of land area)	11.7	2.5	1.7
Population below 5m (% of total)	10.8	10.3	6.5
Population in urban agglomerations > 1 million (%)	..	..	14
Urban pop. growth (avg. annual %, 1990–2010)	4.0	3.3	2.8
Droughts, floods, extreme temps (% pop. avg., 1990–2009)	0.1		
Annual freshwater withdrawals (% of internal resources)	..	10.8	18.7
Agricultural land under irrigation (% of total ag. land)	..		..
Population living below $1.25 a day (% of total)	..	16.8	..
Nationally terrestrial protected areas (% of total land area)	4.3	14.9	9.5
Under-five mortality rate (per 1,000)	14	24	69
Child malnutrition, underweight (% of under age five)	11.7	9.0	31.7
Malaria incidence rate (per 100,000 people)	6,036	525	4,874
Resilience			
Access to improved sanitation (% of total pop.)	52	59	45
Access to improved water source (% of total pop.)	83	88	84
Cereal yield (kg. per hectare)	565	4,860	2,754
Access to electricity (% of total population)	..	90.8	67.3
Paved roads (% of total roads)	23.9	15.9	29.3
Health workers (per 1,000 people)	1.8	2.8	2.6
Foreign direct investment, net inflows (% of GDP)	5.3	3.0	2.4
Invest. in infrastructure w/private participation ($ millions)	35	14,638	81,789
Disaster risk reduction progress score (1–5 scale; 5 = best)	2.0		
Ease of doing business (ranking 1–183; 1 = best)	76		
Public sector mgmt & institutions avg. (1–6 scale; 6 = best)	3.4		
Primary completion rate, total (% of relevant age group)	83	97	88
Ratio of girls to boys in primary & secondary school (%)	100	103	93
GHG Emissions and Energy Use			
CO$_2$ emissions per capita (metric tons)	0.4	4.3	1.6
CO$_2$ emissions per units of GDP (kg/$1,000 of 2005 PPP $)	98.7	827.1	523.9
CO$_2$ emissions, total (MtCO$_2$)	0.1	8,259	3,744
GHG net emissions/removals by LUCF (1994, MtCO$_2$e)	0.0		
Methane (CH$_4$) emissions, total (MtCO$_2$e)	..	1,928	1,705
Nitrous oxide (N$_2$O) emissions, total (MtCO$_2$e)	..	707	687
Other GHG emissions, total (MtCO$_2$e)	..	..	17
Energy use per capita (kilograms of oil equivalent)	157	1,436	680
Energy use per units of GDP (kg oil eq./$1,000 of 2005 PPP $)	40.1	259.5	217.9

National-Level Actions

Latest UNFCCC national communication	10/30/1999 (1st)
Annex-I emissions reduction target	n/a
NAMA submission	
NAPA submission	Yes
Renewable energy target	..

Carbon Markets

Hosted Clean Development Mechanism (CDM) projects	..
Issued Certified Emission Reductions (CERs) from CDM (thousands)	..
Hosted Joint Implementation (JI) projects	n/a
Issued Emission Reduction Units (ERUs) from JI (thousands)	n/a

Venezuela, RB

Population (millions)	28.8	GDP ($ billions)	387.9
Pop. growth (avg. ann. %, 1990–2010)	1.9	GNI per capita (Atlas $)	11,590

Climate

Average daily min/max temperature (1961–90, Celsius)	20 / 30
Projected annual temperature change (2045–65, Celsius)	1.8 to 2.9
Average annual precipitation (1961–90, mm)	1,875
Projected annual precipitation change (2045–65, mm)	-150 to 85
Projected change in annual hot days/warm nights	9 / 27
Projected change in annual cool days/cold nights	-3 / -3

	Country data	Latin America & the Carib.	Upper middle income
Exposure to Impacts			
Land area below 5m (% of land area)	2.3	1.5	1.8
Population below 5m (% of total)	3.7	3.8	6.5
Population in urban agglomerations > 1 million (%)	32	35	22
Urban pop. growth (avg. annual %, 1990–2010)	2.4	2.0	2.3
Droughts, floods, extreme temps (% pop. avg., 1990–2009)	0.2		
Annual freshwater withdrawals (% of internal resources)	1.3	2.0	5.6
Agricultural land under irrigation (% of total ag. land)	..	..	..
Population living below $1.25 a day (% of total)	3.0	8.1	..
Nationally terrestrial protected areas (% of total land area)	53.7	20.8	13.6
Under-five mortality rate (per 1,000)	18	23	20
Child malnutrition, underweight (% of under age five)	3.7	3.8	4.1
Malaria incidence rate (per 100,000 people)	263	206	80
Resilience			
Access to improved sanitation (% of total pop.)	91	79	68
Access to improved water source (% of total pop.)	93	93	92
Cereal yield (kg. per hectare)	3,695	3,337	3,690
Access to electricity (% of total population)	99.0	93.4	98.0
Paved roads (% of total roads)	33.6	28.1	50.5
Health workers (per 1,000 people)	3.1	6.9	4.5
Foreign direct investment, net inflows (% of GDP)	-0.4	2.3	2.7
Invest. in infrastructure w/private participation ($ millions)	423	33,064	26,166
Disaster risk reduction progress score (1–5 scale; 5 = best)	2.8		
Ease of doing business (ranking 1–183; 1 = best)	177		
Public sector mgmt & institutions avg. (1–6 scale; 6 = best)	..		
Primary completion rate, total (% of relevant age group)	95	102	98
Ratio of girls to boys in primary & secondary school (%)	102	102	103
GHG Emissions and Energy Use			
CO$_2$ emissions per capita (metric tons)	6.1	2.8	5.3
CO$_2$ emissions per units of GDP (kg/$1,000 of 2005 PPP $)	516.2	285.6	659.4
CO$_2$ emissions, total (MtCO$_2$)	169.5	1,584	12,860
GHG net emissions/removals by LUCF (1999, MtCO$_2$e)	-14.3		
Methane (CH$_4$) emissions, total (MtCO$_2$e)	61.2	1,009	3,455
Nitrous oxide (N$_2$O) emissions, total (MtCO$_2$e)	14.9	442	1,144
Other GHG emissions, total (MtCO$_2$e)	2.5	21	243
Energy use per capita (kilograms of oil equivalent)	2,357	1,245	1,848
Energy use per units of GDP (kg oil eq./$1,000 of 2005 PPP $)	210.6	130.6	227.1

National-Level Actions

Latest UNFCCC national communication	10/13/2005 (1st)
Annex-I emissions reduction target	n/a
NAMA submission	..
NAPA submission	n/a
Renewable energy target	..

Carbon Markets

Hosted Clean Development Mechanism (CDM) projects	..
Issued Certified Emission Reductions (CERs) from CDM (thousands)	..
Hosted Joint Implementation (JI) projects	n/a
Issued Emission Reduction Units (ERUs) from JI (thousands)	n/a

Vietnam

Population (millions)	86.9	GDP ($ billions)	103.6
Pop. growth (avg. ann. %, 1990-2010)	1.4	GNI per capita (Atlas $)	1,110

Climate
Average daily min/max temperature (1961-90, Celsius)	21 / 28
Projected annual temperature change (2045-65, Celsius)	1.4 to 2.1
Average annual precipitation (1961-90, mm)	1,821
Projected annual precipitation change (2045-65, mm)	-107 to 61
Projected change in annual hot days/warm nights	6 / 14
Projected change in annual cool days/cold nights	-1 / -1

	Country data	East Asia & Pacific	Lower middle income
Exposure to Impacts			
Land area below 5m (% of land area)	17.5	2.5	1.7
Population below 5m (% of total)	42.8	10.3	6.5
Population in urban agglomerations > 1 million (%)	13	..	14
Urban pop. growth (avg. annual %, 1990-2010)	3.1	3.3	2.8
Droughts, floods, extreme temps (% pop. avg., 1990-2009)	1.6		
Annual freshwater withdrawals (% of internal resources)	22.8	10.8	18.7
Agricultural land under irrigation (% of total ag. land)	..	..	..
Population living below $1.25 a day (% of total)	13.1	16.8	
Nationally terrestrial protected areas (% of total land area)	6.2	14.9	9.5
Under-five mortality rate (per 1,000)	23	24	69
Child malnutrition, underweight (% of under age five)	20.2	9.0	31.7
Malaria incidence rate (per 100,000 people)	55	525	4,874
Resilience			
Access to improved sanitation (% of total pop.)	75	59	45
Access to improved water source (% of total pop.)	94	88	84
Cereal yield (kg. per hectare)	5,075	4,860	2,754
Access to electricity (% of total population)	97.6	90.8	67.3
Paved roads (% of total roads)	47.6	15.9	29.3
Health workers (per 1,000 people)	2.2	2.8	2.6
Foreign direct investment, net inflows (% of GDP)	7.7	3.0	2.4
Invest. in infrastructure w/private participation ($ millions)	155	14,638	81,789
Disaster risk reduction progress score (1-5 scale; 5 = best)	..		
Ease of doing business (ranking 1-183; 1 = best)	98		
Public sector mgmt & institutions avg. (1-6 scale; 6 = best)	3.6		
Primary completion rate, total (% of relevant age group)	102	97	88
Ratio of girls to boys in primary & secondary school (%)	93	103	93
GHG Emissions and Energy Use			
CO_2 emissions per capita (metric tons)	1.5	4.3	1.6
CO_2 emissions per units of GDP (kg/$1,000 of 2005 PPP $)	573.2	827.1	523.9
CO_2 emissions, total (MtCO$_2$)	127.4	8,259	3,744
GHG net emissions/removals by LUCF (2000, MtCO$_2$e)	15.1		
Methane (CH_4) emissions, total (MtCO$_2$e)	83.0	1,928	1,705
Nitrous oxide (N_2O) emissions, total (MtCO$_2$e)	23.0	707	687
Other GHG emissions, total (MtCO$_2$e)	0.0	..	17
Energy use per capita (kilograms of oil equivalent)	745	1,436	680
Energy use per units of GDP (kg oil eq./$1,000 of 2005 PPP $)	273.7	259.5	217.9

National-Level Actions
Latest UNFCCC national communication	12/7/2010 (2nd)
Annex-I emissions reduction target	n/a
NAMA submission	..
NAPA submission	n/a
Renewable energy target	Yes

Carbon Markets
Hosted Clean Development Mechanism (CDM) projects	78
Issued Certified Emission Reductions (CERs) from CDM (thousands)	6,646
Hosted Joint Implementation (JI) projects	n/a
Issued Emission Reduction Units (ERUs) from JI (thousands)	n/a

Virgin Islands (U.S.)

Population (thousands)	109.8	GDP ($ millions)	..
Pop. growth (avg. ann. %, 1990–2010)	0.3	GNI per capita (Atlas $)	..

Climate

Average daily min/max temperature (1961–90, Celsius)	22 / 30
Projected annual temperature change (2045–65, Celsius)	1.3 to 1.7
Average annual precipitation (1961–90, mm)	2,263
Projected annual precipitation change (2045–65, mm)	-116 to 44
Projected change in annual hot days/warm nights	12 / 23
Projected change in annual cool days/cold nights	-3 / -3

	Country data	High Income
Exposure to Impacts		
Land area below 5m (% of land area)	31.0	2.2
Population below 5m (% of total)	21.9	7.7
Population in urban agglomerations > 1 million (%)	..	..
Urban pop. growth (avg. annual %, 1990–2010)	0.7	1.0
Droughts, floods, extreme temps (% pop. avg., 1990–2009)	..	..
Annual freshwater withdrawals (% of internal resources)	..	10.4
Agricultural land under irrigation (% of total ag. land)	..	..
Population living below $1.25 a day (% of total)	..	..
Nationally terrestrial protected areas (% of total land area)	15.2	13.4
Under-five mortality rate (per 1,000)	..	..
Child malnutrition, underweight (% of under age five)	..	6
Malaria incidence rate (per 100,000 people)	..	..
Resilience		
Access to improved sanitation (% of total pop.)	..	100
Access to improved water source (% of total pop.)	..	100
Cereal yield (kg. per hectare)	..	5,445
Access to electricity (% of total population)	..	..
Paved roads (% of total roads)	..	87.3
Health workers (per 1,000 people)	..	10.7
Foreign direct investment, net inflows (% of GDP)	..	1.8
Invest. in infrastructure w/private participation ($ millions)	..	
Disaster risk reduction progress score (1–5 scale; 5 = best)	..	
Ease of doing business (ranking 1–183; 1 = best)	..	
Public sector mgmt & institutions avg. (1–6 scale; 6 = best)	..	
Primary completion rate, total (% of relevant age group)	..	97
Ratio of girls to boys in primary & secondary school (%)	..	100
GHG Emissions and Energy Use		
CO_2 emissions per capita (metric tons)	..	11.9
CO_2 emissions per units of GDP (kg/$1,000 of 2005 PPP $)	..	354.4
CO_2 emissions, total (MtCO_2)	..	13,285
GHG net emissions/removals by LUCF (MtCO_2e)	..	
Methane (CH_4) emissions, total (MtCO_2e)	..	1,539
Nitrous oxide (N_2O) emissions, total (MtCO_2e)	..	813
Other GHG emissions, total (MtCO_2e)	..	460
Energy use per capita (kilograms of oil equivalent)	..	4,944
Energy use per units of GDP (kg oil eq./$1,000 of 2005 PPP $)	..	147.0

National-Level Actions

Latest UNFCCC national communication	n/a
Annex-I emissions reduction target	n/a
NAMA submission	n/a
NAPA submission	n/a
Renewable energy target	..

Carbon Markets

Hosted Clean Development Mechanism (CDM) projects	n/a
Issued Certified Emission Reductions (CERs) from CDM (thousands)	n/a
Hosted Joint Implementation (JI) projects	n/a
Issued Emission Reduction Units (ERUs) from JI (thousands)	n/a

West Bank and Gaza

Population (millions)	4.2	GDP ($ billions)	4.0
Pop. growth (avg. ann. %, 1990–2010)	3.7	GNI per capita (Atlas $)	1,250

Climate

Average daily min/max temperature (1961-90, Celsius)	..
Projected annual temperature change (2045-65, Celsius)	2.0 to 2.6
Average annual precipitation (1961-90, mm)	..
Projected annual precipitation change (2045-65, mm)	-40 to -13
Projected change in annual hot days/warm nights	4 / 8
Projected change in annual cool days/cold nights	-2 / -2

	Country data	Middle East & N. Africa	Lower middle income
Exposure to Impacts			
Land area below 5m (% of land area)	14.8	1.4	1.7
Population below 5m (% of total)	11.2	9.7	6.5
Population in urban agglomerations > 1 million (%)	..	20	14
Urban pop. growth (avg. annual %, 1990–2010)	4.0	2.5	2.8
Droughts, floods, extreme temps (% pop. avg., 1990–2009)	..		
Annual freshwater withdrawals (% of internal resources)	51.5	121.9	18.7
Agricultural land under irrigation (% of total ag. land)	4.6	..	..
Population living below $1.25 a day (% of total)	..	3.6	..
Nationally terrestrial protected areas (% of total land area)	..	4.0	9.5
Under-five mortality rate (per 1,000)	22	34	69
Child malnutrition, underweight (% of under age five)	2.2	6.8	31.7
Malaria incidence rate (per 100,000 people)	..	..	4,874
Resilience			
Access to improved sanitation (% of total pop.)	89	84	45
Access to improved water source (% of total pop.)	91	87	84
Cereal yield (kg. per hectare)	1,565	2,512	2,754
Access to electricity (% of total population)	..	92.9	67.3
Paved roads (% of total roads)	100.0	74.3	29.3
Health workers (per 1,000 people)	0.8	3.6	2.6
Foreign direct investment, net inflows (% of GDP)	1.2	2.9	2.4
Invest. in infrastructure w/private participation ($ millions)	47	5,854	81,789
Disaster risk reduction progress score (1-5 scale; 5 = best)	..		
Ease of doing business (ranking 1-183; 1 = best)	131		
Public sector mgmt & institutions avg. (1-6 scale; 6 = best)	..		
Primary completion rate, total (% of relevant age group)	82	88	88
Ratio of girls to boys in primary & secondary school (%)	104	93	93
GHG Emissions and Energy Use			
CO2 emissions per capita (metric tons)	0.5	3.8	1.6
CO2 emissions per units of GDP (kg/$1,000 of 2005 PPP $)	311.3	604.6	523.9
CO2 emissions, total (MtCO2)	2.1	1,230	3,744
GHG net emissions/removals by LUCF (MtCO2e)	..		
Methane (CH4) emissions, total (MtCO2e)	..	287	1,705
Nitrous oxide (N2O) emissions, total (MtCO2e)	..	74	687
Other GHG emissions, total (MtCO2e)	..	7	17
Energy use per capita (kilograms of oil equivalent)	..	1,399	680
Energy use per units of GDP (kg oil eq./$1,000 of 2005 PPP $)	..	213.9	217.9

National-Level Actions

Latest UNFCCC national communication	n/a
Annex-I emissions reduction target	n/a
NAMA submission	n/a
NAPA submission	n/a
Renewable energy target	..

Carbon Markets

Hosted Clean Development Mechanism (CDM) projects	n/a
Issued Certified Emission Reductions (CERs) from CDM (thousands)	n/a
Hosted Joint Implementation (JI) projects	n/a
Issued Emission Reduction Units (ERUs) from JI (thousands)	n/a

Yemen, Rep.

Population (millions)	24.1	GDP ($ billions)	26.4
Pop. growth (avg. ann. %, 1990–2010)	3.5	GNI per capita (Atlas $)	1,070

Climate

Average daily min/max temperature (1961–90, Celsius)	19 / 29
Projected annual temperature change (2045–65, Celsius)	2.0 to 2.6
Average annual precipitation (1961–90, mm)	167
Projected annual precipitation change (2045–65, mm)	-24 to 51
Projected change in annual hot days/warm nights	6 / 13
Projected change in annual cool days/cold nights	-2 / -2

	Country data	Middle East & N. Africa	Lower middle income
Exposure to Impacts			
Land area below 5m (% of land area)	0.6	1.4	1.7
Population below 5m (% of total)	1.8	9.7	6.5
Population in urban agglomerations > 1 million (%)	10	20	14
Urban pop. growth (avg. annual %, 1990–2010)	5.6	2.5	2.8
Droughts, floods, extreme temps (% pop. avg., 1990–2009)	0.1		
Annual freshwater withdrawals (% of internal resources)	161.4	121.9	18.7
Agricultural land under irrigation (% of total ag. land)	3.3	..	
Population living below $1.25 a day (% of total)	..	3.6	..
Nationally terrestrial protected areas (% of total land area)	0.5	4.0	9.5
Under-five mortality rate (per 1,000)	77	34	69
Child malnutrition, underweight (% of under age five)	43.1	6.8	31.7
Malaria incidence rate (per 100,000 people)	1,106	..	4,874
Resilience			
Access to improved sanitation (% of total pop.)	52	84	45
Access to improved water source (% of total pop.)	62	87	84
Cereal yield (kg. per hectare)	1,003	2,512	2,754
Access to electricity (% of total population)	39.6	92.9	67.3
Paved roads (% of total roads)	8.7	74.3	29.3
Health workers (per 1,000 people)	0.3	3.6	2.6
Foreign direct investment, net inflows (% of GDP)	0.5	2.9	2.4
Invest. in infrastructure w/private participation ($ millions)	59	5,854	81,789
Disaster risk reduction progress score (1–5 scale; 5 = best)	2.3		
Ease of doing business (ranking 1–183; 1 = best)	99		
Public sector mgmt & institutions avg. (1–6 scale; 6 = best)	2.9		
Primary completion rate, total (% of relevant age group)	61	88	88
Ratio of girls to boys in primary & secondary school (%)	66	93	93
GHG Emissions and Energy Use			
CO_2 emissions per capita (metric tons)	1.0	3.8	1.6
CO_2 emissions per units of GDP (kg/$1,000 of 2005 PPP $)	458.8	604.6	523.9
CO_2 emissions, total (MtCO$_2$)	23.4	1,230	3,744
GHG net emissions/removals by LUCF (1995, MtCO$_2$e)	-9.7		
Methane (CH_4) emissions, total (MtCO$_2$e)	6.7	287	1,705
Nitrous oxide (N_2O) emissions, total (MtCO$_2$e)	3.3	74	687
Other GHG emissions, total (MtCO$_2$e)	0.0	7	17
Energy use per capita (kilograms of oil equivalent)	324	1,399	680
Energy use per units of GDP (kg oil eq./$1,000 of 2005 PPP $)	143.0	213.9	217.9

National-Level Actions

Latest UNFCCC national communication	10/29/2001 (1st)
Annex-I emissions reduction target	n/a
NAMA submission	..
NAPA submission	Yes
Renewable energy target	..

Carbon Markets

Hosted Clean Development Mechanism (CDM) projects	0
Issued Certified Emission Reductions (CERs) from CDM (thousands)	0
Hosted Joint Implementation (JI) projects	n/a
Issued Emission Reduction Units (ERUs) from JI (thousands)	n/a

Zambia

Population (millions)	12.9	GDP ($ billions)	16.2
Pop. growth (avg. ann. %, 1990-2010)	2.5	GNI per capita (Atlas $)	1,070

Climate
Average daily min/max temperature (1961-90, Celsius)	15 / 28
Projected annual temperature change (2045-65, Celsius)	2.1 to 2.7
Average annual precipitation (1961-90, mm)	1,020
Projected annual precipitation change (2045-65, mm)	-54 to 94
Projected change in annual hot days/warm nights	4 / 18
Projected change in annual cool days/cold nights	-2 / -2

	Country data	Sub-Saharan Africa	Lower middle income
Exposure to Impacts			
Land area below 5m (% of land area)	0.0	0.4	1.7
Population below 5m (% of total)	0.0	2.0	6.5
Population in urban agglomerations > 1 million (%)	11	14	14
Urban pop. growth (avg. annual %, 1990-2010)	2.0	4.0	2.8
Droughts, floods, extreme temps (% pop. avg., 1990-2009)	4.2		
Annual freshwater withdrawals (% of internal resources)	2.2	3.2	18.7
Agricultural land under irrigation (% of total ag. land)	..	..	..
Population living below $1.25 a day (% of total)	..	50.9	..
Nationally terrestrial protected areas (% of total land area)	36.0	11.7	9.5
Under-five mortality rate (per 1,000)	111	121	69
Child malnutrition, underweight (% of under age five)	14.9	24.6	31.7
Malaria incidence rate (per 100,000 people)	13,456	26,113	4,874
Resilience			
Access to improved sanitation (% of total pop.)	49	31	45
Access to improved water source (% of total pop.)	60	60	84
Cereal yield (kg. per hectare)	2,067	1,297	2,754
Access to electricity (% of total population)	18.8	32.5	67.3
Paved roads (% of total roads)	22.0	18.3	29.3
Health workers (per 1,000 people)	0.8	1.2	2.6
Foreign direct investment, net inflows (% of GDP)	6.4	3.6	2.4
Invest. in infrastructure w/private participation ($ millions)	453	11,957	81,789
Disaster risk reduction progress score (1-5 scale; 5 = best)	3.8		
Ease of doing business (ranking 1-183; 1 = best)	84		
Public sector mgmt & institutions avg. (1-6 scale; 6 = best)	3.1		
Primary completion rate, total (% of relevant age group)	87	67	88
Ratio of girls to boys in primary & secondary school (%)	96	89	93
GHG Emissions and Energy Use			
CO_2 emissions per capita (metric tons)	0.2	0.8	1.6
CO_2 emissions per units of GDP (kg/$1,000 of 2005 PPP $)	119.4	428.6	523.9
CO_2 emissions, total (MtCO$_2$)	1.9	685	3,744
GHG net emissions/removals by LUCF (1994, MtCO$_2$e)	3.5		
Methane (CH$_4$) emissions, total (MtCO$_2$e)	19.3	590	1,705
Nitrous oxide (N$_2$O) emissions, total (MtCO$_2$e)	25.1	334	687
Other GHG emissions, total (MtCO$_2$e)	0.0	..	17
Energy use per capita (kilograms of oil equivalent)	617	689	680
Energy use per units of GDP (kg oil eq./$1,000 of 2005 PPP $)	466.8	308.4	217.9

National-Level Actions
Latest UNFCCC national communication	8/18/2004 (1st)
Annex-I emissions reduction target	n/a
NAMA submission	..
NAPA submission	Yes
Renewable energy target	..

Carbon Markets
Hosted Clean Development Mechanism (CDM) projects	1
Issued Certified Emission Reductions (CERs) from CDM (thousands)	0
Hosted Joint Implementation (JI) projects	n/a
Issued Emission Reduction Units (ERUs) from JI (thousands)	n/a

Zimbabwe

Population (millions)	12.6	GDP ($ billions)	7.5
Pop. growth (avg. ann. %, 1990–2010)	0.9	GNI per capita (Atlas $)	460

Climate

Average daily min/max temperature (1961–90, Celsius)	14 / 28
Projected annual temperature change (2045–65, Celsius)	2.2 to 2.9
Average annual precipitation (1961–90, mm)	692
Projected annual precipitation change (2045–65, mm)	–81 to 24
Projected change in annual hot days/warm nights	4 / 13
Projected change in annual cool days/cold nights	–2 / –2

	Country data	Sub-Saharan Africa	Low income
Exposure to Impacts			
Land area below 5m (% of land area)	0.0	0.4	0.7
Population below 5m (% of total)	0.0	2.0	5.1
Population in urban agglomerations > 1 million (%)	13	14	11
Urban pop. growth (avg. annual %, 1990–2010)	2.3	4.0	3.7
Droughts, floods, extreme temps (% pop. avg., 1990–2009)	..		
Annual freshwater withdrawals (% of internal resources)	34.3	3.2	3.7
Agricultural land under irrigation (% of total ag. land)	..		
Population living below $1.25 a day (% of total)	..	50.9	..
Nationally terrestrial protected areas (% of total land area)	28.0	11.7	10.6
Under-five mortality rate (per 1,000)	80	121	108
Child malnutrition, underweight (% of under age five)	14.0	24.6	28.3
Malaria incidence rate (per 100,000 people)	7,480	26,113	16,659
Resilience			
Access to improved sanitation (% of total pop.)	44	31	35
Access to improved water source (% of total pop.)	82	60	63
Cereal yield (kg. per hectare)	450	1,297	2,047
Access to electricity (% of total population)	41.5	32.5	23.0
Paved roads (% of total roads)	19.0	18.3	14.1
Health workers (per 1,000 people)	0.9	1.2	0.7
Foreign direct investment, net inflows (% of GDP)	1.4	3.6	3.2
Invest. in infrastructure w/private participation ($ millions)	301	11,957	4,471
Disaster risk reduction progress score (1–5 scale; 5 = best)	..		
Ease of doing business (ranking 1–183; 1 = best)	171		
Public sector mgmt & institutions avg. (1–6 scale; 6 = best)	2.1		
Primary completion rate, total (% of relevant age group)	81	67	65
Ratio of girls to boys in primary & secondary school (%)	97	89	91
GHG Emissions and Energy Use			
CO_2 emissions per capita (metric tons)	0.7	0.8	0.3
CO_2 emissions per units of GDP (kg/$1,000 of 2005 PPP $)	..	428.6	270.2
CO_2 emissions, total (MtCO_2)	9.1	685	219
GHG net emissions/removals by LUCF (1994, MtCO_2e)	–62.2		
Methane (CH_4) emissions, total (MtCO_2e)	9.5	590	436
Nitrous oxide (N_2O) emissions, total (MtCO_2e)	6.1	334	209
Other GHG emissions, total (MtCO_2e)	0.0	..	..
Energy use per capita (kilograms of oil equivalent)	763	689	365
Energy use per units of GDP (kg oil eq./$1,000 of 2005 PPP $)	..	308.4	303.9

National-Level Actions

Latest UNFCCC national communication	5/25/1998 (1st)
Annex-I emissions reduction target	n/a
NAMA submission	..
NAPA submission	n/a
Renewable energy target	..

Carbon Markets

Hosted Clean Development Mechanism (CDM) projects	0
Issued Certified Emission Reductions (CERs) from CDM (thousands)	0
Hosted Joint Implementation (JI) projects	n/a
Issued Emission Reduction Units (ERUs) from JI (thousands)	n/a

Renewable energy in 2010

2010 saw a new record for global investment in renewable power and fuels[1] of $211 billion. This reflects a 32 percent increase in investments compared to 2009 and nearly seven-fold increase compared to 2004. Investment levels were boosted particularly by wind farm development in China and small-scale solar photovoltaic installations on rooftops in Europe.

Asset finance for utility-scale generation and biofuel projects reached $128 billion in 2010 rising from 19 percent in 2009. Over the same period, investment in small distributed capacity soared 91 percent to $60 billion. Though renewable power capacity remains a small fraction of total world power capacity at around 8 percent (excluding large hydropower), its share in overall new power capacity additions is gradually increasing and has risen from about 10 percent to 34 percent between 2004 and 2010. Investment in renewable energy (excluding large hydropower) is also progressively catching up with investment in fossil fuel–based generation capacity. Investment in small-scale renewable heat (e.g., biomass heating, ground- and air- source heating, and solar water heating) is also gaining traction. In 2010, investment in solar water heating alone was estimated at $10 billion.[2]

Other segments of the value chain also grew over the period 2009–10: venture capital for young firms rose 59 percent to $2.4 billion; equity-raising on the public markets by quoted renewable energy companies grew 23 percent to $15.4 billion; and government-funded research and development increased by 121 percent to $5.3 billion as more "green stimulus" funds arrived in the sector. Only two areas of investment declined over this period. Corporate research, development, and deployment dropped 12 percent to $3.3 billion as companies retrenched in the face of economic difficulties. Expansion capital provided by private equity funds for renewable energy companies also decreased by 1 percent to $3.1 billion.

For the first time, developing countries overtook industrialized countries in financial new investment (i.e., total investment minus small-scale projects and government and corporate research and development [R&D]). Financial new investment exceeded $72 billion in developing countries and just over $70 billion in developed countries. This compares to a ratio of nearly four-to-one for equivalent investment in favor of developed countries in 2004. Importantly, developing countries are starting to host the development of a range of new renewable energy technologies for specific, local applications from rice-husk power generation to solar telecommunications towers.

China attracted the most investment in renewable energy for the second year in a row. In 2010, financial new investment rose 28 percent to almost $49 billion, representing more than a third of global financial new investment. Expenditure in the United States, ranked second, jumped 58 percent in 2010 to just over $25 billion. Developed economies remain well ahead in

---

[1] This includes all biomass, geothermal, and wind generation project of more than 1 megawatt (MW), all hydro projects of 0.5 to 50.0 MW, all solar projects of more than 0.3 MW, all marine energy projects, and all biofuel projects with a capacity of 1 million liters or more per year.

[2] Small-scale renewable heat is not included in the overall renewable energy because it delivers energy services but does not generate power.

Renewable energy in 2010

Table: Global trends in renewable energy investment ($ billion)

Category	2004 ($ billion)	2008 ($ billion)	2009 ($ billion)	2010 ($ billion)
New investment by value chain				
Technology development				
Venture capital	0.4	2.9	1.5	2.4
Government R&D	1.1	1.6	2.4	5.3
Corporate R&D	3.8	3.7	3.7	3.3
Equipment manufacturing				
Private equity expansion capital	0.3	6.6	3.1	3.1
Public markets	0.4	12.8	12.5	15.4
Projects				
Asset finance	18.3	114.7	107.5	127.8
of which re-invested equity	0.0	-4.5	-2.4	-6.0
Small distributed capacity	8.6	21.1	31.2	59.6
Total new financial investment	**19**	**132**	**122**	**143**
R&D, Small distributed capacity	**14**	**26**	**37**	**68**
Total	**33**	**159**	**160**	**211**
Mergers and acquisitions				
Private equity buy-outs	0.8	5.5	2.8	0.8
Public markets investor exits	0.0	1.0	2.0	1.3
Coporate mergers and acquisitions	2.4	18.0	21.6	20.2
Project acquisitions and refinancing	5.3	40.7	39.3	35.6
Total	**9**	**65**	**66**	**58**
Financial new investment by technology				
Biofuels	1.6	18.7	6.9	5.5
Biomass and w-t-e	3.7	10.1	11.5	11.0
Geothermal	1.0	1.6	1.4	2.0
Marine	0.0	0.1	0.2	0.1
Small hydro	1.1	5.8	4.1	3.2
Solar	0.5	33.3	25.3	26.1
Wind	11.3	62.7	72.7	94.7
Total	**19**	**132**	**122**	**143**
Financial new investment by geography Global				
Asia and Oceania	5.6	34.4	45.7	59.3
Europe	9.0	47.6	45.0	35.2
Middle East and Africa	0.3	2.4	2.4	5.0
North America	3.8	32.3	19.7	30.1
South America	0.5	15.7	9.4	13.1
Total	**19**	**132**	**122**	**143**
Select developing countries				
Brazil	0.4	13.2	7.3	6.9
China	1.5	23.9	38.3	48.9
India	1.3	4.1	3.0	3.8
Africa	0.3	1.1	0.7	3.6

Source: UNEP and Bloomberg New Energy Finance (2011).
Notes: New investment volume adjusts for re-invested equity. Total values include estimates of undisclosed deals. R&D = research and development, w-t-e = waste-to-energy.

Renewable energy in 2010

investment for small-scale projects and R&D, which are not included in the financial new investment measure. Germany had the highest investment in small-scale projects in 2010 at $34.3 billion (60 percent of the world total).

Wind remains the leading technology, with solar now a close second. Financial new investment in wind energy and investment in small distributed wind capacity reached $95 billion in 2010 (up 30 percent from 2009). The majority of this investment was asset finance ($90 billion). Financial new investment in solar energy and small distributed solar capacity rose 52 percent in 2010 compared to 2009 to reach $86 billion. Small distributed capacity represented 70 percent of this investment.

Source: UNEP and Bloomberg New Energy Finance (2011).

Urban areas

Country	City	Year	Population (thousands)	GHG Emissions Total (MtCO₂e)	GHG Emissions Per capita
Belgium	Brussels	2005	1,007	7.55	7.5
Brazil	Rio de Janeiro	1998	5,633	12.11	2.1
	São Paulo	2000	10,434	14.22	1.4
Canada	Calgary	2003	922	..	17.7
	Toronto (Metro Area)	2005	5,556	64.22	11.6
China	Beijing	2006	15,810	159	10.1
	Shanghai	2006	18,150	211.98	11.7
	Tianjin	2006	10,750	119.25	11.1
Czech Republic	Prague	2005	1,182	11.03	9.4
Finland	Helsinki	2005	989	6.94	7.0
France	Paris (Île-de-France)	2005	11,532	59.64	5.2
Germany	Frankfurt	2005	3,778	51.61	13.7
	Hamburg	2005	4,260	41.52	9.7
	Stuttgart	2005	2,668	42.57	16.0
Greece	Athens	2005	3,989	41.57	10.4
Italy	Bologna (Province)	2005	900	9.97	11.1
	Naples (Province)	2005	3,087	12.49	4.0
	Turin	2005	2,243	21.86	9.7
	Veneto (Province)	2005	4,738	47.29	10.0
Japan	Tokyo	2006	12,678	62.02	4.89
Jordan	Amman	2008	..	..	3.25
Netherlands	Rotterdam	2005	593	17.64	29.8
Norway	Oslo	2005	1,040	3.63	3.5
Portugal	Porto	2005	1,667	12.14	7.3
Slovenia	Ljubljana	2005	500	4.77	9.5
South Africa	Cape Town	2005	3,497	40.43	7.6
Spain	Barcelona	2006	1,606	6.74	4.2
	Madrid	2005	5,964	40.98	6.9
Sweden	Stockholm	2005	1,890	6.88	3.6
Switzerland	Geneva	2005	432	3.35	7.8
Thailand	Bangkok	2005	5,659	60.44	10.7
United Kingdom	London (Greater Area)	2003	7,364	70.84	9.6
	Glasgow	2004	1,747	15.3	8.8
United States	Austin	2005	672	..	15.57
	Denver	2005	580	11.08	21.5
	Los Angeles	2000	9,519	124.04	13.0
	Minneapolis	2005	388	..	18.34
	New York City	2005	8,170	85.87	10.5
	Portland, OR	2005	683	..	12.41
	Seattle	2005	576	..	13.68

Sources: World Bank, 2010, Kennedy et al., 2009.

Summary of national actions

Renewable energy targets

This table summarizes various renewable energy targets announced by countries. Targets vary significantly with respect to sector coverage, baseline year, methodology, and form, and thus are generally not comparable.

Renewable targets include both voluntary and mandatory targets. Renewable energy targets in italics are expressed as percentages of *primary energy*; other targets are expressed in terms of final energy. Primary energy typically covers direct use at the supply level before transformation or distribution, while final energy covers energy supplied to consumers.

	Renewable energy target	Renewable electricity target
Albania	*18% by 2020*	
Algeria		5% by 2017
		20% by 2030
Argentina		40% by 2015
Australia		20% by 2020
Austria	34% by 2020	
Bangladesh		5% by 2015
		10% by 2020
Belgium	13% by 2020	
Botswana	1% by 2016	
Brazil		16% by 2020
Bulgaria	16% by 2020	
Burundi	2.1% by 2020	
Cape Verde		50% by 2020
Chile		8% by 2020
China	15% by 2020	3% by 2020
Cyprus	13% by 2020	
Czech Republic	13% by 2020	16–17% by 2030
Denmark	20% by 2011	
	30% by 2020	
Dominican Republic		10% by 2015
		25% by 2020
Egypt, Arab Rep.	*14% by 2020*	20% by 2020
Estonia	25% by 2020	8% by 2015
		35% by 2020
Fiji	100% by 2013	
Finland	38% by 2020	
France	23% by 2020	
Gabon	80% by 2020	
Germany	18% by 2020	50% by 2030
	30% by 2030	65% by 2040
	45% by 2040	80% by 2050
	60% by 2050	
Ghana		10% by 2020
Greece	18% by 2020	
Hungary	14.7% by 2020	
India		10% by 2012
Indonesia	*17% by 2025*	
Ireland	16% by 2020	
Israel	50% by 2020	5% by 2016
		7% by 2020
Italy	17% by 2020	26% by 2020
Jamaica	*20% by 2030*	15% by 2020
Japan	*10% by 2020*	1.6% by 2014
Jordan	*7% by 2015*	
	10% by 2020	

Summary of national actions

	Renewable energy target	Renewable electricity target
Korea, Rep.	4.3% by 2015	
	6.1% by 2020	
	11% by 2030	
Kuwait		5% by 2020
Latvia	40% by 2020	
Lebanon	12% by 2020	
Libya		10% by 2020
		30% by 2030
Lithuania	23% by 2020	
	20% by 2025	
Luxembourg	11% by 2020	
Madagascar	54% by 2020	75% by 2020
Malawi	7% by 2020	
Maldives		
Mali	15% by 2020	
Malta	10% by 2020	
Mauritius	35% by 2025	65% by 2028
Mexico		
Moldova	20% by 2020	
Mongolia		20–25% by 2020
Morocco	10% by 2012	20% by 2020
	8% by 2012	
Netherlands	14% by 2020	
New Zealand		90% by 2025
Nicaragua		38% by 2011
Niger	10% by 2020	
Nigeria		7% by 2025
Pakistan		10% by 2012
Peru		
Philippines		40% by 2020
Poland	15% by 2020	
	14% by 2020	
Portugal	31% by 2020	55–60% by 2020
Romania	24% by 2020	35% by 2015
		38% by 2020
Russian Federation		2.5% by 2015
		4.5% by 2020
Rwanda		90% by 2012
Senegal	15% by 2025	
Slovak Republic	14% by 2020	
Slovenia	25% by 2020	
South Africa		4% by 2013
		13% by 2020
		14% by 2050
Spain	20% by 2020	40% by 2020
Sri Lanka		10% by 2017
		14% by 2022
Sweden	50% by 2020	
Switzerland	24% by 2020	
Syrian Arab Republic	4.3% by 2011	
Thailand	20% by 2022	11% by 2011
		14% by 2022
Tonga	100% by 2013	50% by 2012
Tunisia		11% by 2016
		25% by 2030
Turkey		30% by 2023
Uganda	61% by 2017	
United Kingdom	15% by 2020	10% by 2010/11
		15% by 2015/16
Vietnam	5% by 2020	5% by 2020
	8% by 2025	
	11% by 2050	

Source: REN21 Secretariat, 2011.

Summary of national actions

Non-Annex-I country GHG emissions reduction goals

This table summarizes GHG emissions reduction goals included by non-Annex-I countries in their Nationally Appropriate Mitigation Action plans submitted to the UNFCCC. Goals vary significantly with respect to sector coverage, baseline year, methodology, and form, and thus are generally not comparable.

	NAMA emissions goal
Antigua and Barbuda	GHG emission reduction of 25% below 1990 levels by 2020
Bhutan	Efforts to remain GHG neutral
Brazil	GHG reduction of 36.1–38.9% below its BAU emissions in 2020
Chile	GHG reduction of 20% below its BAU emissions in 2020
China	Reduce CO_2 emissions per unit of GDP by 40–45% by 2020 compared to 2005
Colombia	77% of total electric capacity installed will be from renewable sources and 20% of fuel consumption from biofuels by 2020
Costa Rica	Long-term effort to enable carbon neutrality
India	Reduce CO_2 emissions (except agriculture) per unit of GDP by 20–25% by 2020 compared to 2005
Indonesia	GHG emissions reduction by 26% by 2020
Israel	GHG reduction of 20% below its BAU emissions in 2020
Korea, Rep.	GHG emissions reduction by 30% below BAU by 2020
Maldives	Long-term transformational effort to achieve carbon neutrality as a country by 2020
Marshall Islands	GHG reduction of 40% below 2009 level
Mexico	GHG reduction of 30% below its BAU emissions in 2020
Moldova	GHG emissions reduction by 35% compared with the base year 1990, by 2020
Peru	Renewable energy represents at least 33% of total energy used and zero net deforestation by 2020
Singapore	GHG emissions reduction by 16% below BAU by 2020
South Africa	GHG emissions reduction by 34% below BAU by 2020

Sources: UNFCCC, UNEP Risø Centre.

Glossary

Annex-I emissions reduction target is the Annex-I (A1) country's target for reducing economy-wide greenhouse gas emissions by 2020 to the UNFCCC under the Copenhagen Accord. Targets are relative to 1990 emissions unless otherwise specified. Multiple targets indicate that countries have signaled a willingness to accept deeper targets, contingent on commitments by other parties or other conditions. (EU) indicates that the target submitted by the European Union and its member States applies to this country. "n/a" indicates that the country is not an Annex-1 party to the UNFCCC. (UNFCCC on October 21, 2011)

Access to electricity is the percentage of population with access to electricity. Electrification data are collected from industry, national surveys, and international sources. (International Energy Agency, World Energy Outlook 2010; data are for 2008/2009)

Access to improved sanitation is the percentage of population with adequate access to excreta disposal facilities (private or shared, but not public) that can effectively prevent human, animal, and insect contact with excreta. Improved facilities range from simple but protected pit latrines to flush toilets with a sewerage connection. To be effective, facilities must be correctly constructed and properly maintained. (World Health Organization; data are for 2008)

Access to improved water source is the percentage of the population with reasonable access to an adequate amount of water from an improved source, such as piped water into a dwelling, plot, or yard; public tap or standpipe; tube-well or borehole; protected dug well or spring; or rainwater collection. Unimproved sources include an unprotected dug well or spring, cart with small tank or drum, bottled water, and tanker trucks. Reasonable access to an adequate amount means the availability of at least 20 liters a person a day from a source within 1 kilometer of the dwelling. (World Health Organization; data are for 2008)

Agricultural land is arable land, land under permanent crops, and permanent pastures. Arable land includes land defined by the Food and Agriculture Organization of the United Nations as land under temporary crops (double-cropped areas are counted once), temporary meadows for mowing or for pasture, land under market or kitchen gardens, and land temporarily fallow. Land abandoned as a result of shifting cultivation is excluded. Land under permanent crops is land cultivated with crops that occupy the land for long periods and need not be replanted after each harvest, such as cocoa, coffee, and rubber. This category includes land under flowering shrubs, fruit trees, nut trees, and vines but excludes land under trees grown for wood or timber. Permanent pasture is land used for five or more years for forage, including natural and cultivated crops. (Food and Agriculture Organization)

Agricultural land under irrigation is the area purposely provided with water, including land irrigated by controlled flooding. (Food and Agriculture Organization; data are for 2009)

Glossary

Annual freshwater withdrawals are total water withdrawals, excluding evaporation losses from storage basins and including water from desalination plants in countries where they are a significant source. Withdrawals can exceed 100 percent of internal renewable resources because river flows from other countries are not included, because extraction from nonrenewable aquifers or desalination plants is considerable, or because there is significant water reuse. (Food and Agriculture Organization and World Resources Institute; data are for various years; for details, see *World Development Indicators 2011, Primary data documentation*)

Average annual precipitation is the sum of the rainfall and the assumed water equivalent of the snowfall for the year in the country, averaged over the years 1961–1990. Values are based on gridded climatologies from the Climatic Research Unit (Mitchell et al., 2003).

Average daily min/max temperature are the minimum and maximum daily temperatures in the country, averaged for the years 1961–90, based on gridded climatologies from the Climatic Research Unit (Mitchell et al., 2003).

Carbon dioxide (CO_2) emissions are emissions from the burning of fossil fuels and the manufacture of cement and include carbon dioxide produced during consumption of solid, liquid, and gas fuels and gas flaring. (Carbon Dioxide Information Analysis Center; latest data are for 2008)

Carbon dioxide (CO_2) emissions per capita are carbon dioxide emissions divided by midyear population. (Carbon Dioxide Information Analysis Center, World Bank, and United Nations; data are for 2008)

Carbon dioxide (CO_2) emissions per units of GDP are carbon dioxide emissions in kilograms per $1,000 of GDP in 2005 purchasing power parity (PPP) terms. PPP GDP is gross domestic product converted to international dollars using PPP rates. An international dollar has the same purchasing power over GDP that a U.S. dollar has in the United States. (Carbon Dioxide Information Analysis Center and World Bank; data are for 2008)

Certified Emission Reductions—see Issued Certified Emission Reductions (CERs) from Clean Development Mechanism (CDM).

Cereal yield is measured in kilograms per hectare of harvested land and includes wheat, rice, maize, barley, oats, rye, millet, sorghum, buckwheat, and mixed grains. Production data on cereals refer to crops harvested for dry grain only. Cereal crops harvested for hay or harvested green for food, feed, or silage, and those used for grazing, are excluded. The FAO allocates production data to the calendar year in which the bulk of the harvest took place. But most of a crop harvested near the end of a year will be used in the following year. (Food and Agriculture Organization; data are for 2009)

Child malnutrition, underweight is the percentage of children under age 5 whose weight for age is more than two standard deviations below the median for the international reference population ages 0–59 months. The data are based on the World Health Organization's child growth standards

Glossary

released in 2006. (World Health Organization; data are for the most recent year available)

Disaster risk reduction progress score is an average of self-assessment scores, ranging from 1 to 5, submitted by countries under Priority 1 of the Hyogo Framework National Progress Reports. The Hyogo Framework is a global blueprint for disaster risk reduction efforts that was adopted by 168 countries in 2005. Assessments of "Priority 1" include four indicators that reflect the degree to which countries have prioritized disaster risk reduction and the strengthening of relevant institutions (UNISDR, 2009–11 Progress Reports, http://www.preventionweb.net/english/hyogo).

Droughts, floods, and extreme temperatures is the annual average percentage of the population that is affected by natural disasters classified as either droughts, floods, or extreme temperature events. A drought is an extended period of time characterized by a deficiency in a region's water supply that is the result of constantly below average precipitation. A drought can lead to losses to agriculture, affect inland navigation and hydropower plants, and cause a lack of drinking water and famine. A flood is a significant rise of water level in a stream, lake, reservoir, or coastal region. Extreme temperature events are either cold waves or heat waves. A cold wave can be both a prolonged period of excessively cold weather and the sudden invasion of very cold air over a large area. Along with frost, it can cause damage to agriculture, infrastructure, and property. A heat wave is a prolonged period of excessively hot and sometimes also humid weather relative to normal climate patterns of a certain region. Population affected is the number of people injured, left homeless, or requiring immediate assistance during a period of emergency resulting from a natural disaster; it can also include displaced or evacuated people. Average percentage of population affected is calculated by dividing the sum of total affected for the period stated by the sum of the annual population figures for the period stated. (EM-DAT: The OFDA/CRED International Disaster Database—http://www.emdat.be, Université Catholique de Louvain, Brussels [Belgium], World Bank)

Ease of doing business ranks economies from 1 to 183, with first place being the best. A high ranking (a low numerical rank) means that the regulatory environment is conducive to business operation. The index averages the country's percentile rankings on 10 topics covered in the World Bank's *Doing Business*. The ranking on each topic is the simple average of the percentile rankings on its component indicators. (World Bank; data are for October 2011)

Emission Reduction Units—see Issued Emission Reduction Units (ERUs) from Joint Implementation (JI).

Energy use per capita refers to use of primary energy before transformation to other end-use fuels, which is equal to indigenous production plus imports and stock changes, minus exports and fuels supplied to ships and aircraft engaged in international transport. (International Energy Agency; data are for 2009)

Glossary

Energy use per units of GDP is the kilogram of oil equivalent of energy use per $1,000 of GDP in 2005 purchasing power parity (PPP) terms. Energy use refers to use of primary energy before transformation to other end-use fuels, which is equal to indigenous production plus imports and stock changes, minus exports and fuels supplied to ships and aircraft engaged in international transport. PPP GDP is gross domestic product converted to international dollars using PPP rates. An international dollar has the same purchasing power over GDP that a U.S. dollar has in the United States. (International Energy Agency, World Bank PPP data; data are for 2009)

Foreign direct investment, net inflows is investments to acquire a lasting management interest in an enterprise operating in an economy other than that of the investor. They are the sum of inflows of equity capital, reinvestment of earnings, other long-term capital, and short-term capital as shown in the balance of payments. Net inflows refer to new investments made during the reporting period netted against disinvestments. (World Bank and International Monetary Fund; data are for 2010)

GDP is gross domestic product and measures the total output of goods and services for final use occurring within the domestic territory of a given country, regardless of the allocation to domestic and foreign claims. GDP at purchaser values (market prices) is the sum of gross value added by all resident and nonresident producers in the economy plus any taxes and minus any subsidies not included in the value of the products. It is calculated without deductions for depreciation of fabricated assets or for depletion and degradation of natural resources. (World Bank, Organization for Economic Co-operation and Development, and United Nations; data are for 2010)

GHG stands for greenhouse gas, a classification of gases that absorb infrared radiation in the atmosphere. Water vapor, carbon dioxide, methane, nitrous oxide, chlorofluorocarbons (CFCs), hydrochlorofluorocarbons (HCFCs), ozone (O_3), hydrofluorocarbons (HFCs), perfluorocarbons (PFCs), and sulfur hexafluoride (SF_6) are all considered greenhouse gases.

GHG net emissions/removals by LUCF refers to changes in atmospheric levels of all greenhouse gases attributable to forest and land-use change activities, including but not limited to (1) emissions and removals of CO_2 from decreases or increases in biomass stocks due to forest management, logging, fuelwood collection, and so forth; (2) conversion of existing forests and natural grasslands to other land uses; (3) removal of CO_2 from the abandonment of formerly managed lands (e.g. croplands and pastures); and (4) emissions and removals of CO_2 in soil associated with land-use change and management. For Annex-I countries under the UNFCCC, these data are drawn from the annual GHG inventories submitted to the UNFCCC by each country; for non-Annex-I countries, data are drawn from the most recently submitted National Communication where available. Because of differences in reporting years and methodologies, these data are not generally considered comparable across countries (UNFCCC).

Glossary

GNI per capita is the gross national income, converted to U.S. dollars using the World Bank Atlas method, divided by the midyear population. GNI is the sum of value added by all resident producers plus any product taxes (less subsidies) not included in the valuation of output plus net receipts of primary income (compensation of employees and property income) from abroad. GNI, calculated in national currency, is usually converted to U.S. dollars at official exchange rates for comparisons across economies, although an alternative rate is used when the official exchange rate is judged to diverge by an exceptionally large margin from the rate actually applied in international transactions. To smooth fluctuations in prices and exchange rates, a special Atlas method of conversion is used by the World Bank. This applies a conversion factor that averages the exchange rate for a given year and the two preceding years, adjusted for differences in rates of inflation between the country and the Euro area, Japan, the United Kingdom, and the United States. (World Bank; data are for 2010)

Health workers include physicians, nurses, and midwives. Physicians include generalist and specialist medical practitioners. Nurses and midwives include professional nurses, professional midwives, auxiliary nurses, auxiliary midwives, enrolled nurses, enrolled midwives, and other associated personnel, such as dental nurses and primary care nurses. (World Health Organization, Global Atlas of the Health Workforce; data are for 2009 or the most recent year available)

Hosted Clean Development Mechanism (CDM) projects refers to the number of Clean Development Mechanism (CDM) projects registered within the (host) country by the CDM Executive Board. One of the flexibility mechanisms set forth under the Kyoto Protocol, the Clean Development Mechanism is designed to assist developing countries in achieving sustainable development by allowing entities from Annex I Parties to participate in low-emission project activities and obtain Certified Emission Reductions (CERs) in return. (UNEP Risø Centre: as of October 1, 2011)

Hosted Joint Implementation (JI) projects refers to the number of determined Joint Implementation (JI) projects within the (host) country. Joint Implementation is one of the flexibility mechanisms set forth under the Kyoto Protocol whereby entities from Annex I Parties may participate in low-emission project activities in Annex I countries and obtain Emission Reduction Units (ERUs) in return. (UNEP Risø Centre: as of October 1, 2011)

Investment in infrastructure with private participation is the value of infrastructure projects in telecommunications, energy (electricity and natural gas transmission and distribution), transport, and water and sanitation that have reached financial closure and directly or indirectly serve the public, including operation and management contracts with major capital expenditure, greenfield projects (in which a private entity or public-private joint venture builds and operates a new facility), and divestitures. Incinerators, movable assets, standalone solid waste projects, and small projects such as windmills are excluded. Investment in the four sectors are summed by year. The total value shown may not contain data for all sectors. (World Bank; data are for 2010)

Issued Certified Emission Reductions (CERs) from CDM refers to the number of Certified Emission Reductions (CERs) issued to Clean Development Mechanism (CDM) projects within the (host) country. One CER represents a reduction in greenhouse gas emissions of one metric ton of carbon dioxide equivalent. (UNEP Risø Centre: as of October 1, 2011)

Issued Emission Reduction Units (ERUs) from JI refers to the number of Emission Reduction Units (ERUs) issued to Joint Implementation (JI) projects within the (host) country. One ERU represents a reduction in greenhouse gas emissions of one metric ton of carbon dioxide equivalent. (UNEP Risø Centre: as of October 1, 2011)

Land area below 5m is the percentage of total land where the elevation is 5 meters or less. (CIESIN, Place II dataset; data are for 2000)

Latest UNFCCC national communication is the date of the country's most recent National Communication submission under the UNFCCC. The parenthetical number indicates the number of reports submitted by the country. "n/a" indicates that the country is not a party to the UNFCCC. (UNFCCC: as of October 21, 2011)

LUCF stands for Land Use Change and Forestry.

Malaria incidence rate is the number of new cases of malaria per 100,000 people each year. The number of cases reported is adjusted to take into account incompleteness in reporting systems, patients seeking treatment in the private sector, self-medicating or not seeking treatment at all, and potential over-diagnosis through the lack of laboratory confirmation of cases. (World Health Organization, data are for 2008)

Methane (CH_4) emissions are emissions from human activities such as agriculture and from industrial methane production. (International Energy Agency; data are for 2005)

NAMA submission indicates whether a non-Annex I country has submitted Nationally Appropriate Mitigation Actions (NAMAs) to the UNFCCC. "Yes, with Goal" indicates the country included a GHG emissions reduction goal as part of its NAMA. See "Summary of National Actions" for details. "n/a" indicates countries that are not non-Annex I parties to the UNFCCC. (UNFCCC, UNEP Risø Centre: as of September 13, 2011)

NAPA submission indicates whether a country has submitted a National Adaptation Programme of Action (NAPA) under the UNFCCC. NAPAs are part of an effort under the UNFCCC to address the urgent adaptation needs of Least Developed Countries. "n/a" indicates countries that are not considered to be Least Developed Countries. (UNFCCC)

National terrestrial protected areas are totally or partially protected areas of at least 1,000 hectares that are designated by national authorities as scientific reserves with limited public access, national parks, natural monuments, nature reserves or wildlife sanctuaries, and protected landscapes. Marine

Glossary

areas, unclassified areas, littoral (intertidal) areas, and sites protected under local or provincial law are excluded. (World Conservation Monitoring Centre; data are for the most recent year available)

Nitrous oxide (N_2O) emissions are emissions from agricultural biomass burning, industrial activities, and livestock management. (International Energy Agency; data are for 2005)

Other GHG emissions are byproduct emissions of hydrofluorocarbons (byproduct emissions of fluoroform from chlorodifluoromethane manufacture and use of hydrofluorocarbons), perfluorocarbons (byproduct emissions of tetrafluoromethane and hexafluoroethane from primary aluminum production and use of perfluorocarbons, in particular for semiconductor manufacturing), and sulfur hexafluoride (various sources, the largest being the use and manufacture of gas insulated switchgear used in electricity distribution networks). (International Energy Agency; data are for 2005)

Paved roads are roads surfaced with crushed stone (macadam) and hydrocarbon binder or bituminized agents, with concrete, or with cobblestones. (International Road Federation and World Bank estimates; data are for the most recent year available)

Population includes all residents who are present regardless of legal status or citizenship except for refugees not permanently settled in the country of asylum who are generally considered part of the population of their country of origin. Values are midyear estimates. (World Bank; data are for 2010)

Population growth is the exponential change for the period indicated. (World Bank)

Population living below $1.25 a day is the percentage of the population living on less than $1.25 a day at 2005 international prices. (World Bank; data are for the most recent year available)

Population below 5m is the percentage of the total population living in areas where the elevation is 5 meters or less. (CIESIN, Place II dataset; data are for 2000)

Population in urban agglomerations of more than 1 million is the percentage of a country's population living in metropolitan areas that in 2009 had a population of more than 1 million. (United Nations; data are for 2010)

Primary completion rate is the percentage of students completing the last year of primary school. It is calculated by taking the total number of students in the last grade of primary school, minus the number of repeaters in that grade, divided by the total number of children of official graduation age. (United Nations Educational, Scientific, and Cultural Organization [UNESCO] Institute for Statistics; data are for 2009)

Projected annual precipitation change is the projected change in annual precipitation in the years 2045–65, relative to the control period 1961–

2000. The range reflects the 10th and 90th percentiles of results from nine general circulation models (GCMs), employing the A2 storyline and scenario family. Values are then calculated at the country level from 2-degree gridded data. (Modified from Meehl et al., 2007)

Projected annual temperature change is the projected change in annual temperature in the years 2045–65, relative to the control period 1961–2000. The range reflects the 10th and 90th percentiles of results from nine general circulation models (GCMs) at a standardized 2-degree grid, employing the A2 storyline and scenario family. Values are aggregated at the country level. (IPCC Fourth Assessment Report)

Projected change in annual cool days/cold nights are the projected changes in the annual incidence of "cool days" and "cold nights" in the years 2045–65, relative to the control period 1961–2000. Cool days and cold nights are those that fall below the 10th percentile of maximum temperature and the 10th percentile of minimum temperatures, respectively, in the control period. These indicators are useful to understand potentially critical thresholds related to cold stress and frequency of frost in different sectors such as agriculture and energy. The range reflects the 10th and 90th percentiles of results from nine general circulation models (GCMs), employing the A2 storyline and scenario family. Values are then calculated at the country level from 2-degree gridded data. (Climate Systems Analysis Group, University of Cape Town, 2009, calculated from Meehl et al., 2007)

Projected change in annual hot days/warm nights are the projected changes in the annual incidence of "hot days" and "warm nights" in the years 2045–65, relative to the control period 1961–2000. Hot days and warm nights are those that exceed the 90th percentile of maximum temperatures and those that exceeded the 90th percentile in minimum temperatures, respectively, in the control period. These indicators are useful to understand potentially critical thresholds related to heat stress in different sectors such as agriculture and energy. The range reflects the 10th and 90th percentiles of results from nine general circulation models (GCMs), employing the A2 storyline and scenario family. Values are then calculated at the country level from 2-degree gridded data. (Climate Systems Analysis Group, University of Cape Town, 2009, calculated from Meehl et al., 2007)

Public sector management & institutions average. The Country Policy and Institutional Assessment (CPIA) assesses the quality of a country's present policy and institutional framework. "Quality" refers to how conducive that framework is to fostering poverty reduction, sustainable growth, and the effective use of development assistance. The CPIA ratings are used in the International Development Association (IDA) allocation process and several other corporate activities. The public sector management and institutions cluster includes property rights and rule-based governance, quality of budgetary and financial management, efficiency of revenue mobilization, quality of public administration, and transparency, accountability, and corruption in the public sector. (World Bank; data are for 2010)

Glossary

Ratio of girls to boys in primary and secondary school is the ratio of female to male gross enrollment in primary and secondary school. (United Nations Educational, Scientific, and Cultural Organization [UNESCO] Institute for Statistics; data are for 2009/2010)

Renewable energy target indicates whether a country has announced one or more targets for renewable energy production, either as a percentage of electricity production, primary energy or final energy. See "Summary of National Actions" for details. (REN21 Secretariat, 2011)

Under-five mortality rate is the probability per 1,000 that a newborn baby will die before reaching age five, if subject to current age-specific mortality rates. (UN Inter-agency Group for Child Mortality Estimation; data are for 2010, 2011)

UNFCCC stands for the United Nations Framework Convention on Climate Change, the primary forum for international efforts to address climate change.

Urban population is the share of the midyear population living in areas defined as urban in each country.

Urban population growth is the exponential change for the period indicated. (United Nations)

References

Kennedy, C., A. Ramaswami, S. Dhakal, and S. Carney. 2009. "Greenhouse Gas Emission Baselines for Global Cities and Metropolitan Regions." Conference Paper, 5th Urban Research Symposium, "Cities and Climate Change—Responding to an Urgent Agenda." Marseille, France, June 28–29.

Meehl, G. A., C. Covey, T. Delworth, M. Latif, B. McAvaney, J. F. B. Mitchell, R. J. Stouffer, and K. E. Taylor. 2007. "The WCRP CMIP3 Multi-Model Dataset: A New Era in Climate Change Research." *Bulletin of the American Meteorological Society* 88: 1383–94.

Mitchell, T. D., T. R. Carter, P. D. Jones, M. Hulme, M. New. 2003. "A Comprehensive Set of High-Resolution Grids of Monthly Climate for Europe and the Globe: the Observed Record (1901–2000) and 16 Scenarios (2001–2100)." *Journal of Climate:* submitted.

REN21 Secretariat. 2011. *Renewables 2011 Global Status Report.* Paris: REN21 Secretariat.

UN (United Nations) Inter-Agency Group for Child Mortality Estimation. 2011. *Levels and Trends in Child Mortality: Report 2011.* New York: United Nations Children's Fund.

UNEP (United Nations Environment Programme) and Bloomberg New Energy Finance. 2011. *Global Trends in Renewable Energy Investment 2011; Analysis of Trends and Issues in the Financing of Renewable Energy.* New York: UNEP.

World Bank. 2010. *Cities and Climate Change: An Urgent Agenda.* Washington, D.C.: World Bank.

———. 2011. *World Development Indicators 2011.* Washington, D.C.: World Bank.